D1229637

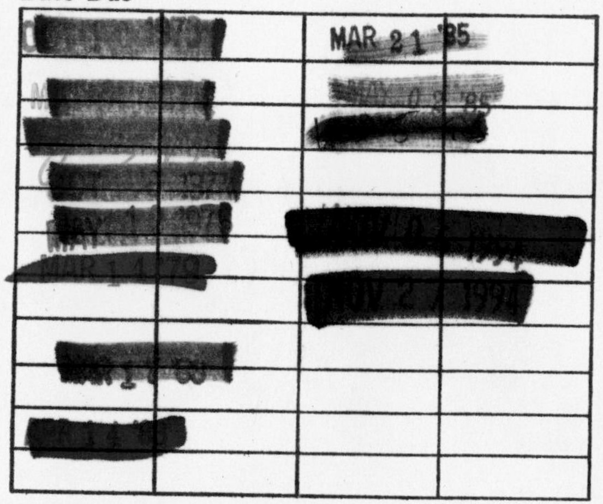
Date Due
MAR 21 '85

WID

The Library of Literature

UNDER THE GENERAL EDITORSHIP OF

JOHN HENRY RALEIGH AND IAN WATT

The Literary Context of Chaucer's Fabliaux

TEXTS AND TRANSLATIONS

LARRY D. BENSON

THEODORE M. ANDERSSON

The Literary Context of Chaucer's Fabliaux

Texts and Translations

THE BOBBS-MERRILL COMPANY, INC.

INDIANAPOLIS & NEW YORK

Library of Congress Catalog Card Number 70–138663

Printed in the United States of America

First Printing

Designed by Starr Atkinson

For B. J. Whiting

Preface

"All judgment is comparative," wrote Doctor Johnson. Nowhere is this truer than in the study of a medieval writer such as Chaucer; the medieval poet, free of the modern obsession with novelty, invites comparison, almost demands that we recognize the twice-told quality of his tale even as we recognize the originality that has made the old tale new. Yet the student who approaches Chaucer for the first time finds this impossible, especially when he turns to what seem (and are) Chaucer's freshest and most original works—his fabliaux: "The Miller's Tale," "The Reeve's Tale," "The Merchant's Tale," "The Shipman's Tale," and "The Summoner's Tale," as well as the similar "Manciple's Tale" and "Friar's Tale." The beginning reader is usually denied the rewards of comparative criticism, the recognition of what is old and the discovery of what is new, because he seldom has at his command the languages or the library facilities that would make accessible even a part of the rich heritage of medieval comic literature that formed the literary context within which Chaucer wrote.

A good sampling of this context was printed in the Chaucer Society's *Originals and Analogues of Chaucer's Canterbury Tales* (London, 1872–1888) and again in *Sources and Analogues of Chaucer's Canterbury Tales*, eds. W. F. Bryan and G. Dempster (New York, 1941; reprinted 1958). But these are specialists' books; constrained by considerations of audience and space, they provide only marginal summaries in English, which are of no help to the beginning student and often of limited help even to the scholar. We have therefore departed from this practice and have printed both the original texts and the full translations. In so doing, our aim is to assist the scholar and advanced student by making available original texts which are in many cases difficult to obtain, and at the same time to introduce the beginner to the values and the pleasures to be gained from the study of the other old languages.

There is necessarily some duplication of what has been printed already. Nine of the thirty-six texts in this volume also appear in *Sources and Analogues*, either in part or in their entirety. We have not included a close Flemish analogue to "The Miller's Tale," since there is a good translation of it in *Sources and Analogues*, and we have likewise excluded the

analogues from Boccaccio's *Decameron*, which is readily available in many translations and editions, and to which the student needs no introduction.

The great majority of texts are here translated for the first time. Some of the French fabliaux have been translated before, in Robert Hellman and Richard O'Gorman, *Fabliaux: Ribald Tales from the Old French* (New York, 1965) and in the anonymous *Norman Tales* (London, 1789); the tale from Apuleius has been frequently translated; the *Novellino* of Masuccio was translated into English by W. G. Waters in the nineteenth century; and Poggio's *Facetiae* were translated in the 1870's and more recently by B. J. Hurwood, *The Facetiae of Giovanni Francesco Poggio Bracciolini* (New York and London, 1968). None of the others have ever appeared in English, and we have made new translations even of those that have been translated, since we wanted to provide texts that are literal enough to be useful to the student who needs help in reading the originals. Nevertheless, we have occasionally departed from the originals—especially in matters of syntax, sequence of tenses, and idiom—in order to make readable versions for those interested only in the translations.

We have not, of course, included all the numerous analogues of Chaucer's fabliaux, but have concentrated on the earlier and closer analogues and excluded modern and very distant versions. In the general introduction to each section we have indicated the most important of the other analogues. However, the student will find here almost all the relevant texts mentioned in *Originals and Analogues* or *Sources and Analogues*, even works of the fifteenth and sixteenth centuries, which often illustrate the later development of Chaucer's tales rather than define the literary situation in his own time. We have also included a good many works not because they are analogues to Chaucer's specific tales but because they illustrate the general nature of his chosen genre, the fabliau. This is particularly true in the sections on "The Merchant's Tale" and "The Shipman's Tale." We have likewise tried to give samples of other medieval genres akin to the fabliau: novella, Shrovetide play, *Märe*, *Schwank*, *facetia*, mock epic, fable, *exemplum*, ballad. We have provided brief discussions of each of these terms in the headnote of the first selection illustrating the genre.

Therefore, we hope that our readers will find this volume more than simply an aid to the study of Chaucer. Our purpose is not only to help the student to study the development of the tales that Chaucer used but also to allow him to gain some understanding of the fact that popular themes did develop and did provide a variety of possibilities to the authors who used them in various genres and for their own various purposes. We hope that our readers will experience the special and rather sophisticated but very medieval pleasure of perceiving the ways in which

a series of talented writers impressed their own individualities upon a common theme, and will come to know and value at least a part of the rich store of comic literature that even today is often mentioned by scholars but seldom read by students.

Professor Hanns Fischer of Tübingen and the G. H. Beck Verlag of Munich kindly gave us permission to use Professor Fischer's text of "Von einem Plinten." The manuscript was typed by the ever patient and efficient Mrs. Benedicte Gilman. The initial suggestion for this volume came from Ian Watt, during an especially wet evening in Cambridge. We hope that the headnotes adequately record our debts to the many scholars on whose work we have drawn.

Lexington, Massachusetts T.M.A.
September, 1968 L. D. B.

Contents

The Miller's Tale and Its Analogues

The Reeve's Tale and Its Analogues

The Merchant's Tale and Its Analogues

The Shipman's Tale and Its Analogues

Some Analogues of Chaucer's Other Tales

The Literary Context of Chaucer's Fabliaux

TEXTS AND TRANSLATIONS

The Miller's Tale and Its Analogues

The literary background of "The Miller's Tale" is usually analyzed in terms of three prominent motifs woven into a story of cuckoldry: 1) the prophesied flood, 2) the misdirected kiss, 3) the hot iron. These motifs are widely distributed in medieval, and in modern oral, literature and occur sometimes individually, sometimes in combination. For the present volume we have selected a few of the earlier and more prominent European analogues which serve to illustrate either a single motif or the story of "The Miller's Tale" as a whole.

The episode from Apuleius' *Golden Ass* is included to remind the reader that the cuckold story in fabliau form reaches back to classical antiquity. It has none of the three characteristic motifs, but it makes an equally novel use of a tub to deceive the husband. "Bérenger au long cul" represents the ultimate elaboration of the misdirected kiss. It also shows a curious reversal of the narrative, since the kiss prepares the way for the cuckolding instead of being an adjunct to it. The two Italian novellas supplement one another: Masuccio uses the misdirected kiss and the hot iron while Morlini uses the prophesied disaster (an earthquake rather than a flood). Heinrich Wittenweiler and Hans Folz incorporate the misdirected kiss in genres other than the fabliau. In addition, Wittenweiler has a counterpart to Absolon's serenade; both scenes parody the courtly manner, but Wittenweiler substitutes rustic farce for Chaucer's light spoof. The *Schwänke* by Hans Sachs and Valentin Schumann date from a later period but preserve the whole story in everything but spirit. "Jankyn" revives in elliptical ballad form the voice, vocation, and avocation of Absolon; and "Old Hogyn" harks back in garbled fashion to the misdirected kiss. The final selection is the Latin verse adaptation of Caspar Cropacius, in which the pastoral setting and classical echoes are incongruous but

charitably veil some of the exhibitionism of the other versions. There is also a fourteenth-century Flemish analogue which assembles all the motifs, but it is not reproduced here since it is printed and translated in *Sources and Analogues of Chaucer's Canterbury Tales.*

Each of these texts has its own interest, but each serves also to define the special nature of Chaucer's achievement. The literary gap between "The Miller's Tale" and what follows here is indeed very great, and nowhere in the analogues will the reader find the same ingenious management of the story.

Chaucer's tale begins by establishing Nicholas' astrological and meteorological expertise ("To demen . . . Whan that men sholde have droghte or elles shoures . . .") so that later his prediction of a flood gains the credence of his landlord with no sacrifice of verisimilitude. The deception in the analogues is not so prepared and the credulity of Hans Sachs's smith and Valentin Schumann's merchant borders on imbecility. Similarly, whereas Chaucer makes Alisoun's trickery credible in terms of her kittenish love of mischief and her rather ingratiating lustfulness, Masuccio's Viola, with her three habitual lovers all entertained in a single night, has no distinguishable characteristics aside from her stamina; her counterpart in Hans Sachs's version is indiscriminately involved with her husband's apprentice and a priest, and the merchant's wife in Schumann's tale is curiously transformed from a virtuous wife into the mistress of two lovers because her husband spends his nights in the ship he has built in anticipation of the deluge. At this point, psychology has yielded to the lamest sort of rational motivation.

The husbands in the analogues fare no better. Viola's husband absents himself and is of no account, while Sachs's smith and Schumann's merchant are impossible simpletons. But Chaucer lends grace even to his poor cuckold John, whose eager cooperation in his own downfall tempers our amusement with sympathy. Despite the fact that he is jealous and "his wit was rude," there is a winning naiveté about him when, tired out by his hopeful labors, he falls asleep in his suspended kneading trough; the reader feels the unkindness of his fall and the misery inflicted on him by his household and his neighbors.

To be sure, Masuccio also makes some headway in the matter of characterization by distinguishing the personalities of the three lovers: the thin-blooded and timorous merchant, the lecherous friar, and the rough and ready smith. But he does not achieve the same sense of rivalry as between "hende" Nicholas and the dandy Absolon. There is a natural antipathy between the self-possessed and self-contained Nicholas with his quick hands and the perpetual lady's man Absolon with his lovelorn warblings, an antipathy which makes the eventual confrontation between the rivals psychologically neater. In the analogues there is not even a hint

that the rival lovers know one another, and the injuries they exchange are therefore more nearly gratuitous. Chaucer even arranges for a fitting distribution of the injuries, since the physically inclined Nicholas is physically chastened while the aesthete Absolon, the promiscuous kisser, with his express squeamishness about such things, undergoes a purely aesthetic indignity. In the analogues the brandings, broken limbs, and stray kisses are indiscriminately allotted and interchangeable. Nor do the analogues have anything to rival the quality of Chaucer's narrative control. At best Morlini has a certain elegance of formulation, and the quaking bed is a nice verbal touch, but neither Morlini nor the others have a sense of the play and interplay of the characters or a sense of dramatic design. Chaucer husbands his story, then brings it to a sudden and unprolonged climax at the moment when the hot iron strikes, John pitches off the roof, and the neighbors scurry to the scene, but Masuccio tarries to detail how the pieces were picked up and even permits a continuation of Viola's exertions. The other analogues stop to moralize.

Finally, Chaucer's tale, for all its cruelties, is more humane. There is, for example, only an angry whack with the brand instead of the pitiless thrust of Masuccio's offended smith using a rod calculatedly kept redhot. In this version, at least for the modern reader, the imagined sensation of pain spoils the comedy. Chaucer's humanity is also apparent in his moral restraint. The analogues cannot refrain from a *fabula docet*: Morlini and Cropacius abstract an odd condemnation of credulity, Hans Sachs comments perfunctorily and impartially that everyone got what he deserved, and Valentin Schumann draws an even more vengeful moral. Only Chaucer looks on with good-natured tolerance.

Apuleius' "Tale of a Poor Fellow's Cuckoldry"

The fabliau is a late medieval genre (largely thirteenth century) and has only scattered precursors in classical antiquity and the early Middle Ages. There is a somewhat putative classical counterpart in the so-called Milesian tales, a group of short, erotic tales written in Greek by Aristides of Miletus (second century B.C.) and referred to by several ancient writers, but now lost. They were translated into Latin, but this collection is also lost except for fragments.

What we do have is a reflection of the Milesian genre in the *Satyricon* of Petronius and the *Metamorphoses* or *Golden Ass* of Apuleius. In classical usage the whole of the *Golden Ass,* which is a medley of satirical, picaresque, and religious materials, was referred to as a *Milesia,* but in modern usage we tend to single out the erotic episodes woven into such narratives and call them Milesian tales. The most famous of such tales is the story of the Matron of Ephesus in the

---

DE ADULTERIO CUIUSDAM PAUPERIS FABULA

. . . cognoscimus lepidam de adulterio cuiusdam pauperis fabulam, quam vos etiam cognoscatis volo.

Is gracili pauperie laborans fabriles operas praebendo parvis illis mercedibus vitam tenebat. Erat ei tamen uxorcula etiam satis quidem tenuis et ipsa, verum tamen postrema lascivia famigerabilis.

Sed die quadam, dum matutino ille ad opus susceptum proficiscitur, statim latenter inrepit eius hospitium temerarius adulter. Ac dum Veneris conluctationibus securius operantur, maritus ignarus rerum ac nihil etiam tum tale suspicans inprovisus hospitium repetit. Iamque clausis et obseratis foribus uxoris laudata continentia ianuam pulsat sibilo etiam praesentiam suam denuntiante. Tunc mulier callida et ad huius modi flagitia perastutula tenacissimis amplexibus expeditum hominem dolio, quod erat in angulo semiobrutum sed alias vacuum, dissimulanter abscondit, et patefactis aedibus adhuc introeuntem maritum aspero sermone accipit: "Sicine vacuus et otiosus insinuatis manibus ambulabis mihi nec obito consueto

Satyricon and there are a number of similar stories in Apuleius.

We have some autobiographical information on the life, studies, travels, and family affairs of Apuleius, which can be gleaned from his oratorical works. He was born in Madaura in North Africa, some distance southwest of Carthage (Tunis), and apparently lived in the second century A.D., since certain contemporary references in his writings indicate the middle decades of that century, but we have no information about the circumstances surrounding the composition of the *Metamorphoses.*

One of the Milesian episodes (VIII, 5–7) has a distant resemblance to "The Miller's Tale" inasmuch as a wife and her lover use a tub to dupe the husband. It is a popular story and was used by Boccaccio as 7,2 in the *Decameron.* It reappears as a French fabliau and again in La Fontaine's *conte* "Le Cuvier." (See Elizabeth Haight, *Apuleius and his Influence* [New York, 1927]). It is reproduced here according to the text of F. Eyssenhardt (Berlin, 1868).

There are a number of modern translations of the *Metamorphoses* easily available to the student, for example those of Robert Graves, *The Transformation of Lucius* (various paperback and hardback editions) and Jack Lindsay, *The Golden Ass* (Bloomington: Indiana University Press, 1962). On the Milesian tales see Ben Edwin Perry, *The Ancient Romances: A Literary-Historical Account of Their Origins* (Berkeley and Los Angeles: University of California Press, 1967), pp. 90–95.

THE TALE OF A POOR FELLOW'S CUCKOLDRY

. . . I heard this amusing story about the cuckoldry of a poor fellow, which I would like you to know.

There was once a working man, who lived in narrow poverty, and who supported himself with the small prices he got from selling the articles he made. But he had a young wife, a very delicate thing, though she was notorious for her extreme lasciviousness.

And one day, as soon as he had hurried off to work in the morning, a bold lecher slipped secretly into his house. As his wife and her lover were fearlessly laboring in the grapplings of Venus, the husband—ignorant of this affair and indeed suspecting nothing of this sort—unexpectedly returned home. And when he found the doors shut and locked, he praised the chastity of his wife and knocked on the door, whistling to announce his presence. Then the ingenious wife—deeply skilled in this sort of shameful business—extracted her lover from her tight embraces and cleverly hid him in a tub that was in a corner, half covered over but otherwise empty; then, throwing open the door, she berated her husband, as he was just coming in, with these bitter words: "So! Are you sneaking home to me again—idle and empty-handed? How do you think we can

labore vitae nostrae prospicies et aliquid cibatui parabis? At ego misera pernox et per diem lanificio nervos meos contorqueo ut intra cellulam nostram saltem lucerna luceat. Quanto me felicior Daphne vicina, quae mero et prandio matutino saucia cum adulteris volutatur."

Sic confutatus maritus: "Ecquid istic est?" ait, "nam licet forensi negotio officinator noster attentus ferias nobis fecerit, tamen hodiernae cenulae nostrae prospexi. Vides istud dolium quod semper vacuum frustra locum detinet tantum et re vera praeter impedimentum conversationis nostrae nihil praestat amplius? Istud ego quinque denariis cuidam venditavi et adest ut dato pretio secum rem suam ferat. Quin itaque praecingeris mihique manum tantisper accommodas, ut exobrutum protinus tradatur emptori."

E re nata fallacia mulier temerarium tollens cachinnum: "Magnum," inquit, "istum virum ac strenuum negotiatorem nacta sum qui rem, quam ego mulier et intra hospitium contenta iam dudum septem denariis vendidi, minoris distraxit."

Additamento pretii laetus maritus: "Et quis ille," ait, "qui tanto pretio praestinavit?"

At illa: "Olim, inepte," inquit, "descendit in dolium sedulo soliditatem eius probaturus."

Nec ille sermoni mulieris defuit sed exurgens alacriter: "Vis," inquit, "verum scire, mater familias? Hoc tibi dolium nimis vetustum est et multifariam rimis hiantibus quassum." Ad maritumque eius dissimulanter conversus: "Quin tu quicunque es homuncio, lucernam," ait, "actutum mihi expedis, ut erasis intrinsecus sordibus diligenter aptum usui possis dinoscere, nisi nos putas aes de malo habere?"

Nec quicquam moratus ac suspicatus acer et egregius ille maritus accensa lucerna: "Discede," inquit, "frater et otiosus adsiste donec probe procuratum istud tibi repraesentem." Et cum dicto nudatus ipse delato lumine scabiem vestustam cariosae testae occipit exculpere. At vero adulter bellissimus ille pusio inclinatam dolio pronam uxorem fabri superincurvatus secure dedolabat. Ast illa capite in dolium demisso maritum suum astu meretricio tractabat ludicre. Hoc et illud et aliud et rursus aliud purgandum demonstrat digito suo, donec utroque opere perfecto acceptis septem denariis calamitosus faber collo suo gerens dolium coactus est ad hospitium adulteri perferre.

live if you don't work? How will you provide for our sustenance? And I, poor thing, work my fingers to the bone day and night at my spinning so that at least we can buy candles to light our miserable room! How much happier than I is our neighbor Daphne; every morning she drinks and feasts and tumbles with her lovers!"

And the confused husband said: "What's all this? Our boss gave us the day off because he had business in court; and nevertheless I have looked after our daily bread. Do you see that useless tub that is always empty, wastes so much space, and, to tell the truth, is good for nothing except to get in our way? I have sold it to a man for five denarii, and he is coming to pay the money and take the tub with him. So please give me a hand for a moment so that we can drag it out and have it ready for the buyer."

Unabashed by this turn of events, the deceitful woman laughed scornfully and said: "What a great husband and shrewd businessman I've gotten! He made a deal for less, when I, a mere woman content to stay in the house, just now sold it for seven denarii!"

The husband, overjoyed by the additional money, cried: "And who is the man who has paid so much?"

"You fool," she replied. "He just now got into the tub to check carefully to see if it was sound."

Her lover was paying close attention to her words and, quickly climbing out, he said: "If you want to know the truth, madam, this tub is very old and it is marred by a great many gaping cracks." And then, guilefully turning to the husband, he said: "Little man, whoever you are, could you quickly bring me a candle? I want to clean the dirt away from the inside so that I can see if the tub can be used—or do you think money grows on trees?"

The husband, with neither suspicion nor delay, eagerly lighted a candle and said: "Come out of there, dear brother, and stand aside while I clean this thoroughly for you." And with these words, he pulled off his shirt, took the candle, and climbed in to clean the ancient filth from the precious tub. Meanwhile, the dashing lover-boy stretched the worker's wife on the tub and, throwing himself upon her, fearlessly gave her a barrel of fun. And she put her head down into the tub and played a whore's trick on her husband; she pointed here and there, indicating this place and that which needed cleaning, until both jobs were finished. The poor worker received his seven denarii and was forced to carry the tub on his own back to the lecher's house.

Guérin's "Bérenger of the Long Arse"

The tale of Bérenger is one of those works classed as "fabliaux"—short, humorous, and often indecent tales in verse written in the thirteenth and fourteenth centuries. There are relatively few fabliaux in English; aside from the works of Chaucer, there is only the thirteenth-century "Dame Sirith." In France the genre flourished (over 160 French fabliaux survive), and Chaucer probably knew a good many of these tales in French. Usually the fabliaux deal with characters of the middle and lower classes, and it has often been thought that these bawdy tales therefore represent the taste of those classes in medieval times; Chaucer's Knight tells a romance, but his Miller and Reeve tell fabliaux. However, the taste for this sort of literature has never been restricted to any one class, and Per Nykrog has shown that sometimes the same authors wrote both fabliaux and romances and probably for the same audience. We have an example of this in the case of Marie de France; she wrote delicate and touching lays, such as *Le Chèvrefeuille,* but she also wrote the fabliaux that we include later in this volume. Likewise, Chaucer places his "Knight's Tale" directly alongside the bawdy tale of the Miller.

The best discussion in English of the technique of the fabliau is in Charles Muscatine's *Chaucer and the French Tradition* (Berkeley, 1957). General studies

---

DE BERANGIER AU LONC CUL

Tant ai dit contes et fableaus
Que j'ai trouvé, viez et noveaus,
Ne finai passez sont dui an,
Foi que ge doi à seint Johan,
Ne cuit que g'en face mais nul
Fors de Berengier au lonc cul;
N'avez vos mie oï encore,
Mais, par mon chief, g'en dirai ore;
Ne cuit que ge targe mais gaire.
10 Oiez que Guerins velt retraire
Que il avint en Lonbardie,
Où la gent n'est gaires hardie,
D'un chevalier qui ot pris fame,

of the genre are Joseph Bédier, *Les Fabliaux* (Paris, 1893); Per Nykrog, *Les Fabliaux* (Copenhagen, 1957), and Jean Rychner, *Contributions à l'étude des fabliaux* (Geneva, 1960). The standard collection is Anatole de Montaiglon and Gaston Raynaud, *Recueil général des fabliaux* (6 vols., Paris, 1872–1890). A still useful collection of summaries and translations into modern French is the four-volume collection by Legrand d'Aussy, *Fabliaux ou Contes,* first published in the eighteenth century. Many of Legrand's versions were translated into English anonymously as *Norman Tales from the French of Mr. Legrand* (London, 1789). Legrand's *Tales* were also turned into French verse by Barthélemi Imbert (Paris, 1788) and English versions of some of the tales (mainly lays rather than fabliaux) were produced by G. L. Way as *Fabliaux or Tales* (2 vols., London, 1796). A useful and recent collection of translations is that by Robert Hellman and Richard O'Gorman, *Fabliaux: Ribald Tales from the Old French* (New York: Thomas Y. Crowell, 1965).

The tale of Bérenger of the Long Arse exists in two different versions, of which we print the longer and better version by Guérin. There is also a German version of "Bérenger" in a chapbook from 1495. It has been photographically reproduced by Karl Schorbach, *Die historien von dem ritter Beringer* (Leipzig, 1893) [Seltene Drucke in Nachbildungen, I]. A similar situation recurs in Hans Folz's "Der arme Bäcker" (see Hanns Fischer, *Studien zur deutschen Märendichtung* [Tübingen, 1968], pp. 397–398).

We include "Bérenger" as an example of the "misdirected kiss," but if Chaucer had known the tale (he probably did not), he would also have relished the fine satiric attack on the "would-be gentleman," and he would perhaps have noted some traits of his own Sir Thopas. Our text is that of Montaiglon and Raynaud, vol. III, pp. 252–262.

BÉRENGER OF THE LONG ARSE

I have told so many tales and fabliaux
Which I have found, old and new,
That I have not finished for the past two years;
By the faith that I owe Saint John
I don't believe that I will compose another,
Except this—of Bérenger of the Long Arse.
You have never heard it before,
And, upon my soul, I shall tell it now;
I don't intend to be slow nor long.
Hear what Guérin would relate **10**
Of what happened in Lombardy
(Where people are not very brave),
Of a knight who had taken as a wife,

Ce m'est vis, une gentil dame,
Fille d'un riche chastelain,
Et cil estoit filz d'un vilein,
D'un usurier riche et conblé,
Et assez avoit vin et blé;
Brebis et vaches, et deniers
20 Ot à mines et à setiers,
Et li chastelains li devoit
Tant que paier ne le pooit,
Ainz dona à son filz sa fille.
Ainsi bons lignaiges aville,
Et li chastelain et li conte
Declinent tuit et vont à honte;
Se marient bas por avoir,
Si en doivent grant honte avoir,
Et grant domaige si ont il;
30 Li chevalier mauvais et vill
Et coart issent de tel gent,
Qui covoitent or et argent
Plus qu'il ne font chevalerie;
Ainsi est noblece perie.
Mais, à ce que ge ai appris,
De chief en chief con l'ai conquis,
Li chevaliers sanz demorer
Fist sa fille bien atorner;
Si la maria à vilain;
40 Sil fist chevalier de sa mein,
Si l'enmena, si con moi sanble:
Plus de x ans furent ensanble.
Li chevaliers amoit repos;
Il ne prisoit ne pris ne los,
Ne chevalerie II auz;
Tartes amoit et flaons chauz,
Et mout despisoit gent menue.
Quant la dame s'est parceüe
Que ses sires fu si mauvais,
50 Ainz pire de li ne fu mais
Por armes prenre ne baillier,
Mielz amast estrain enpaillier
Que manoier escu ne lance,
Dont set ele bien sanz doutance
A ce qu'il estoit si parliers
Qu'il n'estoit mie chevaliers

As I have heard, a noble lady,
Daughter of a rich nobleman,
Whereas he was the son of a churl,
Of a rich and prosperous usurer
Who had plenty of wine and grain;
Sheep and cattle and coins
He had by bushels and barrels; 20
And the nobleman owed him
So much that he could not pay,
And so he gave his daughter to the usurer's son.
Thus good heritage is abased,
And noblemen and counts
All decline and come to shame.
Those who marry beneath themselves for money
Ought to be ashamed of it,
And great harm they have from it.
Evil and lowborn knights 30
And cowards issue from such folk,
Who covet gold and silver
More than doing chivalrous deeds.
Thus does nobility perish.
But to return to that which I began,
From the beginning to the end, as I have gathered it:
The knight without delay
Had his daughter well decked out
And married her to the churl.
Thus he made him a knight with his own hands 40
And raised him in rank, as I have heard.
More than ten years they were together.
The new knight loved repose;
He did not consider the praise and fame
Of chivalry worth two cloves of garlic.
He loved tarts and hot custards,
And he greatly despised the lower classes.
Then the lady perceived
That her lord was so bad
That there was never a worse one than he 50
For taking or using arms;
He loved pressing a mattress better
Than wielding a shield or a lance;
And she knew well without doubt,
Because he was such a boaster,
That he was not at all a knight

Atrais ne de gentil lignaige;
Donc li ramentoit son paraige
Où tant a vaillanz chevaliers:
60 As armes sont hardiz et fiers,
A sejorner n'amoient rien.
Li chevalier entendi bien
Qu'ele nel dit se pour lui non:
"Dame," fait il, "g'ai bon renon;
N'avez nul si hardi parent
Que ge n'aie plus hardement
Et plus valor et plus proëce.
Ge sui chevalier sanz perece,
Le meillor trestot par ma mein;
70 Dame, vos le verroiz demain.
Se mes ennemis puis trouver,
Demain me vorrai esprouver;
Qui m'ont deffié par envie,
Ja nul n'en portera la vie;
Ge les metrai à tel meschief
Qu'à chascun copperai le chief;
Tuit seront mort, que qu'il ennuit."
Ainsi le laissierent la nuit,
Et l'endemain à l'enjornant
80 Li chevaliers leva avant;
Si fist ses armes aporter
Et son cors richement armer,
Quar armes avoit il mout beles,
Trestotes fresches et noveles.
Quant li chevaliers fu armez
Et desus son cheval montez,
Si se porpense qu'il fera,
Comment sa feme engignera
Qu'el le tiegne à bon chevalier.
90 En I bos mout grant et plenier
Qu'il voit mout près de sa maison
Le chevalier à esperon,
S'en vait tot droit en la forest
Que onques n'i fist nul arrest.
Quant en mi le bois fu entrez,
Desoz I arbre est arrestez,
Son cheval aresne et ataiche,
Son escu pant à I estaiche,
A I chaine dedenz le bos.

Descended from noble lineage.
Then she reminded him of her noble family,
In which there were so many valiant knights,
Who in arms are hardy and brave 60
And do not at all love to be idle.
The knight well understood
That she said all this for his benefit.
"Lady," he said, "I have great renown;
You do not have so bold an ancestor
That I don't have a braver one,
More valorous and of more prowess.
I am a knight without peer,
The best of all by my own hand.
Lady, you will see tomorrow; 70
If I can find my enemies,
Tomorrow you will see the proof.
They have defied me out of envy;
Because of that, I can no longer endure this life;
I will put them in such a bad state
That I will chop off all their heads;
All will be dead, whatever the difficulty."
They stopped then for the night,
And the next morning at dawn
The knight rose early. 80
He had his arms brought
And his body richly armed,
For he had very beautiful weapons,
All fresh and new.
When the knight was armed
And mounted on his horse,
He thought about what he could do
In order to trick his wife
Into considering him a good knight.
Into a large and deep wood 90
That he sees near his house
Went the knight spurring,
Straight into the forest,
Without making any stop.
When he arrived in the middle of the forest,
He stopped under a tree;
He reined his horse and tied it,
And hung his shield from a tree
By a chain attached to the wood.

100 Or escoutez que fist li sos;
Adonc a l'espée sachie
Qui estoit bien clere et forbie;
Si fiert en l'escu comme fous,
Mien escient, plus de c cous,
Que tot l'a tranchié et malmis,
Puis avoit son fort espié pris;
Sel brisa en IIII tronçons;
Enprès est montez es arçons
De la sele de son cheval;
110 Poignant s'en vait par mi I val
Tot droitement à sa maison.
De sa lance prent I tronçon,
Et de l'escu n'ot c'un quartier
Qu'il avoit porté tot entier;
Le cheval par la resne tint,
Et sa feme contre lui vint;
Au descendre li tint l'estrier.
Li chevaliers la boute au pié,
Qui ert mout forz de grant maniere:
120 "Traiez vos tost," fait il, "arriere;
Or ce sachiez, n'est mie droiz
Qu'à si bon chevalier touchoiz
Con ge sui, ne si alosé;
Il n'a si preuz ne si osé
En tot vostre lignaige au meins;
Ne sui mie matez ne veins,
Ainz ai los de chevalerie."
La dame fu tote esbahie,
Quant el vit l'escu despecié,
130 Et frait le fust de son espié;
Selonc ce qu'il li fait acroire,
Ne set que dire ne que croire;
Que paor a qu'il ne l'abace,
Quar li chevaliers la menace
Que vers lui n'aut ne que le touche.
La dame tint close sa bouche;
Onques puis mot ne respondi.
Que vos diroie? Ainsi servi
Le chevalier de ceste guille
140 Et tenoit la dame pour ville,
Et despisoit tot son lignaige,
Dont el nel tenoit pas à saige.

Now hear what this fool did: 100
He drew out his sword,
Which was polished and bright;
He beat on his shield as if he were mad—
I tell you, more than a hundred blows—
So that all is hacked and mistreated;
Then he took his stout lance
And broke it into four pieces.
Then he mounted on the bows
Of the saddle of his horse;
Spurring hard he goes through the middle of the valley, 110
Right straight to his house.
He holds a piece of his lance;
Of his shield he has only a quarter
That he had brought back whole.
He reins up his horse,
And his wife comes toward him.
She holds the stirrup for his descent;
The knight pushes her back with his foot,
For he had a very high and haughty manner.
"Get yourself back," he said; 120
"For you should know it is not right
That you should touch such a good knight
Nor one so covered with glory as I am.
There is no one in your family so bold
Or so daring as I am;
I have not been vanquished nor defeated;
Rather I have the prize of chivalry."
The lady was completely astonished
When she saw his pierced shield
And the broken wood of his lance; 130
Because of what he had made her believe
She did not know what to say or what to think;
She was afraid he would beat her,
For the knight so menaced her
That she did not dare go toward him or touch him.
The lady kept her mouth shut.
Not a word could she answer him.
What should I say to you? Thus
The knight served her with this guile,
And held the lady as a peasant 140
And despised all her ancestors,
Which she did not think right.

I jor refu du bois venuz
Li chevaliers, et ses escuz
Refu troez et despeciez,
Mais il n'est navrez ne plaiez,
Ne ses heaumes n'a point de mal,
Ainz est tot sain du chief à val;
Il n'est pas las ne recreüz.
150 De la dame n'est pas creüz
A ceste fois li chevaliers,
Qui dit qu'il a morz ses guerriers
Et ses enemis confonduz
Et à force pris et penduz.
Bien set la dame et aperçoit
Que par sa borde la deçoit,
Et panse, s'il i va jamais,
El bois que ele ira après
Et si verra quanqu'il fera
160 Et comment il se contendra.
Ainsinc la dame est pourpenssée,
Et, quant ce vint la matinée,
Li chevaliers se fist armer
Et dit que il ira tuer
III chevaliers qui le menacent
Et qui grant ennui li porchacent;
Gaitant le vont, dont il se plaint.
La dame li dit qu'il i maint
De ses serjanz ou III ou quatre;
170 Si porra plus seür conbatre:
"Dame, ge n'i merrai nului;
Par moi lor mourai tel ennui
Que ja nus n'en estordra vis."
Atant s'est à la voie mis,
Par grant aïr el bois se fiert,
Et la dame unes armes quiert;
Con un chevalier s'est armée,
Et puis sor I cheval montée.
Cele qui n'a point de sejor
180 S'en vait tot après son seignor,
Qui ja ert el bois enbatuz,
Et ses escuz ert ja penduz
A I chaine, et si le feroit,
A s'espée le detranchoit.
Si fait tel noise et tel martire

One day again from the woods
This knight returned, and his shield
He brought back hacked and pierced.
But he was not wounded nor harmed,
Nor did his helm show any injury,
And he is untouched from head to toe;
He is not at all tired or fatigued.
This time the knight 150
Is not believed by the lady
When he says he has killed his antagonists
And confounded his enemies,
Taken them by force and hanged them.
The lady perceived and well knew
That he had deceived her by some stratagem,
And she determines that if he goes again
To the woods she will follow him
And thus see what he does
And how he conducts himself there. 160
Thus the lady is determined;
When morning comes,
The knight has himself armed
And says he is going to kill
Three knights who menace him
And thus have greatly annoyed him;
They go looking for him—of this he complains.
The lady tells him that he should take with him
Three or four of his servants;
Thus he could be more secure in battle. 170
"Lady, I shall take no one there.
By myself I shall inflict on them such damage
That none shall escape alive."
Immediately he set out on his way.
In a great fury he made for the woods.
And the lady found a suit of armor;
She armed herself like a knight,
And then mounted on a war-horse.
She did not delay at all,
But set out straight after her lord, 180
Who had already plunged into the woods
And had hung his shield
From a chain, as he usually did,
And was hacking at it with his sword.
He made such a noise and raised such havoc

Qui l'oïst, il pooist bien dire
Ce sont c et mile deable;
Ne le tenez vos pas à fable,
Grant noise meine et grant tempeste,
190 Et la dame I petit s'areste;
Et, quant a la chose veüe,
Esbahie est et esperdue,
Et, quant ot assez escouté,
Atant a le cheval hurté
Vers son mari, si li escrie:
"Vassal, vassal, est ce folie
Que vos mon bois me decoupez?
Malvais sui, se vos m'eschapez,
Que ne soiez toz detranchiez;
200 Vostre escu pourquoi laidangiez
Qui ne vos avoit riens meffait?
Mout avez hui meü fol plait,
Mal dahait ore qui vos prise,
Quant à lui avez guerre prise."
Quant cil a le mot entendu,
Esbahiz fu et esperdu;
La dame n'a pas conneüe,
Au poing li chiet l'espée nue,
Et trestoz li sans li foï:
210 "Sire," fait il, "por Dieu merci,
Se ge vos ai de riens meffait,
Gel vos amenderai sanz plait;
A vostre gré mout volentiers
Vos donrai avoir et deniers."
La dame dit: "Se Dieu me gart,
Vos parleroiz d'autre Bernart
Ainz que vos partoiz de cest leu,
Quar ge vos partirai I geu:
Comment que vos jostez à moi
220 Et ge vos creant et octroi,
Se vos cheez, ja n'i faudrez,
Maintenant la teste perdrez
Que ja de vos n'aurai pitié;
Ou ge descendrai jus à pié,
Si me prenrai à abaissier;
Vos me venroiz el cul baisier,
Trés el milieu se vos volez.
Prenez ce que mielz amerez;

That he who heard it would say
There were eleven hundred devils there.
Don't take this for a fable;
He raised a great noise there and a great uproar,
And the lady stopped for a moment. 190
And when she saw what was going on,
She was amazed, struck speechless;
And when she had heard enough,
She straightway galloped her horse
Toward her husband, and she cried:
"Young man, young man! What is this folly?
Why are you cutting down my woods?
I'll be cursed if you escape me
Without being cut into pieces!
Why do you mistreat your shield, 200
Which has never done you any harm?
You have started a crazy business today;
God's hate on him who prizes you
When you thus make war on it!"
When he heard these words,
He was astonished and speechless.
He did not recognize the lady;
The naked sword fell from his hand,
And straightway his senses fled;
"Sire," he said, "for the mercy of God, 210
If I have done you wrong in any way,
I will make it up to you without argument;
Willingly—as much as you want—
I will give you riches and money."
The lady says: "As God may save me,
You will speak of another Bernart
Before you leave this place,
For I will offer you a bargain:
Either you joust with me—
And I swear to you and guarantee, 220
If you fall, without fail
Straightway you lose your head,
For I will have no pity on you—
Or I will dismount on foot,
And I will bend over
And you will come and kiss my arse,
Exactly in the middle, if you please.
Decide now which you prefer

De ce gieu ice vos commant."
230 Et cil qui doute mout forment
Et qui plains est de coardie,
Dit que il ne jostera mie:
"Sire," fait il, "ge l'ai voé,
Ne josterai à home né,
Mais descendez, si ne vos griet,
Et ge ferai ce qu'il vos siet."
La dame ne volt respit querre,
Tot maintenant mist pié à terre,
Sa robe prist à sozlever,
240 Devant lui prist à estuper:
"Sire, metez ça vostre face,"
Et cil regarde la crevace;
Du cul et du con, li resanble
Que trestot li tenist ensanble.
A lui meïsme pense et dit
Que onques si lonc cul ne vit;
Dont l'a baisié de lorde pais
A loi de coart hom mauvais
Mout près du trou iluec endroit;
250 Bien l'a or mené à son droit.
Atant la dame est retornée;
Li chevaliers l'a apelée:
"Beaus sire, vo non quar me dites,
Et puis vos en alez toz quites."
"Vassaus, mes nons n'ert ja celez
Onc mais tel non ne fu trovez;
De mes paraus n'en est il nul;
J'ai non Berengier au lonc cul,
Qui à toz les coarz fait honte."
260 Atant a afiné son conte;
Si s'en est en maison alée;
Au mieus qu'el pot s'est desarmée,
Puis a mandé I chevalier
Que ele amoit et tenoit chier;
Dedenz sa chambre tot aese
L'enmaine, si l'acole et baise.
Atant ez le seignor qui vient
Du bois; cele qui poi le crient
Ne se daigna por lui movoir;
270 Son ami fait lez lui seoir.
Li chevaliers toz abosmez

Of these choices that I offer you."
Then he who was so badly frightened 230
And who is filled with cowardice
Says that he will not joust.
"Sir," he says, "I have vowed
Not to joust with any living man.
So dismount, if it is no trouble,
And I shall do what you please."
The lady would grant no respite
But immediately put foot on ground
And raised her robe
And bent over in front of him. 240
"Sir, put your face here."
And he looked at the crevice
Of the arse and the quim, and it seemed
To him that it was all one.
He thinks and says to himself
That he has never before seen so long an arse.
Then he kissed her with a hearty kiss,
In the manner of an evil cowardly man,
Right at the hole there;
She has well brought him to what he deserved. 250
Straightway the lady turned around,
And the knight cried to her:
"Good sir, I beg that you tell me your name,
And then you can leave here entirely satisfied."
"Young man, my name will never be concealed;
But such a name was never found;
None of my family bears it but me.
I am called Bérenger of the Long Arse,
Who puts all cowards to shame."
As soon as her speech was finished, 260
The lady went back to her house
And disarmed herself as fast as she could,
And then she sent for a knight
Whom she loved and held dear;
In her bedchamber well at ease
She led him and embraced and kissed him.
Straightway, behold the husband who comes
From the wood. She, who little feared him,
Did not deign to move for him;
She had her lover sit next to her. 270
The knight, much chagrined,

S'en est dedens la chambre entrez;
Quant vit la dame et son ami,
Sachiez point ne li abeli:
"Dame," fait il isnelement,
"Vos me servez vileinement
Qui amenez home çaienz;
Vos le conparrez par mes denz."
"Taisiez vos en," fait el, "mauvais!
280 Or gardez que n'en parlez mais,
Quar, se vos m'aviez desdite,
Foi que ge doi seint Esperite,
Tantost de vos me clameroie
Por le despit que g'en auroie;
Si serez vos cous et jalous."
"A qui vos clameriez vous
De moi, par la vostre proiere?"
"A qui? A vostre chier compere,
Qui vos tint ja en son dangier,
290 Et c'est mesire Berangier
Au lonc cul, qui vos fera honte."
Quant il oit que cele li conte,
Mout en ot grant honte et grant ire;
Onques puis ne l'osa desdire,
Desconfit se sent et maté;
Et cele fait sa volenté,
Qui ne fu sote ne vilaine:
A mol pastor chie lous laine.

Explicit de Berangier au lonc cul.

Entered into the bedroom;
When he saw the lady and her lover,
You know he was not at all pleased.
"Lady," he said quickly,
"You serve me churlishly
To bring a man in here;
You will pay for it, by my teeth!"
"Be quiet," she said, "good-for-nothing!
And watch out that you don't say anything more, **280**
For, if you speak wrong to me in any way,
By the faith that I owe the Holy Spirit,
Straightway I shall complain of you
For the scorn that I have had from you,
And you will become a jealous cuckold."
"To whom will you complain of me,
Where make your plea?"
"To whom? To your dear friend
Who had you in his power;
That is my Lord Bérenger **290**
Of the Long Arse, who will put you to shame."
When he heard what she said,
He had great shame and great anger,
But he did not dare to say anything against her.
He felt himself discomfited and defeated;
And she did what she pleased,
She who was neither foolish nor lowborn.
"When the shepherd is weak, the wolf shits wool."

Here ends Bérenger of the Long Arse.

Masuccio's "Viola and Her Lovers"

The erotic story in verse is peculiarly the property of France in the form of the fabliau, but the erotic story in prose is just as peculiarly the property of Italy in the form of the *novella.* The Renaissance *novella* grew from eclectic beginnings and drew on such sources as Apuleius, the fabliaux, sermon anecdotes, troubadour anecdotes, *exempla,* Eastern stories, and so forth. This variety of material was forged into a successful genre by Boccaccio, whose master stroke gave the impetus for numerous imitations and a multiplication of *novelle* through the sixteenth century. Chaucer was in Italy in 1372–1373 and perhaps earlier. His stories suggest knowledge of one, possibly two, *novella* writers, Boccaccio and perhaps Sercambi. Boccaccio provides analogues to "The Reeve's Tale" (*Decameron* 9,6) and "The Shipman's Tale" (*Decameron* 8,1). Neither of these analogues is reproduced in this volume, since they are easily available. In other cases there are correspondences between Chaucer and later *novella* writers (Sacchetti, Masuccio, Morlini) based on common sources.

The chief early collections of *novelle* are the following:

1) *Novellino.* This is a collection of *novelle* without author or title, except in one manuscript, where it is called *Libro di novelle et di bel parlar gientile.* It was first published by Carlo Gualteruzzi at Bologna in 1525 under the title *Le ciento novelle antike.* A second, altered, edition was published by Vincenzo

---

VIOLA E LI SUOI AMANTI

Argomento

La Viola promette a tre suoi amanti in una medesima notte satisfare: va il primo, e dal secondo gli è la preda interdetta: il terzo anda, e dal secondo beffezzato e proibito l'entrare; lui s'accorge dell'inganno e vede la forza, opera l'ingegno, e dell'uno e dell'altro se vendica, e con gran danno del primo e del secondo resta di tale preda ultimo possessore.

Borghini at Florence in 1572 under the manuscript title *Libro di novelle et di bel parlar gientile.* The title *Novellino* (not to be confused with Masuccio's *Novellino* below) now in use derives from the much later Milanese edition of 1836. The dating indices suggest that the original collection was made around 1280.

2) Giovanni Boccaccio (1313–1375), *Decameron* (ca. 1350). The *Decameron* was first printed in Venice in 1470.

3) Giovanni Fiorentino, *Pecorone.* The collection consists of fifty *novelle* exchanged by a friar and a nun and written sometime between 1378 and 1385. The title means "blockhead" and is taken from some deprecatory verses affixed to a manuscript by a disgruntled reader and then reproduced in subsequent manuscripts and editions.

4) Giovanni Sercambi (1347–1424), *Novelliero.* This collection consists of 155 *novelle,* which were probably written for the most part between 1385 and 1387. The frame bears some resemblance to Chaucer's Canterbury fiction since Sercambi tells his stories to a group of travelers, who have left his native city of Lucca in order to escape a plague (as in Boccaccio's frame story).

5) Franco Sacchetti (1335–1400), *Trecentonovelle* (ca. 1388–1395).

6) Gentile Sermini. Sermini wrote forty *novelle* some time after 1424.

7) Tommaso Guardato di Salerno, otherwise known as Masuccio Salernitano, *Novellino* (1476). The collection comprises fifty *novelle.*

8) Giovanni Sabadino degli Arienti (*d.* 1510), *Le Porretane* (1478). A collection of sixty-one *novelle.*

9) Giorlamo Morlini, *Novellae* (1520). A collection of eighty-one *novelle* in Latin.

10) Matteo Bandello (1484–1561), *Novelle* (1554). A collection of 214 *novelle.* A rich survey of early Italian *novella* writing is provided by Lettero Di Francia, *Novellistica* (Milan, 1924).

The text is reprinted from *Novellino: restituto alla sua antica lezione,* Luigi Settembrini, ed. (Naples, 1874), Novella XXIX, pp. 313–321.

VIOLA AND HER LOVERS

The Argument

Viola promises to satisfy three lovers during the same night. The first one comes, but is kept from his booty by the second. The third one comes and, tricked by the second, is prevented from entering, but he sees the trick, has an idea, devises a remedy, takes revenge on both rivals, and is the ultimate possessor of the booty, much to the detriment of both the first and the second lover.

AL MAGNIFICO MESSERE JACOMO AZZAIUOLO
NOBILISSIMO FIORENTINO

Esordio

Improprio e non conveniente saria il mio operare, magnifico e di virtù ornato misser Jacomo, cognoscendote di benigna e gioconda complessione da la natura dotato, se scrivendoti la presente novella, di materia fluematica malinconica e mesta fosse nè poco nè molto tramata overo ordita. Ricevila dunque con piacere te supplico, chè del certo dal principio insino al fine tutta de jocose piacevolezze la troverai edificata, e in manera che a te e agli ascoltanti di soperchio e continuo riso saranno cagione.

Narrazione

Il prossimo passato Jennaro fè un anno che in Napoli fu un bon omo lignaiuolo, il mestiero del quale a niuna altra cosa si estendea che in fare zoccoli, il quale tenea casa a fitto di costa a la Sellaria a un larghetto posto dietro la Zecca vecchia, e avendo una vaga e bellissima moglie, la quale ancora che come a giovane non fosse punto schifa nè sdegnosa dei vagheggiamenti dei suoi quasi infiniti amatori, pure tra la molta brigata tre ne erano da costei, che Viola aveva nome, più che altri amati e favoriti: l'uno era fabro suo vicino, l'altro un mercante genoese, e il terzo un frate, del nome e abito del quale come che non me ne ricordo pure so che era un esperto e famoso corsalo: a li quali tutti tre senza l'uno de l'altro avea promesso come il marito pernottava fuori di casa satisfarli di loro desiderio. Ove accadde che non passaro molti di che il marito andò a Ponte a Selece per condurre un somaro carico di zoccoli smarrati, per poscia polirli in Napoli come era già solito fare, per lo cui bisogno dovendovi insino al seguente dì dimorare, fu da tutti tre gli aspettanti tale partire e pernottare saputo.

E come che ciascuno di loro da per sè si ponesse in ordine, pure el primo che si representò alle battaglie a l'uscio de la nostra Viola, e forse per essere più fervente amante, fu il genoese, e caramente la pregò che la notte lo aspettasse a cena e ad albergo, facendole le più larghe promesse come in simili contratti fare si sogliono, de modo che Viola per non tenerlo in tempo gli disse contentarsi ma che venisse tanto di notte che non fosse dalle brigate della contrada veduto. Il genoese lietissimo rispose, Sia col nome de Dio; e da lei partito se n'andò spacciatamente a la Loggia o tal volta al Pendino, e comparò due avantaggiati caponi grossi bianchi e lunghi, e con pane fresco, e de più maniere d'ottimi vini, occultamente li mandò in casa de la giovene. Il frate celebrati li divini ufficii, desideroso che la

TO THE MAGNIFICENT JACOMO AZZAIUOLO, A VERY NOBLE FLORENTINE

Exordium

My work would be inappropriate and unfitting, magnificent and virtuous Sir Jacomo, if, knowing you to be endowed by nature with a benign and agreeable temper, I had in composing for you the present story stitched or embroidered it with either much or little phlegmatic, sad, and melancholy matter. Receive it then, I pray you, with pleasure, since surely you will find it from beginning to end composed entirely with pleasant humor, and in such a manner that it will cause you and other listeners uproarious and repeated laughter.

The Story

A year ago last January there was a good wood-worker in Naples, whose trade consisted solely in making wooden shoes. He rented a house next to the saddlers' quarter in a nice little spot behind the old mint and had a wife who was charming and very beautiful. Although young as she was, she was not at all averse or disdainful to the suits of her almost countless lovers, still there were in this large number three whom the young woman (Viola by name) favored and loved above the others: one was her neighbor the smith, the second a Genoese merchant, and the third a friar (though I don't remember his name and order, I know he was an expert and notorious adventurer). She had promised all three of these privily that she would satisfy their desires as soon as her husband spent a night away from home. Now it happened that not many days passed before her husband went to Ponte a Selece to accompany a packass loaded with unfinished wooden shoes in order to have them polished in Naples, as he was accustomed. Since he was obliged to remain on this business until the following day, all three hopefuls were apprised of his departure and his night away.

Though each of them made his own preparations, the first to appear on the battlefield at the door of our Viola, perhaps because he was the most ardent lover, was the Genoese. He asked her sweetly to await him that night with dinner and lodging, making her the most extravagant promises, as is the custom in such arrangements, so that Viola without further delay told him to rest content, but to come late enough at night so as not to be seen by anyone in the neighborhood. The Genoese replied joyfully, "Farewell in God's name!" And leaving her he went off hurriedly to the Loggia, or perhaps it was the Pendino, and bought two extra-large capons—big, white, and fat—and together with fresh bread and several excellent wines had them sent secretly to the young woman's house. When the friar had

fatta promessa gli fosse osservata, postasi la via tra' piedi, traversando di molte strate, come famelico lupo s'abattesse in alcuna smarrita pecora de la greggia, pervenne ove era la Viola, e chiamatala le disse che lui intendea per ogni modo venire a stare la notte con lei. Viola che per cosa alcuna il Genoese averia ingannato; e per conoscere il frate temerario e fastidioso molto, non gli averia di contentarlo possuto negare, così confusa non sapea che deliberare; pur come a prudente di subito le occorse con acconcia maniera a tutto provvedere, e al frate con piacevolezza rispose, essere al suo volere presta, ma che non venesse prima de le cinque ore, per cagione che un piccolo suo cognato venea a stare con lei, il quale insino a tale ora non saria addormito; e satisfatto che avesse il suo desiderio se n'andasse subito con Dio. Il frate vedendo che pur era ricevuto, non curando del resto, disse di farlo, e andò via.

Il fabro che in Doana era stato insino al tardo occupato al traere de certo ferro, retornandosene verso casa trovò Viola a la fenestra, e le disse: Pur questa notte che tuo marito non vi è mi potrai ricevere in grazia, e ben per te se il fai altrimenti tieni per fermo ogni tuo disegno da me ti sarà turbato. Viola che molto lo amava, e non poco lo temeva, pensando pur che tempo le avanzava de la lunga notte di tutti e tre li avventori poter liberare, come a li due aveva trovata maniera, così propose al terzo, ancora che ultimo fosse, dare recapito, e gli disse: Mauro mio, tu sai come ne sono io male tollerata in questa contrada, e quanto tutte con giusta cagione cercheriano di cacciarmene; e sono di quelle che me fanno la guardia sino a mezza notte, e imperò a tale che loro insidie non me abbiano a offendere, dimora a venire per sino all'alba, a quell'ora che solito se'levarti, e faraimi segno, che io te aprirò, e staremo un pezzo insieme per questa prima volta, che col tempo provvederemo per migliore cammino. Il fabro canoscendo che lei con colorate ragioni si movea, e che lui pur averia sua intentione, senza altro replicare restò a tale ordine contento.

Lo Genoese come notte fu occultamente se n'entrò in casa di Viola, il quale ancora che da lei fosse lietamente raccolto, e più volte baciatisi, nondimeno da la sua infreddata natura non gli essendo concesso senza caldo di letto o di altri argomenti li concupiscibili appetiti svegliare, si pose a cavallo e cominciò a fare sua salatuccia fin che i caponi si penavano ad arrostire per mal foco o che altro ne fosse stata cagione, ancora che la giovene tutta si andasse struggendo, dubitando non le sopravvenesse la seconda vivanda avanti che avesse la prima assaggiata: pure erano già sonate tre ore, e la loro cena non era incominciata. E in questi termini sentero piccare l'uscio: il genoese molto impaurito disse: Ei mi pare che l'uscio nostro sia tocco. La giovene rispose: Tu di'vero, e certo io dubito che sia mio fratello; ma non temere che io provvederò che non te vederà:

celebrated the divine offices, he was eager for the fulfillment of her promise; and hurrying at top speed through the streets, like a famished wolf attacking some sheep strayed from the flock, he arrived at Viola's house. He called out to her and told her that he had every intention of coming to spend the night with her. Viola, who would not have deceived the Genoese for anything, but who knew that the friar was bold and very insistent, had no mind to refuse him satisfaction and was so confused that she did not know what to do. Still, as befits a prudent woman, it suddenly occurred to her how to make suitable provision for all contingencies and she replied pleasantly to the friar that she was at his disposal, but that he should not come before eleven o'clock because a little relative was staying with her and would not be asleep until that time, and with this satisfaction he should take his leave quickly in God's name. The friar, seeing that he had been received and caring for nothing else, said he would do as she wished and went on his way.

The smith, who had been in the customs house until late, busy with the release of some iron, found Viola at her window on his way home and said to her, "Tonight when your husband is out, you can make me welcome, and it will be well for you if you do, for if you do not, you may be sure that I will upset any other plans of yours." Viola, who loved him well and feared him not a little, thought that indeed there was time enough during the long night to attend to all three customers; and having found a way with the first two, she proposed to make delivery to the third as well, though he came last. She said to him, "Dear Mauro, you know how disliked I am in this neighborhood and how all the women (with good reason) are trying to get rid of me; some of them spy on me even in the middle of the night. But to prevent my being caught in their snares wait until dawn, at the hour you are accustomed to get up, and signal to me to let you in. We can be together for a short while this first time and later we will find a better way." The smith, seeing that she had plausible reasons and that he had achieved his purpose, was satisfied with the arrangement without further ado.

At nightfall the Genoese secretly entered Viola's house, but though he was given a gay reception and many kisses, still his sluggish nature did not permit him to satisfy his fleshly appetites without the warmth of a bed and other inducements. He mounted his steed and began to go through his paces, since the capons were slow to roast either from a lack of heat or for some other reason. Meanwhile the young woman was all anxiety, fearing to be anticipated by the second course before she had savored the first. Nine o'clock had already struck and their dinner was not even begun. At this point they heard a knock at the door. The Genoese was much alarmed and said, "Alas! I believe someone is knocking at the door." The young woman replied, "That's true and I am very much afraid it's my little

e però esci per questa fenestra, e poniti a sedere a questo arvarello de erbicciole che è qui, che io vederò chi è, e quello che vole dire, e ne lo manderò presto. Il genoese più timido che caldo d'amore, come che una minuta pioggia facesse da freddissimo vento menata che molti per neve l'avrebbeno giudicata, pure fe'quanto per Viola gli fu ordinato; la quale serratogli dietro, e, per estimare chi era colui che aveva picchiato, occultata la cena, se ne venne all'uscio; e certificata che era l'importuno frate, alquanto turbata gli disse: Tu sei molto presto venuto, e non hai servato l'ordine te donai: trista me che per non aspettare un poco de tempo vorrai che io sia morta. E con queste ed altre simili parole pur gli aperse; il quale entrato, senza cerimonie di baci come il genoese fatto avea, rattissimamente a non serrar l'uscio le donò per una volta plenaria remissione, non per autorità che il generale gli avesse donata ma da sua poderosa natura concessagli: e credendo Viola che quello gli bastasse a farnelo contento ritornare, il vide che montava in casa: di che lei serrato l'uscio seguendolo per le scale, gli dicea: Vattene per l'amore di Dio, che mio cognato non è anco addormito, e del certo ti sentirà. Il frate non curando del suo dire, salito su, e trovato ancora il foco calente, scalfatosi un poco, appicciata un'altra volta la Viola cominciò a sonare un novo ballo, con più piacevole melodia che quella che il poveretto Genoese col battere dei denti pel soverchio freddo facea; il quale per le fessure della finestra ogni cosa vedendo, quanto da tale dolore, dal timore d'essere sentito e dal gran freddo che senteva fosse afflitto, ciascuno a sè pensando ne potrà fare giudicio. E più volte del saltare lui avria il partito preso, se non che la oscurità era si grande che non gli facea l'altezza scorgere, e anco che pur dimorava in speranza che il frate per essere più del dovere satisfatto, e da la giovane de continuo al partirsi sollicitato, se n'andasse. Ma il frate dal piacere della bella giovene riscaldato, senza togliersi la Viola di braccia avendo di più e diversi tratti de moderni balli non che a lei ma al Genoese che con poco piacere li mirava insegnati, avea deliberato di mai partirsi di là fin che dalla chiarezza del giorno non ne fosse cacciato.

E così stando insino alle dieci ore, sentì il fabro che col preso segno inquietava l'uscio di Viola: el che lui alla giovene rivolto disse: chi tocca il tuo uscio? Lei rispose: Egli è il continuo stimolo di questo fabro mio vicino, il quale nè con bona nè con rea risposta me l'ho possuto togliere dinanzi. Il frate che facetissimo era subito gli occorse fare una nova piacevolezza, e rattissimo se ne venne giù a l'uscio, e con sommessa voce, come Viola fosse, disse: Chi se'tu? Lui rispose: Sono io, non mi conosci tu? aprimi, ti prego, che tutto mi bagno. Esso disse: Dolente me, che io non posso per questo uscio che aprendolo fa tanto rumore che ne seguiria scandalo. Lui non avendo dove fuggir l'acqua sollicitava che gli aprisse, che tutto si

friar, but never fear, I will make sure that he doesn't see you. So climb out the window and sit down on this little window-box full of plants until I see who it is and what he wants, and I'll send him away quickly." The Genoese, more timorous than hot with love, and despite the fact that a fine rain was falling whipped by such a cold wind that many people would have considered it snow, did exactly what Viola told him. She locked him out and, having guessed who was knocking, she hid the dinner and went to the door. She found that it was the importunate friar and, somewhat confused, said to him, "You have come too early and have not followed the directions I gave you; poor me, whom you would see dead rather than wait a little while." And with these and other similar words she let him in. Once inside, and without any kissing ceremony such as the Genoese had used, he was so avid that he did not even lock the door, but gave her plenary absolution on the spot, not by the authority vested in him by his superior but by the authority granted by his own potent nature. Viola, who thought that this was enough to satisfy him and send him on his way, now saw him go upstairs. Therefore, bolting the door, she followed him up the stairs and said, "Be off for the love of God; my little relative is not asleep yet and he is sure to hear you." The friar took no notice of what she said, entered, found the fire still hot, warmed himself a little, and embracing Viola once again began a new dance with a pleasanter melody than the one the poor Genoese made with the chattering of his teeth in the bitter cold. The latter saw everything through the cracks in the window and the reader may judge for himself how he was afflicted with chagrin, with the fear of being detected, and with the terrible cold. He was about to jump down several times, but it was too dark for him to judge the height and he continued to wait in the hope that the friar, who had gotten more than his due and whom the young woman repeatedly asked to leave, would go away. But the friar was kindled by the pleasure of the beautiful girl and did not let Viola out of his arms, since he knew a number of new dance steps to teach her (and the Genoese as well, who looked on with no particular pleasure) and had decided not to leave until daylight drove him away.

Thus he stayed until four o'clock and heard the smith making a commotion at Viola's door with the agreed signal. Turning to the young woman he said, "Who is knocking at your door?" She replied, "It's that continual nuisance, my neighbor the smith, whom I haven't been able to get rid of with good words or bad!" The friar, who was a practical joker, suddenly got an idea for a new bit of fun; he quickly went out to the door and with a very high-pitched voice, as if he were Viola, he said, "Who is it?" The other replied, "It's me, don't you recognize me? Open up, I beg you, I'm sopping wet." The friar said, "Alas, I can't open the door because it would make so much noise that there would be a scandal." The smith could not get out of the rain and en-

struggea per amore suo. Il frate che con gran piacere lo tenea in tempo per farlo ben bagnare gli disse: Anima mia, baciami un tratto per questa fessura che è ben larga, per sino a che vederò di piano aprire questa maledetta porta. Il fabro sel crese, e molto lieto a baciare s'acconciò: il frate che fra quello mezzo s'avea cavate le brache gli porse la bocca per la quale si rigetta il soverchio de la sentina: il fabro credendosi appicciare i dolci labbri di Viola, de continente cognobbe e par tatto e per odore ciò che di ver già era, ed estimò quello essere altro cacciatore il quale più sollecito di lui gli aveva tolto il piacere e dipoi in tale maniera il beffeggiasse. Di che subito propose tale ricevuto scorno non passare irremunerato; e facendo vista di mordere e leccare, gli disse: Viola mia, fra questo mezzo che tu vederai di aprirme io anderò per un mantello, che non posso più durare l'acqua. Il frate rispose: Va col nome di Dio e torna presto, ridendo con la giovene in maniera che non si posseano in piedi tenere.

Il fabro entrato in bottega fe'spacciatamente una verga di ferro a modo di spido e ben focante lasciò stare, e disse al garzone: Sta attento, e quando io sputo e tu leggiero te ne vieni a me con questa verga. E ciò detto si ritornò a tenere in trame dell'entrare, e da una parola a un'altra il fabro disse, Baciatemi un'altra volta. Il frate che era più presto a tale volgimento che una scimia, subito gli porgè la solita voragine: Mauro dato il segno, al suo garzone, prestissimo gli presentò il focante ferro, il quale recatosi in mano, e preso tempo, gli donò una stoccata presso vallescura che ve lo pose quasi un palmo dentro. Il frate sentendo la fiera percossa fu costretto a buttare un grido che toccò il cielo, e mugliando di continuo come un toro ferito. Tutti i vicini destatisi con lumi in mano si faceano per le finestre, e ognuno dimandava di tale novità la cagione. Il dolente genoese che era in maniera assiderato che poco più gli bisognava stare che convertito in giazzo ivi si averiano i suoi giorni terminati, udendo tale rumore, e vedendo tanti lumi per la contrada, e già appressare l'alba, per non essere quivi trovato a modo di ladro posto in vergogna, preso per ultimo partito di buttarsi giù; e pigliato core, e raccomandandosi a Dio così fece. E gli fu la fortuna cosi favorevole che al percotere in terra trovò una pietra sopra la quale dato il piede e voltatosi in maniera che si fraccò una gamba in più pezzi; il quale dal fiero dolore oppresso non meno che il frate fu costretto al gridare fortissimo i suoi oimai. Il fabro correndo al rumore, e trovato e cognosciuto il Genoese, e vista la cagione del suo gridare, alquanto pietoso divenuto, con aiuto del suo garzone con difficoltá non piccola il menorono in bottega, e saputo da lui tutto il fatto come era andato, e chi era il frate, si cavò fuori e pose silenzio al molto abbaiare

treated her to open the door because he was burning with love for her. The friar, who took great pleasure in putting him off in order to give him a thorough dousing, said, "My love, give me a little kiss through this crack, which is large enough, while I see if I can get this cursed door open quietly." The smith believed him and, all agog, made ready for the kiss. The friar, who in the meantime had let down his trousers, stuck out the mouth which spews out the excess bilge. The smith, who thought he was kissing Viola's sweet lips, immediately realized by both touch and smell what it really was and decided that this was another hunter who, quicker than himself, had bagged the game and then mocked him this way. Having suffered such a disgrace, he straightway determined not to let it pass unavenged and, pretending to smack his lips, he said, "My Viola, while you are seeing how to open the door, I will go after a cloak because I can no longer stand the rain." The friar replied, "Go in God's name and return quickly"—at the same time laughing with the young woman so hard that they could hardly keep their feet.

The smith entered his workshop, quickly forged an iron rod into a spit, let it heat well, and said to his apprentice, "Pay good attention and when I spit, come to me right away with this rod." With this he returned to carry out his plan for gaining entrance. One word led to another and the smith said, "Kiss me again." The friar, who was quicker than a monkey to take advantage of this turn of events, immediately proffered him the usual orifice. Mauro gave the sign to his apprentice who instantly handed over the red-hot iron, which he took in his hand and with which he carefully delivered a thrust hard by the dark valley so that it went in almost a hand's breadth. The friar, feeling the fierce blow, perforce uttered a yell which echoed from the high heavens and kept on roaring like a wounded bull. All the neighbors were roused and came to the windows with lights in hand, and each asked the reason for such a disturbance. When the wretched Genoese, who was so frozen that little more was left for him but to end his days there turned into ice, heard such a clamor and saw so many lights in the neighborhood and realized that dawn was approaching, he finally resolved to jump down so as not to be found there like a thief caught red-handed. Summoning up his courage and commending himself to God, he jumped. And fortune smiled so kindly on him that when he landed, he struck a rock with his foot in such a way that he broke his leg in several places. Overcome by the fierce pain no less than the friar, he was forced to vent his woes in a loud voice. The smith, attracted by the noise, found and recognized the Genoese, and seeing the reason for his screams, he took a little pity on him and with the help of his apprentice and with no little difficulty they carried him to the workshop. The smith, when he learned from him the whole story and what had happened, and who the friar was, went outside and silenced the commotion among

dei vicini, dicendo che erano stati due suoi garzoni che si avevano feriti. Ed essendo ognuno quieto, come il frate volse, la Viola chiamò piano il fabro, il quale in casa intratogli e trovato il frate mezzo morto, dopo molti e diversi debatti, col suo fante sel posero in spalla e insino al suo convento nel condussero; e ritornato ne fece il Genoese sopra un somaro portare a la sua stanza. E lui in casa di Viola rientrato essendo omai dì, mangiatisi insieme i caponi, e oltre a ciò satisfatto intieramente al suo desiderio, lietissimo se ne tornò a battere il martello. E così il maestro come ad ultimo corretore fe'restare i compagni con beffe e danno e con dolore.

Masuccio

Di non piccola prudenza potrà essere la nostra Viola e meritamente commendata per avere a tutti tre gli amanti in una medesima notte con acconcia maniera recapito donato; e come che li due con lor grandi interessi se ne ritornassero a casa accompagnati donde soli se n'erano partiti, pur lei con la plenaria remissione più volte datale dal venerabile patre restò a insegnare al fabro la nova maniera dei balli, che il Genoese con poco piacere mirandoli avea già imparati.

the neighbors, saying that two of his apprentices had been at each other's throats. When all was quiet, Viola, as the friar desired, called softly for the smith, who entered the house and found the friar half dead. After much discussion he and his servant put him on their shoulders and took him to his monastery. Then they returned and had the Genoese brought to his lodging on an ass. But the smith himself reentered Viola's house at dawn and when they had eaten the capons together and otherwise completely satisfied their desires, he merrily returned to wielding his hammer. And thus Master Mauro, though he came last, left his rivals disgraced, injured, and in pain.

Masuccio

Our Viola is a clever girl and deserves to be congratulated for having made suitable provision for all three lovers in one and the same night. And while two of them, with all the interest on their investment, returned home escorted, though they had come alone, Viola, having received plenary absolution several times from the venerable father, remained to teach the smith the fashionable new dances which the Genoese had already witnessed with such little edification.

Morlini's "The Monk Who Prophesied an Earthquake"

Giorlamo Morlini's *Novellae* are a good illustration of the vernacular literature's influence on the more learned Latin language, with the old popular tale

---

DE MONACHO QUI VENTURUM TERRAE MOTUM VATICINATUS EST

Monachus, oratoriae facultatis instructus, ordinis Minorum, V. dictus, Neapoli, ustus amore cujusdam venustissimae ac hujusmodi civitatis nobilissimae mulieris, ut cum ea concumberet cavillum excogitavit, viamque reperit quae propositum ad exitum produceret: vaticinium profiteri, nocte terrae motum fore quo tota gens civitatis peribit; et hoc non alio adinvenit nisi ut, recedentibus domesticis e lare Glycerii suae, tutius cum ea per noctem baccharetur in venerem. Sicque desiderans quod cogitaverat exsequi, quum primum rota solis lucidam diem peperit, in pulpitum ascendens, magna dicendi ubertate sub aenigma ratione ostentare coepit Deum optimum maximum criminibus hominum praeparasse ruinam, sibique renuntiatum esse tertia post hac nocte terrae motum venturum, cujus violenti vibratione atque concussione cuncta civitatis moenia dissipatum et erutum iri: Et non alio noctu hoc eventurum auspicor nisi ut incautos oppressosque somno omnes aeque puniat. Cujus quidem apparens sermo, licet mendax, adeo populum formidine repletum reddidit, quin commodum in paludibus sub divo tuti excogitabant exstare. Quid dicam? Praeambula hora vaticinatae noctis, Parthenopeus populus, credulus, ut ita dicam, nimium, civitatem deseruerunt, et per campos, paludes campestriaque tentoria tendere videbantur: pars vero per templa supplices accedebant; pars quantumcumque minima, praeparata fuga, aedes custodiebant. Monachus quidem (non monachus, sed chalconida sociatus), cum sua Glycerio cubans, ob veneream colluctationem terrae motum in cubile, nec in terra, intulit. Sicque pro se tantum vaticinatus fuit, populumque fefellit.

Novella indicat maximum vitium esse faciliter credere, et maxime falsis vaticinatoribus, qui, quum sint mortales, ostentant se temere coelestia scire.

turned into elegant Latin prose complete with rhetorical flourishes (such as "Quid dicam?"—"What should I say?"). The moralizing conclusion to Morlini's tale also shows how easily a tale could slip from one genre to another, since here Morlini almost turns his tale into an *exemplum* (see p. 366–367). Our text is from Eugen Kölbing, "Zu Chaucers Erzählung des Müllers," *Zeitschrift für vergleichende Literaturgeschichte*, XII (1898), 449.

THE MONK WHO PROPHESIED AN EARTHQUAKE

A monk of Naples, named V . . . , who belonged to the Minorite Order and had a gift for oratory, conceived a passion for a certain very beautiful and, for this city, very noble woman. He hit on a scheme to enable him to sleep with her and found a way which would lead to that desired end: namely to predict that at night there would be an earthquake in which the whole population of the city would perish. And he invented this for no other reason than that, after the servants had left the house of his Glycerium, he could more securely revel in love with her during the night. And thus wishing to carry out what he had planned, as soon as the rays of the sun brought forth bright day, ascending the pulpit, he began with great eloquence and secret design to show that Almighty God had prepared the destruction of mankind for their sins and that it had been announced to him that there would be an earthquake on the third night, which with its violent trembling and rending would crumble and destroy all the walls of the city: "And I prophesy that this will happen at night for no other reason than to punish all equally while they are unmindful and overcome by sleep." And when this sermon was known, though false, still it filled the people with fear so that they thought it advisable to seek safety in marshes under the open sky. What should I say? Just before the prophesied night the people of Naples, credulous to a degree in my opinion, left the city and could be seen putting up their tents in fields and marshes. Some to be sure went to the churches in supplication; some, though a small party, having prepared for flight, remained at home. The monk however, (no monk, but an associate of . . . .)*, lying with his Glycerium, what with the struggle of love, caused an earthquake in bed and not in the earth. And thus the prophecy applied only to him and deceived the people.

The novella suggests that it is a great fault to be credulous and especially to believe false prophets who, although they are mortal, claim to know heavenly matters.

* The meaning of *chalconida* is unknown.

Heinrich Wittenweiler's "Ring"

Wittenweiler's *Ring* is a mock-romantic and mock-didactic (though not always facetious) epic of 9699 verses preserved in a single manuscript. The dialect places it in what is now Switzerland. What we know of the author and his title is contained in the opening lines, where he announces, "Ein puoch, daz ist 'Der Ring' genannt/ (Mit einem edeln stain bechlait),/ Wan es ze ring umb uns beschait/ Der welte lauff und lert auch wol,/ Was man tuon und lassen schol." ["A book entitled 'The Ring' (adorned with a precious gem) because it rings us with the way of the world and teaches what one should and shouldn't do"]. A

WITTENWEILER'S RING

Bertschi Triefnas, a hero in the village of Lappenhausen, has his heart set on Metzi Rüerenzumph, whose ill-favored appearance is described in alienating detail.

In good romance tradition, the courtship is preceded by a test of prowess in the form of a tournament. Bertschi and his peasant cohorts, mounted on an assortment of nags, asses, and draught animals, stumble into battle and find themselves aligned against a courtly stranger named Neidhart, a legendary reincarnation of the poet and peasant baiter, Neidhart von Reuenthal. One after the other the heroes are dumped or drubbed until only two remain, who are so frightened that they make abject confessions to Neidhart in anticipation of imminent death. In a sequel to the tourney the peasants fare no better, since on Neidhart's advice they fight with bundles of straw, while Neidhart himself secretes an iron mace in his straw bundle. In the meantime the very unladylike peasant girls in the gallery give a raucous display of enthusiasm to the point where one of them falls out of the gallery and is killed.

Undeterred by his ill fortune in the tourney, Bertschi continues to besiege Metzi with his attentions. One night he awakens the piper Gunterfai ("Faker") to assist him in a serenade. Gunterfai's reluctance is overcome by money and the two set out helter-skelter, Gunterfai trouserless because he has been unable to locate them. It is at this point that the motif of the misdirected kiss is inserted, though in so truncated a form that the kiss does not actually take place. The hundred verses or so covering this serenade scene are translated here in order to give the reader an idea of the rollicking tone and broad humor of the original.

few lines later the author names himself and substitutes for the usual appeal for attention an expression of indifference toward the reader's reaction, "Secht es aver ichts hie inn,/ Das weder nutz noch tagalt pring,/ So mügt irs haben für ein mär,/ Sprach Hainreich Wittenweilär." ["But if you see anything in it that affords neither profit nor pleasure, you may regard it as a lie, said Heinrich Wittenweiler."]. Heinrich's exact identity is a matter of conjecture and the chronological indications in the text are so vague that the usual dating around 1400 is about equally conjectural. A poem of such length and ambition is entirely isolated in the German literature of the period, though it inherits and combines didactic and satirical attitudes from the thirteenth and fourteenth centuries.

The whole of the epic is conveniently available to the English-speaking student in a translation by George Fenwick Jones, *Wittenwiler's Ring, Colkelbie Sow: Two Comic-Didactic Works from the Fifteenth Century* (Chapel Hill: University of North Carolina Press, 1956). A summary follows.

But he didn't want to stop **1282**
And served Lady Metzi day and night.
With heart and soul
He could not be untrue to her.
At night he regularly went out
And sneaked off to her father's house.
He tore the clay from off the wall
And chewed it: to him it wasn't sour.
He prowled about here and there, **1290**
His mind was set on entering the door.
Time and tide were too long for him.
How often he began to sing:
"I long to pine for you,
I long to die for you."
With that he crept up to the window
On the chance that he could see her there.
He found nothing; that stirred his gall,
For thus his song was wasted.
He did this often and repeatedly; **1300**
Alas it didn't help him worth a nickel.
And so he crept to the piper's house
And said: "My dear companion, up
And help me tonight with your art;
I suffer from the rut of love!"
Gunterfai was snoring hard:
He dreamed he was fishing in the sea.
What should the hero say?

His throat was dry.
1310 My Triefnas was undeterred:
He called the musician louder still
And struck the housedoor
With two great stones.
He banged on the door with a stick
And said: "Get up, good fellow!"
At the same moment
The musician began to awaken
And jumped up like a wild hare.
"What's this all about?"
1320 He cried forthwith.
His wife he threw out of bed;
He thought that she had done it.
"You dissembler," said the man,
"Why do you plague me all night long?"
Bertschi would have laughed aloud.
Then the flame of love tormented him
So much that his nose bled.
When that dried up, he pounded the door;
He moved off and called the man:
1330 "For God's sake get up
And go with me; I've need of you!"
Gunterfai was full of wrath
And in addition he'd drunk his fill.
He cried: "Be off, you son of a mare,
And knock no more; that's best for you!"
Bertschi was offended by the scolding
And still more by the insolence.
He thought: "I'll be a villian!
If I didn't need you so,
1340 I'd maim your calves and cows
And break your back on top of that!
Now I have to sing your tune,
But the day will come when I get even!"
Sweetly he began to speak:
"Don't be angry, dear piper.
It's me, Triefnas; come with me.
I'll give you seven pence."
When Gunterfai heard this,
He began a different cry:
1350 "Oh, dear sir, is it you?
I didn't recognize you, forgive me!"

Then he got up immediately;
He wiped his eyes with straw.
He looked for his pants, but they were lost.
He could have done without them nicely
Except that at the moment his purse
Was attached to these same pants.
He couldn't be without it then;
He wanted to put his money in it.
The search, forsooth, lasted so long **1360**
That Bertschi thrice jumped up and down
From the anger that he felt.
"Aren't you coming?" he shouted to the man.
"Yes," he said, "right away,
As soon as I can find my pants."
Then Triefnas replied forthwith:
"Come, let the breeches be!
I'll give you both money and the purse,
I'll give you beer and the bottle too."
Who was happier than Gunterfai? **1370**
He didn't give a hang for the breeches
And came flying out
In a rush and a flurry
With his brand-new pipes.
Bertschi said: "Now blow and blow
And let us court tonight.
I'll pay you fourfold for it!"
The pipes resounded everywhere
So that mountain and valley echoed.
They came to Metzi's house. **1380**
She offered her arse at the window.
Then Bertschi said right off:
"Oh fortunate am I that I have seen
Your shapely face!
Lean toward me, dear Metzi, lean!"
The noise began to displease the neighbors;
They would rather have slept.

Eventually the neighborhood is aroused by the ruckus and the serenaders are driven off.

The following evening Bertschi tries to visit Metzi while she is milking in the barn, but she raises an outcry which brings her father Fritz and the neighbors running. The poor cow is startled and butts wildly in all directions while Bertschi makes good his escape. Three nights later

Bertschi is again overcome by his burning desire and tries to get a glimpse of Metzi from the roof of her house. He ends by tumbling down the chimney so that, as the poet tells us, he burns both outside and inside. The outraged father now locks her in a loft, where she discourses with herself in a variant on the motif later more elaborately developed in Diderot's *Les Bijoux indiscrets.*

Bertschi, more feverishly in love than ever, appeals to his cousin, the scribe Nabelreiber, who gives him a quantity of advice on the art of love and composes a suitably courtly love letter for him. Bertschi tosses it through Metzi's window attached to a stone, which unfortunately hits her squarely on the head and knocks her unconscious. When she comes to, she discovers the letter, but, being unable to read, can make nothing of it. She laments the deceitfulness of the world, which puts her in doubt about whom to entrust with the reading of the letter, and finally decides to approach the village doctor Krippenkra, whom she can plausibly consult for her head injury in any event. The doctor promptly blackmails her with the letter and makes her pregnant with miraculous instantaneousness, though he reassures her by giving her an elaborate prescription to restore her virginity. At the same time he composes a favorable and even more elaborate response to Bertschi's letter, complete with mythological and allegorical apparatus. The letter is entrusted to a bawd who delivers it to an overjoyed Bertschi. Bertschi assembles his relatives to ask advice, and after a protracted debate on the pros and cons of matrimony, decides to marry Metzi. Two of the relatives are dispatched to win over the bride's father. It is now his turn to assemble a family council, to which Bertschi is summoned to prove his worth. He passes the initial test by reciting the Lord's Prayer, Hail Mary, and the Creed and is then treated to a series of edifying harangues (in a serious vein) on learning, religion, hygiene, morals, and domestic affairs. Eventually the wedding is celebrated amid general festivities, including a banquet at which every rule of social deportment recommended by the medieval books of etiquette is systematically trampled under foot. The merrymaking ultimately degenerates into a brawl, which in turn develops into a war between the villages of Lappenhausen and Nissingen.

But before the war achieves full-scale proportions, the bridal night takes place. Thanks to the doctor's prescription and the bride's theatrics, Bertschi is persuaded that all is well.

The war is then resumed and the opposing camps take counsel and seek allies on a truly universal scale, from real, fictional, and legendary realms. The fighting rages back and forth until Lappenhausen is betrayed to the enemy by a disgruntled female inhabitant. On the final day Bertschi defends himself valiantly as he is besieged on a haystack but escapes only to discover that Lappenhausen is pillaged and destroyed.

He is led to reflect on the transitoriness of the works of man and, in an unexpectedly devout ending, he retires as a recluse to the middle of the Black Forest.

Hans Folz's "Mirthful Peasant Play"

A *Fastnachtspiel* or Shrovetide play is a performance connected with the carnival period before Lent most familiar to Americans from the Mardi Gras festivities. The Church tended to condone an interlude of relaxation and license before the period of fasting and religious preoccupation, and the celebrations thus sanctioned seem to have been boisterous. The *Fastnachtspiele* reflect this tone and are known for projecting low humor with an insistence and stamina beside which Chaucer's occasional pricklings look very incidental. The famous German literary historian Gödecke was led to pronounce in disgust that "every speaker is a pig, every line a vulgarity, and every joke an obscenity." Contemporary students may still blanch, but their devotion to history is more likely to outweigh considerations of taste.

The *Fastnachtspiele* are peculiar to the fifteenth and sixteenth centuries (ca. 1430–1600) and flourished particularly in Nürnberg, where the best known writers in the fifteenth century were Hans Rosenplüt and Hans Folz, the author of the following example. These little plays were performed by groups of guild journeymen, perhaps at first extemporaneously and later more formally; the players circulated from house to house or acted in a tavern. The form represented here is typical: a prologue-speaker, a sequence of players speaking mono-

---

GAR AIN VAST SPOTISCH PAURNSPIL GAR KURZWEILIG ZU LESEN. SAGT IETLICHER WAS IM AUF DER PUOLSCHAFT GEGENT IST.

Der Einschreier:

Got grues all, die wir hinnen sechen!
Ir herren, es ist ain anschlag gschechen,
Welich paur das aubenteurischst sag,
Das im mit puolen begeget sein tag,
Den wirt man mit aim kranz begauben
Und wirt darzuo den vortanz haben.
Darumb wer iederman still hinnen,
So wert ir hubscher schwenk noch innen.

logues on a given theme illustrating some form of folly, an epilogue-speaker, and a concluding dance. Hans Folz, as he tells us at the end of the piece, was a barber-surgeon and a native of Worms, though he moved to Nürnberg in 1479 and stayed there until his death sometime between 1506 and 1515. In a period of little literary distinction in Germany he looms relatively large as a writer of *Meistersang,* of didactic poems, and of *Schwänke* (see p. 64), as well as of *Fastnachtspiele.* He is mentioned in a number of documents from Nürnberg, for example, a decree from January 19, 1486, authorizing a performance: "It is granted to Master Hans, the barber, and his associates, to perform a seemly *Fastnachtspiel* in rhyme provided that they perform it decently and take no money for it." The work here will indicate to what extent Master Hans heeded the city fathers' plea for decency. It suggests what sort of company the motif of the "misdirected kiss" might normally keep and tends to put Chaucer in a relatively genteel light.

Information about the *Fastnachtspiel* is most conveniently available in Eckehard Catholy, *Fastnachtspiel* (Stuttgart: Metzler, 1966). A brief statement in English is given in Derek Maurice van Abbé, "What is Fastnachtspiel?" *AUMLA* [*Journal of the Australasian Universities Language and Literature Association*], 12 (1959), 36–44.

The language of the fifteenth century presents certain difficulties to the student who approaches it with a knowledge of modern German, and there is no special dictionary for the period. In order to facilitate the use of the German text, we have footnoted the forms of difficult words as they occur in Grimm, *Deutsches Wörterbuch.* In many cases the passage in question is cited by Grimm. The text is taken from Adelbert von Keller, *Fastnachtspiele aus dem 15ten Jahrhundert,* (Stuttgart, 1853) I, 330–336.

A VERY MIRTHFUL PEASANT PLAY, VERY PLEASANT TO READ. EACH SAYS WHAT HAS HAPPENED TO HIM ON HIS LOVE ADVENTURES

Prologue:

God's greetings to all whom we see here!
Good folk, a proposal has been made,
That whichever fellow tells the best tale
Of love adventures that have happened to him
Will be rewarded with a wreath
And will be leader of the dance besides.
Therefore let everyone be silent here,
And you will hear some merry tales.

Der erst paur:

Ir herren, ich kam eins an ain end
10 Und gab meim puolen zuo verstend
Durch ein warzeichen, das ich es wer,
Und weiss nit, wie si ungefer
Ein *hafen* mit dreck rauss wirt schwingen,
Das mir die scherben am hals behiengen,
Dan das mir ainss zuo guot geschach,
Mich jagten fier durch ainen pach,
Da *zabelt* ich in als in aim *nuosch*,
Piss ich mich gleich wol wider gewuosch.

Der ander paur:

Was geheustu dich mit deiner puolschaft an?
20 Solstu mir auch ain halbe nacht stan
Und auf aine an aim laden warten,
Als ich auf meine, die vil zarten,
So stuond ich wol piss sechs in die nacht.
Erst kum der verheit sack der ungeschlacht
Und sprach: Mein Künzlin, pistu do?
Do sprach ich: Ei pox leichnams willen jo.
Und die weil ich also auf si laus,
Reckt si den ars zuom venster rauss.
Do wolt ich ganz wen, es wer der kopf,
30 Und hielt mich hin zuo, ich verheiter dropf,
Und meinet si kussen an den munt
Und draf ir eben den hinteren *spunt*.
Do plies si mir ain staub under die augen,
Das mir kaum *klegkt* ein kübel voll laugen,
Pis ich des gschmachs ain wenig ward frei.
Acht selb, welcher ain pesser puoler sei.

Der dritt paur:

Schweig! Ich eilt eins zuo meim puolen
Und meint mein herz mit ir zuo erkuolen;
So kumpt einr ungefar darzuo
40 Und fragt mich, was ich pei der tuo,
Ich soll des teufels nam naher gen,
Was ich nu pei der sein hab zuo sten.

13. hafen 17. zappeln; nusch 32. spund 34. klecken (4)

The first peasant:

Good folk, I once came to a place
And gave my mistress to understand 10
By a sign that it was me,
And I don't know how it came to pass
That she flung out a crock of refuse
So that the splinters hung around my neck;
Then so that something good would happen to me,
Four fellows chased me through a brook.
There I squirmed as in a trough
Until I washed myself clean again.

The second peasant:

Why make so much of your adventure?
You should stand half a night like me 20
And wait for a wench at a window,
As I waited for mine, the gentle creature!
I waited a good six hours into the night.
Only then came the cursed wretch, the monster,
And said: "My little Kunz, is it you?"
Then I said: "Yes, by God's wounds, it's me!"
And while I'm listening for her,
She sticks her arse out the window.
I thought for sure it was her head
And bent toward it, stupid fool, 30
And thought to kiss her on the mouth
And hit her right on the hinder mouth.
Then she blew dirt in my face
So that a whole tub of lye was hardly enough
To free me a little from the smell.
Judge yourself who is the better lover!

The third peasant:

Silence! I hurried once to my mistress
And thought to cool my desire with her;
Then someone comes along by chance
And asks me what I'm doing at her house 40
And bids me be off in the devil's name,
Whatever I'm doing standing by his mistress' house.

Ich waiss nit, wie ich hin wider prum
Und auch mit worten an in kum,
Das er mich pei dem har erknaust
Und rempt mir des angesichts mit der faust,
Das mirs maul geschwall als ainr krotten,
Und in mein allergrösten nöten
Stuont die verheit huor und *kuttert* stet,
50 Als der si mit willen gekutzelt hett.

Der fiert paur:

Auf mein sterben, du manst mich dran,
Eins det ich ain *karren* mit meiner an,
Ich wolt mich in ir pet ie wagen.
Samer pox leichnam, was sol ich sagen,
Ob ich zuo fruo oder zuo spat was kumen?
Es hetten fier das haus ein genomen
Und zankten sich umb den *verheiten* sack,
Do kam ich so eben auf den kirchtak,
Das si des kriegs under in vergassen
60 Und wurden iren zorn an mir auss lassen
Und *firkelten* mich hin und erwider,
Ein stiegen auf, die ander nider,
Pis ich uber ein glender ab fill,
Dan ains ich mich drin riemen will,
Het ich die tür als pald nit funden,
Ich het des puolns hart uberwunden.

Der funft paur:

Nun höra, lieber, was ir ist gschechen!
Do gwan mir aine an ain *nechen*,
Der ich ungfer kam an ir thür;
70 So spricht si: Freunt, wie schleicht ir für?
It wolt mir zuo hoffertig sein.
In dem tritt ich zuo ir hin ein
Und will wen, die huor ken mich gleich eben,
Und thet mir als pald anleutung geben
Ein stiegen auf pis an ir pett;
So pald und ich ain drit drein tätt
Und het mein klaider abgezogen
Und plos under die deck geschmogen,

49. **kittern** 52. **karren** (4) 57. **verheien** 61. **firgeln** 68. **necken**

I don't know how I mumbled back
And gave answer to his words
That made him seize me by the hair,
And he twisted my face with his fist
So that my lip swelled like a toad's,
And in my greatest hour of need
The cursed whore stood and giggled away
As if he had tickled her on purpose. **50**

The fourth peasant:

Upon my death, you remind me
That once I conspired with my mistress
That I would venture into her bed.
God's wounds, what should I say,
Did I come too early or too late?
Four fellows had invaded the house
And were fighting over the lascivious hussy.
I came to the party just in time
So that they forgot their quarrel
And vented their wrath on me **60**
And tugged me back and forth
Up one stair and down another
Until I fell over a railing.
But in one respect I praise my luck,
If I hadn't found the door right off,
I would have been well cured of love adventures.

The fifth peasant:

Now listen, good fellow, what happened to me!
A girl played a trick on me
When by chance I came to her door.
She spoke thus: "Friend, why do you sneak by? **70**
You seem to be too proud for me."
With that I step into her house
And forsooth she sees I'm not proud;
And she gave me directions right away
Up a stair and to her bed.
As soon as I had stepped in
And had taken off my clothes
And crawled under the blanket bare,

So fall ich durch ab in ain stall;
80 Do war ainr mit aim knüttel als pall
Und schluog mich, das ich kam entran,
Und streich auch was ich mocht darvon,
Und muost meins gelts und klaider enperen.
Wie mainst, kund die nit drucken scheren?

Der sechst paur:

Ach got, es will nichts mit euch sein.
Ich puolt eins wol ain jar umb ein,
Pis sie mir eins zilt in ein fas,
Do ein schweinsmuoter mit jungen in was.
Ich klopf dran und sprach: Pistu do?
90 Sich straupt die sau und sprach: Jo, jo.
Wer froer, dan ich? Und want, si wers,
Und daucht mir lauter kains gefers
Und wolt des schimpfs bald machen ent
Und nestelt mich vor auf behent
Und puckt mich und will zuo ir hin ein,
So rumpelt si mir her zwischen die pein
Und mit mir durch den hof auss drat
Piss in ain allerdüefest kot.
Do ich mit marter von ir kam,
100 Den laf ich zuo meim haus hein nam.
Dan was darf man hie weiter fragen?
Ich was mit dreck also uberzogen,
Das ich het ab zuo keren mit aim pesen.
Rot, wer ist do am *reisigosten* gewesen?

Der sibent paur:

So narr, waistu sunst nichts, dan das?
Jo wer ich, do ich nechten was,
Do puolet ich schier ain stund umb aine,
Das was ain hübsche und ein raine,
Des mir das herz gleich nach ir echzet,
110 Als ain hunlin, das an der sunnen lechzet,
Die pot mir ir hant gar nachet zwir,
Als sanft was der verheiten krotten mit mir.
Mainst nit, het ich mir der weil genomen,
Ich wolt auch eins guoten sein bekomen?

104. **reisig** (3)

I fell right through into a stall.
There was a fellow with a cudgel 80
And hit me so that I barely escaped
And ran away as hard as I could
And had to do without my money and clothes.
I ask you, didn't she know a dodge?

The sixth peasant:

Good Lord, your stories aren't worth a groat.
Once I wooed a girl for a year
Until she finally arranged a sty for me
In which there was a sow with her young.
I knocked and said: "Is it you?"
The sow moved and grunted: "Yup, yup." 90
Who was happier than I? I thought it was she
And expected no danger at all
And wanted to finish the game on the spot
And quickly unbuttoned in front
And bent down and wanted to get in to her;
Then she rushed between my legs
And ran out into the yard with me
Into the very deepest mud.
When I got away from her all battered,
I took off for my house. 100
What more is there to ask?
I was so covered with filth
That I had to sweep it off with a broom.
Guess, who is now the bravest fellow?

The seventh peasant:

Well, fool, have you nothing better than that?
I wish I were where I was last night,
Where I was wooed hour after hour.
She was pretty and virtuous
So that my heart longs for her
Like a puppydog for the sun. 110
She gave me her hand, all naked, twice,
So loving was the nasty bitch with me!
Don't you think that if I'd stayed a while
I would have enjoyed something good?

Der acht paur:

Ach schweig, du verheites göffelmaul!
Jo wer ich mein tag nit gwesen so faul,
Ich wolt mein *neun* gnuok han erpuolt.
Ich han wol ainr so süess *gespuolt,*
Das si mir ein wörtlin stach in ein or
120 Und ist halt freilich noch nit ein jor.
Ja sichstus, mein lieber hautgesell,
Do het ich gen einr ain sollichs gefell,
Das ich mein, wer ich lenger da pliben,
Ich wolt mich pas mit ir han zuo geriben.

Der neunt paur:

Ach ir narren, wie habt ir ein riemen!
Ir mochts doch aller teufel nam verplüemen,
Und hett irs als guot, als ichs gehabt han,
Ich main, ir *geüt* eur lebtag darvan,
Wan ich kam neulich an ain stat,
130 Do hetten mich ir drei geren gehabt,
Ich liess si aber als ungluck han,
Si petten mich dann vor darumb gar schon
Und hetten darzuo zuo spannen auss,
Das ich ess und drunk und lept im sauss
Und ritt in der stat spacieren um.
Sunst denk mir keinr, das ich zuo ir kum.

Der zechent paur:

Ach du verheiter eselskopf,
Dir *laust* wol ein nar im schopf,
So du dein ruomes dich nit schempst,
140 Jo wen du mein puolschaft recht vernempst.
Ich schut ainr hubschlich ab die *aglen,*
Das ir die pein gen perg auf *gaglen,*
Dan far ich umher mit aim raschen
Und wird ir zuo dem puosen naschen,
So hept si ain lachen und kütren an
Und weist mich seiberlich hindan.
Wan ir euch also zuo künt flicken,
Es hett all welt mit euch zuo schicken.

116. **neune** 117. **spulen** (4) 128. **gäuen** 138. **lausen** 141. **agen** 142. **gaglen** where these verses are explained

The eighth peasant:

Oh shut up, you gawking fool!
I would never in my life have been so slow,
I would have made my wench for sure.
I have talked so sweetly to a girl
That she whispered a little word in my ear
And it hasn't even been a year! **120**
There you see, my dear fellow,
I was so pleasing to a girl
That I believe, if I had stayed there longer,
I would have rubbed her up better!

The ninth peasant:

Oh you fools, what idle boasts!
You could swear it by all the names of the devil
If you had had the luck I've had.
I think you'll gape your whole life long
That I recently came to a place
Where three of them would have liked to have me. **130**
But I told them to go to the devil
Unless they begged me prettily
And in addition exerted themselves to see
That I ate and drank and lived in luxury
And went riding about the town.
No one should think that I would take her otherwise!

The tenth peasant:

Oh you blasted fool,
You have bats in your belfry
That you are not ashamed of your boasting,
Especially when you hear my adventure. **140**
I politely brushed the chaff off one
So that her legs flew in the air.
Then I come around in a rush
And get a touch of her bosom.
Then she begins laughing and giggling
And tells me daintily to go away.
If you could bring it off this way,
You would have the world in the palm of your hand.

Der ailft paur:

Ach got, was hört ir an dem ding?
150 Hört, wie es mir ains mals ergieng
Gen ainer paurenmaid, weil si malk.
Da kam ich in ain raine walk.
Ich kützelt si ain weng unter den üchsen,
Do weis si mich zuo der *gaugelpüchsen*,
Und als wir straichten pei der kuo,
Schmitzt si mit paiden fuessen zuo,
Stirzt uns die *gelten* ubern kopf,
Das nit drin plaib ain ainiger dropf,
Und erschracken freilich sider,
160 Als gieng ain wolkenprunst dernider.
Do wurden wir im mist umb walgen
Und uns in dem küedreck *bedalgen*,
Als het man uns aus ainr *laimgruob* zogen,
Des wir uns in ein egen schmogen.
Do gewan ich ir erst ain *rank* an,
Das si sprach: Du hast mir *och* getan.
Ich wolt lang fragen, ob du schliefst,
Pis ich sach, das du darvon liefst.
Was *gheit* ir euch mit euer puolerei?
170 Kum ainer, dem ain söllichs begeget sei!

Der zwelft paur:

Mich ant, das ir sölch esel seit,
Oder was teufels auss euch speit.
Es *gheit* mich, das ir so grob mügt sein.
Ich hab ain puolschaft, das ist nit *nein*.
Do pin ich selbs ganz herr im haus,
Ich gee recht ein oder gee auss,
So tuot man alweg auf mich harren.
Ich liess euch aber unsinig werden, ir narren,
Das ich si also wolt beschamen.
180 Gept her den kranz aller teufel namen
Und fragt nit weiter mer dar no!
Nun pfeif auf, pauker, juch heia o!
Mach uns ain seuberlichs denzlin behend,
Wan ich hab noch sin an ein end,

154. **gaukelbüchse** 157. **gelte** (1b) 162. **betalken** 163. **leimgrube** 165. **rank** 166. **och,** interj. 169. **geheien** 173. **geheien** (3d) 174. **nain** (6c)

The eleventh peasant:

Oh Lord, what kind of thing is that to listen to?
Hear the adventure I once had 150
With a farmer girl, while she was milking;
There I got into a real brawl.
I tickled her a little under the arms,
Then she directed me to the "charm purse"
And as we cuddled by the cow,
It kicked with both hind feet
And knocked the bucket over our heads
So that not a drop remained within,
And we took a fright indeed,
As if a cloudburst had come down. 160
There we rolled in the manure
And wallowed in the cow dung,
As if we had been pulled out of a clay-pit,
And so we crawled into a corner.
There I finally got the better of her
So that she said: "You've hurt me!
I wanted to ask if you were asleep
Until I saw that you ran away."*
How can you boast with your adventures?
There's hardly one to whom such has happened. 170

The twelfth peasant:

I think you're asses
Or that the devil comes out of your mouths.
It angers me that you're so gross.
I have a mistress who doesn't say no.
There I am myself the lord of the house,
I come and go as I please
And am always expected.
I'd rather have you all go mad, you fools,
Rather than shame her thus.
Give me the wreath in the devil's name 180
And ask no more about it.
Now pipe up, piper, heigh ho!
Quick, make us a merry dance,
For I have wit enough

* The sense of these lines escapes us.

Des eur kainr nit wirt gewar,
Es füer in dan der teufel dar.

Einer, der die pauren vodert:

Nun dar, ir paurendrollen dret her für!
Dan wan ich euer ein verlur,
So leg einr dorfgmein so gross dran,
190 Das mich der pfarrer verkünt in pan.
Dan wen ich voder mit eim wort,
Der drett schnell her auf disen ort!
Ruodolt, Seututt und Molkenknoch,
Maulfrank, Lüllars, und Lausansloch,
Langhals, Schlotmock und *Küestrick*,
Holzpock und Lüllzapf, merket mich,
Was ich eur genennet hab,
Drett auf die seit und weich kainr ab,
Dan wann ich nit lieber ain laus verlür,
200 Dan eur ein, das eüch der teufel hinfüer!

Der auszschreier:

Ir herren, habt uns nit verübel,
Der ain straucht neulich uber ein kübel
Und hat das maul zuo fallen so gar,
So lauft der ander her und dar,
Als ob in die amaissen paisen.
Der dritt drapt umb, sam well er scheissen,
Der fiert kan auf dem ars nit sitzen,
So kan der fünft vor grossen witzen
Kaum wissen, wau er pleiben soll.
210 Der sechst steckt pös gespeis so voll,
Das im das maul nimer gestet.
Ir ieder kan etwass, wie es get.
Solt ich dan lenger pei euch pleiben,
Ich west euch auch ein guoten muot zuo verdreiben,
Dan got der bewar eüch hin als her,
Spricht Hans Folz von Wurms barbierer.

*

Est magnum mirum, quod mulier volt regere virum.

195. **kühstrick** idiom

So that none of you will discover her
Unless the devil takes him there.

One who marshalls the peasants:

Now forward, you peasant louts, step forward!
If I were to lose one of you,
It would be such a loss to the village
That the priest would excommunicate me. **190**
Now whom I order with a word,
Let him step forward quickly to this place!
Rudolt, Sowteat, and Milkbone,
Bigmouth, Suckarse and Louseinhole,
Longneck, Chimneyheap and Cowrope,
Sawhorse and Sucktap, pay attention,
The ones of you I've named
Step aside and don't move,
For if I wouldn't rather lose a louse
Than one of you, let the devil take you! **200**

Epilogue:

Good sirs, don't take it amiss:
One just tipped over a bucket
And has a fat lip,
Another runs to and fro
As if he had ants in his pants;
The third walks around as if he had to shit;
On his arse the fourth can't sit;
The fifth is such a clever fellow
That he hardly knows where he is.
The sixth is so full of bad food **210**
That his mouth never stops.
Each knows something of how it goes.
If I were to stay with you longer,
I would use up your patience,
God preserve you here and there,
Says Hans Folz, surgeon of Worms.

*

It's a great marvel that a woman wants to govern a man.

Hans Sachs's "The Smith in the Kneading Tub"

Hans Sachs (1494–1576) was by all odds the most prolific German writer of the sixteenth century. Born to an artisan family in Nürnberg, he received his schooling and apprenticeship there, spent several years as a journeyman in other cities, and returned in 1515 to his birthplace, where he spent the remainder of a long

---

DER SCHMIT IM PACHDROG

In des Romers gesanckweis

1.

Zw Dettelpach ein schmid sas, ein einfeltig man,
Der het ein schoͤnes weib, das puelet der caplon.
Nuͤn war der schmit dag unde nacht im hawse,
Das der pfaff kuͤnt den seinen aufrit haben nicht;
Daruͤmb er ein selczame abentewer dicht.
Am suͤntag frwe, als die predig war ause,
  Sprach er: "Ir lieben kint, habt acht!
Es wirt ein grose wasser guͤes vuͤr rinnen,
Wen sich heint schaidet tag und nacht.
10 Fliecht auf den perg und wie ir muͤegt entrinnen."
Des schmides haus stünd an dem pach;
Wie pald wart er im einen sin erdencken
Und wart hinauͤf unter das tach
Sein pachtrog an vier starcke wiede hencken
Und leget sich haimlich darein,
So palt das wasser keme,
Das er sich den abschnit allein
Und sitlich fein
Herab fiel in dem pachdrog sein
20 Und auͤf dem wasser schweme.

2.

  Zw nacht meint die schmidin, es wer der schmit darfon,
Und schicket heimelicḥ(e) ir maid nach dem caplon,
Der kam in ir kamer heimlich geschlichen.
  Auch het die schmidin vor gepuͤlt mit dem schmidknecht,
Der selbig mainet auͤch, er wer allein der recht,

life as master cobbler and poet. In his capacity as *Meistersinger*, familiar from Wagner's opera, he composed more than four thousand *Meisterlieder*. In addition he wrote 125 tragedies and comedies, eighty-five Shovetide plays, and hundreds of assorted shorter poems, fables, epigrams, and *Schwänke* such as the following. His themes were as varied as the genres he cultivated and were drawn from classical, sacred, and popular sources. A selection of the *Schwänke* is available in the translation of William Leighton, *Merry Tales and Three Shrovetide Plays by Hans Sachs* (London: D. Nutt, 1910). The text printed here is from Edmund Goetze and Carl Drescher, eds., *Sämtliche Fabeln und Schwänke von Hans Sachs* (Halle: Max Niemeyer, 1900), III, 163–165.

THE SMITH IN THE KNEADING TUB

To Romer's Melody

1.

In Dettelbach there was a smith, a simple man;
He had a beautiful wife, whom the chaplain wooed.
Now the smith was at home night and day,
So that the priest couldn't pay his visit;
Therefore he devised a strange adventure.
Sunday morning, when the sermon was over,
He said: "Dear children, hearken!
A great cloudburst will come down
Today between day and night.
Flee to the mountain or wherever you can escape." 10
The smith's house was at the brook;
How quickly he thought of a plan
And up under his roof
He hung his kneading tub on four strong ropes
And secretly lay down in it
So that as soon as the water came,
He would only have to cut it down
And neat as you please
Fall down in his kneading tub
And float on the water. 20

2.

At night the smith's wife thought the smith was out
And secretly sent her maid to the chaplain,
Who slipped into her chamber secretly.
The smith's wife had also had amorous doings with the smith's apprentice,
Who thought he was the only candidate

Gedacht, der schmid wer aus dem hauͤs entwichen.
   Pald sich die schmidin niderlegt,
Kam der knecht an ir kamertuer zw klopfen
Und mit vil pitten sie auf wegt.
30 Sie sprach: "Ge nuͤr von mir weg, allers dropfen,
Wan es muͤs heint gestorben sein."
Er sprach: "Kuͤest mich doch vor, e den wir sterben."
Die kamer het ein fensterlein,
Der pfaff fur auf, hielt im darfuer sein kerben;
Der schmidknecht kuͤest [in] auͤf das loch,
Das leichnam ubel stancke.
Der schmidknecht sich des kuͤmert hoch,
Gedacht idoch,
Es kem her von dem pfaffen noch,
40 Erdacht er im ein rancke.

3.

   Er ging hin vur die ess und macht ein eysen hais,
Ging darmit zw dem fensterlein und es auͤfrais,
Sprach: "Kuest mich zw lecz, kert euͤch an kein hasser!"
   Der pfaff recht nauͤs sein ars und den schmidknecht anplies,
Das gluͤent eysen er im ein die kerben sties;
Der pfaff schray: "Wassrio, wasser, o wasser!"
   Das gschray erhoͤrt der guͤete schmid,
Unter dem dach lag in dem pachdrog muͤnder,
Aufuͤer er und die wied abschnid
50 Und vil herab, als schlueg ins haus der duͤnder.
Der pfaff schmiczt nackat hinden nauͤs,
Vermaint, er hoͤret einen doner knallen.
Der schmid lag unden in dem hauͤs
Und het schir all sein rib im leib zerfallen.
Der schmid war zw einfeltig gar,
Muest den *oͤllgoczen* dragen;
Der pfaff was gar zw listig zwar,
Den zalt man par,
Wie er gemessen het vurwar,
60 Und dorft es niemant klagen.

Anno salutis 1537, am 20 tag Januarii.

56. **ölgötze** Grimm s.v.

And thought the smith had left the house.
As soon as the smith's wife had lain down,
The apprentice came knocking on her chamber door
And aroused her with his begging.
She said: "Just go away from me, you fool, 30
For today we must die."
He said: "But kiss me before we die."
The chamber had a little window,
The priest jumped up and held his rump out for him;
The smith's apprentice kissed him on the hole;
There was a villainous stink.
The smith's apprentice was very grieved
But thought
It came from the priest
And devised a trick against him. 40

3.

He went to the forge and made an iron rod hot,
Went with it to the window and opened it
And said: "Kiss me one last time, don't heed the envious!"
The priest stuck his arse out and let a wind at the apprentice.
He thrust the redhot iron in his rump.
The priest cried: "Water ho, water, oh water!"
The good smith heard the cry
At ease in the kneading tub under the roof;
He jumped up and cut the rope
And fell down as if thunder had hit the house. 50
The priest crept naked out the back door
And thought he heard a thunderclap.
The smith lay below in the house
And had broken all the ribs in his body.
The smith was far too gullible
And had to bear the brunt.
The priest was all too crafty
And was paid
In his own currency forsooth
And could not complain to anyone. 60

The year of our Lord 1537, on the 20th day of January.

Valentin Schumann's "The Merchant Who Was Afraid of Judgment Day"

Though the earlier French fabliau found willing and competent imitators in Germany, the Italian *novella* did not. The closest equivalent is provided by a series of *Schwankbücher* clustering for the most part around the middle of the sixteenth century. They do not represent a literary event, as will be more than evident from the examples in this volume. They tend to be reduced versions of Latin and Italian as well as indigenous models and the reduction applies equally to narrative dimension, style, tone, and quality of wit. (The contrast between the Morlini and Schumann analogues is indicative.) The general impression

---

EIN ANDERE HYSTORIA, VON EINEM KAUFFMANN, DER FORCHTE SICH VOR DEM JÜNGSTEN TAGE

Ein reicher kauffmann ist vor zeyten zu Nördlingen gesessen, des namen ist mir unbekandt, aber es solt doch war sein. Der kame auff ein zeyt in ein kirchen, da höret er, das der predicant saget, wie es zur zeyt des jüngsten tags wurde zugehen, das es da wurde feür regnen und verbrennen alles, was auff erden were, unnd was das feür wurde uberlassen, das wurde das wasser erseüffen. Der kauffmann gedachte: "Wie möchte ich doch disem wasser entrinnen?" unnd gieng heim, liess ihm ein schiff machen, dasselb liess er mit eysenem blech wol beschlagen und mit bech auff das allerbeste vergiessen. Als es nun fertig was, da liess er im ein gross starck sayl machen und des nachtes allerley speiss sampt wein unnd bier, auch was zur leibs narung gehört, in das schiff tragen und liess das schiff auffziehen und also hangen für und für. Wann es dann nacht war, so stige er auff einem brett inn das schiff und lag also alle nacht in dem schiff.

Nun hett der kauffmann ein auss der massen schön weib, der thet wehe, das der mann alle nacht in dem schiff lag, und hette vil lieber gesehen, er were bey ihr an dem beth gelegen; dann sie hett wol bedürfft und lag ir vil an dem nachthunger, das man ir den gebüsst hette. Dardurch die gut fraw in liebe entzündet ward gegen einem jungen pfaffen und auch gegen einem schmidt, damit, wann der mann des nachts in das schiff stige, dz

is not enhanced by the frequent appending of an uncongenial moral. The humor is predominantly sexual or very broadly satirical, and the favored victims of the jokes and anecdotes are priests and peasants, as befits a Protestant urban literature. The only virtue these little stories can claim is that they are terribly easy reading, which is clearly what they were intended to be.

The chief collections in Germany are the following:

Johannes Pauli, *Schimpf und Ernst* (1522)
Jörg Wickram, *Rollwagenbüchlein* (1555)
Jakob Frey, *Gartengesellschaft* (1556)
Martinus Montanus, *Wegkürzer* (1557)
———, *Gartengesellschaft II* (ca. 1560)
Michael Lindener, *Rastbüchlein und Katzipori* (1558)
Valentin Schumann, *Nachtbüchlein* (1559)
Bernhard Hertzog, *Die Schildwacht* (1560)
Hans Wilhelm Kirchhof, *Wendunmut*, 7 vols. (1563–1603)

The story printed here is taken from Valentin Schumann's *Nachtbüchlein*, ed. Johannes Bolte, *Bibliothek des litterarischen Vereins in Stuttgart*, 197 (Tübingen, 1893), 12–14.

ANOTHER STORY OF A MERCHANT WHO WAS AFRAID OF JUDGMENT DAY

In Nördlingen there once lived a rich merchant, whose name is not known to me, but the story is supposed to be true. He came once to a church where he heard the preacher say how it would be at the Last Judgment, how fire would rain down and burn everything on earth, and whatever was left over by the fire would be engulfed by the water. The merchant thought, "How could I escape this water?" and went home and had a boat made for himself which he reinforced with metal and caulked thoroughly with pitch. When it was ready, he had a great hawser made and at night he had all sorts of food and wine and beer and whatever the body requires put into it and had the boat hoisted up and suspended. When night came, he entered the boat on a plank and spent the whole night in the ship.

Now the merchant had an uncommonly beautiful wife, who was grieved that her husband spent every night in the ship and would much have preferred him to lie with her in the bed; for she was needy and much beset by night-hunger, which she wanted satisfied. For this reason the good woman fell in love with a young priest and also with a smith, so that when her husband went on board the boat at night they would still her night-

sie ir dieweil den nachthunger büssten. Dessen die frau gar wol zukam und zufriden was, auch der mann nichts wusste von solchen sachen, vermeinet, er hett ein frommes weib. Nun trug sich zu, das auff ein zeyt der pfaff bey der frawen war, mit ir schertzt; nach dem zusamen sassen, truncken und assen unnd waren frölich. In dem so kompt der schmid auch, wolt zu der frawen, klopfet an dem fenster an; da fragt die fraw: "Wer ist da?" Der schmid antwort: "Fraw, thund auff!" Die fraw fragt den pfaffen: "Herr, soll ich auffthun?" Der pfaff sprach nein. Da sprach die kauffmännin zum schmid: "Ich kan euch jetzt warlich nicht herein lassen." Da sprach der schmid: "Liebe fraw, so lasst mich euch doch nur einmal kussen zu guter nacht!" Das hört der pfaff und sprach: "Halt, fraw, ich will ihm recht thun!" und zoch das gesesslin ab und wuscht mit blossem arss zum fenster zu. Der gut schmid mainet, es were die fraw, unnd kusst den pfaffen auff den arss; der sprang von dem banck und schlug das fenster zu.

Der schmid gieng haimwertz, und fiel im auff dem weg ein, der pfaff wurd da sein unnd wurd ihm ein schalckheit haben gethan, gieng heim und namm ein gross eysen, macht das glüet heiss, gieng wider an das fenster, klopfet an. Die fraw fragt wider, wer da sey. Der schmid sprach: "Liebe fraw, thund auff!" Die fraw fragt den pfaffen widerum, ob sie solt aufthun. Der pfaff sprach nein, sie antwort wie vor. Da bat sie der schmid, sie solt in nur noch einmal kussen lassen. Da sprach der pfaff wider: "Halt, fraw!" und wider das gesesslein herab zoch und mit dem arss zum fenster nauss. Das merckt der schmid und nam das heyss glüend eysen, stiess das dem pfaffen inn den arss hinnein, so tieff als er kundt, darvon der pfaff ward springen und in der stuben anfieng zu schreyen: "Wasser, wasser, wasser!" und mit dem geschrey zum hauss hinauss lieff, schrey immer fort. Das hört der kauffmann oben in seinem schiff, das der pfaff so laut schrye: "Wasser, wasser, wasser!," vermeinet, es käme der jüngste tag, wuschte von stund an auff unnd schnit das seyl ab, vermeinet, er wolt also dahin faren. Da fiel er darnider, dass das schiff zu stucken und zu drümmer fiel, auch der kauffman halber tod auss dem schiff in sein hauss wurd tragen.

Also der kaufmann durch sein verstandt und weltliche weisshait kam umb sein gut und bracht sein weib umb ir ehr, auch sich umb leib und leben, auch der pfaff umb sein grobe schalckhait umb seine gesundthait. Ich wolte, das es allen also gienge, die den frommen männern ire weyber nicht wolten mit friden lassen, sondern tag und nacht mit bitt unnd geschenck nachlauffen, wie der schmid, und ihn die frawen liessen in hindern kussen; so behielt mancher mann ein frommes weib.

hunger all the while. The woman thrived on this and was content, and her husband knew nothing of such doings and thought he had a virtuous wife. Now it happened that once the priest was with the woman and regaled her, after which they sat together, ate and drank, and were merry. At that moment the smith came too, wanted to visit the woman, and knocked on the window. Then the woman asked, "Who's there?" The smith replied, "Woman, open up!" The woman asked the priest, "Sir, should I open up?" The priest said no. Then the merchant's wife said to the smith, "In truth, I can't let you in." Then the smith said, "Dear lady, then let me just kiss you once goodnight." The priest heard that and said, "Wait a moment, woman, I'll give him what he deserves!" and pulled off his pants and went to the window with a bare arse. The good smith thought it was the woman and kissed the priest on the arse; he jumped up from the bench and shut the window.

The smith went home, but on the way it occurred to him that it was probably the priest who had played a trick on him. He went home and took a big rod, made it redhot, went back to the window, and knocked. The woman asked again who was there. The smith said, "Dear lady, open up!" The woman asked the priest again if she should open up. The priest said no, and she answered as before. Then the smith asked her to kiss him just once more. Then the priest said again, "Stop, woman!" and pulled off his pants again and stuck his arse out the window. The smith saw this and took the redhot iron, stuck it into the priest's arse as far as he could, which caused the priest to jump up and shout in the room, "Water, water, water!" and run out of the house still shouting. The merchant in his boat heard the priest shouting so loudly, "Water, water, water!" and thought the Day of Judgment was at hand, got up immediately, and severed the hawser, and thought that he would sail off this way. Then he plummeted down so that the ship broke into bits and pieces and the merchant was taken out of the boat and into the house half dead.

Thus the merchant through his wit and worldly wisdom lost his property and deprived his wife of her honor and himself of life and limb, and the priest for his gross villainy lost his health. I wish that everyone would fare this way, who refuses to leave the wives of good men alone and day and night pursues them with prayers and presents, like the smith, and the women would let them kiss their arse. Thus many a man would keep a virtuous wife.

"Jankyn and Aleyson"

Chaucer's clever clerks, such as Nicholas, appear in many secular lyrics, similar to this brief poem about a clerk who, like Absolon in "The Miller's Tale," takes

---

JANKYN AND ALEYSON

"Kyrie," so "Kyrie,"
Jankyn singeth merie
With "Aleyson,"

As I went on a Yol-day in our prosession,
Knew I jolly Jankyn by his mery ton,
Kyrieleyson.

Jankyn began the offis on the Yol-day
And yit me thynketh it does me good so merie gan he say
"Kyrieleyson."

Jankyn red the pistil ful fair and ful wel,
And yit me thinketh it dos me good, as evere have I sel,
Kyrieleyson.

2. **merie** merrily 3. **Aleyson** Kyrie Eleison ("Lord have mercy on us"), which the clerk Jankyn sings in the Mass, with a pun on Aleyson's name 5. **ton** tone, voice 7. **offis** Office, church-service 8. **me thynketh** it seems to me 10. **the pistil** Epistle 11. **sel** joy, bliss.

advantage of his ecclesiastical duties to woo an Alyson. The poem survives in a fifteenth-century manuscript and has been reprinted many times. The best and most recent edition is that of R. H. Robbins, *Secular Lyrics of the XIV and XV Centuries* (Oxford, 1952). We have regularized the spelling and some of the forms of the text.

Jankyn at the sanctus crakit a merie note,
And yit me thinketh it dos me good; I payid for his cote.
Kyrieleyson.

Jankyn crakit notes an hunderid on a knot,
And yit he hakkyt hem smaller than wortes in a pot.
Kyrieleyson.

Jankyn at the angnus beryt the pax brede,
He twinkelid, but said nowt, and on my fot he trede;
Kyrieleyson.

Benedicamus domino, Crist fro schame me schilde!
Deo gracias therto. Alas, I go with child.
Kyrieleyson.

13. **sanctus** part of the mass **crakit** cracked, sang 17. **hakkit** hacked **wortes** roots 19. **angnus** part of the Mass (Agnus Dei—Lamb of God) **pax brede** the communion bread 20. **twinkelid** winked **nowt** nothing 22. **Benedicamus domino** bless we the Lord **schilde** shield 23. **Deo gracias** thanks be to God (This and the preceding Latin phrase marked the close of the Mass.)

"Old Hogyn's Adventure"

This late ballad version of the climax of "The Miller's Tale" survives only in a manuscript of the sixteenth century (Balliol Coll. Oxford MS. 354), though the

---

OLD HOGYN'S ADVENTURE

Hogyn cam to bowers dore,
Hogyn cam to bowers dore;
He trilled upon the pin for love,
Hum, ha, trill go bell!
He trilled upon the pin for love,
Hum, ha, trill go bell!

Up she rose and let him in,
Up she rose and let him in;
She had a went she had worshipped all her kin,
10 Hum, ha, trill go bell!
She had a went she had worshipped all her kin,
Hum, ha, trill go bell!

When they were to bed brought,
When they were to bed brought,
The old churl he could do nought,
Hum, ha, trill go bell!
The old churl he could do nought,
Hum, ha, trill go bell!

1. **bowers dore** The bedroom door 3. **he trilled upon the pin** he turned the door-latch
9. **She had a went** she believed

poem itself is probably from an earlier period. It is notable mainly for its crudity and for its demonstration of what happens to a fabliau theme when it is reduced simply to a dirty joke. Yet there must have been many such simple and crude versions of the fabliaux circulating in the Middle Ages, transmitted orally in the same manner as modern dirty jokes, and "Old Hogyn's Adventure" may stand as an example of what must have been a flourishing genre in Chaucer's time. The text is reproduced, with some regularization of the spelling, from the version first printed by Ewald Flügel in *Anglia*, XXVI (1903), 273–274.

Go ye forth to yonder window,
Go ye forth to yonder window, 20
And I will come to you within a throw,
  Hum, ha, trill go bell!
And I will come to you within a throw,
  Hum, ha, trill go bell!

When she him at the window wist,
When she him at the window wist,
She turned out her arse and that he kissed,
  Hum, ha, trill go bell!
She turned out her arse and that he kissed,
  Hum, ha, trill go bell! 30

Ywis, leman, ye do me wrong,
Ywis, leman, ye do me wrong,
Or elles your breath is wonder strong,
  Hum, ha, trill go bell!
Or elles your breath is wonder strong,
  Hum, ha, trill go bell!

21. **a throw** a short while 25. **she him at the window wist** she knew he was at the window 31. **Ywis, leman** indeed, sweetheart 33. **elles** else

Caspar Cropacius' "Fable of a Priest and a Simple Rustic"

Caspar Cropacius enjoys a virtually undisturbed obscurity in the humanistic literature of sixteenth-century Germany and has escaped the attention of the standard reference works on German literary bibliography and biography. Jöcher's *Allgemeines Gelehrtenlexicon* has a brief note on him, but it looks as if this information was taken from the preface of Cropacius' collection of

---

FABULA DE SACERDOTE ET SIMPLICI RUSTICO

Tempus erat, pecori quo pandit ovilia pastor,
  Aureus Hesperias Phoebus adibat aquas:
Forte sua digressa domo speciosa petebat
  Femina vicinae proxima tecta casae,
Quae, licet agrestis coleret cum coniuge villae
  Rura nec Attalica sorte beata foret,
Attamen eximiis naturae dotibus aucta
  Divino formae munere dives erat.
Viderat hanc gressu properare decente sacerdos,
10 Viderat et caeco captus amore fuit.
Utque leves stipulae subiectis ignibus ardent,
  Uritur et vetitum tentat obire nefas.
Mille modos captat; quis enim modus adsit amori!
  Nescit amor posita vincula lege pati.
Iamque ardet penitus, furor ima perambulat ossa,
  Vulnere crudeli saucia corda dolent.
Festa dies aderat, qua rustica tuba colonum
  Divinis rebus sedula mane vacat.
Conveniunt igitur solito pro more, parati
20 Excipere attenta dogmata mente dei;
Quin etiam sacri studiosior assecla verbi
  Formosae uxoris praes ibi nuptus erat.
Callidus ante dolis instructus et arte sacerdos
  Incipit ad populum verbaque sancta facit.
"Puniet omnipotens," inquit, "peccata creator,

poems. According to Jöcher, Cropacius was born in the Bohemian city of Pilsen and died there on January 13, 1580. After his death his poems were collected by Paulus Melissus and published in Nürnberg in 1581 under the title *Poemata.* This volume is not slender (377 pages), but it is rare; the only copies we have located are in the British Museum and the University of Michigan Library.

Jöcher describes Cropacius as "one of the best poets of his time," and though we are in no position to evaluate this statement, the following poem does not belie it. Along with Morlini's novella it is easily the most readable and graceful treatment of "The Miller's Tale." The idyllic setting and pastoral reminiscences create a rather effective ironic contrast, and even the moral is made palatable by the fable form.

The text printed here is from Valentin Schumann's *Nachtbüchlein,* ed. Johannes Bolte, *Bibliothek des litterarischen Vereins in Stuttgart,* 197 (Tübingen, 1893), 355–357.

FABLE OF A PRIEST AND A SIMPLE RUSTIC

It was the time when the shepherd opens the sheepfold for his flock
And when golden Phoebus approached the western waters.
By chance a beautiful woman leaving her house
Sought out the nearby confines of the neighboring cottage,
A woman who, though with her husband she cultivated the soil
Of her rustic estate, was not blessed with Attalian fortune [wealth].
However, endowed with the extraordinary favors of nature,
She was rich in the divine gift of beauty.
A priest saw her hastening with decorous steps,
He saw and was seized with blind love. **10**
As the dry straw burns when ignited by fire,
He burns and tries to accomplish the forbidden crime.
He takes a thousand measures; for what measure does love observe!
Love knows not how to suffer the chains imposed by law.
He is deeply inflamed, a fury circulates in his very bones,
His grieved heart suffers a cruel wound.
A holiday was at hand, on which the rustic crowd of tillers
Is free and attends the morning services.
Thus they come together in the accustomed way,
Ready to listen to the teachings of God with attentive minds. **20**
Being indeed also a devoted follower of the sacred word,
The husband of the beautiful woman was present.
The artful priest had previously devised his cunning wiles
And began to address sacred words to the people.
"The almighty Creator," he said, "will punish sins,

Qui quatit ultrici dira flagella manu.
Iamque senescentem statuit submergere mundum
Diluvio humanum sicque abolere genus.
Prae foribus letum. Decima deus omnia luce
30 Perdet aquis, ultra nec superesse sinet.
Consimili veteres olim ratione parentes
Puniit omnipotens ob malefacta deus,
Provida cura Noae tamen est hac clade levata,
Nave cava mediis dum veheretur aquis."
Discedunt maesti sortem versantque futuram
Ruricolae et largis fletibus ora rigant.
At memor ante alios tanti discriminis alto
Pectore posterius vir bene dicta notat,
Cuius pulchra domi curabat prandia coniux
40 Lauta volens cupido fercula ferre viro.
Ille dapes blandaeque nihil bona verba moratus
Coniugis exiguam construit arte ratem
Sublimique domus in culmine reste ligatam
Occupat hanc vitae praesidiumque vocat,
Expectans tristis gemitum planctumque diei,
Cum deus effusis omnia perdet aquis.
Interea fretus fallaci fraude sacerdos
Comprimit uxorem, credule mule, tuam.
Quid non tentat amor, quid non perducit ad actum!
50 Parent aligero femina masque deo.
Dumque ita bella movent, dum miscent oscula amantes,
Gaudia dum Veneris nocte silente fovent,
Forte Cupidineis transfixus pectora telis
Ante fores pulsans alter adulter erat.
Illa domi lecti socium causata iacere
Differt in certum tempus amoris opus.
Ille tamen caeco nimium stimulante furore
Oscula, dum reliquum non datur, orat amans.
Hoc ubi sollicita perceperat aure sacerdos,
60 Gaudia rivali praecipit illa suo,
Exponens pingues, ut figeret oscula, clunes.
Hac lusit cupidum calliditate virum.
Ille dolum foetore notans exardet in iram
Et velut accepto vulnere ardet aper.
Arripit ergo nocens dentata forcipe ferrum
Et rapido massam versat in igne rudem
Ignitamque morae impatiens avidusque nocendi
Eximit adque fores supplice voce redit,

He who brandishes the fierce scourge with a vengeful hand.
Already He has determined to submerge the aging world
In a flood and thus destroy the human race.
Death stands before the door. On the tenth day hence, God
Will destroy all things in water and allow nothing to survive. 30
For a similar cause our ancient ancestors once
Were punished by almighty God for their misdeeds,
But the provident care of Noah avoided this destruction
When he sailed in the midst of the waters in his hollow ark."
The villagers depart troubled and weigh their future fate
And wet their cheeks with abundant tears.
But more mindful than the others of the great peril,
The man takes careful note in his heart of what has been said,
The man, whose beautiful wife prepared a dinner at home,
Wishing to bring tasty dishes before her hungry husband; 40
But undeterred by the good words and dainties of his alluring
Wife, he artfully constructed a tiny craft,
And lashing it to the rooftop of his house with a rope,
He enters it and calls it the refuge of his life,
Awaiting with troubled spirits and sighs and laments the day
When God with a downpour of water will destroy all things.
In the meantime the priest, relying on fraud and deceit,
Besets your wife, oh credulous mule!
What does Love not attempt, what deed does it not carry out!
Man and woman obey the winged god. 50
And as they struggle thus, and as the lovers mingle kisses,
As the joys of Venus prosper in the silent night,
By chance, his breast transfixed by Cupid's dart,
Another lover stood before the door.
Pleading that her husband was at home,
She defers the work of love to another time.
But the lover, with the blind raging of desire,
Begs for kisses when all else is refused.
When the priest, listening attentively, heard this,
He accords this pleasure to his rival, 60
By thrusting out his fleshy rump for him to kiss.
With this cunning he tricked the panting fellow.
Realizing the filthy trick, he burns with wrath
And rages like a wounded boar.
With ill intent he seizes an iron with serrated tongs
And turns the rough rod in a hot fire
And having fired it, impatient of delay and eager to do harm,
He removes it and returns to the door with a suppliant voice:

Si vir adest, sibi ne tamen oscula ferre recuset,
70 Oscula pro Veneris grata futura vice.
Illa nihil contra. Plenus levitate sacerdos
Prosiliit turpes exseruitque nates.
Ignitum mota vicinus forcipe ferrum
Admovet atque ait, "Haec praemia fraudis habe!"
Territus exclamat cogente dolore sacerdos
Et pleno largas gutture poscit aquas,
Poscit aquas. Pavidus pendens sub culmine coniux
Extremum fati retur adesse diem,
Nec mora, vincla manu pallens nodosa relaxat,
80 Culmine suspensam quae tenuere ratem.
Laxat, et infelix stulta pietate maritus
In silices casu praecipitante cadit.
Non est danda fides nullo discrimine rerum;
Nam cito qui credit, fallitur ille cito.

If her husband is at home, she should not refuse to give him a kiss,
A kiss for the future delights of Venus. 70
She is nothing loath. The priest, light on his feet,
Leaped up and presented his nasty buttocks.
With his tongs he moved up the heated iron
And said, "Take this reward for your deceit!"
Terrified and compelled by pain the priest cries out
And calls with a loud shout for much water,
And again for water. The fearful husband hanging on the roof
Thought the Day of Judgment was at hand,
And without delay he looses with his hands all pale the knotty ropes
Which held the craft suspended from the roof. 80
He looses them and the unfortunate husband in his foolish devotion
Crashes onto the rocks with a headlong plunge.
No credence should be given when no danger impends,
For he who is quick to believe is quickly deceived.

The Reeve's Tale and Its Analogues

In the case of "The Miller's Tale" we were obliged to deal with the literary background largely in terms of motifs. For "The Reeve's Tale" no such atomization is necessary. The story exists as a whole in a number of apparently independent versions, one Italian (*Decameron* 9,6), two French ("Le Meunier et les II clers" and "De Gombert et des II clers"), two German ("Das Studentenabenteuer" and "Irregang und Girregar"), and Chaucer's story in English. These versions are similar enough so that we can abstract a single plot to cover all six, as follows:

> Two youths take lodging in the house of a man with a handsome wife, a pretty daughter, and an infant. After the evening meal and some conviviality the family and the guests retire. During the night the first youth gets up and visits the daughter in her bed. In the meantime the second youth takes the baby's cradle from the mother's bed and places it by his own. When the mother goes out for a moment and returns, she is confused by the misplaced cradle and goes to bed with the second youth, thinking it is her husband. He is not slow to take advantage of the confusion. The first youth now wishes to return to his bed but is also confused by the cradle and gets into bed with his host, whom he mistakes for his companion and to whom he boasts of his adventure. The father is incensed and a struggle ensues. In the end the host is either thoroughly beaten or deluded into believing that nothing has really happened. The next morning the youths depart.

This story is schematically analyzed below for each of the six versions in order to make clear what features they have in common and what features set them apart one from the other. The outlines are organized according to the eight episodes into which all six stories seem naturally to fall.

	SETTING	TRIP	LODGING (AND THEFT)	ENTERTAINMENT
De Gombert et des II clers	Two clerks find themselves without means, having spent their money more on foolishness than on learning.	They return from school.	They seek lodging from the peasant Gombert and are received. One falls in love with the wife, the other with the daughter.	While the baby is being fed, the second clerk takes a ring from a pan on the hearth. They are given simple but plentiful fare. During the evening the first student cannot take his eyes off the wife.
Le Meunier et les II clers	Two poor clerks, who are companions and countrymen, live in an isolated monastery and suffer want. One borrows a sack of wheat, the other a mare, and they decide to become bakers.	They take their wheat to a lonely mill to be ground.	While they are out looking for the miller, he steals their horse and wheat. They search for it in vain, then ask for and are given lodging.	The miller has a wife and baby and a pretty daughter who sleeps locked in a bin. During supper one clerk takes a ring from an andiron on the hearth. They see their stolen wheat.
The Reeve's Tale	Location of a mill and description of the miller, his wife, and daughter. The marriage ambitions for the daughter.	Two scholars come to grind their grain, intent on not being cheated.	The miller sets their horses loose and while they are off in hot pursuit, he cheats them with a vengeance. They return late and ask for lodging for the night.	The scholars are ready with their silver and the daughter is sent for food and drink. They eat and especially the miller drinks deeply.
Decameron 9, 6	A good man lives in the village of Mugnone. To earn money he lodges wayfarers or sometimes even acquaintances in his single room. He has a handsome wife, a daughter of 15 or 16 years, and a baby boy of one year. A Florentine youth (Pinuccio) sees the daughter (Niccolosa), is enamored, and determines to take lodging with her father in order to spend the night with her.	He hires two horses and sets out with his friend Adriano.	They ask for lodging. The host protests his inability to entertain such fine guests, but finally receives them.	They dine on provisions provided by the youths and retire to three beds in one small room.

Das Studentenabenteuer	The sons of two good friends distinguish themselves at school and decide to study music at Paris. The fathers dissuade them at first, but finally agree and equip their sons generously.	They set out. At Arras they exchange greetings with a lady and her daughter returning from the baths. One youth conceives a passion for the daughter and they decide to seek lodging in her house.	Her father readily agrees.	The students provide food and drink. The lover takes the girl aside to help her read her psalter; instead he woos her, displaying the usual symptoms of love. Dinner is accompanied by lovelorn glances. The host promises to lodge his guests in his own room for their better protection and all retire.
Irregang und Girregar	Two youths decide to travel abroad to study. They are wealthy, courteous, and handsome.	They pass through a town, where one of them is dazzled by a girl. He pretends that illness prevents him from proceeding further and they decide to seek lodging in the girl's house.	Her father deprecates his resources and refuses at first, but he relents when his daughter intercedes for the travelers.	The youths order drink and the daughter decks herself out in her best finery. The host gets sleepy from the drink and goes to bed while the others stay up and converse longer before retiring.

	LOVEMAKING WITH DAUGHTER	LOVEMAKING WITH MOTHER	THE HOST APPRISED TUSSLE	THE BEATING (OR HOODWINKING) OF THE HOST (AND SEQUEL)
De Gombert et des II clers	At night the second clerk visits the daughter in bed and gives her the ring from the pan.	Gombert gets up to go out. The first clerk removes the baby's cradle to his own bed and hides. Gombert returns, is misled, goes to the clerk's bed, thinks his wife is out too, and lies down. The clerk goes to the wife's bed. Thinking it is her husband, she compliments him on his prowess.	The second clerk returns from the daughter, gets into bed with Gombert, and mistaking him for his companion, boasts of his adventure. A struggle ensues.	The wife hears the uproar and tells her supposed husband that the clerks are fighting. He offers to separate them and joins his companion in pommeling Gombert. Departure.
Le Meunier et les II clers	At night the clerk gains admittance to the daughter's bin and wins her favors in exchange for the andiron ring, which he alleges to have a stone capable of restoring virginity.	The wife gets up to go out and the second clerk, who envies his companion's luck, sets out to trick her. He brings the baby's cradle to his bed and tweaks the baby's ear; the crying brings the mother to his bed when she returns and he takes his pleasure with her.	The first clerk gets up when the cock crows and returns to his bed, but is confused by the misplaced cradle. He lies down with the miller, whom he mistakes for his companion, and boasts of his conquest. A struggle ensues, but the miller is weaker and escapes.	The miller lights a fire and discovers his wife in bed with the other clerk. He calls her a whore and she counters by calling him a thief. The clerks beat the miller and repossess their wheat. Departure.
The Reeve's Tale	At night Aleyn makes his way to the daughter's bed and is received.	John laments his bad luck and hits on the idea of moving the baby's cradle to his bed. The miller's wife goes out, is confused on her return, and goes to John's bed. He is quick to take advantage of the error.	Aleyn leaves the daughter and returns to his bed, but is confused by the misplaced cradle. He lies down next to the miller, and thinking it is John, regales him with the night's adventure. A struggle ensues.	The scholars beat the miller and recover their grain. Departure.
Decameron 9, 6	Pinuccio makes his way to Niccolosa's bed and they take their pleasure.	The housecat causes a clatter and the wife gets up to investigate. In the meantime Adriano also gets up to go out and moves the cradle, which is blocking his way. On her return the wife is confused by the misplaced cradle and goes to Adriano's bed, where she gets an amorous reception.	Pinuccio, afraid of falling asleep, returns to his bed, is confused by the misplaced cradle, and lies down next to the host. Thinking it is Adriano, he tells his adventure. A struggle ensues.	The wife hears the quarrel and becomes aware of her bedmate's identity when he speaks. She lies down next to Niccolosa and claims to have been there all night so that Pinuccio could not possibly have visited her; she accuses her husband of drinking too much and dreaming. At the

				same time Adriano explains that Pinuccio is a sleepwalker. Pinuccio, taking the cue, pretends to wake up, rub his eyes, and speak nonsense, which puts the host in a good humor. Departure amidst general merriment next day. Pinuccio later found other ways to visit Niccolosa.
Das Studentenabenteuer	The amorous student makes his way to the daughter's bed and they take their pleasure.	The second student is disconsolate. The mother gets up to go out and during her absence he moves the baby's cradle. He tweaks the baby's ear and on her return she is attracted to his bed by the crying. She twits her supposed husband for his unusual amorousness, suggesting that wine is the cause.	The first student returns to his bed, is confused by the misplaced cradle, and lies down next to the host. Thinking it is his companion, he boasts of his adventure. A struggle ensues.	While the mother brings a light, the second student retrieves the first student and they pretend to be asleep, leaving the spouses to solve the riddle. The mother understands what has happened and advises her husband to say nothing. The students take leave merrily the next morning.
Irregang und Girregar	The lovesick youth debates at length with himself, then makes his way with infinite care to the girl. She is coy and resists for a long time before allowing the youth to "warm himself" in her bed.	The second youth is disconsolate. The mother gets up to latch a door and the youth moves the baby's cradle to mislead her. She lies down next to him and is received accordingly. Thinking it is her husband, she twits him for his amorousness.	The first youth leaves the girl at dawn and returns to his bed. He loses his way and lies down next to the host. Thinking it is his companion, he boasts of his adventure. There is a struggle and the youth takes to his heels.	The wife persuades her husband he has had a nightmare and the youths read a mock prayer over him. They prolong their stay and gain access to the daughter by lowering a basket into her room. The father falls into it by mistake, is raised, then dumped. In a dazed state he is chided by his wife and told to remain silent. Bedmates are switched again and the lovemaking continues. The host, intending to make love to his wife, is confused by the sex of his bedmate. Another quick switch completes his befuddlement. He is now convinced of his madness. The daughter conjures over him and drives off the alleged demons, Irregang and Girregar. The host now holds his peace no matter what he sees or hears. The frolicking continues both now and many times later.

Though the plot is the same for all versions, the details are clearly variable. If we take the stories section by section, the more obvious differences are these:

1) The youths are clerks or scholars in all versions except Boccaccio's, where they are young men of Florence. In "Le Meunier" and "The Reeve's Tale" the host is a miller, elsewhere his livelihood is not specified. In Boccaccio's story one youth knows and has fallen in love with the daughter before the action begins. In the German versions and "Gombert" the youths develop their passionate attachments on the spur of the moment, and in "Le Meunier" and "The Reeve's Tale" there are no romantic overtones at all. In "Gombert" the mother is the primary attraction, elsewhere it is the daughter. Only Boccaccio and Chaucer provide names for most of their characters.

2) In "Le Meunier" and "The Reeve's Tale" the youths come to have their grain milled. In "Gombert" they are penniless and in need of lodging. In the German stories the students seek lodging after one of them has by chance seen and fallen in love with the pretty daughter. In Boccaccio's story the visit is a preconceived plan to facilitate a night with the daughter.

3) In "Le Meunier" and "The Reeve's Tale" the youths ask for lodging because their efforts to recover their lost (or stolen) horses prevent them from returning home before nightfall. In Boccaccio's story the youths conspire to be delayed and are unable to return to Florence. In "Gombert" and the German stories the lodging is a station on a longer journey. In the miller versions, there is an additional motif, according to which the host robs the youths; this justifies the seductions as a form of vengeance. Chaucer is alone in making the seductions particularly ironical by emphasizing the snobbishness, fastidiousness, and social ambitions of the women, and the jealousy of the miller.

4) In all versions but the French the youths provide food and drink. The host partakes liberally so that he becomes sleepy ("Irregang und Girregar"), snores loudly (Chaucer, "Meunier"), or is later accused of drunkenness (Boccaccio and the German versions). The French tales are also isolated by the motif of the ring, which gives the youth access to the daughter in "Le Meunier" and is simply a spurious gift to her in "Gombert."

5) The first youth encounters no resistance from the daughter, except in "Irregang und Girregar" where the seduction is accompanied by the casuistries of German courtly literature, and to a lesser extent in "Gombert."

6) According to Boccaccio's version the seduction of the mother is involuntary; the second youth moves the cradle only because it blocks his way. Elsewhere he deliberately brings the cradle to his bed in order

to attract the mother or the father. "Gombert" is the only version in which the host instead of the hostess is misled by the cradle. In all versions the mother thinks her lover is her husband, but in "Gombert" and the German versions she also teases him for his unexpected amorousness.

7) The confusion of the first student when he leaves the daughter's bed, lies down next to the host, and tells of his adventure is described in almost identical form in all the variants. The outcome of the tussle, which is described most vividly by Chaucer, varies according to the version. In "Gombert" the host is soundly beaten by both clerks, in "Le Meunier" the miller escapes, in the English story the wife knocks her husband senseless by mistake, in the Italian story the wife intervenes to quell the disturbance, in the shorter German story the second youth retrieves his beleaguered companion from the host's bed, and in the longer German story the youth takes to his heels.

8) "Le Meunier" is the only version in which the host learns that not only his daughter but also his wife has been seduced. This provokes an angry response, which in turn causes the wife to reveal her husband's theft and paves the way for his beating. In Chaucer's story the miller is beaten without further ado since the scholars know already that he is a thief. In "Gombert" the host is also beaten, while in the other versions he is not beaten but rather deluded by the wife (and daughter) conspiring with the youths. The delusion is practiced most elaborately and with the addition of several new motifs in the longer German version. In the French, English, and shorter German versions the youths simply take their leave in the morning. In Boccaccio's story we learn that this is only the beginning of the affair between Pinuccio and Niccolosa and in the longer German version we are told that both youths later continued their capers with the ladies of the house.

In addition to the five medieval analogues, all of which are earlier than Chaucer, there are a number of derivative reworkings of the story. There is a Flemish translation of Jean Bodel's "Gombert" entitled "Een bispel van II clerken, ene goede boerde" and published by Eelco Verwijs in *Dit sijn X goede boerden* (The Hague, 1861), pp. 11–18. There are some minor deviations from Bodel's text which will be specified in the headnote to "Gombert."

The tale reappears again in a rare book by Aloyse Cynthio degli Fabritii, *Libro della origine delli volgari proverbi* (Venice, 1526) under the heading "Tu vai cercando Maria per Ravenna," in a collection of anecdotes "De generibus ebriosorum et ebrietate vitanda" appended to later editions of the *Epistolae obscurorum virorum,* in Hans Sach's *Schwank* "Die zwei Gesellen beim Wirt, der nur ein Kammer het," as number twenty-four in Michael Lindener's *Rastbüchlein und Katzipori* (1558),

as number eighty-six in Martinus Montanus' *Gartengesellschaft* (ca. 1560), and ultimately in La Fontaine's *conte* "Le Berceau." These materials are not mentioned in *Sources and Analogues of Chaucer's Canterbury Tales*, but they are accounted for, among other places, in Martinus Montanus, *Schwankbücher*, ed. Johannes Bolte (Tübingen, 1899), p. 620, and in A. Collingwood Lee, *The Decameron: Its Sources and Analogues* (London, 1909), pp. 281–287.

All of the later versions are simple paraphrases of Boccaccio, with the exception of the Flemish "Gombert" and the anecdote in "De generibus ebriosorum." We have reprinted the latter, which appears to derive from one of the medieval German analogues, perhaps the "Studentenabenteuer." In addition we have printed a Danish ballad version not previously included among the analogues. It tells the story of two companions who come to a miller with a sack of grain, in which one of the companions is hidden. In due course he seduces the miller's daughter, but the story dispenses with the motif of the switched beds, and it ends on a curious note of Danish melancholy. Finally, there is a sixteenth-century English version entitled "A Verie Merie Historie of the Milner of Abington." It is too close to Chaucer's story to be worth reprinting and may be found in Varnhagen's article referred to below (p. 195).

As the analogues show, every action in the plot of "The Reeve's Tale" has its parallel in some earlier form of the story, and from a superficial viewpoint it therefore seems that Chaucer's plot is controlled by the tradition, that the miller steals the clerks' grain and they seduce his wife and daughter simply because that is what always happens in the tale. But "The Reeve's Tale," because its analogues so clearly define the plot, demonstrates more obviously than any of Chaucer's other fabliaux his peculiar genius for characterization and for deftly uniting plot and character. The actions in Chaucer's tale may be generally the same as those in the analogues, but in Chaucer's version the actions grow out of the characters of the participants. The proud and snobbish miller is annoyed that the clerks think they can outwit him by carefully watching the milling of their grain; that is why he sets their horse free and steals their grain. He says to himself:

> They wene that no man may hem bigyle,
> But by my thrift, yet shal I blere hir ye,
> For al the sleighte in hir philosophye.
> The moore queynte crekes that they make,
> The moore wol I stele whan I take. (4048–4052)

That night, the miller is so pleased with his success that he cannot resist a sly dig at the learned clerks whom he has so cleverly outwitted:

Myn hous is streit, but ye han lerned art;
Ye konne by argumentes make a place
A myle brood of twenty foot of space. (4122–4124)

The clerks know that they have been fooled, and they have their pride too. When they discover their loss, they are not so concerned with the theft as with the fact that

men wil us fooles calle,
Bathe the wardeyn and oure felawes alle,
And namely the millere, weylaway! (4111–4113)

The seduction of the daughter is not therefore the result of simple love or lechery, as in the other versions, but revenge of a particularly clerkly variety. As Aleyson explains while the two clerks lie listening to the miller's family snore,

Som esement has lawe yshapen us;
For, John, ther is a lawe that says thus,
That gif a man in a point be agreved,
That in another he sal be releved. (4179–4182)

Likewise, John's trick on the wife is not the result of lechery so much as worry about what men will think when they hear he has been outwitted:

And when this jape is tald another day,
I sal been halde a daf, a cokenay!
I wil arise and auntre it, by my fayth! (4207–4209)

The ingenuity of his trick—the shifting of the cradle—guarantees that he will be known as anything but "a daf, a cokenay."

In none of the other analogues is each step of the action motivated in this way—by the pride of the miller and his determination to outwit the clerks, and by the clerks' own pride and their determination to revenge the insult. Nor in any of the other analogues is there the delicious social comedy of the pretensions of the miller and his "noble" wife (the daughter of a priest), pretensions which lend a poetic justice to the *dénouement*, in which the clerks avenge themselves in the most insulting way possible. Characterization and action beautifully blend at the moment when Symkyn discovers that John has seduced his daughter:

Who dorste be so boold to disparage
My doghter, that is come of swich lynage? (4271–4272)

"The Reeve's Tale" and its analogues allow us a more rewarding glimpse than any of Chaucer's other tales of what Charles Muscatine calls "Chaucer's typical investiture of the naked fabliau jest with the substance of a rather deeper poetry" (*Chaucer and the French Tradition*, p. 199).

Jean Bodel's "Gombert and the Two Clerks"

Jean Bodel, who was born about 1165–1170 and died in 1210, is best known to students of medieval literature as the author of the lively miracle play, *Le Jeu de Saint Nicholas,* but he also wrote an epic, the *Chanson des Saisnes (The Song of the Saxons),* some charming pastourelles, nine fabliaux (more than any other French author is known to have written), and the fascinating *Congés (Farewell),* in which Jean, stricken with leprosy, bids farewell to his friends and begs them to find him a place in a leprosarium. In 1202 Jean entered the leper-hospital at Beaurains, where he died eight years later.

"Gombert and the Two Clerks," which Bodel wrote in the years between 1190 and 1194, is clearly based on the same story as "The Miller and the Two Clerks"; for a comparison of the two tales, see Charles Foulon, *L'Œuvre de Jehan Bodel* (Rennes, 1958) pp. 48–53. "Gombert" was apparently the more popular version, for it is mentioned in other fabliaux, it survives in three manuscripts (a large number for a fabliau), and it was translated into Flemish. The Flemish translation has a special interest for the student of Chaucer, since this very close rendering contains two passages which survive in none of the French texts of "Gombert" but which are suggestive of passages in "The Reeve's Tale." Probably these passages were in the French manuscript used by the Flemish translator. The first passage occurs when Gombert retires for the night (line 44 below); in the Flemish version we have a hint of the drinking that accompanies dinner in "The Reeve's Tale" and we learn that (as in Chaucer) both Gombert and his wife snore:

DE GOMBERT ET DES II CLERS

En cest autre fablel parole
De II clers qui vienent d'escole;
Despendu orent leur avoir
En folie plus qu'en savoir.
Ostel quistrent chiés un vilain;
De sa fame, dame Guilain,
Fu l'un des clers, lués que là vint,
Si fols que amer li convint;
Mès ne set coment s'i acointe,

Die dochter ginc oec slapen, 59
Ende biede die vremde knapen,
Die weys ghenoech hadden gedroncken,
Ende die weert ginc liggen roncken,
Ende die weerdinne oec wel saen.

(The daughter also went to sleep
And both the visiting clerks,
Who had drunk in wise moderation,
And the host went to stretch out and snore,
And the hostess did the same.)

In the second passage, which occurs when the first clerk comes to the daughter's bed (line 56 below), we have, more clearly than in the French, some of the same mock-courtliness which characterizes the speedy seduction in Chaucer:

Die clerc antworde hoofschelike:
"Hebt mijns ghenade suverlike! 73
Ic en hebbe niet die cracht,
Dat ic van u scheiden macht,
Ic en mach mi jegen u niet veizen."

(The clerk answered in a courtly way:
"Have mercy on me graciously!
I do not have the power
To take myself away from you.
I will not rub against you.")

The Flemish version is printed in Eelco Verwijs, ed., *Dit Sijn X Goede Boerden* (The Hague, 1861), pp. 11–18. The following text is from Montaiglon and Raynaud, II, 238–244; for a more recent edition see Pierre Nardin's edition of the *Fabliaux* of Jean Bodel (Dakar, 1959).

GOMBERT AND THE TWO CLERKS

This next fabliau tells
About two clerks who were returning from school;
They had spent all their money,
More on foolishness than on wisdom.
They sought lodging at the house of a peasant,
By whose wife, Dame Guile,
One of the clerks, as soon as he came there,
Was so overcome that he fell in love.
But he could not help it,

10 Quar la dame est mingnote et cointe;
Les iex ot vairs come cristal.
Toute jour l'esgarde à estal
Li clers, si qu'à paine se cille,
Et li autres ama sa fille,
Qui adès i avoit ses iex.
Cil mist encor s'entente miex,
Quar sa fille est et cointe et bele,
Et je di qu'amor de pucele,
Quant fins cuers i est ententiex,
20 Est sor toute autre rien gentiex,
Comme li ostors au terçuel.
Un petit enfant en berçuel
Paissoit la bone fame en l'aistre.
Que qu'ele entendoit à lui paistre,
Uns des clers lez li s'acosta;
Fors de la paelete osta
L'anelet dont ele pendoit;
Si le bouta luès en son doit
Si coiement que nul nel sot.
30 Tel bien com sire Gombers ot
Orent assez la nuit si oste,
Lait boilli, matons et composte;
Ce fu assez si come à vile.
Cele nuit fu moult dame Guile
Regardée de l'un des clers;
Ses iex i avoit si aers
Que il nes en pooit retrère.
Li preudom, qui ne sot l'afère
Et n'i entendoit el que bien,
40 Fist lor lit fère près del sien;
Ses coucha, et les a couvers.
Lors se couche sire Gombers
Quant fu chaufez au feu d'esteule,
Et sa fille jut toute seule.
Quant la gent se fu endormie,
L'uns des clers ne s'oublia mie;
Molt li bat li cuers et flaele;
A tout l'anel de la paele
Au lit la pucele s'en vint.
50 Oiez coment il li avint;
Lez li se couche, les dras œvre:
"Qui est-ce, Diex, qui me descuevre?"

For the lady was beautiful and attractive; 10
Her eyes were gray as glass.
All day the clerk stared at her
So hard he barely blinked his eyes.
And the other clerk loved the daughter
And continually had his eyes on her.
He chose much the better,
For the daughter was elegant and lovely,
And I say that the love of a girl,
When a courtly heart is set on it,
Compared to all others is as much more noble 20
As is the hawk to the tercel falcon.
A tiny infant in a cradle
The good wife was feeding by the hearth.
While she was busy feeding him,
One of the clerks slipped by her
And took away from the cooking pan
The little ring by which it hung.
He slipped it quickly on his finger
So quietly that no one noticed it.
The best that Sir Gombert had, 30
Those guests had in plenty that night:
Boiled milk, cottage cheese, and mixed fruits—
It was more than enough, as usual on a farm.
That evening Dame Guile was closely
Watched by one of the clerks;
His eyes were so fixed on her
He could not take them away.
The husband, who did not know what was going on,
And who thought all was well,
Had their bed placed next to his own; 40
He put them to bed and covered them up.
Then Sir Gombert went to bed,
After he had warmed himself at the straw fire;
And his daughter slept all alone.
When the people had fallen asleep,
One of the clerks did not let his chance slip by;
His heart beat rapidly and tormented him;
With the ring from the cooking pan
He went to the girl's bed.
Listen to what happened to him: 50
He lay down by her, drew back the covers.
"Lord! Who is this who uncovers me?"

Dist-ele quant ele le sent.
"Sire, por Dieu omnipotent,
Que querez-vous ci à ceste eure?"
"Suer," dist-il, "se Diex me sequeure,
N'ai talent qu'en sus de vous voise;
Mès tesiez vous, ne fetes noise,
Que vostre père ne s'esveille,
60 Quar il cuideroit jà merveille,
S'il savoit que o vous géusse;
Il cuideroit que je éusse
De vous fètes mes volentez;
Mès, se vos mes bons consentez,
Granz biens vous en vendra encor,
Et si aurez mon anel d'or,
Qui miex vaut de IIII besanz;
Or sentez comme il est pesanz;
Trop m'est larges au doit m'anel."
70 Et cil li a bouté l'anel
Ou doit, si qu'il passa la jointe.
Et cele s'est près de lui jointe,
Et jure que jà nel prendroit.
Toutes eures, mi tort, mi droit,
L'uns vers l'autre tant s'amolie
Que li clers li fist la folie.
Et, quant il plus l'acole et baise,
Plus est ses compains à malaise,
Quar ressouvenir li fesoit;
80 Ce qu'à l'un paradis estoit
Sambloit à l'autre droiz enfers.
Lors se liève sire Gombers;
S'ala à l'uis pissier toz nuz;
L'autre clers est au lit venuz:
A l'esponde par de devant
Prist le berçuel o tout l'enfant,
Au lit le porte où a géu.
Or est dant Gombert decéu;
Quar adès à coustume avoit
90 La nuit, quant de pissier venoit,
Qu'il tastoit au berçuel premier.
Si come il estoit coustumier,
Lors vint tastant sire Gombers
Au lit, mès n'i ert pas li bers;
Quant il n'a le berçuel trové,

She said when she felt him;
"Sir, by God Almighty,
What are you doing here at this hour?"
"Sweetheart," he said, "as God may save me,
I only want to go in there beside you.
But be quiet, don't make a sound,
Lest your father should awake,
For he would think this strange indeed; 60
If he knew that I was in bed here with you
He would think that I had
Made you do my pleasure.
But, if you will consent to my wishes,
Great good will come to you from it,
And you will have my golden ring,
Which is worth more than four besants;
Now feel how heavy it is;
It is too large for my ring finger."
And he pushed the ring 70
On her finger, so that it passed the joint,
And she pressed herself close to him
And swore that she would never leave him.
Immediately, half by trickery, half openly,
The one became so tender to the other
That the clerk accomplished his foolish desire.
And the more he embraces and kisses her,
The more uncomfortable is his companion,
For it made him think of his lady;
What to the one was paradise 80
Seemed to the other true hell.
Then Sir Gombert got up;
Stark naked, he went out the door to piss.
The other clerk came to his bed,
Right from in front of the headboard
He took away the cradle with the baby
And carried it to the bed where he lay.
Now Dan Gombert is tricked,
For he always had the habit
At night when he came back from pissing 90
That he would first grope for the cradle.
Thus, as was his custom,
Sir Gombert soon came groping
To his bed, but there was no cradle there;
When he did not find the cradle,

Lors se tient à musart prové;
Bien cuide avoir voie marie.
"Li maufez," dist-il, "me tarie,
Quar en cest lit gisent mi oste."
100 Il vint à l'autre lit encoste,
Le bers i trueve et le mailluel,
Et li clers jouste le pailluel
Se trest, que nel truist le vilain.
Moult fu sire Gombers en vain,
Quant il n'a sa fame trovée;
Cuide qu'ele soit relevée
Pissier et fère ses degras.
Li vilains senti chaus les dras,
Si se couche entre II linceus;
110 Li sommaus li fu pris des eux;
Si s'endormi isnel le pas.
Et li clers ne s'oublia pas;
O la dame s'en vait couchier;
Ainz ne li lut son nez mouchier
S'ot esté III fois assaillie.
Or a Gombers bone mesnie;
Moult le mainent de male pile.
"Sire Gombers," dist dame Guile,
"Si viez hom com estes et frailes,
120 Moult avez anuit esté quailes;
Ne sai or de qoi vous souvint;
Pieça mès qu'il ne vous avint;
Ne cuidiez-vous que il m'anuit?
Vous avez ausi fet anuit
Que s'il n'en fust nus recouvriers;
Moult avez esté bons ouvriers;
N'avez guères esté oiseus."
Li clers, qui ne fu pas noiseus,
En fist toutes voies ses buens,
130 Et li lesse dire les suens.
Ne l'en fu pas à une bille
Cil qui gisoit avoec la fille;
Quant ot assez fet son delit,
Penssa qu'il r'ira à son lit
Ainz que li jors fust escleriez.
A son lit en est reperiez,
Là où gisoit Gombers ses ostes.
Cil le fiert du poing lèz les costes

Then he felt like a real fool.
He supposed indeed that he had lost his way.
"The devil," he said, "afflicts me,
For my guests are sleeping in this bed!"
He came alongside the other bed, 100
And he found there the cradle and the baby.
And the clerk had crouched down
Next to the bed, so that the peasant did not find him.
Sir Gombert was greatly surprised
When he did not find his wife.
He thought that she had gotten up
To piss and do her business.
The peasant felt the warmth of the bedclothes
And lay down between two sheets;
Slumber pressed upon his eyes 110
And he straightway fell asleep.
And the clerk did not miss his chance;
He went to get in bed with the lady,
And he did not so much as let her wipe her nose
Before he had attacked her three times.
Now Gombert had a good household
But he ran it with a weak stick.
"Sir Gombert," said Dame Guile,
"For so old and weak a man as you are,
You have been very hot tonight; 120
I don't know what you are thinking of;
It has been a long time indeed since you have been like this;
Aren't you afraid you will tire me?
You have done as much tonight
As if our salvation depended on it;
You have been a very good worker,
You have not been lazy."
The clerk, who did not make a sound,
Continually did his pleasure
And let her say what she pleased. 130
And he was no stick of wood,
He who was lying with the daughter;
When he had done enough of his pleasure,
He thought that he would go back to his bed
Before day had dawned.
So he returned to his bed,
There where his host, Gombert, was lying.
He punched him with his fist in the ribs,

Grant cop du poing, o tout le coute:
140 "Chetiz, bien as gardé la coute,"
Fet-il, "tu ne vaus une tarte;
Mès, ainz que de ci me departe,
Te dirai jà grande merveille."
A tant sire Gombers s'esveille;
Esraument s'est apercéuz
Qu'il est trahis et déçeuz
Par les clers et par lor engiens.
"Or, me di," dist-il, "d'ont tu viens?"
"D'ont?" dist-il, si noma tout outre,
150 "Par le cul bieu, je vieng de foutre,
Mès que ce fu la fille l'oste;
Pris en ai devant et encoste;
Aforé li ai son tonel,
Et se li ai donné l'anel
De la paelete de fer."
"Ha! ce soit de par cels d'enfer,"
Fet-il, "à cens et à milliers."
A tant l'aert par les illiers;
Si le fiert du poing lez l'oïe,
160 Et cil li rent une joïe
Que tuit li œil li estincelent.
Si durement s'entreflaelent
Entre els, qu'en diroie-je el,
C'on les péust en I tinel
Porter tout contreval la vile.
"Sire Gombert," dist dame Guile,
"Levez tost sus, quar il me samble
Que no clers sont meslé ensamble;
Je ne sai qu'ils ont à partir."
170 "Dame, j'es irai departir."
Lors s'en vint li clers cele part;
Trop i dust estre venuz tart,
Que ses compains ert abatuz,
Puisque cil i fu embatuz.
Le pior en ot dans Gombers,
Quar il l'ont ambedui aers;
L'uns le pile, l'autres le fautre.
Tant l'ont debouté l'un sor l'autre
Qu'il ot, par le mien escientre,
180 Le dos aussi mol que le ventre.
Quant ainsi l'orent atorné,

A great blow with the fist and with the whole elbow:
"Poor fellow, you have guarded our mattress well," 140
He said, "you are not worth a tart,
But before I leave here,
I will tell you a great wonder."
With that Sir Gombert awoke;
He immediately realized
That he had been betrayed and deceived
By those clerks and their tricks.
"Now, tell me," he said, "where are you coming from?"
"Where?" he said, and he announced straight out,
"By God, I come from fucking! 150
And it was our host's daughter, no less!
I took her from the front and from the side;
I breached her wine barrel,
And gave her the ring
From the iron cooking pan!"
"Ah! Let him be with those in hell!"
He said, "With the hundreds and the thousands!"
With that he grabbed him by the flank
And hit him in the eye with his fist,
And he gave him such a blow 160
That both his eyes saw stars.
They were so intent upon thrashing
One another that I would say
That one could have put them in a barrel
And carried them through the village.
"Sir Gombert," said Dame Guile,
"Get up quickly, for I believe
Our clerks are fighting each other;
I don't know what they have to fight about."
"Lady, I will go separate them." 170
Then the clerk went in from the side;
He almost came there too late,
For his companion had been thrown down
Just as he came rushing there.
Dan Gombert had the worst of it,
For both of them set upon him;
The one stomped him and the other punched him.
They so kicked him from one to the other
That, so it seems to me,
His back was as soft as his belly. 180
And when they had done this,

Andui sont en fuie torné,
Et l'uis lessent ouvert tout ample.
    Cis fabliaus moustre par example
Que nus hom qui bele fame ait,
Por nule proière ne lait
Clerc gesir dedenz son ostel,
Que il li feroit autretel;
Qui plus met en aus, plus i pert.
190 Ci faut li fabliaus de Gombert.

Explicit de Gombert et des II clers.

The two of them fled away,
Leaving the door wide open.
  This tale shows us by its example
That a man who has a pretty wife
Should never allow, despite his prayers,
A clerk to sleep in his house,
For he will do this same thing.
The more one trusts them, the more one loses.
There is no more of the fabliau of Gombert. 190

Here ends Gombert and the Two Clerks.

"The Miller and the Two Clerks"

This fabliau, the closest of the known analogues to Chaucer's "Reeve's Tale," was written by an anonymous author in the thirteenth century. Because of the many close resemblances, it is likely that Chaucer knew this fabliau, but not in the exact form in which it has survived.

There are two manuscripts, one printed by Montaiglon and Raynaud, V,

---

LE MEUNIER ET LES II CLERS

Dui povre clerc furent jadis
Né d'une vile et d'un païs;
Conpeignon et diacre estoient
En un boschage, o il menoient,
O il orent esté norri,
Tant c'uns chiers tans lor i sailli,
Con il fait mout tost et sovant:
C'est domage à la povre gent.
Li clerc virent la mesestance;
10 Si en orent au cuer pesance,
Ne il ne sevent conseillier,
Car il ne sevent rien gaaignier
N'en lor pais, n'en autre terre;
Honte avroient de lor pain querre,
Tant por lor hordre, et tant por el.
Il n'avoient point de chatel
Don se poïssent sostenir,
Ne il ne sevent où ganchir.
I diemanche, après mangier,
20 Sont alé devant lo mostier;
Illuec se sont entretrové,
Puis s'an sont de la vile alé,
Por dire I po de lor secroi.
Li uns dist à l'autre: "Antan moi;
Nos ne nos savon conseillier,
Car ne savon rien gaaignier,

83–94, the other first printed by H. Varnhagen in *Englische Studien,* IX (1885), 241–246. Chaucer's tale has some detailed similarities to passages peculiar to each of the two manuscripts. It seems likely, therefore, that the version Chaucer knew was a slightly longer manuscript containing those passages found now only in one or the other of the two manuscripts. We have printed the longer and better version as it appears in Montaiglon and Raynaud, but we have added in brackets those passages from the other manuscript (labeled *B*) that contain details which, some scholars believe, reappear in "The Reeve's Tale." This method of editing is somewhat arbitrary, but it produces a version that contains all the passages of interest to the student of Chaucer. For a full discussion of those passages, see Germaine Dempster, "On the Source of the Reeve's Tale," *JEGP,* XXIX (1930), 473–488. A more recent edition is that of Jean Rychner, *Contributions à l'étude des fabliaux* (Geneva, 1960), II, 152–160.

THE MILLER AND THE TWO CLERKS

Once there were two poor clerks,
Born in the same town and in the same country;
They were fellow deacons.
In the forest where they lived,
Where they had been nourished,
Very hard times assailed them,
As happens so often;
It is a sad situation for poor folk.
The clerks considered their sad state;
They had such heavy hearts — 10
They could not think what to do,
For they did not know how to earn anything,
Neither in their own country nor anywhere else.
They were ashamed to beg for their bread,
As much because of their Order as for anything else.
They had no possessions at all
With which to support themselves,
And they did not know where to turn.
  On Sunday, after dinner,
They went out of their church — 20
And met one another there,
And went out of the town
To speak a bit about their problem.
  The one said to the other: "Listen here,
We do not know what to do
Because we don't know how to earn anything;

Et voiz là fain qui nos destraint,
C'est une chose qui tot vaint;
Nus ne se puet de li deffandre,
30 Ne nos n'avon rien nule o prandre.
As tu nule rien porveü
Par quoi nos soions maintenu?"
L'autre respont: "Par saint Denise,
Je ne te sai faire devise,
Mais que jo ai un mien ami,
Je lo que nos aillon vers li,
Por prandre I setier de fromant,
A la vante que l'an lo vant;
Et il m'an querra les deniers
40 Mout longuemant et volantiers
Jusq'à la feste saint Johan,
Por nos giter de cest mal an."
Li autres a lors respondu:
"Il nos est trés bien avenu;
Car j'ai un mien frere ensemant,
Qui a une grasse jumant;
Je la prandrai, pran lo setier,
Et si devandron bolangier.
L'an doit toute honte endosser
50 Por soi de cest mal an giter."
Ensi lo font, plus n'i atant:
Au molin portent lor fromant.
Li molins si loin lor estoit,
Plus de II liues i avoit.
C'estoit lo molin à choisel,
Si seoit juste un bocheel:
Il n'ot ilueques environ
Borde, ne vile, ne maison,
Fors sol la maison au munier,
60 Qui trop savoit de son mestier.
Li clerc ont tost l'uis desfermé,
Si ont lo sac dedanz gité:
Après ont mis en un prael
La jumant, joste lo choisel.
Li uns remest por tot garder,
L'autre ala lo munier haster,
Que il les venist avancier.
Mais il s'an fu alé mucier:
Bien ot les clers veü venir,

And see now how this famine afflicts us.
It is a thing that conquers all;
No one can defend himself against it.
We have nothing to draw upon. 30
Have you set aside anything
With which we can support ourselves?"
The other answered: "By Saint Denis,
I do not know what to say to you,
Except that I do have a good friend;
I advise that we go to him
To fetch a quarter of wheat
At the price it goes for this year,
And he will grant me credit for its cost
For a long time and willingly, 40
Until the feast of Saint John,
For us to use in this bad year."
The other then answered:
"That is very good for us,
For I have a very good brother indeed,
Who has a fat mare;
I will get her, get the quarter of wheat,
And we will become bakers.
The times will excuse the shameful things
A man must do in this bad year." 50
Thus they did without delay.
To the mill they carried their grain.
The mill was far away,
More than two leagues it was.
It was a mill at a millstream,
And stood next to a small wood.
There was nothing around there,
Not hut, nor town, nor house,
Except for the house of the miller,
Who knew his trade too well. 60
The clerks soon opened the gate
And threw their sack of grain inside.
Then they put the mare
In the meadow next to the millstream.
The one stayed to watch everything,
The other went to rouse the miller
So that he would come to help them.
But he had gone into hiding.
He had indeed seen the clerks coming,

70 Je cuit à aus voldra partir.
Chiés lo munier en vient corant,
La dame a trovée filant:
"Dame," fait il, "por saint Martin,
O est li sires do molin?
Bien fust que il nos avançast."
"Sire clers, point ne m'an pesast;
En ce bois lo porroiz trover,
Se il vos i plaist à aler,
Qui ci est joste ce molin."
80 Et li clers se mest au chemin,
Querre lo vait mout vistemant.
A son conpeignon qui l'atant
Poise mout qu'il demore tant;
En la maison en vient corant:
"Dame," fait il, "por amor Dé,
O est mon conpeignon alé?"
"Sire, si aie je hanor,
Il en vait querre mon seignor
Qui orandroit issi là hors."
90 Ele ot bien ce mestier amors:
L'un des clers après l'autre envoie,
Et li muniers aquiaut sa voie;
Si vient au molin auramant,
Lo sac lieve sor la jumant
O sa fame qui li aida,
En sa maison tot enporta.
Tant a en sa maison mucié,
Puis est au molin repairiez;
Et li clerc ont tant cheminé
100 Que il sont au molin torné.
"Munier," font il, "Deus soit o vos!
Por amor Deu, avanciez nos."
"Seignor," fait il, "et je de quoi?"
"De nostre blé qu'est ci, par foi."
Qant durent prandre lo fromant,
Ne trovent ne sac ne jumant.
L'uns d'aus a l'autre regardé:
"Qu'est ice? somes nos robé?"
"Oïl," fait ce l'uns, "ce m'est vis!
110 Pechiez nos a à essil mis."
Chascuns escrie: "Halas! halas!
Secorez nos, saint Nicolas!"

And I believe he wanted to separate them. 70
One came running to the miller's house
And found the wife at her spinning.
"Lady," he said, "by Saint Martin,
Where is the lord of the mill?
He should come to help us."
"Sir Clerk, don't bother me about that;
You could find him in that wood—
If you please to go there—
That is next to the mill."
And the clerk is on his way; 80
He goes very quickly to seek him.
His companion, who was waiting for him,
Was so bothered by the long delay
That he came running to the house:
"Lady," he said, "for the love of God,
Where has my friend gone?"
"Sir, on my honor,
He has gone to seek my lord,
Who went out just a little while ago."
She knew well the tricks of the trade. 90
She sent one clerk after the other,
And the miller got on his way
And came running to the mill.
He threw the sack on the mare,
With his wife who helped him,
And carried everything into his house.
As soon as he had hidden it in the house,
He returned to the mill.
And the clerks have wandered so long
That they returned to the mill. 100
"Miller," they say, "God be with you!
For the love of God, help us."
"My lords," he said, "Help with what?"
"With this grain here, in faith."
But when they go to fetch their grain,
They find neither sack nor mare.
One looked at the other:
"What is this? Have we been robbed?"
"Yes," said one, "that is what I think,
Sin has brought us to ruin!" 110
Each cried: "Alas, alas!
Save us, Saint Nicholas!"

Fait li muniers: "Qu'est ce c'avez?
Por quoi si durement criez?"
"Munier, ja avon tot perdu;
Malemant nos est avenu,
Car n'avons ne jumant ne el:
Tot i estoit notre chatel."
"Seignor," fait il, "n'en sai noiant."
120 "Sire," font il, "ne vos apant
Fors tant que de nos asener
Quel part nos poïssiens aler
Querre et tracier nostre domage."
"Seignor," fait il, "en cest bochage:
Ne vos sai je pas conseillier,
Mais en cel bois alez cerchier,
Qui ci est joste cest molin."
Li clerc se mestent au chemin.
Maintenant sont el bois entré,
130 Et li muniers s'an est alé
[Tant ont et haut et bas alé
Que le soleil fu escoussé;] (B, 113–114)
Li uns clers à l'autre parla:
"Certes," font il, "voir dit i a,
Fous est qui en vain se travaille;
Avoir vient et va comme paille,
Alons nos huimais herbergier."
"Nos? en quel leu?" "Chiés lo munier,
O no alon en cel molin,
140 Deus nos doint l'ostel saint Martin!"
Errant vindrent chiés lo munier.
Lor venir n'avoit il point chier,
Ainz lor demande aneslopas:
"Que vos a fait saint Nicolas?"
"Munier," font il, "ne I ne el."
"Or gaaigniez autre chatel,
Car de cest estes vos trop loing;
Ne l'avroiz pas à cest besoing."
"Munier," font il, "ce puet bien estre:
150 Herbergiez nos, por saint Servestre,
Ne savon maishui o aler."
Et li muniers prant à panser,
Or seroit il pire que chiens,
S'il ne lor faisoit aucun bien
Del lor, car il lo puet bien faire.

Said the miller: "What is the matter?
Why are you crying so loud?"
"Miller, we have lost everything;
Evil has fallen upon us,
For now we have not mare nor anything;
Those were all our possessions."
"My lords," he said, "I know nothing about this."
"Sir," they say, "it does not concern you, 120
Unless you can tell us
Where we should go
To search and seek out our loss."
"My lords," he said, "look in this wood.
I do not know how to advise you,
But you can look in this wood
That is next to this mill."
The clerks set out on their way;
When they had entered the woods,
The miller went on his way. 130
[They went up and down so long
That the sun had set,]
And one clerk spoke to the other:
"Indeed," he said, "it is truly said
That he is a fool who labors in vain.
Possessions come and go like straw.
Let us go now and stay for the night."
"Us? Where?" "At the miller's,
Where we went to the mill;
God grant us the hostel of Saint Martin!" 140
They went quickly to the miller's house;
He was not at all happy at their arrival,
But he asked them straightway:
"What has Saint Nicholas done for you?"
"Miller," they said, "not a thing."
"Then go earn some other goods,
For you are too far away from what you lost,
And you will not have it for this business."
"Miller," they said, "that may well be.
Give us lodging, by Saint Sylvester! 150
We don't know where else to go at this hour."
Then the miller began to think
That he would be worse than a dog
If he did not do something for them
With their own goods, since he could easily do it.

"Seignor," fait il, "nient fors l'aire
Ice avroiz, se plus n'en avez."
"Munier," font il, "ce est assez."
Li vilains n'ot pas grant cointie:
160 Il n'ot que soi, cart de maisnie,
Sa fille q'an doit metre avant,
Sa fame, et un petit enfant.
La fille estoit et bele et cointe,
Et li muniers, qu'el ne fust pointe,
En une huche la metoit
Chascune nuit, o el gisoit,
Et l'anfermoit par de desus,
Et li bailloit par un pertuis
La clef, et puis s'aloit cochier.
170 A noz clers devons repairier.
La nuit, qant ce vint au soper,
Li muniers lor fait aporter
Pain et lait, et eues, et fromage,
C'est la viande del bochage;
Aus II clers assez en dona.
L'un o la pucele manja,
L'autre o la dame et lo munier.
En l'aitre ot un petit andier,
O il avoit un anelet,
180 Que l'an oste sovant et met.
Cil q'o la pucele manja
De l'andier l'anelet osta,
Bien l'a et repost et mucié.
La nuit quant il furent cochié,
Li clers de li grant garde prist:
Bien vit que li muniers li fist;
Con en la huche la bouta,
Et par de desus l'anferma;
Con il li a la clef bailliée,
190 Par un pertuis li a lanciée.
[Adont se couche et ronfle fort
Icel mouner et tost s'endort.] (B, 177–178)
Qant il furent aseüré,
Il a son conpaignon bouté:
"Conpainz," fait il, "je voil aler
A la fille au munier parler,
Qui est en la huche enfermée."
"Viaus tu," fait cil, "faire mellée,

"My lords," he said, "there is only this hall;
You will have that if you have nothing more."
"Miller," they said, "it is enough."
The churl did not have a great establishment;
He had only himself, a quarter of the household, 160
His daughter, whom one ought to put first,
His wife, and a tiny baby.
The daughter was pretty and agreeable,
And the miller, lest she be too agreeable,
Put her into a bin
Each night, where she slept,
And he locked it from the outside
And through a little opening he gave her
The key, and then went to bed himself.
We must return to our clerks: 170
At night, when suppertime came,
The miller had brought to them
Bread and milk and eggs and cheese—
This is the food of the countryside.
He gave plenty of it to the two clerks.
One ate with the daughter,
The other with the miller and his wife.
In the fireplace there was a small andiron,
On which there was a little ring
That moved it in and out. 180
The one who ate with the young girl
Took the little ring from the andiron
And concealed and hid it well.
That night when they were in bed,
That clerk paid close attention
And he saw all that the miller did—
How he put her in the bin
And locked it from the outside,
How he gave her the key,
Threw it through a little window. 190
[Then he went to bed and loudly snored.
The miller was fast asleep.]
When all were settled down,
He nudged his companion:
"Friend," he said, "I am going to go
Talk to the miller's daughter,
Who is locked up in that bin."
Said the other: "Do you want to raise an uproar

Et estormir ceste maison?
200 Verité est, tu ies bricon,
Tost nos en porroit mal venir."
"Je ne voldroie por morir,
Que ne m'en aille à li savoir
S'el me porroit de rien valoir."
A la huche vient erraumant,
I petit grate, et el l'antant:
"Q'est ce," fait ele, "là defors?"
"C'est celui qui por vostre cors
Est si destroiz et mal bailli,
210 Se vos n'avez de lui merci,
Jamais nul jor joie n'avra.
C'est celui qui o vos manja,
Qui vos aporte un enel d'or,
Onques n'aüstes tel tresor;
Bien est esprové et saü
Que la pierre en a tel vertu
Que ja fame, tant soit legiere,
Ne tant par ait esté corsiere,
Qui chaste et pucele ne soit,
220 S'au matin en son doi l'avoit.
Tenez, gel vos en faz presant."
Errant cele la clef li tant,
Et il desferme errant la huche,
Dedanz se met, ele s'acluche.
Or puent faire lor deduit,
Car ne trovent qui lor anuit.
La fame o munier, ainz lo jor,
Se leva d'enprès son seignor;
Tote nue vait en la cort.
230 Par de devant lo lit trescort
Au clerc, qui en l'aire gisoit.
Li clerc au trespasser la voit;
Qant il la vit, si l'esgarda,
De son conpaignon li manbra,
Qui en la huche fait ses buens;
Mout convoite faire les suens.
Pansa que il la decevroit
Au revenir, se il pooit:
Puis repansoit no feroit mie,
240 Tost en porroit sordre folie.
I autre angin li est creüz:

And stir up the household?
It is true, you are a fool; 200
Evil can soon come to us from this."
"I would rather die
Than not go to find out
If she can do me any good."
He comes quickly to the bin
And scratches lightly, and she hears him.
"Who is out there?" she says.
"It is one who for your body
Is so anguished and tormented
That if you do not have mercy on him, 210
He will never again have joy.
It is he with whom you dined,
Who has brought to you a little golden ring:
You have never handled such a treasure,
For it is well proven and known
That its stone has such power
That any woman, no matter how easy in virtue,
Nor how often she has whored about,
Will yet be chaste and a maiden
If she has this on her finger in the morning. 220
Take it; I make you a present of it."
Quickly she gives him the key,
And he immediately unlocks the bin.
He gets in, she crouches over,
And now they can take their delight,
For they find no one to bother them.
The miller's wife, before dawn,
Gets up from the side of her lord.
Stark naked she walks into the courtyard.
She passes directly by the bed 230
Of the clerk who was sleeping in the hall.
The clerk saw her passing by;
When he saw her and considered her well,
He thought of his companion,
Who was doing well for himself in the bin.
He greatly desired to do something for himself.
He decided that he would trick her
When she returned, if he could.
Then he thought again he would not do it;
Straightway it would cause some mischief. 240
He was struck by another idea.

S'anprès est de son lit chaüz,
A l'autre lit s'an va tot droit,
Là o li muniers se gisoit;
L'anfant à tot lo briez aporte,
Et qant la dame entre en la porte,
Li clers tire à l'anfant l'oroille,
Et l'anfes crie, si s'esvoille.
Cele ala à son lit tot droit,
250 Qant ele oït o cil estoit;
Puis est erraument retornée,
Au cri de l'anfant est alée:
Lo briez trove, don s'aseüre,
Puis solieve la coverture,
Dejoste lo clerc s'est cochiée
Et cil l'a estroit enbraciée.
Vers soi l'atrait, formant l'acole,
A son deduit tote l'afole;
Si sofre tot, si se mervoille.
260 Et l'autres clers si s'aparoille,
Qant il oït le coc chanter,
Car il cuidoit trop demorer.
De la huche s'an est issuz,
[A la pucele congié prent,] (B, 247)
Puis est droit à son lit venuz:
Lo briez trove, si s'esbaïst;
N'est pas mervoille s'il lo fist.
Il ot peor, et neporqant
I petit est alez avant;
270 Et qant II testes a trovées,
Erraumant les a refusées.
A l'autre lit o se gisoit
Li muniers, s'an va cil tot droit.
Dejoste li s'estoit cochiez,
Ne s'est pas encore esveilliez,
Ne ne s'est mie aparceüz.
"Compainz," fait li clers, "que fais tu?
Qui toz jorz se tait rien ne valt,
Or sai je bien, se Deus me salt,
280 Que j'ai aü boene nuitiée:
Mout est la pucele envoisiée,
La fille à cest nostre munier;
Mout par si fait mal anvoisier
Et si fait trop bon foutre en huche.
Conpeignon, car va, si t'i muce,

He leaped out of his bed
And went directly to the other bed,
There where the miller was lying,
And carried away the baby in its cradle.
When the lady comes through the doorway,
The clerk pulls the baby's ear,
And the infant wakes and cries.
She was going straight to her bed
When she heard where the baby was, 250
And she straightway turned
And went toward the baby's cry.
She found the crib and, reassured,
She then lifted the blanket
And laid herself down next to the clerk,
And he immediately seized her,
Turned her toward himself, and stoutly grasped her;
In his pleasure he quite batters her.
She suffers all, she is so amazed.
Then the other clerk got dressed 260
When he heard the cock crowing,
For he was afraid to delay too long.
He came out of the bin,
[Took his leave of the girl]
And went straight to bed.
He found the crib and he was amazed;
It is no wonder that he was.
He was afraid, but nevertheless,
He came a bit nearer,
And when he found two heads, 270
He quickly drew back.
He went to the other bed where lay
The miller, and he quickly got in.
He lay down next to him,
Who was not yet awake
And as yet had discovered nothing.
"Friend," said the clerk, "what are you doing?
'He who is always silent gains nothing.'
Now I know well, as God may save me,
That I have had a good night. 280
That girl is very accommodating,
That daughter of our miller.
It is very hard work to amuse oneself in that way
And to do so much good screwing in the bin.
Friend, now go, if you can keep it quiet,

Et si pran do bacon ta part;
Assez en a jusq'à la hart;
Par VII foiz l'ai anuit corbée,
Dès or sera boene l'asnée,
290 El n'a fors l'anel de l'andier;
Si ai je bien fait mon mestier."
Qant li muniers entant la bole,
Tantost prant lo clerc par la gole
Et li clers lui, qui s'aparçoit
Tantost lo met en si mal ploit
A po li fait lo cuer crever;
Et la dame aquialt à boter
L'autre cler, qui o lui gisoit:
"Sire," fait ele, "ce que doit?
300 Se viaus, car nos levon tost sus,
Ja s'estranglent cil cler laissus."
"Ne te chaut," fait il, "lai ester,
Lai les musarz entretuer."
Il savoit bien, si n'ot pas tort,
Que ses conpainz ere plus fors.
Qant li muniers pot eschaper,
Tantost cort lo feu alumer;
Et qant il sa fame aparçoit,
Qui avoc lo clerc se gisoit:
310 "Or sus," fait il, "pute provée,
Qui vos a ici amenée?
Certes, il est de vos tot fait."
"Sire," fait ele, "autremant vait,
Car se je sui pute provée,
Par engin i fui atornée;
Mais vos estes larron provć,
Qui en cez clers avez emblé
Lor sac de blé et lor jumant,
Dont vos seroiz levez au vant:
320 Tot est en vostre granche mis."
Li dui clerc ont lo vilain pris;
Tant l'ont folé et debatu
Par po qu'il ne l'ont tot molu,
Puis vont modre à autre molin.
Il orent l'ostel saint Martin,
Et ont tant lor mestier mené
Q'il se sont do mal an gité.
[A deu et a seint Nicolas
Entendent grasces haut et bas.] (B, 293–294)

And get your share of the bacon;
There is enough of it left over;
Seven times tonight I screwed her,
And yet there is enough there to load down an ass.
And she has nothing for it but the ring from the andiron, 290
I carried on my trade so well!"

When the miller understood the trick,
Straightway he grabbed the clerk by the throat
And the clerk him, when he understood what was happening;
The clerk had him in such an evil plight
That the miller was nearly strangled.

The lady began to nudge
The clerk who lay beside her.
"Sir," she said, "what's to be done?
If you please, let's get right up; 300
Those clerks are strangling one another over there."

"Don't get excited," he said, "let them be;
Let the rascals kill one another."
(He knew well, and he was not wrong,
That his companion was the stronger.)

When the miller was able to escape,
He went quickly to light the fire,
And when he saw his wife,
Who was lying in bed with the clerk:
"Get up," he said, "you proven whore! 310
Who has brought you to this?
Indeed, it was all your own doing!"

"Sir," she said, "it is not so;
For if I am a proven whore,
I was brought to it by a trick,
But you are a proven thief,
You who stole from these clerks
Their sack of grain and their mare,
For which you should be hanged on high,
For it is all in your barn!" 320

The two clerks took the churl
And so kicked and beat him
That he was nearly ground up himself.
And then they went to grind at another mill.
They had the hostel of Saint Martin,
And they carried on their trade so well
That they managed in that bad year.
[To God and to Saint Nicholas
Give thanks both high and low.]

"The Students' Adventure"

Unlike England, Germany has a rich fund of medieval stories equivalent in form, tone, and technique to the French fabliaux. However, compared to the fabliaux, the German stories are much neglected, to the point where there is not even a firmly established term for the genre. They have sometimes been designated simply and colorlessly as Middle High German *Versnovellen;* more recently the term *Märe* has come into use, but it has not yet acquired the currency and clear set of associations which establish a literary term. In English one is tempted to call these stories "German fabliaux" out of the same terminological embarrassment that prompts us to speak of "Chaucer's fabliaux."

The German genre developed a little later than the French, with about the same lag that separates the development of courtly literature in these countries. The *Mären* began early in the thirteenth century, reached maturity around the middle of that century, and continued in the fourteenth and fifteenth centuries. Some of them were written by well-known authors of the

---

THE STUDENTS' ADVENTURE

It is said that good companions are bound like brothers. Two honest burghers were such companions until the time each had a son; they were the same age. The companions were wealthy and were men of honor. They steadily increased their property and possessions. The children also learned to be fond of one another.

When they came of age, they were admitted to school; their master was promised both gold and silver on their behalf—that made the master beholden to them. It was his job to stay with them; he taught the boys to read and sing, one better than the other. They pursued their studies until they understood very well whatever a young man should know, and they perfected their singing to the point that they were the best musicians there. They were told that at another place there was a school of great distinction where the priesthood held sway and taught the art; the place was called Paris. One of them spoke up immediately, "Indeed, good comrade, if you consent to accompany me there, and stay a year, we would derive both honor and advantage from it."

The other said, "Assuredly. I praise the Lord that I have learned this from you. I will gladly go with you." They swore troth and vows to one another.

thirteenth century, and later, in the fifteenth century, the genre was kept alive by the Nürnberg writers, Hans Rosenplüt and Hans Folz, mentioned in connection with the *Fastnachtspiele* (p. 46), but along the way many of them were written anonymously and are quite impossible to date. The total number extant is roughly the same as in France, around two hundred. They are in the four-beat rhymed verse of the Middle High German epic and vary in length from something over one hundred lines to about two thousand. Thus "Das Studentenabenteuer" (464 lines) is about average and "Irregang und Girregar" (1450 lines) is one of the longest. For a general treatment of the *Mären* the reader should turn to Hanns Fischer's *Studien zur deutschen Märendichtung* (Tübingen: Max Niemeyer Verlag, 1968).

Despite the general dearth of information available on the *Mären,* there is a full monograph on "Das Studentenabenteuer": Wilhelm Stehmann, *Die mittelhochdeutsche Novelle vom Studentenabenteuer* (Berlin, 1909). On the basis of a linguistic investigation and a comparison to texts which can be located and dated (Konrad von Würzburg), Stehmann concludes that the story was written in the middle of the thirteenth century in the North Alemannic, South Frankish region west of Strassburg. Since the text is well edited by Stehmann in his book, and in order to conserve space, we have printed only a translation of it. The language and style of a Middle High German *Märe* is amply illustrated by the succeeding text, "Irregang und Girregar."

When they went home from school, their fathers received them—they were sitting outside waiting with supper for them. One said, "Now tell me, children, what does it mean that you are so late tonight? What do you have on your minds? Can you tell us?"

One of them said, "Yes, we can. We want to go away to school and want you to support us. We have sworn oaths to this effect to one another. It would be wasted effort that you have spent on us unless we spend a year where there are priests."

Now they were loath to lose their children and said, "Children, stay here! What our fathers left to us we have increased. You are very well instructed in what a layman should know. We will provide well for you during these years here at home, in a way to do you honor. You should not be involved with the priests."

Then one of them spoke up, "It would be very foolish if we remained for that reason and passed our days with work and worry. We will not stay longer than tomorrow; then we will go by foot rather than remain here longer."

Then the elders spoke again, "Now God forbid that you should go where you will suffer want. If you have nothing in your purses, you will be unwelcome guests to the French. They don't care a farthing for anyone who comes to them without silver and doesn't spend money lavishly;

such a man they all loudly declare a fool. You should be courteous and wait until we equip you properly. You are well-bred youths; do justice to yourselves and you will have honor and benefit from it. We have no other children, you are our pride and joy."

In a short time they were provided with horses, books, and clothes. They sent two pages with them who took care of them wherever they spent the night, so that they didn't lose their silver, and who chose good hosts for them and made sure that they ate heartily but modestly.

The youths did not delay; they took leave and rode away. It was a difficult parting for both the fathers, but the children rode off joyfully and with no remorse.

Now they came riding into the good city of Arras. There a lady greeted them with a courteous demeanor; she was going from the baths with her daughter, who greeted them as well. Whatever qualities one in any way can praise and honor in virtuous ladies, of these qualities they were perfect paragons. The two young men thanked her courteously and asked God to reward her. The mother was very decorous; the maiden was never equalled in virtue and worthiness, she was altogether ideal.

When one of them looked at her carefully, he said to his companion, "Have you seen the girl? You have to admit that you never saw a prettier maid. I'll pine away and perish on the spot if I can't win her. Now don't be in too much of a hurry; let's ride behind them and see where she lives so we can take lodging there or nearby until we get a good look at her."

"Well spoken. I agree."

As soon as she stepped into her house, he asked the gentleman who sat by the door to lodge them that night if he was master of the house.

The host said, "I am a man who can do nothing on a business basis and you are probably merchants. I will tell you what I'll do: if you wish to stay here, both bread and wine will be at your disposal and whatever comfort I can provide."

"Mercy, sir, that would be too much. Let me state our wishes: we are on our way to the school in Paris and if you allow us to stay here, we will provide for bread and wine and whatever one has with it far better than any merchant."

Then the host said, "So be it. I will make good cheer. I was never so glad to welcome guests."

When he learned that they were to lodge within, he [one companion] said, "Dear comrade, now lay in good provisions so that I will always be beholden to you. Bring us the best wine and mead available in town for the host and his household so that they will be of good cheer. If the cost is too great for you, I will pay for it alone, if you wish."

His companion carried out the commission well; wine and mead were brought so that the house was liberally stocked. The maiden was brought a

casket in which a beautiful psalter lay. The lady of the house bade her daughter read. I don't know in what curious way it was written which prevented her from finding the right place. The student took the psalter in his hand and read like a learned man.

The maiden said, "If I could only read as well as you! Sir, teach me. My mother slaps me whenever I miss a word."

Then the mother began to laugh. She said, "If he could make you read the way he does, he would be a welcome guest to you and would save you from many a blow. Sir, take her aside under the arbor by the door, go together there; there no one will bother you, nor will the smoke, and there is light."

When he got away from the others, I wager it didn't grieve him. He was supposed to read the psalter to her, but he began to plead his woe and said, "Dear maiden, I want to be your very own; I am overcome with love for you, maiden; hear me and by your courtesy and honor release me from my heartache and from my affliction. Don't let me pine away and I will praise your virtue, your beauty, your courtesy, and your youth."

"Sir, how can this be? I have never seen you before and would pay for my fault by losing my father's affection and my mother's as well. Where would I be then? In addition I would lose my honor. I will always be well disposed to you, come what may, but whatever your feelings are, I will not risk my honor."

He was supposed to teach her the psalter, but he began firmly to increase her knowledge of what she didn't know before, until she was caught by the toils of love. He persisted so long that love's pincers drew her into its snare. They cast many a glance, their hearts were fired so that they could not turn their eyes aside. They looked at one another until they quite lost their senses. They lost their color and went pale; the bond of love held them fettered. His companion found them sitting thus; he scolded them harshly and said, "Do you want to lose your honor and your life here for the sake of this girl's love? Whoever becomes so pale betrays the signs of love; a wise man recognizes them easily."

He took his companion away and said, "Maiden, take heart. We and our property must all remain here. Your wishes must be fulfilled, but in such a way that you don't risk your honor too easily. Your secret will not be revealed."

Then the maiden began to take cheer and recovered her color. They sat down by one another until a page told them that the meal was ready.

Now the host was a courteous man and showed his breeding by not dismissing the maiden; he bade her kindly eat with the youth with whom she had been seated. His favorite dish was to look at her constantly. The other companion, who was seated there also, didn't forget anyone and gave them all plenty of the best wine that was available and could be found for sale.

He didn't begrudge it them at all. The host's household all drank apace so that they forgot their troubles.

When they were sitting after the meal, he asked them to tell whither their trip took them.

"We wish to travel to Paris and must be careful to choose hosts with whom we don't lose anything, and I'll tell you why: we have with us here what we need for a whole year."

Then the host said:

"If that is true, I will take good care of you. I will lodge you in my chamber where you can come to no harm. There you can remain securely until the morrow."

Then they were delighted and pleased with their luck in finding lodging there. Everything went according to plan; they went straightway to bed. The maiden was reminded of her pledge lest she forget something and remain seated too long. They were accommodated splendidly at one end of the chamber as it befits rich guests. The host lay by the wall and the maiden slept in a place I have indicated to you before.

Soon they went to bed. The host's servant returned and said, "Master and mistress, you should not remain here any longer lest you awaken the guests and startle them out of their sleep. They are tired and have had a long ride."

"That is a reasonable request," said the host immediately. He took his wife by the hand and the handsome maid and they retired together.

Now there was a newly-weaned child whom the lady had taken and put down at the foot of her bed, after which she lay down with the host; she was very sleepy. The student went to the maiden. She received him lovingly; they both rejoiced and had their pleasure. I'll cut this story short.

The other companion lay alone and got no sleep; he thought, "Alas, poor wretch, that I can achieve nothing and that I gain no honor, yet half of what we consume is mine."

As he was turning these things over in his mind, it happened that the lady went out, for what reason I do not know. The student took the cradle and set it down at the foot of his bed. Now when the lady came back and wanted to lie down by the host and settle down to sleep, the student took the child and pulled it by the ear so that it began to cry. The lady went to the cradle and told the child to shush and lay down by the student thinking it was her bed. Behold, when she lay down next to him, the doughty student played the part of a man who knows how to serve women and didn't let her lie idly. She said, "I would hardly have expected that you would ever touch me, as drunk as you were."

She kissed him and was at his disposal. This made him overjoyed and eager. She said, "Tomorrow morning I'll give you good wine to drink. Drinking is good for you if it makes you so enterprising. If you wish, I'll

buy the whole keg for you so that you will feel in the mood just that much longer."

In the meantime his companion, the one who had lain with the maiden, arrived (he thought the sun had risen) and wanted to go to bed. There he found the cradle and heard the man and woman. He turned right around and went back quickly and lay down by the host. Then the host said:

"Where were you?"

"You know where I was; I have slept with the maiden and have had good love and great pleasure with her."

Then the host fell into a rage:

"You are as drunk as a dog!"—and struck the student in the mouth. He thought it was his wife.

The student thought, "Upon my life, my companion is envious that the maiden has shown me such courtesy. For the sake of kindness I will overlook it and lie down to sleep."

The host prevented him with lusty blows. He struck him two blows with his left hand so that he couldn't fail to take notice of it.

"Since you don't mind fisticuffs, I'll pay you back, if that's what you want!"

He grabbed the host by the hair and vice versa; they both tugged with all their might.

Then the lady got worried. She said to the student:

"Listen, our guests are in a fight."

Now he understood what was up and how it had happened.

"A light," he said, "so that we can see what has happened to the guests."

The lady went to fetch the light, the student gathered up the cradle and put it down at the end of her bed; he pulled his companion back to bed with him. That was done very softly. They lay down at their ease and pulled the covers over their heads. The lady came quickly and brought a light with her. When she saw the host sitting—his nightcap was pulled off and hair was pulled out of his scalp—she spoke a blessing to herself and said, "God have mercy on us!" She clutched her heart and said, "Who has been wrestling with you?"

"You have, you devil!"

"Indeed, not I, dear husband! Should I fight with you when you have been so nice to me tonight? You haven't been so merry in a whole year!"

The host went with the light to where the guests were lying. Although they weren't asleep, they pretended they were in a deep slumber. When he saw them sleeping thus, he said to his wife, "The guests are innocent, the devil did this to me, he has deceived us both. How could you lie to me and tell me I was merry tonight?"

The lady was quick to understand and said, "We must let it rest. Be quiet for my sake so that the guests don't notice anything; they'll travel

on tomorrow and won't know anything about it. But if anyone asks about it, deny everything." Thus the deception was complete.

When it now began to dawn, the students took leave and went on their way. They laughed uproariously about this merry prank and that their luck and fortune's wheel had taken such a turn.

Now I advise my friends, he who lodges strangers (though he take good care of them otherwise) should not put them in his room and should take good care that what happened to the host not happen to him. If he does that, all will be well, because opportunity makes the thief.

Rüdiger von Munre's "Waywardwight and Lustymite"

Judging from certain linguistic criteria (such as declined possessive pronouns) and from the very fact of its elaboration, the longer German version would appear to be somewhat later than the shorter version. However, the courtly mannerisms, which are more imitation than burlesque, suggest that it is not too much later. Perhaps a dating around 1300 is not too far off the mark. The author, Rüdiger von Munre, names himself, but we have no other works by him and no information concerning him. Nor can Munre be located satisfactorily. The language of the poem places it to the north of "Das Studentenabenteuer," perhaps in the neighborhood of Aachen, the native city of one of the youths (line 1297).

There are two distinguishing features which set "Irregang und Girregar" apart from the other analogues. One is the sequel which it attaches to the original events of the story. Lines 1–700 correspond roughly to what we have in "The Reeve's Tale" and the other versions, but to this are added another 750 lines in which the youths prolong their stay, continue their frolic with mother and daughter, and subject the poor host to renewed humiliations and deceptions. After each prank, he is deluded into believing that he has been tricked by his imagination or by evil demons. His ailment is remedied successively by mock prayers, magic incantations, and a heathenish exhortation to expel the intruding demons, Irregang and Girregar. He is ultimately driven to resolve never to trust his senses again and steadfastly ignores all later commerce between his women and their lovers.

The two new pranks are the "basket motif" (lines 826–910), which finds the lover lowered into his mistress's chamber in a basket, and the "substitution

---

IRREGANG UND GIRREGAR

Diz mære heizet Rüediger,
unt sprichet von zwein gesellen.

Von gemelîchen dingen
sagen unde singen,
swer daz gerne vernimet,
daz der jugent wol an zimet,
swen in diu wîle dunket lank,

motif" (lines 1093–1234), according to which one youth disguised as a woman takes the wife's place in the host's bed. The "basket motif" is connected with the popular medieval story of Virgil in the basket (see John Webster Spargo, *Virgil the Necromancer* [Cambridge, Mass., 1934]); Stehmann (Studentenabenteur, pp. 114–117) points out parallels in a French fabliau and a later German story. The "substitution motif" (Stehmann, p. 118) is perhaps most familiar from the *Decameron* 7,7 (a man disguised as a woman) and 7,8 (a bed substitution). The gross details are Rüdiger's own.

The second distinguishing feature of "Irregang und Girregar" is the courtliness of the first half, which stands in such clear contrast to the farcical humor of the continuation that one would pause to doubt whether the same writer is responsible for both parts, were it not that Rüdiger names himself both at the beginning and at the end of the poem. The courtly atmosphere is explicit in a dozen passages: the cultivated behavior of the youths (23–40), the sudden kindling of love accounted for by Cupid's arrow and accompanied by conventional love pathology (72–80), the host's deprecation of his hospitality (144–150), the greeting formulas (180–189), the girl's adornment (200–208) and perfect beauty (209–224), the elaborate politeness of the youths (229–235), the polished conversation with the ladies (249–257), the sleeplessness of the enamored youth (273–285), his anguished doubts (286–311), his beseeching of his lady's favors and her demure protests (363–457), and the parting scene described according to the conventions of the dawn song in courtly *Minnesang* (526–560). All these passages echo the stereotypes of German courtly epic and make "Irregang und Girregar" as peculiarly German as the emphasis on characterization in "The Reeve's Tale" is peculiarly Chaucerian and the emphasis on wit in Boccaccio is peculiarly Italian.

The text is reprinted from the only available, though rather unsatisfactory, edition by Friedrich von der Hagen, *Gesammtabenteuer* (Stuttgart and Tübingen, 1850, III, 43–82. We have rationalized the punctuation and capitalization to make it somewhat more readable. Parentheses in the text indicate von der Hagen's additions and square brackets indicate his deletions.

WAYWARDWIGHT AND LUSTYMITE

Rüediger tells this story
and speaks of two companions.

Anyone who likes
to hear the telling
of a merry tale
well fit for youth
and who finds time heavy on his hands,

der sage Rüedigêre dank
ob er sîn gelachet,
wan er hât gemachet
vremdiu âventiure
10 der vröude ze stiure,
diu nû der werlde mak gezemen.
Ouch wil er ze lône nemen,
daz ir ez merket rehte.
Zwêne guote knehte
zesamene geswuoren,
daz si daz lant durch vuoren
hübischlîchen sunder ruom
durch manger hande wîstuom,
der dâ lit an den buochen.
20 Vrâgen unde suochen
beide begunden si dar nâch,
zuo der verte was in gâch.
Uz vuoren si in dem lande,
die knappen âne schande,
mit zühten hübeschlîche,
wande si ouch rîche
des guotes beide wâren;
ouch kunden sie gebâren
vil wol nâch ir rehte.
30 Wie möht' ich ir geslehte
baz gesagen oder künden,
wan daz si sich gevründen
wol kunden swar sie kwâmen,
und sulher site râmen
alsô man dâ ze lande pflak.
Vür wâr ich iu daz sagen mak
mit rehter rede, sunder wân,
si wâren beide alsô getân,
swer si in der werlde gesach,
40 der in ie des besten jach.
Eines tages ûf dem wege
alsus gênde nâch ir pflege,
kwâmen si zuo einer stat,
dâ si wek unde pfat
hin geleitet hæte.
Dâ vunden si guot geræte
von koufe manger slahte.
Diu stat was ûzer ahte

should, if he is moved to laugh,
thank Rüediger,
for he has fashioned
strange adventures
to while away the time 10
and please the public.
The reward he asks
is that you pay close attention.
Two good youths
agreed together
to travel abroad,
with propriety and not for glory,
in order to learn
what is available in books.
They began to cast about 20
and make inquiries
and were eager to be off.
These reputable youths
set out abroad
in cultivated style,
for both were wealthy
in worldly goods
and could conduct themselves
according to their station.
How could I describe 30
their breeding better
than to say that they made friends
wherever they went
and adapted themselves to the customs
of foreign lands?
I can tell you
most assuredly
that they were both handsome fellows;
whoever saw them
spoke only well of them. 40
One day as they were proceeding
on the road according to their wont,
they came to a town
to which their route
had led them.
There they found good provisions
of many kinds for sale.
The town was quite out of the ordinary,

guot, rîch unde wît.
50 Dennoch was ouch der zît
des selben tages alsô vil,
daz si ir wege zil
geleget hâten vürbaz.
Ir beider muot sich des vermaz.
Dô gesach der eine
blikke glesten kleine
von einer sizzenden maget,
glîche schînen, sam ez taget
durch des morgens rôten glast.
60 Dô gewante der gast
sîn ougen an daz palas,
dâ diu maget schœne was
inne gesezzen,
an der Got niht vergessen
hâte an irme lîbe,
swaz ie man an wîbe
loben unde prîsen sol,
daran was diu maget wol
vol komen garwe,
70 ir antlize und ir varwe,
wan daz si einiu maget hiez.
Dô schôz in der Minne spiez
sô vaste in daz herze,
daz die senede smerze
in vil unsanfte ane kwâmen
und im den [stæten] muot benâmen,
den er hâte brâht dar.
Bleich unde missevar
wart er an den stunden
80 von den tiefen wunden.
Der gewunte sieche saz
vröude lôs, wan er vergaz
sîner besten wizze.
In der selben hizze
sprach er dem geverten zuo,
"Waz wil tû daz ich tuo?
Ich enmak niht kumen hinnen;
wes sol ich beginnen?
Mir ist worden alsô wê,
90 ist ez, daz ich hinnen gê,
sô muoz ez mîn tôt (ge)sîn.

rich and spacious.
However, the day 50
was not so far advanced
that they had covered
the distance they intended,
as they both agreed.
Then one of them saw
a maiden seated
with dainty eyes sparkling,
shining like the sun
through the red brilliance of dawn.
The traveler turned 60
his eyes to the place
in which was sitting
the lovely maiden,
from whose beauty God
had omitted nothing
one could ever praise
or value in a woman,
neither in countenance
nor complexion,
in all a perfect woman, 70
except that she was still a maid.
Then Cupid lodged love's arrow
so deeply in his heart
that longing desire
assailed him immoderately
and deprived him of the composure
he had shown hitherto.
He immediately turned
pale and livid
from the deep wound. 80

The stricken youth sat
ill and joyless
and all but lost his wits.
In his fever
he spoke to his companion,
"What would you have me do?
I can't go on.
What would I do with myself?
I am so afflicted
that if I move from here, 90
it will mean my death.

Rietes dû ez, geselle mîn,
daz ich tâlank belibe
unde daz ich vertribe
ein teil mîner swære?"
Daz es im liep wære,
sprach der geselle dô,
"Ich bin des vil unvrô,
daz dir iht gewirret,
100 daz wir sîn verirret
dâvon unsers gewerbes;
ê dan dû aber verderbes,
sô blîbe wir über naht;
dir sol, hoffe ich, dîn maht
morgen wol werden wider;
dar nâch schaffe wir ez sider."
In der selben riuwe
sprach der vil getriuwe,
alsô der beste dikke tuot,
110 "Geselle, wâ dunket dich guot,
daz wir mit gevüegen siten
solhe herberge biten,
dâ wir vinden guot gemach?"
Der gesunde sieche sprach,
"Geselle, möht' ez uns geschên,
alsô ich hân ersên
und erkorn hie zestunt,
sô wurde ich lîhte gesunt
von mîner starken suht;
120 dâ dunket mich diu luft
süeze unde reine;
ez ist dâ stille und eine,
sunder gebrehte.
Dâ gê wir rehte
und versuochen unser heil;
ez ensenftet mir ein teil."
Nâch diseme râte
giengen si vil drâte,
die zwêne unkunden,
130 dâ si den wirt vunden
vor sîner tür sizzen.
Mit gevüegen wizzen
bâten in die zwêne,
wan ez stuont in ze vlêne,

Would you advise, good friend,
that I remain a day
and recover from the worst
of my illness?"
To please him
his companion spoke,
"It grieves me
that you are so ill
that we are diverted 100
from our business;
but rather than have you perish,
let us spend the night here;
I hope tomorrow
will restore your health,
then we'll make up time."
Though grieved,
the loyal youth spoke
as befits a good man,
"Companion, where do you think 110
we might courteously
ask for lodging
and find some comfort?"
The healthy invalid replied,
"Companion, if we
could find lodging
in the place I've just seen,
I would undoubtedly recover
from my grave illness.
The air there seems 120
sweet and pure,
it is quiet and isolated
and there is no racket.
Let us go without delay
and try our luck there;
it will do me good."
Following this advice,
the two strangers
went directly
to where they found the master 130
of the house sitting by his door.
The two of them
asked him courteously,
as it behooves supplicants,

daz er si hielte über naht,
wande si dar müediu brâht
und siechiu lit hæten.
Swie vil si gebæten,
daz versagete der alde
140 und in des gewalde
stuont daz gefæze.
Swie er sich vergæze,
doch tet er dikke daz beste.
"Ich enmak solher geste,"
sprach der wirt, "niht gepflegen;
ich habe mich des bewegen,
daz ich niht veile hân;
darumbe muget ir wol gân,
dâ ir bezzer gemach habet
150 und iuwern müeden lîp labet."
Des wirtes tohter diu maget,
dô disen knappen was versaget
der herberge gemach,
ze irem vater si dô sprach,
"Herre, wie ist dir nû geschên?
Ich hân doch selden gesên
deheinen wege müeden man,
der sich genâde an dir versan,
dû(ne) gewertes si joh ie.
160 Swie tump ich nû sie,
ich kan doch wol gemerken daz,
daz dû, herre, nirgen baz
dîn hûs maht bewenden,
den an disen enelenden.
Ich hab' ouch daz erkorn,
si mugen wol sîn geborn
von grôzem geslehte,
daz merke selbe rehte;
si sint alsô werltlîch
170 und sô gezogen, dunket mich,
si mugen wol guotiu kint sîn.
Dû solt si durch den willen mîn,
vater, al hie behalden."
Dô geliebet' ez dem alden,
und schuof, daz ein bote lief,
der den knappen wider rief.
Des wurden die knappen dô

to lodge them overnight,
because sore and weary limbs
had brought them there.
But despite their protestations
the old gentleman,
who was responsible for hospitality, 140
refused them.
Though he forgot himself now,
he often did his best.
"I cannot accommodate such guests,"
the host said;
"I have borne myself in such a way
that I have nothing to offer.
Therefore you should go
where you can find more comfort
and refresh your weary limbs." 150

When the youths
were denied lodging,
the maiden, the host's daughter,
spoke to her father:
"Sir, what are you thinking of?
I have seldom seen
a weary traveler
ask your favor
without your granting it.
Though I am only a silly girl, 160
I can tell, sir,
that you can make
no better use of your house
than to shelter these poor strangers.
I have also perceived
that they are well born
and of high lineage.
See for yourself:
they are such gentlemen
and so accomplished 170
that it seems to me they must be good youths.
For my sake, father,
you should keep them here."
This was pleasing to the old gentleman
and he sent a messenger
to recall the youths.

The courteous youths

mit zühten hübisch unde vrô,
daz si solden kêren wider.
180 "Sît willekomen und sizzet nider,"
sprach der wirt, "ob ir sîn gert,
sô sullet ir sîn gewert
der herberge tâlank."
Beide genâde unde dank
sageten im die knappen des.
Er sprach, "Ir enwizzet [nicht] wes,
ir danket umbe ein klein gemach;
swaz ich aber ê des sprach,
ich schaffe (dennoch) iu genuok."
190 Ein bette man dar truok
und ein bank lachen;
der wirt hiez in machen,
daz si wol gesæzen,
und daz si vergæzen,
swaz in ie geschach ze leide.
Dô vröuweten si sich beide;
er nam ir deste baz war.
Die knappen liezen tragen dar
mête, wîn, lûtern trank.
200 Ouch was diu maget von der bank
in eine kamere gegangen;
dâ hâte si hangen
ir kleider an eime rikke,
diu ir dâ vor vil dikke
liebe hâten getân.
Si leite sich schône an
und begunde her vür gân,
die geste wolde si enpfân.
Diu senfte, wol getâne,
210 reine und valsches âne,
schœner varwe rîche,
enpfienk gezogenlîche
die werden jungelinge.
Wie si dar ze ringe
gevazzet komen wære,
daz wær' ein langez mære,
solde ich iu daz künden;
er enwolde sich [denne] sünden,
swer si rehte gesach,
220 sîn herze im (wol) des verjach,

rejoiced that they
were to return.
"Welcome, and be seated," 180
said the host.
"If you wish,
shelter is yours for today."
The youths thanked him
profusely for this.
He said, "There is little comfort
to thank me for.
But whatever I said before,
I will make good provision for you."
A couch and coverings 190
were brought.
The host ordered
that they be seated comfortably
and that they forget
whatever unpleasantness had befallen them.
They were both overjoyed,
and he took so much the better care of them.
The youths ordered
mead, wine, and claret.
The maiden had arisen from her bench 200
and gone into a chamber
where she had her clothes
hanging on a rack;
they had often
served her well before.
She decked herself out
and issued forth
to receive the guests.
Gentle, stately,
pure, frank, 210
and endowed with a beautiful complexion,
she greeted the worthy youths
graciously.
If I were to tell you
how she was dressed
when she came to the group,
it would be a long story.
Anyone who took a proper look at her
would be a sinner
if he did not admit in his heart 220

ez wære maget oder wîp,
daz nirgen wertlîcher lîp
wære in keime lande
von sô schœnem gewande.
Dô bekanten ir die geste;
swaz der wirt weste,
daz sîn êre was getân,
daz erwarp er sunder wân.
Die jungelinge verwizzen,
230 mit zühten si sich vlizzen,
daz daz gesinde wurde vrô;
ouch gevuogeten si ez alsô,
daz in des wart gestatet,
daz si wurden gesatet
vollen rîcher spîse.
Dô trank der alde grîse
durch sîner geste liebe,
daz im des slâfes diebe
slichen in die stirne;
240 den kleinen wîn virne
trank er dâ sô vaste,
des latte er ze eime gaste
den slâf in daz houbet,
daz er wart betoubet.
Er enweste niht waz tuon,
wan daz er mit den schuon
vil kûme an daz bette kwam;
daz gesinde tet alsam.
Diu wirtin mit der maget saz
250 bî den knappen dennoch baz
durch ir kurze wîlen;
muozeklîchen, sunder îlen,
begunden si sich dennoch êren.
Diu hûs vrouwe begunde kêren
an ir geste (guot) gemach;
tugentlîchen si besach,
daz in wol gebettet wart.
Des knappen herze stuont gekart
vaste an die schœnen maget;
260 mit den ougen unverzaget
maz er zuo ir dikke
vil minneklîche blikke
unt trat si mit den vüezen.

that there was nowhere in the world
so stately a woman
in such beautiful raiment,
whether maid or matron.
The guests acknowledged her greeting
and the host willingly performed
whatever he thought
his honor demanded of him.
  The prudent youths
politely made certain 230
that the servants were satisfied
and arranged that
they were allowed
to have their fill
of the abundant food.
Then the old man drank
to please his guests
so that Morpheus began
to weigh down his eyelids.
He drank so freely 240
of the old vintage
that he admitted
sleep to his mind
and became so groggy
that he had no choice
but to shuffle
off to bed.
The servants did the same.
  But the hostess and the maiden
sat up longer with the youths 250
to enjoy their company.
In leisure and without haste
they began to compliment one another;
the lady of the house catered
to the comfort of her guests
and graciously saw to it
that they were seated at their ease.
The young man's heart
was full of the lovely maiden.
Boldly he shot 260
loving glances
at her persistently
and touched her foot with his;

Diz tougentlîche grüezen
hat' er in der liebe erdâht.
"Got gebe iu guote naht!"
Diu hûs vrouwe dô sprach,
"Hætet ir nû guot gemach,
daz sæhe wir vil gerne."
270 Diu liebe wunschel kerne
mohte dâ niht lenger sîn,
dô neik in daz meidîn.
Daz volk allez slâfen gienk,
der si schiere under vienk,
wan er was in allen
vil vaste zuo gevallen,
grôzen unde kleinen,
sunder dem al einen,
der dâ lak gebunden
280 von der unkunden.
Seneder minne er pflak,
von gedanken er lak
sêr beswæret und geladen;
entweder vrumen oder schaden
getrûwete er des enpfân;
er gedâhte, "Mak ich dar gân?
Oder sol ich ez lâzen?
Ê des dô wir sâzen
bî dem wîne, âne wân,
290 mich dûhte daz diu wolgetân'
gar senftes muotes wære;
dô enmoht' ich ir mîner swære
niht vür baz kunt getuon,
wan daz ich si mit den schuon
lîse trat ûf iren vuoz.
Vernam si dô mînen gruoz,
des enweiz ich niht, si sweik,
wan daz si mir geneik,
dô si wolde slâfen gân.
300 Sol ich nû ûf den wân
mînen lîp dar wâgen?
Ich weiz wol, sunder vrâgen,
daz si ez tet durch ire zuht.
Ie doch hât mich des bedûht,
daz ir munt stüende zegliten
rehte nâch sulhen siten,

love had taught him
to devise this secret greeting.
"God give you good night,"
the hostess said,
"we are eager that you
should be comfortable."
The perfect paragon of love 270
could remain no longer
and the maiden curtsied to her guests.
Everyone went to bed and
sleep soon overcame them
because it had firmly
taken hold of all of them,
both young and old,
except the one
who lay fettered
by the thought of the unknown maiden. 280
He longed for love
and lay there oppressed
and burdened by his thoughts.
He anticipated
either joy or grief.
He thought, "Do I dare approach her?
Or should I refrain?
While we were sitting
over our wine,
it certainly seemed to me 290
that the beautiful girl had a gentle heart.
I could not express
my longing more openly
than by touching her foot
lightly with mine.
I do not know whether
she understood me since she was silent,
except that she nodded to me
when she went to bed.
Shall I risk it 300
on a chance?
Of course I know she only did it
for the sake of courtesy.
But still it seemed to me
that she had a twinkle in her eye
as if she wanted

als si mir wolde lachen zuo.
Swie kintlîchen ich nû tuo,
ich wil versuochen iren muot;
310 si ist sô rehte wol gemuot,
daz si niht vertrîbet mich."
An den trôst geliez er sich.
Mit vorhten er begunde
des er niht enkunde,
wan daz in diu minne
an deme beginne
gemachet hâte wîse;
mit den vüezen lîse
begunde er vil wîten
320 von ein ander schrîten
und greif vür sich mit der hant.
Michel ungeverte er vant,
vil stüele unde mange bank.
Slîchen, strîchen [und] stillen gank
lernete er dô tougen;
die hende vor den ougen
die benâmen im der stœze vil,
biz er kwam an daz zil,
dar sîn herze hin wolde.
330 Swen er sezzen solde
den vuoz ûf die erde,
mit vremder geberde
über lank kwam er dô nider.
Dikke trat er ouch wider,
nâch gemelîchen siten,
alles nâch mit kranches schriten,
swen er iht (dâ) vernam,
biz daz er doch ze leste kwam,
dâ diu junkvrouwe slief.
340 Sînen willen, âne brief,
tet er der megede kunt;
sus wart der sieche gesunt.
In der kamer ein kumber
huob sich, wan der tumber
greif, sam ê die blinden;
er enmohte ir niht vinden,
wan er niht (dâ) gesach.
Ein heil im doch geschach,
daz der junk vrouwen bein

to wink at me.
I may be a fool now,
but I want to test her feelings;
she is so good-natured
that she won't turn me out." **310**
This was the consolation he relied on.
Fearfully he began
the uncertain enterprise,
inexperienced except
that love had taught him
how to go about it.
Tiptoeing lightly
and with long steps
he made his way, **320**
groping ahead with his hands.
He found a veritable obstacle course
of chairs and benches.
He learned to creep and crawl
in silence and in secret.
His hands, stretched out before his eyes,
saved him from many a jolt
before he reached the goal
his heart had set him.
When he had to set **330**
a foot forward,
he misjudged the distance
and came down awkwardly.
Often he pulled it back
with a ludicrous movement
and with a crane's gait
when he thought he heard something,
until he finally came to the place
where the maiden slept.
He made his wishes known, **340**
and not in writing.
This was the cure for his illness.
There was trouble in the chamber
because the foolish fellow
groped like a blind man;
he couldn't find her
because he could see nothing.
But he had a piece of good luck
since the maiden's leg

350 mit snêwes varwe erschein,
sam ez wære endekket.
Daz hâte si gestrekket
ûf eine kolter brûn var;
dâ bî wart er ir gewar.
Mit vil schemelîcher nôt
sîn herze im daz gebôt,
daz er greif an ir kinne,
wan in diu liebe minne
machte küene unde balt.
360 Dô was sîn hant alsô kalt,
daz diu junk vrouwe erschrak
ûz dem slâfe, dâ si lak.
"Besworn sîs dû vil tiure,
weder bistu gehiure?"
Sprach si, "Waz wekket mich?"
Er sprach, "Junk vrouwe, daz bin ich."
"I(ch)," sprach si, "wer ist daz?"
Er sprach, "Der nehten bî iu saz,
ein minniklîcher jungelink."
370 Si sprach, "Her, schaffet iuwer dink;
wes habet ir iu gedâht?"
"(Junk) vrouwe, mich hât her brâht
iuwer minne, diu mich twinget."
Si sprach, "Ich wæne, daz ir ringet
noch mê umbe diz gewant,
den umbe der minne bant,
ob ir daz möhtet versteln.
Ich enwil ez iuch niht heln,
und gêt ir niht von hinnen,
380 ez wirt iu zuo unminnen,
swen ich ez den liuten künde."
Er sprach, "Des hetet ir sünde,
wande ir hât mich missezigen;
ir muget wol an mir gesigen,
wan iu mîn herze dienen wil."
Si sprach, "Des dunket mich ze vil,
daz ir mit [der] rede sît sô balt."
"(Junk) vrouwe, an iuwer gewalt
sezze ich guot unde lîp."
390 [Si sprach,] "Werbet umbe ein ander wîp,
wan ich getuo(n) ez nimmer."
"Vrouwe, sô muoz ich immer

lay revealed 350
and shone with the color of snow.
She had stretched it
on a dark blanket
and this guided him to her.
Shamefacedly he was
compelled by his heart
to touch her face,
for love made him
bold and daring.
But his hand was so cold 360
that the maiden was startled
from her sleep, there where she lay.
"Have pity, precious girl,
if you are kind."
She said, "What wakes me?"
He said, "Maiden, it is I."
"I?" she said, "Who is that?"
He said, "The one who sat beside you
this evening, a handsome youth."
She said, "Sir, state your business. 370
What is on your mind?"
"Maiden, love for you has brought me here,
love overcomes me."
She said, "I'll wager
you're more interested
in stealing my cloak
than in stealing love.
I will make no secret of the fact
that, unless you're off,
it will be a loveless encounter 380
when I call the servants."
He said, "That would be a sin
because you misjudge me.
I'm an easy victim
since my heart desires to serve you."
She said, "It's too much
that you make so bold."
"Maiden, in your power
I place life and limb."
"Woo another woman, 390
for I will never consent."
"Lady, then I will always

kwelen unt verderben."
[Si sprach,] "Der halp muget ir ê sterben,
ê ich ez immer getuo,
ez envüege anders sich dar zuo."
"Vrouwe, nû bedenket iuch baz."
Si sprach, "Umbe waz?"
Er sprach, "Umb rehte hübischeit."
400 Si sprach, "Sô gæbe ich liep umb leit."
"Nein, iu kwæme leit ze liebe."
Si sprach, "Ir redet eime diebe
harte glîche, dunket mich,
iuwer rede ist sô kündeklîch."
"Vrouwe, nû bin ich ouch."
Si sprach, "Nû sît ir ein gouch,
daz ir mir es sult verjên."
"Vrouwe, ez ist mir von iu geschên,
ich wolde iuwer minne steln."
410 "Weiz Got, ir sulet lange kweln,
ê dan ich daz tæte;
ir man sît sô unstæte,
daz ir ez immer ûz schellet,
swie iu daz gevellet,
swen iu liebez wider vert."
"Vrouwe, ist mir daz heil beschert,
daz ir mich machet gesunt,
ich sol vaste mînen munt
berigelen und besliezen;
420 ob mich alle die sagen hiezen,
die in der werlde sint betaget,
ez enwurde nimmer gesaget."
Dô diu maget dâ gesach
des knappen swære und [sîn] ungemach,
daz in zitterte unde vrôs,
iren zorn si dô beslôz
und hiez in an daz bette treten,
"Des ir mich habet (ê) gebeten,
des blîbet ir ungewert,
430 ez ensî ob ir sîn noch gert,
daz ir ot erwarmet,
wan ir mich erbarmet.
Ob iuch daz nû dunket guot,
daz ir anders niht entuot,
daz wil ich ûz dingen:

be in pain and agony."
She said, "Unless there are better reasons,
as far as I am concerned,
you can die before I will ever consent."
"Lady, reconsider."
She said, "Reconsider what?"
He said, "The rules of proper courtesy."
She said, "Then I'd be giving love for loss." 400
"No, you would learn to love your loss."
She said, "It strikes me
that you talk just like a thief,
your words are so artful."
"Lady, that's what I am."
She said, "You're a fool
to admit it."
"Lady, it's your fault
that I wanted to steal your love."
"God knows, you'd have to suffer a long time 410
before I consented;
you men are so inconstant
that you always trumpet abroad
how well pleased you are
when you have your will."
"Lady, if the good luck befalls me
that you heal my illness,
I will lock and bolt
my mouth so tightly
that if a plenary session of the world 420
commanded me to speak out,
I would never do it."
When the maiden had seen the distress
and disconsolateness which assailed the youth
so that he trembled and shivered,
she relinquished her anger
and told him to approach her bed,
"What you have asked me
cannot be granted unless it be
that you only want 430
to warm yourself,
because I feel sorry for you.
This you are free to do,
but on the condition
that you do nothing else.

spotten, âne ringen,
des wirt iu hie gestatet.
Swen ir iuch des gesatet,
sô gêt wider an iuwer stat."
440 "Vrouwe, des selben ich bat,
ich engere nihtes mêr;
ir habet mir mînes herzen sêr
wol vertriben mit gewalt,
nû bin ich junk, ê was ich alt."
In ir genâde dô nam
diu junk vrouwe lustsam
den gesunden siechen.
Der begunde kriechen
zuo (z') ir an daz warme,
450 dâ sô vant der arme
nâch sînem willen guot gemach.
Ob er sîn gelübde brach,
des enwirt iu niht gesaget,
wan daz im diu junge maget
ze vlîze wol gunde,
ob er sich [er]wermen kunde.
Waz sol iu des gesaget mê?
In beiden was dâ niht ze wê,
wan er lak nâch sîner ger.
460 Under des erwachete der,
den er slâfende liez,
biz sich er (. . .) gestiez.
Dô er sîn vermiste,
er dâhte wol und wiste,
daz er was gegangen
sich nâch minne drangen,
oder spreche sîn gebet.
Under des knarrete ein bret
an einer want dâ vüre;
470 des getrat zuo der türe
diu stolze wirtinne;
si dûhte an ir sinne,
daz si unbeslozzen wære.
Dem knappen was vil swære,
daz er eine solde ligen,
wan im der rât was verswigen.
In disme zorn alsus er kwal;
doch stuont er ûf unde stal

You are permitted free conversation
but no liberties
and as soon as you have had enough,
go back to bed."
"Lady, this is what I wanted 440
and no more.
You have quite dispelled
my heartache;
now I feel young again."
The lovely maiden then took
the convalescent invalid
into her good graces.
He began to creep
toward her warmth,
there the poor fellow found 450
comfort according to his wishes.
Whether he broke his oath
I will not tell you,
but only that the young maiden
did not begrudge it
if he could warm himself.
What more should I tell you?
Both of them were hardly discontented,
for he lay as he wished.
In the meantime the youth 460
whom he had left behind,
asleep, woke up.
When he missed him,
he thought he knew
that he had gone
in search of love
or that he was at his prayers.
At the same time a board
creaked in a wall nearby.
This made 470
the proud hostess
go to the door,
thinking it was unlatched.
The youth was unhappy
that he was obliged to lie alone
and he had no solution to his plight.
He was tormented by this predicament,
but he got up and stole away

daz kint mit der wiegen;
480 dâ mite wolde er liegen
der vrouwen die wider vart;
daz was ir liep unde zart.
Vür sîn bette er ez truok,
den wek er ir versluok.
Wan daz kint schrei unde gal;
dô si gehôrte den schal,
unrehte si sich kêrte,
als si der dôn gelêrte,
und leite sich bî dem jungelink.
490 Sunder langez teidink
ir kint si gesweigete
(. . . . .
. . . .)*
Des wart si vröuden rîche.
Der selbe niuwe wiegen diep,
im was daz stelen worden liep.
Diu vrouwe was wol an ir tugent
und hâte guoter mâze jugent,
si was schœne unt vlætik(lîch).
500 Da engegen vröuwete sich
der knappe, der dâ bî ir lak,
guoter kurze wîle er pflak;
vil ebene nâch dem alten site
spilte er ir gemelîchen mite
und uebete alsô vil daz [selbe] spil,
daz si es dûhte ein teil ze vil.
Si sprach, "Got gesegene mich,
wie bist dû sô wunderlîch
worden an dirre naht,
510 oder waz hâst dû gedâht,
daz dir nû sus ernest ist?
Ich wæne, dû noch trunken bist;
daz muoz ich dir verwîzen:
du ensoldes nie mer enbîzen
keines starken trankes.
Swenne dû nû krankes,
sô wil dû, daz es mîn schult sî."
Doch gedâhte si dâ bî,
si liez' ez gerne alsô sîn,

* The rhymes show that two lines are missing from the manuscript here.

the baby and the cradle.
By doing this he meant to mislead 480
the lady on her return
(she was nothing loath).
He took the baby to his bed
and diverted her course
because it screamed and howled
and when she heard the rumpus,
she made the wrong turn,
following the noise,
and lay down by the youth.
Without much ado 490
she pacified the child.
(. . . . .
. . . .)
She was well content
and the cradle thief
enjoyed the theft.
The lady was worthy
and in her prime;
she was fair and full of life.
This pleased the youth 500
who lay next to her
and he enjoyed himself;
according to the ancient custom
he plied her so lustily
and kept up the game so long
that she began to think it a bit too much.
She said, "God bless me,
what has taken possession
of you tonight?
What are you thinking of 510
that you are so eager?
I think you're still drunk.
I should warn you
not to partake
of such strong drink again.
If you get ill now,
you'll blame it all on me."
But she thought to herself
that she had no objection

520 daz er (von) solhem edelen wîn
trunken wurde[n] mêre,
beide, vaste und sêre.
Sus hâten die unkunden
vremde minne vunden,
der si beide wâren vrô.
Jener knappe sprach dô,
der dâ lak bî der maget,
"Vrouwe liebe, ich wæne, ez taget,
ich muoz mich heben hinnen,
530 daz man's iht werde innen."
Si sprach, "War umbe tuot ir daz?
Wermet iuch noch (michels) baz.
Es ist noch vil guot(iu) zît,
ich lâz' ez gerne, âne nît,
daz ir iuch (er)wermet wol."
"Vrouwe mîn, diu wort ich sol
verdienen immer [mêre] gerne;
es stêt mir zuo enberne,
doch tuon ich(z) michels mêre,
540 vrouwe, durch iuwer êre,
denne durch die mîne;
ich wil [immer] senede pîne
durch iuch gerne lîden,
und alliu wîp vermîden."
Dô nam si in sider an den arm
und machte in vollîchen warm,
ê er dannen schiede.
Nû merket amme liede,
ob er sîner zuht genôz,
550 daz die vrouwe niht verdrôz,
swie lange er wære beliben,
er wære von ir unvertriben;
helsen, küssen tûsent stunt
gap im ir rôsenrôter munt.
Dô si sich schieden beide,
dô weinete si vor leide,
daz er sô schiere was genesen.
Ir wære, weiz Got, liep gewesen,
daz in dennoch lenger vrüre,
560 wær' ez gestanden an ir küre.
Wol gevröuwet und gemeit,
der knappe tougenlîchen schreit

either to how much 520
or how often he got drunk
on this noble wine.
Thus the strangers
had found unfamiliar love,
with which they were both well content.
The other youth,
who lay by the maiden, said,
"Dear lady, I think the dawn is coming
and I must get away
lest someone discover us." 530
She said, "Why do you do that?
Warm yourself a little longer,
there is still time enough.
I have no objection at all
to your getting thoroughly warm."
"My lady, I am eternally
indebted to you for your words.
I am loath to leave,
but I do it much more
for your honor 540
than for mine.
I will always gladly
suffer longing for you
and will renounce all women."
Then she took him in her arms
and warmed him through and through
before he left.
Now mark my story and decide
whether he benefited from his courtesy
so that the lady would not have been grieved 550
no matter how long he remained,
as long as he was not taken from her.
Her rosy mouth bestowed
a thousand kisses and embraces.
When they parted,
she wept for sorrow
that his ill was cured so soon.
God knows, she would have liked him
to shiver a little longer
if she had had her choice. 560
Well pleased and glad of heart
the youth crept secretly

ze sînem bette hin wider,
daz er sich legete nider.
Dô vant er die wiege und daz kint,
daz dar kwam verstolen sint.
Hœret, wes er gedæhte,
"Ich bin ot unrehte
her gegangen, dunket mich."
570 Alsus bedâhte er sich,
daz er tougenlîchen trat
hin zuo (z')einer bette stat,
dâ der wirt selbe lak;
dem gab er einen senften slak
und stiez in an die sîten,
"Dû slæfest ze allen gezîten
und bist ein slæfære;
wer solde sich sô swære
ze allen zîten machen!
580 Woldest dû nû wachen,
ich sagete dir ein mære,
daz harte vremde wære."
Der wirt erwachete unde sprach,
"Habe, vrouwe, dîn gemach.
Wie bist dû sô wunderlîch,
war zuo wekkest dû mich,
oder, waz wilt dû mir sagen?"
Er sprach, "Ich enkan es niht verdagen;
nehten, dô dû sliefe,
590 swie vil ich dir geriefe,
dû læge vür dich als ein stein;
dô wart ich (des) in ein,
daz ich durch kurze wîle gienk
dar, dâ man mich enpfienk
vil genædeklîchen wol,
dâ ich rîcher vröuden vol
bin gewesen über naht,
als ez von wunsche wære erdâht,
bî des wirtes tohter."
600 Weiz Got, dô enmoht' er
niht lenger verswîgen daz;
er rihte sich ûf unde saz:
"Waz bist dû?" sprach er dô,
"daz dû mich beswærest sô?
Dû muost daz mære koufen."

back to bed
and lay down.
Then he found the cradle and the child
which had been stolen.
Hear what he thought,
"It seems to me that I
have lost my bearings."
And so he reconsidered 570
and quietly stole
to the bed
where the host himself lay.
He shook him softly
and poked him in the ribs,
"You do nothing but sleep
and are a lazy lout!
How can someone always
be such a sluggard!
If you would only wake up, 580
I would tell you
quite a story."
The host woke up and spoke,
"Wife, hold your peace.
What has gotten into you
to wake me up this way?
What do you want to tell me?"
He said, "I can't keep it to myself.
Tonight, when you were asleep,
no matter how I called to you, 590
you slept like a log.
Then I decided,
for the sake of company,
to go where I was received
very graciously indeed.
There I have spent
a very pleasurable night,
the kind one might dream about,
with the host's daughter."
God knows, at that moment 600
the host could no longer contain himself
and started up in bed,
"Who are you," he said,
"That you insult me this way?
You'll pay for this story!"

Er begunde in sêre roufen
unde gab im mit der hant
ein wol gemezzen nase bant,
dar zuo mangen mûl streich;
610 die wîle im diu kraft niht entweich,
sô gab er im der genuok;
kurze wîle er im vertruok,
daz geborgete er im vergalt,
er warf in nider mit gewalt
von dem bette bî dem hâre,
er pflak sîn z'wâre
mit ungevüegen glîten.
Dô gienk ez an ein strîten.
Doch enmohte der alde,
620 vor des lîbes ungewalde,
deme knappen niht gevehten;
dô rief sînen knehten
und gerte der helfe.
In disme schalles gelfe
der jungelink sich versan,
er warf in nider, und entran.
Diu wirtinne geloufen kwam,
alsô schiere als sie vernam
disen ungevüegen schal;
630 si sprach lûte über al,
"Herre, waz ist hie geschên?"
"Daz maht dû (vil) wol gesên,
daz ich wol zebluwen bin;
hie kwam einer her in
und sagete mir ze mære,
daz er gelegen wære
bî mîner tohter über naht."
"Herre, nû bis baz bedâht,"
sprach diu vrouwe, "durch Got,
640 ez ist ein ungevüeger spot,
daz dû sô bewirrest
und ze allen zîten irrest
an swachem gelouben;
nû lâz dich niht berouben
dîner wizze, nim ir war;
dich hât geriten der mar,
ein elbischez âs,
dû solt daz übele getwâs

He began to manhandle him sorely
and gave him with his fist
a well-placed blow on the nose
and many a hefty punch.
As long as his strength lasted, 610
he wasn't stingy with his fists.
He spoiled his fun
and took payment for the loan,
he seized him by the hair
and slung him out of bed.
In truth he plied him
with intemperate tumbles.
Then the fight began in earnest.
But the old man
with his frail limbs 620
was no match for the youth.
So he called his lackeys
and asked their help.
In the midst of the uproar
the youth thought better of it,
threw his opponent down, and took to his heels.
The hostess came on the run
as soon as she heard
the wild commotion.
She called out in every direction, 630
"My lord, what's happened here?"
"You can see yourself
that I've been battered black and blue.
Someone came in here
and told me to my face
that he had spent the night
with my daughter."
"For goodness' sake, lord,
use your head," the lady replied,
"It's embarrassing 640
that you're always
so confused
and gullible.
Don't lose your wits entirely,
but take care of what you have.
You've had a nightmare
and an infernal visitation;
drive off the devilish apparition

mit dem kriuze vertrîben."
650 "[Sêt,] daz hât man von iu wîben,
swenne uns mannen iht geschiht,
daz ir immer des jeht,
uns (be)triege der alp;
wære ez dir doch worden halp,
sô möhtest dû mir gelouben;
ez gezæme eime touben,
daz er sô vil gesliefe.
Swie vil ich dir geriefe,
du enwoldest nìht erwachen;
660 waz wiltu ûz mir machen?"
Alsus stuont er unde vaht
in sîme zorne über maht,
biz er wart alsô krank,
daz er al dâ nider sank.
Dô wart diu wirtinne gewar,
daz der knappe brâhte dar
binnen des diu wiege und daz kint;
dô sach si wol, daz si sint
was bî vremden vründen.
670 Si hiez ein lieht enzünden,
daz si baz erkente sich.
Si sprach, "Got gesegene mich,
wer getorste dich slân?
Dir enhat nie man niht ge(tân),
wan sô vil, daz dich zoumete
ein alp, dâ von dir troumete;
den vare der sunnen haz!
Ez ist immer etewaz,
dâ von dû sus verirret bist.
680 Nû slæfet allez daz hie ist;
dîne geste ligent dort,
die kunnen diu Gotes wort
unde mangen guoten segen,
ich wil dich des wol verpflegen.
Si sint alsô versunnen,
daz si dich [wol] gelêren kunnen,
wie man sol gestiuren
den übelen ungehiuren."
Alsus versluok si im den muot,
690 daz den wirt gedûhte guot,
daz er schiere gesweik;

with your cross."
"That's just like you women; 650
whenever anything happens to us men,
you tell us
we are seeing things.
If half as much had happened to you,
you'd believe it.
Only a deaf man
could have slept through it.
No matter how much I shouted,
you refused to wake up.
What are you making me out to be?" 660
So he stood there
and ranted in his anger
until he became so weak
that he collapsed.
Then the hostess saw
that in the meantime the servant
had brought the cradle and the child
and she realized that she had been
with a newfound friend.
She had a candle lit 670
so that she could see better
and said, "God bless me,
who would dare to strike you?
No one has hurt you,
it's only some hobgoblin
who has seized you in your dreams—
may he perish!
It's always some such thing
that muddles your thinking.
Here everyone's asleep. 680
Your guests are lying close by,
they know the Scriptures
and many a good blessing
with which I'll ask them to attend you.
They're well informed
to teach you
how to cope
with the Evil One."
Thus she disarmed his anger
so that he saw fit 690
to lapse into silence.

an sîn bette er geseik,
unde bat si, daz si swige.
Nâch disme listigen sige
begunde si die rekken
gezogenlîchen wekken;
dô wart gevlêhet und gebeten,
daz si beide wolden treten
dar zuo eime segene,
700 dem wirte ze wegene.
Nâch irem willen daz geschach,
der knappen ietweder sprach,
kriuzende hin unde her,
"Got dich immer gewer,
daz dir heil belîbe,
ein affe der wîbe,
und daz dich al[lez] daz tœre,
daz wîben zuo gehœre!
Diz ist ein kündiger segen,
710 der sol unser wirtes pflegen."
Dô machten si einen rouch:
daz si den (vil) tumben gouch
volleklîchen gouchten,
si sprâchen unde rouchten
alsô, alsi es im gunden.
Die andern niht enkunden
si dar umbe strâfen.
Dô giengen si wider slâfen.
Daz ander bövel slief.
720 Dô gedâhte der alde gief,
"Herre, wie ist mir sust geschên,
wes mag ich dar umbe jên,
daz ich sô zebluwen bin?
Triuget mich nû der sin,
sô getet er mir ez nie;
wer wære sô balt hie,
daz er mir hæte gekündet,
ob sich mit im gevründet
alsô mîn tohter hæte?
730 Ich weiz wol, daz entæte
der jungelinge nirgen kein.
Wie wurden si aber in ein
der vriuntschaft alsô schiere?
Ez gezæme eime tiere,

He sank on his bed
and bade her be quiet.
After this crafty triumph
she began to wake
the youths courteously
and begged and implored them
to be good enough
to oblige the host
with a blessing. 700

It was done according to her bidding.
Both youths said,
crossing themselves up and down,
"God grant you
the good fortune
always to be a woman's fool
and may a woman's wiles
always confound you!
That is a blessing tried and true
to comfort our host." 710
Then they rigged a charm
and thoroughly duped
the old fool.
They talked and charmed away
and said exactly what they thought;
the others could hardly
scold them for it.
Then they went back to bed again
and while the others were asleep,
the old fool thought, 720
"Lord, how did this happen to me
and whose doing is it
that I have been thrashed this way?
If I am deceived by my senses,
I have never been so deceived before.
Who would be so bold here
as to tell me to my face
that my daughter had become
so intimate with him?
I know perfectly well 730
that neither of the youths would do it.
And how would they become such fast friends
with my daughter so quickly?
That would befit

daz in dem walde liefe.
Ich enweiz, ob ich sliefe;
mir tuont die slege harte wê.
Wes mag ich gedenken mê,
ich enswîge stille und lâz' ez varn,
740 wan ich sol daz bewarn
mit gevüeger gedult.
Ist ez ie mannes schult,
der hier inne gewesen ist,
daz mak in kurzer vrist
an iren geberden
wol ervaren werden."
Die knappen, âne swære,
sageten iriu mære,
ûfm bette, dâ si lâgen;
750 ir sagen und ir vrâgen
was ir kurze wîle guot.
Si gewunnen mangen muot,
wie si mit gevüegen listen
sich künden gevristen,
daz si mit den wîben
lenger müesten blîben:
si gerieten, daz er sagete,
der knappe der sich ê klagete,
dem wære worden alsô wê,
760 daz er nirgen möhte kumen mê.
Gegen dem morgen diz geschach.
Diu hûs vrouwe wider in dô sprach,
"War woldet ir dan[ne] kêren?
Ich kan iuch wol gelêren,
sît iuwer geselle niht enmak,
so belîbet aber disen tak
in hûse und in dache
und in sulhem gemache,
swaz wir iu gedienen kunnen,
770 des sol ich iu wol gunnen."
Der wirt ouch des selben sprach,
daz si hæten ir gemach.
Des wurden die knappen vrô,
unde volgeten in dô,
alsô si in gerieten.
Des tages si sich genieten
minniklîcher blikke

the beasts in the forest!
I don't know if I was dreaming,
but the bruises are very painful.
What else can I do
but be silent and let it pass,
for I must bear it 740
with becoming patience.
If it was the fault of someone
who was in here,
it will become apparent
from his actions
soon enough."
The youths merrily
exchanged stories
in the bed as they lay there;
telling and listening 750
was jolly entertainment.
They had in mind to
hit on some scheme
to prolong their stay
and spend more time
with the women.
They decided that the youth
who had previously complained
should say that he had become so ill
that he could not move. 760
Toward morning this was done.
The lady of the house then answered them,
"Where would you want to go?
My advice,
since your companion is unable to move,
is that you stay at home today
under our roof
and in whatever comfort
we can provide for you.
I am entirely at your service." 770
The host said the same thing
and bade them make themselves at home.
The youths were overjoyed
and followed
their advice.
That day they enjoyed
loving glances

beide [gnuok] vil und dikke.
Der wirt in sîn gemüete nam,
780 daz im sint unebene kwam,
von zwîvelhaften sinnen,
er wolde werden innen,
weder daz vremde mære
getroumt oder wâr wære;
wan in dennoch (ge)rou,
daz in jener sô sêre blou,
der die botschaft dâ warp.
In den gedanken er verdarp;
diz nam er alles in sich,
790 doch tet er nirgen dem gelîch,
alsô er sich dô kwalte,
wan daz er sich gestalte
in also getâne huote,
daz si ez alle muote,
beide, tohter und muoter.
Vil kurze wîle guoter
wart des tages dâ gemiten;
mit guoten zühten si daz liten
beidenthalben über maht,
800 biz an die vinster naht.
Mit zühten wart dâ vil gezert;
doch hâte sich der wirt erwert,
daz er niht sô vil getrank.
Des wart hoffenunge lank,
die dâ nâch minnen strebeten
und in dem wâne swebeten.
Doch enmohte niht geschên,
alsô si gerne (dâ) gesên
hæten, die gelieben.
810 Mit irem gedanken briuwen
begunde(n) si daz swinde.
Dô gienk daz gesinde
slâfen und der alte,
der die huote gestalte.
Sich wolde mit der wiegen
gerne lâzen liegen
diu stolze wirtinne, als ê;
der junk vrouwen tet ouch wê,
daz si des niht geahten
820 kunden, noch getrahten,

thick and fast.
The host made a decision
that he later rued. 780
Beset as he was by doubts
he wanted to find out
whether the strange occurrence
was real or dreamt
for he still resented
that the fellow who had borne the tale
had given him such a thrashing;
his mind was full of anguish.
But he swallowed his anger
and gave no indication 790
of how he felt,
except that he put himself
on guard in such a way
that both mother and daughter
were dismayed.
Much good sport
was omitted that day.
They suffered it with a good grace,
though it was almost beyond their endurance,
until nightfall. 800
There was much gracious dining,
but the host avoided
drinking too much.
This prolonged the expectations
of those who longed for love
and found their hopes suspended;
nothing the lovers
would have liked
could come to pass.
But they began 810
to hatch a plan.
The servants went to bed
and likewise the old man
who kept watch.
The proud hostess would gladly
have let herself be deceived
with the cradle as before.
The maiden
was also afflicted
that they could devise 820

wâ si die list næmen,
daz si ze samne kwæmen,
si und ouch ir amîs.
Mit gedanken mange wîs
ir herze si bewegeten.
Nâch râte sich dô legeten
die zwêne gesellen ûf ein dach,
dâ der tohter (ir) gemach
was geschaffen under;
830 dâ lak si besunder,
beide dâ vor und ouch dô,
über ir was ein himeliz' hô,
dâ si durch gesprâchen.
Si rieten, daz si brâchen
dâ durch ein venster alsô grôz,
daz der eine slâf genôz
wol mit vuoge slouf dar in,
sunder pîne und ungewin.
Swie si ez geschüefen sider,
840 sus kwam er zuo (z')ir hin nider
in eime korbe geriten;
den hâten si mit guoten siten
gebunden ze eime seile.
Ze sîme unheile
wart der wirt des gewar;
er lief mit zorne dar
und wolde in begrîfen.
Die vüeze begunden im slîfen
unt ze eime valle werben.
850 Sus viel er in die kerben
einen kreftigen val,
daz vil lûte erschal
unde regete sich daz seil,
"Waz sol mir diz unheil?"
gedâhte der geselle,
"ich wæne, er diz geschelle
wolde mîden unde vlien:
dû solt in wider ûf zien!"
Diz ergienk ouch alsô.
860 Der wirt gedâhte dô,
"Ez mak vil wol etwaz sîn,
daz mir daz gesinde mîn
sagete von mîme tobene."

no ruse whereby
she and her lover
could come together.
They searched their minds
high and low for a solution.
According to the plan, the two companions
climbed onto a roof,
under which the daughter
had her room;
there she slept apart. 830
She had above her now as always
a high ceiling,
through which they spoke.
They determined to break
a hole through it large enough
to allow one of the companions
to slip through it
safely and comfortably.
However they managed it,
he came riding down to her 840
in a basket,
which they had neatly
tied to a rope.
To his own misfortune
the host became aware of what was going on;
he ran up in a rage
and wanted to seize the culprit,
but his feet began to slip
and prepared him for a fall.
He tumbled heavily 850
into the basket
so that there was a loud thump
and the rope quivered.
"What does this danger signal mean?"
thought the youth above.
"I imagine he wants to get away
from this uproar and escape,
and I should pull him up again."
This is what he did.
The host thought then, 860
"There may be something
to what my people tell me
about my madness."

Jener knappe dar obene
zôch in vaste an daz loch;
er wânte alles dennoch,
daz er sich ot vorhte,
und daz er hilfe dorfte.
Der alde in dem korbe saz,
870 vor zorne er sich selber az,
in bedûhte, daz er vlüege,
oder daz in lîhte trüge
ein alp in sîme troume.
Dô aber sîn goume
der knappe obene wart gewar,
daz der wirt kwæme dar,
der si mit der huote
al ze vil gemuote,
er liez in vallen ûz der hant,
880 beide korp unde bant;
des vlugen si ze wette
nider zuo dem bette.
Der wirt mit dem korbe vlouk:
ir beider vliegen si betrouk
wan si wâren veder lôs.
Dô der jungelink erkôs,
daz der wirt lak da nider,
er zukte sîne kerben wider.
Sus nam sîn vliegen ende,
890 dô er bî der wende
nider was gerûschet;
des wâren im zetuschet
vreislîchen alliu sîniu lit,
daz er muoste geben vride
tougenlîcher minne,
wande im die sinne
entwichen wâren und diu kraft;
des wart er alsô zwîvelhaft,
daz er die sprâche legete.
900 Niht anders er sich regete,
wan daz man daz vallen
sô lûte hôrte schallen,
daz es diu wirtin wart gewar;
diu gienk gezogenlîchen dar
und hiez ein lieht enzünden.
Ob si den knappen vünden

The youth above
pulled him quickly up to the hole;
he still thought
that his companion had taken
a fright and needed help.
The old man sat in the basket
and was ready to chew nails. 870
He thought that he had taken wing
or that a hobgoblin
was tricking him with a dream.
When the youth on top realized
that the host,
who had given them so much trouble
with his spying,
was on his way,
he let him fall,
both rope and basket. 880
They flew down to the bed,
one faster than the other,
and the host flew with them.
Their flight tricked them
because they had no feathers.
When the youth saw
that the host was laid out below,
he pulled the basket back up.
The host's flight came to an end
when he was dumped 890
down by the wall.
His limbs were
fearfully bruised
and he, for one,
was in no mood for loveplay,
since he was deprived
of strength and senses;
they were in such a doubtful state
that he refrained from speech.
His descent was such 900
and the fall
resounded so loudly
that the hostess heard it.
She courteously went to investigate
and had a candle lit.
Do you think they found the youth

ûf dem bette bî der maget?
Daz sî iu wider saget,
wand er was gegangen
910 hin wider ungevangen.
Ein michel weinen wart erhaben
von der vrouwen, dô si laben
muoste den wirt, dâ si in vant
alsus ligende bî der want,
rehte alsam er wære erslagen;
vil manger hande wart ir klagen,
swie ez von herzen niht enwas.
Der wirt des selben doch genas,
daz er ûf wert gesach.
920 Diu vrouwe im (dô) zuo gesprach,
"Mahtu, vriunt, berihten mich,
wie stêt ez alsô umbe dich?
Oder waz gewinnest dû dâmite,
daz dû verkêrest dîne site,
die dû hâtest hie bevorn?
Sullen die nû sîn verlorn,
wie möhte ich des vrô gesîn?
Stüend' ez nâch dem willen mîn,
ich riete sicherlîchen daz,
930 wan ez gezæme michel baz,
daz dû mit zühten læges
und sulher ruowe pflæges,
als ûf dem bette wære,
den elbischer gebære."
Mit kranker stimme er dô sprach,
"Mir ist ot diz ungemach
wunderlîchen komen zuo.
Waz wiltu nû, daz ich tuo,
nû ez mir allez missekümet,
940 daz mîn(em) armem lîp gevrümet,
oder swes ich beginne?
Mich dûhte an mîme sinne,
daz jener komen wære,
der mir daz leidige mære
ze dem bette nehten brâhte.
Dô stuont ich ûf und gedâhte,
daz ich in wol[de] begriffe;
ich enweiz, ob ich sliffe
oder waz mir geschach,

in bed with the girl?
That must be disclaimed
for he made off,
undetected. 910
The lady broke
into a torrent of tears
when she had to revive the host
where she found him lying
by the wall as if he were dead.
Her lamentations were manifold,
though they were counterfeit.
But the host recovered
and opened his eyes.
The lady spoke to him, 920
"Can you tell me, love,
what this is all about?
What are you accomplishing
by changing
your old ways?
If they are all to be cast aside,
how can I be expected to approve?
If it were up to me,
I would advise you:
it would surely be more fitting 930
if you would lie down properly
and repose in your bed
rather than indulging
in such elfin pranks."
In a weak voice he said,
"This accident befell me
in a strange way.
What should I do,
now that everything
I undertake in my own interest 940
goes wrong?
I thought I had detected
the fellow who brought
that atrocious story
to my bed last night.
I got up and thought
to lay hands on him.
I don't know if I slipped
or what happened to me,

950 wan daz ich daz wol sach,
daz mich jener ûf zôch
in eime korbe vil hôch,
unde liez mich vallen nider.
Alsus kwam ich her wider
mit grôzem ungeverte;
wan daz mich Got ernerte,
ich wære des selben valles tôt.
Mir wære guotes râtes nôt,
wan ich niht mak genesen;
960 woldes dû mir guot (ge)wesen,
die wîle (daz) ich leben sol,
sô tætes dû, vrouwe, vil wol."
"Gote sî unser leit geklaget,"
sprach diu muoter und diu maget,
"daz dû sus beginnes!
O wê dînes [reines] sinnes,
wer hât dir, herre, den benomen?
Dû bist doch an dîn alder komen
wol mit grôzen êren;
970 sol sich daz nû verkêren,
wir enmugen nie mer werden vrô."
Den tumben truogen si dô
hin wider an sîn gemach.
Diu tohter im dâ zuo (ge)sprach,
"Daz weiz Got, lieber vater mîn,
dû tuost mir harte wol schîn,
daz ich dir vil unmære bin,
nû dû mînes herzen sin
mit schalle sô beswæres,
980 und mich alsus vermæres.
Ob dich der tiuvel triuget,
der dir ouch von mir liuget,
dû ensoldes niht getriuwen.
Mich mak wol (ge)riuwen,
daz ich mich habe gespart
sô lange und mit êren bewart,
ob ich nû daz tæte,
des ich laster hæte
under mîme kunne,
990 daz was ein gearnte wunne."
"Liebe tohter, nû enruoch',"
sprach diu muoter, "nim dîn buoch

except that I saw 950
the other fellow pull me
way up in a basket
and then let me drop again.
It was a perilous trip
down here.
If God hadn't saved me,
the fall would have killed me.
I'm in need of good counsel
because I can't take care of myself.
If you would treat me kindly 960
as long as I'm still alive,
you would be doing a good deed, dear wife."
"God have mercy on us,"
said mother and daughter,
"that you carry on so!
Who robbed you
of your reason, master?
You've grown old
with your honor intact;
if this is to be changed now, 970
we'll never have a happy day."
Then they carried the poor fool
back to his room.
The daughter spoke to him,
"God knows, dear father,
you make it quite apparent
that you don't love me
when you make
such noisy accusations
and compromise me this way. 980
Even if the devil deceives you
with such lies
you shouldn't believe it.
Having preserved
my honor so long,
I would certainly rue the day
were I now to do something
which would discredit me
in the eyes of my family;
that would be an unprofitable pleasure." 990
"Dear daughter, pay no heed,"
said her mother, "Take your prayerbook

und sprich dîn gebet über in,
daz im Got sînen sin
genædiklîchen sende,
daz er uns iht schende.
Es ist ein geslehte,
ich weiz wol, daz er rehte
sîn hulde hât verlorn,
1000 wan in dar an hie bevorn
versûmet hât sîn muoter.
Er solde sîn ein guoter
und ein pilewiz geheizen;
dâ von ist, daz in reizen
die übelen ungehiuren.
Got der müeze in stiuren,
sô daz si sîn vergezzen."
Berouchen unde mezzen
begunden si in beide;
1010 alsam in wære leide,
was ir geberde getân.
Daz brâht' in genzlîche an den wân,
daz er des wol hæte gesworn,
daz ez im wære an geborn.
"Got gebe sulher muoter leit,"
sprach er, "diu sô grôze arbeit
ir[me] kinde hât gemachet!
Des bin ich gar verswachet.
Nû swîget stille und lât ez varn,
1020 ez enkan nie man bewarn,
daz dem manne geschehen sol."
"Nû kan ich dich gelêren wol,"
sprach si, "daz dir hulflich ist,
habe ot einen ganzen list,
daz dû nimmer niht verjehes,
swaz daz sî, daz dû gesehes.
Bedunket dich aber ihtes
keinerlei gesihtes,
ze hant tuo zuo dîn ougen,
1030 ensage niht dîn tougen,
sô beginnet si es verdriezen."
"Si ensulent es niht [vil] geniezen,

and say a prayer over him
that God may graciously
return him to his senses
and prevent him from dishonoring us.
It's a congenital ill;
I know full well
that he has quite lost God's grace
because his mother neglected **1000**
him when he was a child;
he should be called
a goody and an imp.*
For this reason
the evil demons beset him.
May God guide him
so that they release him."
They began to send up smoke
and make magic signs;
they went about it **1010**
as if they took pity on him.
That persuaded him completely,
to the point where he would have sworn
that he was congenitally mad.
"The devil take such a mother,"
he said, "who has caused her child
so much suffering.
I'm quite overcome.
Now be still and let it pass,
no one can save **1020**
a man from his fate."
"I can tell you
what will help you," she said.
"Be devious and never
tell people what you see,
no matter what it is.
But if you catch sight
of anything,
close your eyes immediately
and don't tell your secret **1030**
lest it offend them."
"It won't do them much good

* These lines are not quite clear, but the meaning in general is that the host was somehow bedeviled as a child and therefore continues to be a prey to demons. On *pilewiz* see Jacob Grimm, *Deutsche Mythologie*, 4th ed. (Berlin, 1875), I, 391–395.

sint ez mir ist bescheinet,
waz disiu rede meinet;
si ensol ir triegen niht vervân."
Die tohter hiez er slâfen gân.
Slâfen gienk diu guote,
sicher vor der huote,
si mit irme amîse;
1040 si wurden von prîse
vrô, sunder vorhte,
wan er dô worhte
die lieben kumpânîe
mit stolzer banekîe
alsô lange in behagete.
Der wirt vil gar gedagete,
swes sô in bedûhte;
von der sorgen truhte
was er in den zwîvel brâht.
1050 Dô wart vil ange (dâ) gedâht
umb [ein] niuwez barâtieren
von den gespilen vieren,
wie si des gedæhten,
daz si den wirt bræhten
gar von sîme sinne.
Ouch wolde diu wirtinne
kumen von ir[me] wâne,
dâ si des zwîvels âne
wurde mit der wârheit;
1060 des wart ir der jungelink bereit.
Der wirt der lak bedekket,
wan er was erschrekket;
sîn houbet drukte er under,
in nam michel wunder,
waz im die sinne benæme,
swie sô diz allez kwæme.
Der süeze slâf geriet im daz,
daz er der sorgen doch vergaz.
Daz lieht ouch geleschet wart;
1070 lenger wart des niht gespart,
swes si gedenken kunden.
Eines si begunden,
als ich iu bescheide,
die knappen kwâmen beide,
der eine jungelink der trat

since what you say
is very clear to me.
Their deception won't profit them!"
Then he told his daughter to go to bed.
The good girl,
safe from spies,
went to bed with her lover.
They took their pleasure 1040
without fear
and he exercised
his dear companion
with a gallant joust
as long as he pleased.
The host held his tongue
no matter what he thought,
he was reduced to despair
by his train of calamities.
Then the four companions 1050
set about thinking up
a new trick;
they imagined
how they could drive the host
completely out of his mind.
The hostess too
wanted more than wishful thinking
and wanted to exchange her doubtful expectations
for the real thing;
the youth was nothing loath. 1060
The host, who was all aghast,
lay under the covers
and pressed his head down;
he was dazed
at what had befuddled his senses
and how this had all come to pass.
But sweet sleep helped him
to forget his troubles.
The candle was extinguished.
They delayed no longer 1070
in carrying out their plans.
I'll tell you
what they did:
the two youths approached;
one came to the bed

und legete sich an die [selben] stat,
dâ diu wirtinne was gelegen,
daz dise ander zwei gepflegen
ires willen deste baz;
1080 mit gevüegen listen was daz
gevüeget und getrahtet.
Ein bette was geahtet,
dar ûfe si gelâgen.
Daz endarf nie man vrâgen,
ob in iht sanfte wære.
Er kunde die gebære,
diu ir vil wol behagete;
dâ mite er verjagete
allez sorgen und [allez] trûren.
1090 Diz was bî einer mûren,
dâ wart sprechen gar verlobet.
Wie möhten si baz sîn gehovet!
Vernemet ein (vil) vremde dink,
wie der eine jungelink
die stolzen wirtinne verpflak:
bî dem alden er gelak
mit gewande, sam ein wîp
was gevazzet im der lîp
mit [einer] hûben und [mit] gebende;
1100 sus lak der enelende
gezogenlîchen stille.
Dô was des wirtes wille,
dô er von dem slâf erwachete,
daz er vrô gemachete
sich und ouch die wirtin;
ein vil tumber sin
tôrlîchen an sîn herze kwam,
der sîner tobeheit an gezam:
es nam in michel hæle,
1110 er rank, daz er verstæle
einen alden hælink.
Sus wart der alte sûrink
vollelîchen getœret,
als ir wol gehœret.
Swaz der wirt dâ begienk,
der jungelink ez allez enpfienk
mit sulher gebære,
sam er entslâfen wære.

and lay down in the place
where the hostess had lain
so that the other two
could do their will all the more easily.
This was arranged and done 1080
with all the necessary guile.
A bed was made,
on which they lay.
No one need ask
if they were comfortable.
He knew how to behave
in a way to please her;
he put to flight
all worries and sadness
there next to the wall. 1090
They made do without conversation;
how could they be better lodged?
Now listen to a strange thing.
As one youth was obliging
the proud hostess,
the other was lying next
to the old man
dressed like a woman
and adorned with a headdress.
Thus the stranger lay 1100
quietly and considerately.
Then the host awoke
from his sleep
and desired to pleasure himself
and his wife—
a foolish desire
in a foolish heart
and quite worthy of his madness.
He was mysteriously seized
with the wish to steal 1110
the secrets of the ancient mystery.
The old fool
was completely deceived,
as you will hear.
Whatever the host did,
the youth
acted as if
he were asleep.

Den wirt des dô wol geluste,
1120 er helste unde kuste
in vil dikke unt vaste.
Daz was (dô) dem gaste
ze vertragen' unmugelîch;
ie doch verduldete er sich,
daz er ez allez versweik.
Der wirt dô mit vlîze kreik,
daz er die süeze minne
verstæle, in deme sinne
daz hemde er ir ûf las;
1130 dô vant er dâ, rehte als ez was
von Gote dar geschaffen.
Daz machte dem affen
sîn trüebe gemüete swære,
in wunderte, waz ez wære;
die hant zukte (er) snel[lek]lîchen dan
und greif aber wider dar an,
dô was ez aber alsam;
des wart er an den sinnen lam.
"Wer hât mir vervelschet daz wîp?
1140 Si hât nû (gar) mannes lîp;
diu vremde mære ich nie mê vernam.
Mir ist Got wol mit vlîze gram,
dâ von ich sus verirret bin.
Nû gedenke ich an den sin,
den mich mîn bâbe lêrte,
daz ich mich dar an niht kêrte,
ob mich ihtes bedûhte.
Sol ich in dirre suhte
alsus immer mêr mich kweln,
1150 ich enmak es niht verheln,
ich enkünd' ez etesweme,
der mir den swæren muot beneme.
"Wache," sprach er, "vrouwe mîn,
lâ dîn slâfen lenger sîn,
kêrâ dich umbe, unde sprich."
Dô regete der knappe sich
und sprach, "Waz wiltu mîn nû?"
"Patriz! vrouwe, jâ bist dû
worden, dunket mich, ein man."
1160 "Wie wære mir geschehen dan?
Wan ich daz nie mê gesach.

The host was very eager,
he kissed and embraced him 1120
hard and fast.
That was almost impossible
for the guest to endure,
but he suffered it
and held his peace.
The host strove energetically
for sweet love
and with this in mind
he pulled up her nightshirt.
Then he found things 1130
exactly as God had created them.
This troubled the poor fool
and dampened his spirits;
he wondered what was wrong.
He quickly pulled back his hand
and then took another feel,
but it was just the same.
His mind was paralyzed.
"Who has falsified my wife?
Now she has the body of a man. 1140
I've never heard such a strange thing.
God is angry with me in earnest
since I am so led astray.
But now I remember the advice
my beldam gave me,
that I should pay no attention
to what I seem to notice.
But if I am always going to be
tormented by this ill,
I can't conceal that I would be grateful 1150
to anyone who would relieve me
of such a depressing thought.
Wake up, wife," he said,
"you've slept enough,
turn around and speak."
The youth bestirred himself and said,
"What do you want from me now?"
"Wife, it seems to me
that you've become a man."
"How could that happen? 1160
I've never seen such a thing!

Habe, herre, dîn gemach;
dû enweist niht, waz dû sagest.
Nû dû nimmer niht verdagest,
waz dir sulhes wider vert,
sô ist dir ungemach beschert.
Nû sage ich dir ez wol, daz
dich bedunket aber etewaz;
daz kiuse ich (vil) wol dar an,
1170 daz dich dunket, ich sî ein man:
nein ich, z'wâre, ich bin ein wîp.
Nû hâst dû doch mînen lîp
manik jâr (vil) wol bekant:
versuoch' ez baz mit dîner hant;
sint daz dû mîn wil lâgen,
sô endarf dich es niht betrâgen."
Dô der wirt mit der hant
selbe daz wol ervant,
wie daz dink was getân,
1180 "Ich kan mich," sprach er, "wol verstân,
daz ez ist ein mannes mâl;
diz möhte ein vremde Westevâl
wol, âne mich, gemerken."
"Nû wiltu aber sterken
dîn ungevüege tobeheit,
ez sî mir liep oder leit,
ich sihe wol, daz dû elbisch bist.
Nû gip mir eine kleine vrist,
daz ich ein lieht enzünde,
1190 und daz ich dir gekünde,
waz dich Westevâlet,
oder wie ich bin gemâlet.
Ich wæne, ich dich wol gewere
eines wîbes, als ich here
bin gewesen manik jâr;
des soltu werden (wol) gewar.
Nû volge sîner lêre,
des hâstu lüzzel êre,
der dich alsô verleitet
1200 und dîne schande breitet!"
Von dem bette er getrat
wider ze sîner bette stat;
der geselle volgete mite.
Diu vrouwe trat snelle trite

Be still, husband,
you don't know what you're talking about.
When you never know enough to hold your tongue
about what happens to you,
you're in for trouble.
I can tell that you've
been seeing things again.
I gather that much from the fact
that you think I am a man. **1170**
Not I, forsooth, I am a woman.
After all, you've been familiar
with my body for many years;
test it again with your hand.
Since you're so eager for it,
you shouldn't object to it."
When the host
found with his hand
how the thing was shaped,
he said, "I know the mark **1180**
of a man when I see it;
even a simple-minded Westphalian
could tell!"
"Now you're just adding
to your lunacy;
whether I like it or not,
I can see you're mad.
Now give me a moment
to light a candle
so that I can show you **1190**
what's "Westfailing" you
and how I'm shaped.
I wager, I'll prove
to be a woman as well
as I've been for many a year,
you can be sure of that.
You do yourself no credit
by putting your trust in the One
who is misleading you this way
and making public your disgrace!" **1200**
He went from the bed
back to his own bed.
His companion went with him.
The lady stepped quickly

hin zuo dem viure:
"Ein elbische ungehiure,"
sprach si, "dû sîs verwâzen!
Dû möhtes mich wol lâzen
hînte mit gemache leben;
1210 wie ist mir armen sus vergeben,
oder waz hân ich getân!"
Vür daz bette gienk si stân,
daz lieht si in der hant truok;
si sprach, "Des dunket mich genuok,
daz dû mich sus umb trîbes
und dînes eigen wîbes
niht erkennes; daz ist wol,
sint ich dir'z nû zeigen sol,
sô grîf vil ebene unde sich,
1220 bekenne mich (nû) baz, und sprich,
daz ich vür wâr ein wîp bin.
Waz gæbe ich umbe den sin,
der [n]iht bezzer wære!
Ez wirt ein schœnez mære
von uns hin vürder mêre;
ouch habe wir's lüzzel êre.
Mich dûhte daz noch rehte guot,
daz dû dînen tumben muot
an mînen rât gewentes,
1230 und ein teil baz erkentes
der übelen ungehiuren site,
die pflegen dir des immer mite,
wilt dû ez allez gesagen,
daz si dir ze den ougen tragen."
"Eijâ, mînes herzen trût!"
sprach der tôre über lût,
"nû vergib mir mîne schult,
vrouwe, mit grôzer gedult.
Ich sihe wol, waz mir wirret,
1240 ich bin ot verirret
leider [mir] mîner sinne;
swie sô ich es beginne,
ez engeschiht mir nimmer mê,
wære mir alle tage wê
mêr den niun stunt an eime tage,
daz ich nimmer mêr gesage
keinen swachen gelouben.

to the hearth:
"May you be cursed
for a hellish demon!" she said.
"You could have let me sleep
in peace tonight.
What have I done, poor wretch, **1210**
to deserve this?"
She went to the bed and
brought the candle in her hand
and said, "It's too much
that you run me ragged
and don't recognize
your own wife, and it's a good thing
I can give you proof now.
So take hold and see,
admit it and say **1220**
that I am indeed a woman.
What wouldn't I give for a husband
with a little more sense!
We'll get a pretty reputation
for this sort of thing
and little honor.
It seems to me that it would be a good thing
if you with your foolishness
would turn to me for counsel
and recognize better **1230**
the ways of those evil demons
who are forever causing you
to announce whatever
they put before your eyes."
"Alas, my heart's desire,"
exclaimed the fool,
"forgive me for my error
and be patient with me, lady.
I can see now what ails me;
alas, I am deprived **1240**
of my senses.
Whatever I do
and whatever happens to me,
I'll never again give way
to my gullibility,
even if I'm beset
nine times a day.

Eime blinden touben
dem wold' ich mich gelîchen,
1250 möht' ich dâ mite entwîchen
alsus getânen sachen;
mîn zürnen und mîn lachen
mak mich allez niht vervân.
Ouch lêrte mich daz mîn wân,
daz dû mich lîhte selbe truges
unde mir sô vor zuges,
alsô der kazzen, den halm.
Nû sprich ot dînen salm
über mich, vrouwe, durch Got,
1260 daz der liute smælîcher spot
mich alsus iht under var.
Ouch nim (dû) ir selbe war,
rehte als ich dir getrouwe,
swen ich die liute schouwe,
sô sage in, mîn unkraft
mache mich sô zwîvelhaft,
daz von ir vrâge
grôzlîche mich betrâge."
"O wê, lieber," sprach si dô,
1270 "möhte ich gewinnen sô,
als ich gerne tæte
und als ich willen hæte,
des wære mir vil nôt:
mir tæte senfter (wol) ein [reiner] tôt,
sold' ez lenger an dir weren,
ich hæte senfter einen beren
ze dirre naht gebunden.
Sint ich nû habe bevunden,
waz disiu rede meinet,
1280 so entouk es niht geweinet;
wir sulen Got dar umbe ane beten."
Sie hiez die tohter dar treten,
si lâsen unde bâten,
rehte als ez was gerâten.
Si sprach, "Weiz Got, ich kan
einen vluoch und einen ban,
daz ich mich wol gereche,
swen ich den gespreche:
Bî deus salter ich dich swer,
1290 und bî Wutungis her,

I'll act blind
and dumb
if I can only avoid 1250
this sort of thing.
Nothing can make
me laugh or cry.
My hallucination even made me
think that you yourself deceived me
and led me on
like a cat with a straw.
Now for the love of God, lady,
say a psalm over me
and protect me from 1260
the mockery of spiteful people.
And see to it,
as I trust you will,
that when I am among people,
you tell them that my infirmity
makes me so confused
that I am terribly vexed
by their questions."
"Alas, dear husband," she said,
"if I could do 1270
as I like
and as seems best,
it would be good for me.
I would rather die
if your condition persists,
and I would liefer
have subdued a bear tonight.
Now that I've found out
what the trouble is,
tears are no help. 1280
We must pray to God for relief."
She told her daughter to approach;
they read and prayed
as was needful.
She said, "God knows,
I have a curse and an exhortation
that will take effect
when I speak it:
By God's psalter I conjure you
and by Odin's rout, 1290

bî P(e)ters ban bast
banne ich dich vil vast,
swaz dû sîes, ob dû lebes,
daz dû mir antwürte gebes,
war umbe tuostu uns ungemach?"
Mit kleiner stimme dô sprach
ein jungelink von Ache,
reht in koboldes sprâche,
"Lâz dîn bannen alsô vil,
1300 ez wirt ein vil bœsez spil;
wer lêrte dich diu starken wort?
Daz sîn vröude sî verstôrt!
Du enmaht mich niht vertrîben,
ich wil hie lenger blîben."
Des erschrak der wirt vil sêre,
und bat si bannen mêre.
"Jâ," sprach si, "daz weste ich wol,
wan daz man's iu niht sagen sol,
ez ist ein vil übelez âs.
1310 Nû sagâ mir, elbischez getwâs,
vil rehte dînen namen."
"Ich mache dînen gamen,"
sprach er, "tâlank alsô grôz."
Dô nam si über iren schôz
aber wider daz buoch,
sus begunde si da iren vluoch
ander weide bannen
von wîben und von mannen:
"Bî künik Karlins brükken,
1320 und bî Getanis krükken,
bî des herzogen Wolwis granen,
beide bannen unde manen,
mit aldes wîbes vluochen,
daz si dich verruochen
und vermeinen müezen;
bî den vünf eseles vüezen,
die die Beijere brâhten über mer:
daz dich Hasehart verzer,
dû entuos mir dînen namen kunt,
1330 ich banne dich an den (grunt)!"
Mit grôzer stimme er dô schrei,
"O wî!" sprach er, "und ac(h)ei!
Daz mîne wer ist alsô krank!

by Peter's exhortation
I conjure you amain,
whoever you are, if you are a living creature,
give me answer:
why do you disturb us?"
Then with a little voice
the youth from Aachen spoke
in goblin speech,
"Cease your awful conjuring,
it's a perilous game. 1300
Who taught you the potent words?
May he perish!
You cannot banish me!
I've a mind to stay here longer."
The host was all aghast
and bade her conjure more.
"Yes," she said, "I knew all along
it was an evil wight,
except you wouldn't listen.
Now, demon spirit, tell me 1310
truthfully your name."
"I'll make you play my game
all day," he said.
Then she took her book
on her lap again
and began once more
to pronounce her curse,
invoking men and women:
"By King Charles's bridge
and by Getani's crutch, 1320
by Duke Wolwi's beard
I conjure and admonish you
with a granny's curse
that they may scorn
and hex you;
by the five hooves of the ass
which the Bavarians brought across the sea,
may Hasehart consume you;
unless you reveal your name to me,
I'll banish you to Hell!" 1330
With a great voice he cried aloud,
"Alas," he said, "and alack,
that my resistance is so weak!

Vrouwe, ich heize Irregank,
mîn bruoder heizet Girregar,
sint ich iuch niht verswîgen tar,
unser ambet ist alsô getân:
wir brengen dikke an den wân
vil mangen wizzigen man,
1340 daz er niht weiz, waz er kan.
Wan daz dû sô vil kans,
und uns des gemaches vergans,
müeste wir hie beharren,
wir solden girregarren
und machen sulhen irregank,
daz der wirt ân' sînen dank
des nimmer gedenken möhte."
"Nein!" si sprach, "daz entöhte;
dû solt dich anders wâ bestaten,
1350 wan ich wil dich hie gesaten
mit bannen und mit vluochen,
dû endarft hie niht mêr suochen.
Ich gibe dir, daz dû hinnen vares
unde vürder mê bewares,
daz dû immer kumes her."
Er sprach, "Daz geschiht nâch dîner ger,
ich muoz von hinnen varen."
Er begunde alsô gebâren
mit einer stangen umb den hert,
1360 daz er erschrekkete diu pfert;
er stalte grôz ungestiure
mit den stüelen bî dem viure,
daz si erwachten alle.
In diseme grôzen schalle
sleich er zuo dem bette wider.
Des wart wol gelachet sider,
dô si beide ze samene
kwâmen in ir gademe.
"Nû sehet, wie er hinne vert!"
1370 sprach si, "doch ist im erwert,
weiz Got, (nû) sîn irregank;
er muos' âne sînen dank
hie rûmen diz gemach."
Der wirt dô vrôlîchen sprach,
"Des müeze Got gelobet sîn,
daz diu liebe tohter mîn

Lady, my name is Waywardwight,
my brother's name is Lustymite,
and since I dare not be silent,
our office is
to delude
many a sensible man
into not knowing what he knows. 1340
Were it not that you are so powerful
and refuse to grant us peace,
we would remain here;
we would lustify
and waywardize
so that the host all unknowing
would never find it out."
"No," she said, "that would be of no avail.
Go elsewhere,
for I will give you such a bellyful 1350
of curses and conjurations
that you'll find no more business here.
I tell you to get hence
and make sure
you never come again."
He said, "That shall be done
according to your wish; I must leave."
He began to thrash
about the hearth with a stick
so loudly that he frightened the horses; 1360
he made such a rumpus
with the chairs by the fire
that they all awoke.
In the midst of this commotion
he slipped back to bed.
Then they had a good laugh
when both of them were back
together in their room.
"Now see how he takes to his heels,"
she said. "God knows, 1370
his waywardness is stymied now.
Willy nilly he must
leave this room."
The host said cheerfully,
"God be praised
that my dear daughter

ie gelêrte sulhiu wort,
dâ von mîn sorge wirt zestôrt.
Nû sol ich mit gemache leben.
1380 Got müeze uns daz ze heile geben,
daz er uns welle mîden!"
"Wir müezen," sprach si, "lîden,
daz Got mit uns allen tuot.
Diu rede ist ie doch vil guot,
sint er vürhtet mînen ban
und sulhiu wort diu ich kan.
Sô mahtu wol ân' angest wesen;
ich wil ir sprechen unde lesen
über dir genuok und alsô vil,
1390 daz ich dich verpflegen wil,
daz er dich vürder mê verbirt."
Dô klagete der unwîse wirt,
daz im unsanfte wære
worden von der swære,
die er mit grôzen sorgen truok.
Sint wart er dikke und genuok
betœret und gelürzet;
daz sî iu gekürzet.
Vröude und âventiure,
1400 sunder ungestiure,
der wart dâ under geüebet;
si bliben unbetrüebet
sô lange sô si wolden.
In wart vil wol vergolden,
waz dâ was geborget;
lüzzel wart gesorget
in dirre vriuntlîcher schar;
si nâmen vil kleine war
von sagen unt von lieden.
1410 Die knappen dannen schieden,
dikke kwâmen si ouch wider,
wan der alde wirt sider
niht vürder mê verjach,
swaz er nâch der zît gesach.
Ir habet dikke wol gesên,
daz wunders vil ist geschên
von den jungen wîben,
die den paras trîben;
nû muoz ez blîben ungewundert,

learned words
which end my troubles.
Now I can live in peace.
God grant us the good fortune 1380
that this creature keep away from us."
"We must all," she said,
"abide by God's will,
but my formula is good.
Since he fears my curse
and the words I know,
you can be secure.
I will speak and read
enough of them over you
to take good care 1390
that he will avoid you in the future."
Then the foolish host lamented
the pain and discomfort
he had grievously endured
with such great sorrow.
Many a time since then
he has been fooled and deceived,
but I'll cut the story short.
Pleasure and adventure
were indulged in 1400
all the while without disturbance;
they remained unvexed
as long as they desired.
They were well repaid
for what was borrowed there.
There was little grief
in this gay company.
They paid little attention
to tales and ditties.
The youths took their leave 1410
but often returned
since the old host
never again told
of what he saw.
You have often observed
that strange things are brought to pass
by young women
who practice deception.
So it can come as no surprise

1420 uns ist ein niuwer alp gesundert,
Irregank und Girregar;
der sult ir alle nemen war,
und gehüetet iuch dâ vüre,
tuot ein kriuze vür die türe,
daz er iuwer gast iht werde
iu schadet sîn geberde
noch mê den ein dunre.
Rüediger von Munre
an disen rât iuch kêret.
1430 Nû hânt diu wîp gelêret,
daz si niht werden nunnen,
die sus girregarren kunnen
an Irreganges leichen.
Drî guote knütele eichen
ze guoter mâze wol gewegen
die wæren dâ der beste segen,
und bezzer den ein bannen,
die hulfen (wol) den mannen
disen Irregank vertrîben,
1440 so entörste dâ niht blîben
weder Irregank, noch Girregar;
si wisten daz wol vür wâr,
daz man si begunde regen
mit ungevüegen hals slegen.
Dâ mite lâzet mich nû vrî.
Swen ir welt und iu liep sî,
sô erwerbet iu daz lachen:
ich enkan iu niht gemachen
die rede gemelîcher,
1450 noch ouch der vröuden rîcher.

that new demons have been born— 1420
Waywardwight and Lustymite.
You should all be on the lookout
and guard against them;
make a cross on the door
lest they become your guests—
their actions do more damage
than a thunderbolt.
Rüediger of Munre
gives you this advice.
Now women have learned 1430
that those who lust
to the tune of Waywardwight
don't make good nuns.
Three good oaken cudgels
nicely measured would be
the best blessing for this case,
and better than a curse;
they would help husbands
banish such a Waywardwight.
Neither Waywardwight nor Lustymite 1440
would dare remain.
They would know for a certainty
that they would be belabored
with lusty thumps on the head.
And now dismiss me.
If you are willing and wish to do so,
give way to mirth.
I cannot make
my tale gayer
or more entertaining. 1450

"Two Students Who Intoxicated Their Host Together With His Wife and Daughter"

We have a Latin synopsis of "The Reeve's Tale" in a collection of anecdotes illustrating the vagaries of drink and entitled "De generibus ebriosorum et ebrietate vitanda" ("On Drunks and Avoiding Drunkenness"). The anecdote is regularly referred to among the analogues, but, as far as we can ascertain, it has not been printed since the seventeenth century. "De generibus . . ." is usually mentioned as an appendix to the famous German humanist lampoon *Epistolae obscurorum virorum* (first edition 1515), to which it was added in 1556 or 1557 (see Eduard Böcking's *Ulrichi Hutteni equitis operum supplementum: Epistolae obscurorum virorum cum inlustrantibus adversariisque scriptis* [Leipzig, 1869], II, 1, p. 15). However, according to Karl Goedeke's *Grundriss zur Geschichte der deutschen Dichtung* (Dresden, 1884), I, 437, there was an independent edition in 1516. The full title of this edition is: *De generibus ebriosorum et ebrietate vitanda. Questio facetiarum et urbanitatis plena quam pulcherrima optimorum scriptorum flosculis referta. In conclusione quodlibeti Erphurdensis anno Christi 1515 circa aequinoctium scholastico more explicata.*

ALIA HISTORIA DE DUOBUS STUDENTIBUS, QUI HOSPITEM CUM UXORE ET FILIA INEBRIARUNT

Non multum dissimile est aliud. Fuerunt Erfurdiæ duo studentes, qui cum in oppido quodam, quod erat in partibus Franconiæ, ad hospitem non publicum, sed privatum eis notum, noctu divertissent, haberetque idem hospes uxorem et filiam formosam, alter ad alterum*: utinam, inquit, eas vino replere possemus, quis scit, si convertantur et admittant. Quod hactenus pro voluntate eis cessit: iamque hospes cum uxore et filia, et ipsi duo studentes madidi, in eodem cubiculo, in quo tres duntaxat erant lecti, recipiuntur. Apparebant enim ingenui et morati iuvenes. Impleverunt

In line with the moral of the stories in this collection, the feature of drunkenness, common to most versions, is singled out and made into a horrible example. We have come full cycle from Boccaccio's story, which is conceived as illustrating a woman's wit and has no moralistic implications. Hermann Varnhagen, in his article "Die Erzählung von der Wiege," *Englische Studien*, IX (1886), 240–266, was inclined to derive the Latin anecdote from a hypothetical French story halfway between "Gombert et les II clers" and "Le Meunier et les II clers" (p. 259), but it seems more likely that it derives from one of the German versions. Despite the brevity of the anecdote, there are two features which associate it more closely with "Das Studentenabenteuer" than with "Irregang und Girregar." One is the emphasis on the learning of the two scholars, who in the *Märe* are consummate musicians and in the Latin version thoroughly versed in Aristotle. The other feature is the conclusion, in which the wife simply realizes what has happened and urges her husband to be silent "ne domesticam maculam propalaret." On the other hand, the description of the youths as "ingenui et morati" more nearly coincides with "Irregang und Girregar."

The topical allusions in the story are a little difficult. The eleven books of *Ethics* are puzzling, since the *Nicomachean Ethics* comprise ten books. Perhaps this is a witticism akin to "working twenty-five hours a day." Perhaps also the knowledge of ethics and physics has an ironical application to the physical but unethical situation in the story. Schildgen is still a place name in the vicinity of Erfurt, but we are unable to locate Sperlingsberg. St. Gotthard was a church in Erfurt and perhaps the reference here is to a cathedral school attached to it. St. Gotthard (960–1038) was Bishop of Hildesheim and founder of a school there, so that he had a reputation as an educator and could well have given his name to a school. (Incidentally, he also gave his name to the Saint Gotthard Pass). One suspects that there are jokes in this passage which would be clear to someone familiar with the scholastic debates of the period.

The text printed here is from *Epistolae virorum obscurorum* (Frankfurt, 1643), pp. 441–443.

ANOTHER STORY ABOUT TWO STUDENTS WHO INTOXICATED A HOST TOGETHER WITH HIS WIFE AND DAUGHTER

There is another rather similar story. There were two students of Erfurt, and when they stopped for the night in a certain town in Franconia, not at a public inn but at a private lodging known to them, and the host had a wife and a beautiful daughter, one said to the other, "If only we could fill them with wine, who knows whether they might be won and admit us to their favors." And this turned out just as they desired. The host together with his wife and daughter and the two students, a little tipsy, retired in the same room, in which there were only three beds, for they seemed to be

namque undecim libros Ethicorum Erphurdiæ apud S. Gothardum, *Auff dem Schiltgen,* et posteriorum Scoti, et Physicorum, *auff dem Sperlings Berg.* Noctu igitur surgens alter, qui iuvenculam amabat, leniter eius lectulum (sola namque iacebat) accedens, eamque consolari volens, nullo discrimine facile est admissus. Interim nescio quid strepitus in domo audiens uxor ebria, ab ebrio marito consurgens, cupiebat videre quid esset: cum interim alter quia adhuc solus dormiebat, invento dolo, cunas in quibus infans apud maritalem thalamum erat repositus, ad suum lectum trahens, ipsa redeunte coepit movere cunas infantis: quod ipsa audiens, strepitum cunarum secuta, lectum adulteri sponte conscendit, putans illic esse suum maritum ubi cunas invenisset. Ille vero dissimulans, dedolavit uxorem alienam egregie et multis vicibus. Illa insolitam viri potentiam admirata, inquit: *Ey ia mein lieber Mann, vvie seyd ihr heind so geil vvorden?* Ille nihil, preter tace, respondens, ne vocis indicio proderetur, sæpius a principio rem petiit. Luce vero appropinquante, surgens ille qui filiam stupraverat, ad lectum mariti pervenit, quoniam sonus eum cunarum, quarum indicio ipse maritalem lectum cognoverat, ad sese traxerat. Cum vero hospitem suum socium esse credens, gloriatur cum hospitis filia se concubuisse, hospes iam sobrius factus dolum sentiens uxorem vocat, quæ ibidem se apud adulterum esse cognoscens, errorem confessa, filiam de stupro non increpavit, maritoque persuasit, ne domesticam maculam propalaret: eius enim id omne culpa accidisse clamitabat, etc. Ita fit nonnunquam, ut quod sobrii, ne cogitamus quidem, ebrii facile admittamus.

* Text: *adulterum* (a bad pun?).

worthy and reputable youths. Indeed, they had completed the eleven books of the *Ethics* at Erfurt at St. Gotthard at Schildgen under the followers of Duns Scotus and the *Physics* at Sperlingsberg. Now getting up in the night, the one who loved the girl softly approached her bed (for she slept alone) and, wishing to solace her, with no struggle he was easily admitted. In the meantime the intoxicated wife, hearing I don't know what noise in the house, arose from her intoxicated husband and wanted to see what it was. In the meantime the other student, because he was now sleeping alone, having devised a ruse, drew to his bed the cradle in which the infant was placed next to the conjugal bed and when she returned, he began to rock the baby's cradle. When she heard this, she followed the noise of the cradle and entered the bed of her adulterous spouse, thinking that her husband was where she found the cradle. By dissimulating he tricked the other man's wife in excellent and repeated fashion. Amazed at the unaccustomed prowess of her husband, she said, "What ho, my dear husband, why are you so merry tonight?" But he answered nothing lest he be betrayed by the evidence of his voice and began anew several times. When the dawn now approached, the one who had debauched the daughter arose and came to the husband's bed because the sound of the cradle, by which indication he knew the conjugal bed, guided him. Believing then that the host was his companion, he boasted that he had lain with the host's daughter. The host by now somewhat sobered and perceiving the trick, called his wife, who, realizing that she was likewise with an adulterer, admitted her error, did not rebuke her daughter for her disgrace, and persuaded the husband not to publicize the family's shame. For she protested that it had all happened through his fault, etc. Thus it sometimes happens that what we would hardly contemplate when sober, we do readily when we are intoxicated.

"The Miller's Daughter"

The most interesting and best represented literary product of medieval Scandinavia (aside from Iceland) is the ballad, and among the Scandinavian countries Denmark has the richest remnants of the ballad tradition. Judging from the matter they contain, these ballads seem to have flourished during the feudal age in the thirteenth and fourteenth centuries, though no written versions survive from this period. They were transmitted orally, and it was not until the middle of the sixteenth century that the first substantial collection was made. The Renaissance collections have since been supplemented by later broadsides and in modern times by the recordings of the folklorists, so that the number of ballads and ballad versions is very large. The most common forms are a four-line stanza and a two-line stanza, as in the following example. They seem originally to have been used as a dance accompaniment, and they still survive in this function in the Feroe Islands.

The subject matter is varied—erotic, heroic, historical, supernatural, and, at

---

MØLLERENS DATTER

Der stode to Skalke og tænkte Raad—
Ja hvad skulde man tænke?
De vilde til Møllerens Datter gaae.
Foroventil var hun Mø forneden var hun Enke.

O hvad har du i Sækken din?
Ja hvad skulde man tænke?
Jeg haver Rug og hveden fin.
Foroventil var hun Mø forneden var hun Enke.

Du sæt din Sæk hos min Datters Seng!
Ja hvad skulde man tænke?
Der kommer ingen Rotter til den.
Foroventil var hun Mø forneden var hun Enke.

Og der blev mørk udi i hver en Vraa,
Ja hvad skulde man tænke?
Den sæk begyndte at krybe og gaa.
Foroventil var hun Mø forneden var hun Enke.

a later period, jocular. There is nothing medieval about the ballad printed here, except perhaps for the melancholy ending, in which the hostess is not accorded the same treatment as her daughter, but is drowned in the mill-pond for her interference. Whether the miller's punishment in our earlier versions of the story has somehow been transferred to his wife, whether the mother has become associated with and a victim of the wicked stepmother motif popular in the ballad, or whether her behavior is dictated by the traditional ballad feature of a mother's overconcern with her daughter's honor is hard to tell. Indeed, this may not be the same story at all, though the arrival of two companions at a mill with a sack of grain and the subsequent seduction of the miller's daughter is more than a little reminiscent of "The Reeve's Tale." Another curious reminiscence is the cat to which the daughter attributes the disturbance; in Boccaccio's story the housecat is in fact responsible for the noise that arouses the mother.

The text is preserved in broadsides which are undated but probably from the eighteenth century. It is reprinted from R. Nyerup, *Udvalg af danske viser fra midten af det 16de aarhundrede til henimod midten af det 18de* (Copenhagen, 1821), II, 154–156. The most recent collection of Danish ballads available in English translation is Erik Dal, *Danish Ballads and Folk Songs*, trans. Henry Meyer (Copenhagen and New York, 1967).

THE MILLER'S DAUGHTER

There stood two wags and hatched a plan—
  Oh, what should one think?
They wanted to go to the miller's daughter.
  Above the waist she was a maid, below she was a widow.

"And what do you have in your sack?"
  Oh, what should one think?
"I have rye and wheat so fine."
  Above the waist she was a maid, below she was a widow.

"Put down your sack by my daughter's bed!"
  Oh, what should one think?
"There no rats will get at it!"
  Above the waist she was a maid, below she was a widow.

Darkness came to every corner,
  Oh, what should one think?
The sack began to creep and walk.
  Above the waist she was a maid, below she was a widow.

O, kjær Fader! I tænder Lys,
  Ja hvad skulde man tænke?
Der er kommen Tyve i Møllerhus.
  Foroventil var hun Mø forneden var hun Enke.

Han klappede hende ved hviden Kind:
  Ja hvad skulde man tænke?
Og du skal være allerkjæreste min.
  Foroventil var hun Mø forneden var hun Enke.

O, min kjær Fader! I slukker Ljus.
  Ja hvad skulde man tænke?
Det var den kat han tog en Mus.
  Foroventil var hun Mø forneden var hun Enke.

Det svared' den Kjerling i Bænken laa:
  Ja hvad skulde man tænke?
Den Kat han havde to Støvler paa.
  Foroventil var hun Mø forneden var hun Enke.

Og ti du Kjerling! det du faae Skam!
  Ja hvad skulde man tænke?
I Morgen skal du i Mølledam.
  Foroventil var hun Mø forneden var hun Enke.

Og Kjerlingen sank og Pelsen flød,
  Ja hvad skulde man tænke?
Den arme Mand sad paa Landet og græd.
  Foroventil var hun Mø forneden var hun Enke.

"Oh, father dear, please light a candle,"
Oh, what should one think?
"Thieves have come to the miller's house."
Above the waist she was a maid, below she was a widow.

He patted her on her cheek so white:
Oh, what should one think?
"Now you will be my sweetheart dear."
Above the waist she was a maid, below she was a widow.

"Oh, father dear, put out the light,"
Oh, what should one think?
"It was the cat; he caught a mouse."
Above the waist she was a maid, below she was a widow.

The old shrew answered, who lay in bed:
Oh, what should one think?
"I trow that cat had on two boots."
Above the waist she was a maid, below she was a widow.

"Be quiet, you shrew! A curse upon you!"
Oh, what should one think?
"Tomorrow I'll throw you in the pond."
Above the waist she was a maid, below she was a widow.

And the old shrew sank and the cloak stayed afloat,
Oh, what should one think?
The poor man sat on the shore and wept.
Above the waist she was a maid, below she was a widow.

The Merchant's Tale and Its Analogues

A large number of analogues of Chaucer's "Merchant's Tale" are collected in *Originals and Analogues of Some of Chaucer's Canterbury Tales* and *Sources and Analogues of Chaucer's Canterbury Tales.* Versions have circulated as far afield as Ceylon, India, Persia, and Turkey, but we restrict the present selection to western variants. Among these there are two fairly distinct types. According to one (which corresponds to the eastern versions) the deluded husband, before whom the wife sports with her lover, is not blind but is persuaded by his wife that he is the victim of an optical illusion caused by a magical tree. According to the other the husband is old, jealous, and blind; he miraculously regains his sight at the crucial moment and discovers his young wife with her lover in a pear tree, where she has sought refuge from his jealous supervision. Nothing daunted, she quickly protests that her act is a secret remedy for her husband's blindness, thus not only allaying his suspicions but even earning his gratitude. Boccaccio's version in *Decameron 7,9* belongs to the first of these two types and Chaucer's "Merchant's Tale" to the second.

One of the features which distinguishes Chaucer's "Reeve's Tale" from its analogues is the more fully developed domestic comedy. The analogues reveal very little about the household which the two young men are about to invade, and the fun lies simply in the seduction of the two women. Chaucer, on the other hand, provides a good deal of information on Symkyn's marriage, his wife, her parentage, their conpensatory snobbishness, and their plans for their daughter's future. This background enriches the farcical situation with a sense of comic demise and social satire which is as appropriate to the middle class scene in the twentieth century as it was in the fourteenth.

Chaucer's procedure in "The Merchant's Tale" is similar. Like "The Miller's Tale" and "The Reeve's Tale" it has a fabliau nucleus—adultery

in a pear tree; but it is twice as long as these tales and is expanded with an even more elaborate domestic framework. The situation is reminiscent of "The Miller's Tale" and draws on that inexhaustible source of humor, the cuckold comedy. But whereas "The Miller's Tale" concentrates on characterizing the erring young wife and rather neglects John, "The Merchant's Tale" lavishes most of its attention on the old cuckold, January. The actual denouement is preceded by the old man's decision to marry a young girl, his rosy flights of imagination about his anticipated marital bliss, his soliciting of advice and complacent rejection of well-founded warnings, his palpitations and lecherous delights, and the corresponding distaste of his young bride. These are dramatic ironies later exploited by the stage practitioners of cuckold comedy, but they are not typical of fabliau literature, which is more exclusively interested in demonstrating the wiles of women. Thus, most of the analogues to "The Merchant's Tale" are concerned not with the portrait of a cuckold, but with the mechanics and the outrageousness of the deception.

The most extreme form of the deception is provided by the first and longest of our analogues, the "Comoedia Lidiae." This text belongs together with *Decameron* 7,9 and typifies the story in which the cuckolded husband witnesses all and is made to believe that a magical pear tree has deluded him. Not only is this final delusion outrageous, but it is preceded by three other brazen tests of the husband's credulity. In "Lydia," unlike "The Merchant's Tale," it is the woman who falls in love with the young man and must find the means to satisfy her passion. The youth (Pyrrhus) at first repulses her because he doubts her sincerity and, before committing himself, he demands three proofs of her love: she must kill her husband's favorite falcon, pull five hairs out of his beard, and extract one of his teeth (the tooth motif recurs independently in the German fabliau "Der Zahn" and is later used twice by Heinrich Kaufringer [Hanns Fischer, *Studien zur deutschen Märendichtung*, pp. 426, 429, 481]). Lydia not only undertakes these tasks but outdoes her doubting swain by promising to make love to him before her husband's very eyes. She duly accomplishes all she has promised and leaves her spouse none the wiser. This twelfth-century Latin fabliau is so close to Boccaccio's novella that it must be regarded as Boccaccio's immediate source.

The second group of analogues which we have included represents a type rather closer to Chaucer. In the *Novellino* story, the fable of Adolphus, and "Von einem Plinten," the cuckold is old and blind and is given his sight by God in order to catch his wife with her lover in the pear tree. She promptly disarms his wrath by taking credit for the restoration of his eyesight. In the Italian and German versions it is furthermore the young man who initiates the suit and not, as in "Lydia" and the *Decameron*, the wanton lady. There as also brief prose adaptations of this version in Latin

and French, which add nothing substantial to the story and are available in *Sources and Analogues.*

The third group of analogues we have chosen has far less to do with "The Merchant's Tale" and simply illustrate the very abundant medieval literature on feminine wiles, the theme par excellence of the fabliau, especially in France. There are many examples of women hopelessly compromised who free themselves from suspicion by having their wits about them: the Apuleius story at the beginning of this volume ushers in a long tradition. For example, the earliest collection of medieval fabliau material, Petrus Alphonsus' *Disciplina Clericalis,* contains an anecdote (no. 12) according to which a woman is caught with her lover by her returning husband. She saves the situation by making her lover stand mute with drawn sword as the husband enters; she then dispels his confusion by explaining that the man has taken refuge from would-be assassins, and her husband obligingly congratulates her on averting a murder. In the fables of Marie de France printed here the ocular evidence is explained away once as an optical illusion and once as a hereditary omen of death, which transforms the husband's wrath into abject fear that he will lose his wife (and her dowry). "The Lady Doctor" provides a twist on the theme: the husband, though not a witness to the adultery, is told in great detail exactly what has happened, but in such a way that he does not have wit enough to understand. Here the deception is aural rather than ocular. The final example, "The Priest Who Peeked," reverts to the alternate version of the pear tree story, according to which a woman and her lover indulge themselves before the husband's eyes and persuade him that his vision is distorted by magic.

Ocular deception belongs also to the repertory of German fabliau writers. In "Der Wirt" (Fischer, *Märendichtung,* p. 481) a husband is abused before his very eyes by three rogues, one of whom uses exactly the same trick as in Boccaccio's story and the "Comoedia Lidiae." The same story is later revived in Hans Rosenplüt's "Der Wettstreit der drei Liebhaber" (Fischer, p. 452). These two German stories also use the test-of-strength motif that appears in "The Priest and the Lady" (below, pp. 328–337).

The pear tree story itself survived the Middle Ages to be reworked in La Fontaine's "La Gageure des trois commères" (using Boccaccio's version) and in Pope's "January and May" (using Chaucer's version).

"The Comedy of Lydia"

The following text belongs to a little publicized group of some fifteen comic stories in Latin written in the second half of the twelfth century or a little later and designated as *comoediae.* Some are anonymous; some have identifiable authors (notably Vitalis of Blois and Matthew of Vendôme); most were written in France, but a few may be English, such as those of Geoffrey of Vinsauf and John of Garland. They range in length from twenty-two to 792 verses, but three hundred to five hundred verses is customary. They are almost all in elegiacs.

The term *comoedia* derives partly from the usage of the authors themselves and partly from the thematic similarity to Roman comedy: Vitalis of Blois ("Aulularia" 11) refers to Plautus, and William of Blois ("Alda" 14) to Menander. In fact, however, the derivation from Roman theater is at best indirect and some of the familiar sounding titles are misleading; Vitalis' "Aulularia" and the "Miles Gloriosus" (by the anonymous author of our "Lydia") have, for example, nothing to do with Plautus' counterparts. The literary term *comoedia* seems to have been misunderstood or expanded in the Middle Ages and was

---

COMOEDIA LIDIAE

Postquam prima equitis ludentis tempora risit,
    Mox acuit mentem musa secunda meam.
Ut nova Lidiades veteres imitata placeret,
    Finxi femineis queque notanda dolis.
Cautius ut fugeres docui quid femina posset;
    Esse potest una Lidia quoque tibi.
Audit et in Getam ridet premiturque cachinno,
    Qui Pirrum nescit vel pira missa piro.
Quis stupet insidias Iovis aut facinus deitatis,
10   Si recolit que sit Lidia quidve potest?
Quis Iove miratur lusum semel Amphitruona,
    Cum lusit Decium Lidia fraude quater?
Credere quod nihil est aliquid fuit Amphitruoni,
    Quod vidit Decius credidit esse nihil:
Conveniens parili fraus fraude fefellit utrumque;
    Lusus uterque dolo non putat esse dolum.
Invide, qui palles, negat hic cornicula risum:
    Qui nitet his plumis est meus ille color.

used in the case of these texts to describe works which are dramatic only by virtue of interlarding the narrative with a good deal of lively dialogue.

The classical study on the *comoediae* is Edmond Faral's "Le Fabliau latin au moyen âge," *Romania* 50 (1924), 321–385. Faral was led to this subject by his interest in twelfth-century rhetorical treatises, and he shows how in all probability the *comoedia* originated in the rhetorical preoccupations of the schools at Chartres, Fleury, Blois, and Orléans. The *comoediae* are heavily laden with rhetoric; "Lydia" is rich in the pyrotechnics of diction and very fond of wordplay, for example, the tireless punning on *Lidia / ludere* and *Pirrhus / pirus / pirum*. Faral suggested further that the *comoediae* are models for the later fabliaux since they have a very similar repertory of erotic and farcical themes. Whether the relationship is derivative or parallel, the *comoediae* along with the German *Mären* and the Italian *novelle* are very close to the fabliaux in spirit.

The *comoediae* are conveniently available in a two-volume edition with French translations under the general direction of Gustave Cohen: *La "Comédie latine" en France au XIIe siècle* (Paris, 1931). Our text is based on this edition (I, 226–246) with some changes in normalization and the adoption of a few variant manuscript readings. The translation by Edmund Lackenbacher was of great assistance, but we have deviated from his solutions in a relatively large number of instances. Because of its rhetorical ambitions the text is on occasion rather difficult, and each reader will have to make his own decisions.

THE COMEDY OF LYDIA

After the first had smiled at the measures of the sportive warrior,
  A second muse sharpened my mind once more.
So that a new Lydian comedy modeled on the old might please,
  I have devised matters remarkable for women's wiles.
I have taught what a woman can compass so that you may escape;
  You too may have your Lydia.
The scoffer hears and is overcome by laughter at Geta [Sosia],
  Not knowing Pyrrhus and the pears thrown down from the pear tree.
Who will be amazed at the tricks of Jove or the misdeeds of the gods
  If he remembers who Lydia is and what she is capable of? **10**
Who will wonder at Amphitryon deluded by Jove but once,
  When Lydia led Decius astray four times with deception?
Amphitryon was obliged to believe that something was nothing;
  Decius believed that what he saw was nothing.
Like deceits fooled both with similar deceptions;
  Each was deluded with a trick, but thought there was no trick.
Reader green with envy, the crow disclaims any mimicry here;
  The color which shines in these feathers is mine.

Invide, ne serpas; murmur compesce labelli:
20 Crescit et excurrit per mala verba pudor.
Invide: si nescis, ratio non omnis in uno est;
Ut labor exquirit, unus et alter habet.
Se pater Helyadum pennarum ditat honore
Et vult fenicem vivere posse diu.
Psittacus, hoc uno potior, minus invidet illis,
Quod canit humanis assimulata modis.
Si labor et studium Grecis prefecit Homerum,
Nec sibi quem voluit alteritate parem,
Huic nostri similis respondet musa Maronis,
30 Arte nec inferior nec ratione minor.
Pirrus eques, Decius dux est et Lidia coniux.
Est ducis hic fidus, hic gravis, ista levis.
Quid gravitas, quid fidus amor valet aut operatur?
Ista dolo fidum surripit, arte gravem.
Arte, dolo, studio, furit, allicit, insidiatur;
Femina fit virus ut necet illa virum.
Acrius insurgit furor, anxius in muliere
Instat et est preceps impatiensque more.
Cum libet illicitum, citius licito properatur;
40 Cumque procul pudor est, fit scelus arte prope.
Stat; cadit; errat; hebet; nunc huc, nunc affluit illuc:
Spes, pudor, ingenium, mens vaga, cecus amor.
Cum duce quando sedet, si transit Pirrus, et illa
Incumbit lateri, languida visa, ducis.
Inter verba frequens Pirri pars nominis heret:
Altera sepe subit, altera sepe cadit.
Nocte vigil, si quando tamen sit victa sopore,
Sompniat, et "Pir! Pir!" garrula lingua sonat.
Parte thori vacua, Decio sine, letior illa;
50 Sic, cum sola iacet, sic sibi verba iacit:
"Heu mihi! nec morior et sum mortua vivo;
Vivo, sed ut peream, Pirre, perire facis."
Sic subit assidue sermo; suspiria ducit;
Ingemit, et venis saucia vulnus alit.
Mens tandem melior egre sibi contulit artem;
Invenit ars aditum quo gradiatur amor.
Una ministrarum fidissima ferre iubetur
Pirro que Decium verba latere decet.
Vadit et explorat animum blandeque profatur
60 Nuntia consilium calliditatis habens:
"Vive, vale, Pirre; te Lidia sepe salutat;

Envious reader, do not be a serpent; suppress the murmur of your lips.
  Honor overflows and is dissipated by evil words. 20
Envious reader, if you know it not, reason is not the property of one man;
  One and another possess it as their endeavors provide.
Apollo enriches himself with an adornment of feathers
  And wishes that the phoenix may live a long life.
The parrot envies them less, more powerful only in this,
  That he sings with his voice adjusted to human speech.
If assiduous study placed Homer at the forefront of the Greeks
  And he admitted no other as his equal,
To him replies the equal muse of our Virgil,
  Not lesser in art nor inferior in argument. 30
Pyrrhus was a gentleman, Decius a duke, and Lydia his wife.
  The first was faithful to the Duke, he earnest, she frivolous.
What good is earnestness? What can faithful love accomplish?
  She snatches faith with wiliness and earnestness with art.
With cunning, wiles, and stratagems she raves, lures, and plots.
  A woman turns to poison to kill her husband.
The fury wages sharper, besets the woman,
  Is headlong and impatient of delay.
When illicit designs attract her, they outstrip the licit.
  And when shame is banished, villainy is near at hand. 40
She stops, faints, wanders, moons; now she rushes here, now there.
  Hope, shame, character become confusion and blind love.
When she sits with the Duke, if Pyrrhus passes by,
  She appears to be faint and leans on the Duke.
Among her words part of Pyrrhus' name frequently clings;
  One part frequently sounds, and the other frequently drops.
Wakeful at night, but if now and again overcome by sleep
  She dozes, her talkative tongue says, "Pyr! Pyr!"
With half the couch vacant and Decius absent she is happier.
  Thus, when lying alone, she talks to herself: 50
"Alas, I do not die, but am dead to the living.
  I live, Pyrrhus, but you cause me to die."
Thus she speaks repeatedly; she breathes, sighs,
  Groans, and, hurt to the quick, nurses her wound.
But at last her mind brought art to bear on its illness;
  Art found an access by which love could enter.
The most faithful of her servants is ordered to bear
  To Pyrrhus words which were best concealed from Decius.
The messenger goes and explores his mind and speaks
  Flatteringly with the knowledge of cunning: 60
"Greetings and salutations, Pyrrhus; Lydia greets you as ever,

Qua, si vis, poteris sepe salute frui.
Illa quidem pro te moritur, palletque rubetque,
Et dolor hic animi querit amantis opem.
In te suspirat, in te gemit, et malesana
Languet, nec quisquam vellet ut illa pati.
Luce vagam, sompno stupidam, cum coniuge fictam,
Hanc necat, hanc lacerat, hanc tuus urit amor."
Exanimant Pirrum preludia vocis;
70 Verba stupor resecat, corque tremore micat;
Et stupet, et dubitat, et mens a mente vagatur;
Huc, illuc animum fertque refertque suum:
"Nuntia, me ludis forsan, sed ne male ludas,"
Pirrus ait, "ludus sit procul iste tuus!
Non Decii coniux, Decius mihi mente vagatur;
Hunc amo, neque amem quod sibi turpe putet.
Lusca, precor, ludus absit quem Lidia poscit!
Culpatur ludens si male ludus eat.
Ut Pirrus fidus, sic est sibi Lidia fida."
80 Est modo vel facilis vel modo nulla fides:
Dux amat hanc, non illa ducem; male ducitur ille;
Quo vult, quo non vult, Lidia ducit eum.
Mel sibi propinat verbis rebusque venenum,
Que fido lateri vipera nexa iacet.
Dux, vigila! vigilare decet ne mordeat illa,
Que gravius reliquis vipera virus agit;
Et si dux vigilet, vigilantem lambere novit;
Ludere dissimulans ledere cauda solet.
Ne se conservet, ne sit sibi commodus ipse,
90 A se feminea fraude recedit homo.
"Nuntia, dic domine, si qua ratione potitur,
Non mihi sed fame consulat egra sue!"
Dixit et ingemuit, et eo sermone resistit
Quem solet in media flectere voce dolor.
Lusca redit, secum loquitur: "Pater Hercule, non est
Iste furor qui sit in muliere furor.
Femina fit demens, solaque cupidine fortis
Audet et aggreditur, temptat agitque nefas.
Hec furit, hec gannit, hec gestit versa lepore;
100 Subtus agit leporem, dum salit ipse pudor.
O faciles mores! Uni non sufficit unus;
Isti nec Decius nec puto posse decem.
Omnes sunt tales, en Messalina veretur?
Nulla timet, nulla denegat, immo petit.

A greeting which, if you wish, you may often enjoy.
Indeed, she dies for you, she blanches and blushes,
And the anguish of her spirit seeks the help of a lover.
For you she sighs, for you she moans, and ailing
She languishes; nor would anyone wish to suffer as she does.
Distracted in daytime, dazed at night, dissembling with her husband,
Her love for you burns her, lacerates her, kills her."
Pyrrhus is stunned by the drift of her opening words;
A stupor cuts off his speech and his heart trembles with fear. **70**
He is dazed and incredulous and his mind is adrift;
He casts his mind hither and thither:
"Messenger, you make sport of me perhaps, but it is ill sport,"
Pyrrhus said; "Such sport as this is far from my mind.
It is not Decius' wife but Decius himself who misleads me.
I am devoted to him, nor will I love what he deems a disgrace.
Lusca, I pray you, let that sport never be, which Lydia demands.
The player is guilty if the game is dishonest.
As Pyrrhus is faithful, so is Lydia faithful to herself."
This is an easy fidelity or no fidelity at all. **80**
The Duke loves her, not she the Duke; he is led astray.
Lydia leads him, willy-nilly, hither and yon.
She offers honeyed words but poisonous deeds,
Who lies by his faithful side like a viper.
Duke, be vigilant! It behooves you to be vigilant lest she bite,
The viper that poisons worse than others.
But if the Duke is vigilant, she knows how to tame the vigil;
Pretending to play, the tail is accustomed to sting.
Unless he saves himself and serves his own interests,
A man surrenders to feminine wiles. **90**
"Messenger, tell your mistress, if she is in command of her senses,
That in her illness she consult not me, but her honor!"
He spoke and sighed and resisted with words
Which trouble broke in mid-speech.
Lusca returns and says to herself, "Good Lord, this is not
A fury as furious as in the woman.
The woman is mad; made strong by love alone
She dares and ventures, attempts and carries out a crime.
She raves, she yelps, she is hot on the trail of the hare;
She pursues the hare while shame itself departs. **100**
O easy morals! One man is not enough for one woman;
For this woman, I think, neither Decius nor ten men would suffice.
They are all this way; does Messalina know shame?
None hesitates, none refuses, rather they offer themselves.

Non habet una modum, nec in omnibus una modesta;
Illud quando movet est modus absque modo.
Turpis, formosa, trux, mitis, dives, egena,
Sulcat, arat, vellit, quassat, aduncat, hiat.
Parva puella suos preludens sincopat annos;
110 Immemor etatis fervida fervet anus.
Pruritum scit queque suum sudatque lacuna
Omnibus; ha! pudor est scire pudoris opus.
Miror et est mirum: quod habet non curat habere
Femina; cui res est maxima, parva placet.
Hec grosso graciles preponit, et, o pudor! illa
Usa diu longo captat habere brevem.
Lidia sic Decio didicit servire parata,
Ut probet arte viri quemlibet esse virum.
Femina vile forum de se facit; haud pudet ullam;
120 Omnibus est una Lidia, nulla tamen.
Aula ducis larga est; quia non pudet, accipit omnes;
Ianitor invitat, fit vis, porta patet.
Unum post alium, quod adest, de more, vicissim;
Malleus incude terque quaterque sonat;
Sustinet hos et adhuc aperit fabrilia quassans.
Invitat Pirrum ut premat ille femur.
Hec rogat, ille negat; tamen hec quod hic invidet optat,
Sollicitatque virum femina falsa viro.
Quid nunc coniugium, quid nunc sponsalia iura,
130 Quid confert socii gratia lege thori?
Nusquam Penelope, nusquam Lucretia dudum;
Utraque neutra quelibet esse potest.
A simili subit omne malum, repetique videtur
Illicita Thaydis altera lege Thays.
Parva fides hodie, minor est inde in muliere:
Omnes si muneres, nulla Sabina manet.
Sola viro fida frons est; si cetera queris,
Invenies zephyro blanda venena suo.
Omnia sunt nota Lusce que Lidia novit;
140 Femina feminei scit bene queque doli.
Sed mihi quod prodest levitas lascivia confert:
Non tam cara forem si sibi casta foret.
Si gravis esset hera, mihi quid gravitate lucrarer?
Est levis, illius sum levitate potens.
Parca quidem gravis est, quia nil frons nuda veretur;
At lasciva viri prodiga spargit opes.
Lidia si ludit que cura? quid inde? quid ad te?

Not one is moderate, nor is there a single modest woman among them;
When she is moved by this thing, she behaves without measure.
Ugly, beautiful, fierce, gentle, rich, poor,
She furrows, ploughs, uproots, breaks, bends, opens.
A young girl shortens her years with premature play,
The passionate old woman burns unmindful of her age. 110
Each knows her own itch and all sweat with desire.
Shame? Ha! Shame is to test the works of shame.
I am astounded and it is a wonder indeed; what she has she disdains.
The woman who has the greatest thing desires the smallest.
She prefers the small to the large and, oh fie,
Long accustomed to the tall, she longs to have the short.
Thus Lydia has learned to serve Decius so willingly
That she knows by her knowledge of man the nature of any man.
A woman makes a cheap market of herself; none knows shame;
Everyone has a Lydia, but, having her, has none. 120
The Duke's hall is large; since she has no shame, she receives all;
The doorkeeper beckons, a way is made, the doors are flung open.
By custom whoever is there is admitted, one after the other in turn.
The knocker falls and sounds three and four times;
The door sustains these blows and, shaking the knocker, opens again.
She invites Pyrrhus to press her thighs.
She solicits, he refuses; but she wishes what he spurns
And the woman, false to her man, desires a man.
What does marriage mean now, what mean the conjugal vows,
What means the law of the nuptial couch? 130
Penelope is gone and Lucretia long departed;
Neither could be either now.
With such a woman all evil begins, by established law
One libertine Thais follows another.
There is little faith today and therefore less in a woman;
If you count them all, not a single Sabine remains.
Only their faces are true to a husband; if you search beyond,
You will find the poison in their gentleness.
All things are known to Lusca which Lydia knows;
Every woman is well acquainted with feminine wiles. 140
But her wanton frivolity profits me;
I would not be so dear to her, if she were chaste herself.
If my mistress were earnest, what gain would I have from her earnestness?
She is frivolous and I am made powerful by her frivolity.
An earnest woman is stingy, for an open countenance has nothing to hide,
But a wanton woman is prodigal with her husband's wealth.
What does it matter if Lydia sports? What then? What concern of yours?

Lusca, tace; scelus hoc quod cupit esse bonum est.
Vir favet uxori, tibi quid si Lidia ludit?
150 Quid tibi si Decius desidiosus adest?
Et timet et dubitat, quia sum sibi conscia, crimen;
Fida licet taceam me putat ipsa loqui.
Me vocat et mecum loquitur luditque loquendo:
Sum reliquis ludo carior inde suo.
Velle meum faciunt famule, possumque iubere.
Omnia sunt Lusce, Luscaque iure vocor.
A simili mihi nomen adest omenque figurat,
Quod prestat stellis previa luna iubar.
Descripsit in me nuper que Lidia novit,
160 Nescio que memorans, sed puto signa poli.
'Lusca, quidem nescis causam cur Lusca voceris;
Ut reor, a luna nomen et omen habes.
Quinta fuit, fateor, subducens cornua matris,
Cum redit in lucem parturientis onus.
Esse vagam tua te tibi constellatio prebet:
Hinc pernox vigilas, mobilitate vigil.
Nocte placet quod agis; tibi lux est emula, Lusca.
Constat servitio nominis umbra sui.
Claudicat artis opus in te trutinumque, trocheo
170 Flexa pedem nervo sillaba longa brevem.
Et tamen ampla fores facie vultuque rotunda,
Sed pudor est oculis, nec minus alter adest.'
Discite, pulchra lupanaris haud femina nunc est,
Et tamen ad ludum, discite, Lusca valet."
His incedit ovans dictis dominamque revisit,
Expediens blandis singula verba iocis:
"Lidia, perdidimus quia nil maris edit harena;
Perdidimus sterili semina lapsa solo.
Quod cupis, ille negat; quod vis, non vult; vocat illud
180 Illicitum sibi quod non tibi velle licet.
Obstat amor domini, domine ne temptet amorem;
Pretendit fedus federe fidus amor.
Audes, ille timet; properas, sed et ille moratur;
Quod fingis tibi fas est sibi velle nefas."
Illa diu cunctata loqui, tristisque repulsa
Heret et interius saucia sepe gemit.
Et rubor et pallor vultum subit, inficit ora:
Alterat alterius signa colore color.

Lusca, be silent. This crime which she desires is good.
The husband abets the wife, why should you care if Lydia sports?
What do you care if Decius stands idly by? 150
She fears her crime and hesitates because I am an accomplice.
Even though I am faithful and silent, she thinks that I speak.
She calls me and speaks to me and deceives as she speaks.
I am dearer to her than others because of her game.
Her servants do my bidding and I can command.
All things are at Lusca's disposal, and I am rightfully called Lusca,*
My name is appropriate and describes my nature,
A light which is like the moon before the stars.
Lydia told me once what she knows of me,
Recalling I know not what, but I think the signs of the heavens: 160
'Lusca, indeed you know not the reason you are called Lusca;
You have, as I think, the name and the nature of the moon.
It was the fifth moon, I say, when, relieving your mother's womb,
The burden of birth saw the light of day.
Your constellation destines you to be unstable;
Therefore you remain awake at night, alert to changefulness.
You prefer to act at night; the light is jealous of you, Lusca,
And its shadow destines you to be a servant.
The work of nature limps in you, and the balance, a long
Syllable altered into a short foot in a vigorous trochee. 170
And still you would be of ample countenance and with a full face,
But there is modesty in your eyes, not less because you have but one.'
Know that she is now hardly a beauty of the brothel,
But be certain that Lusca knows the game!"
Saying this she proceeded joyfully and sought out her mistress,
Delivering her words with pleasant wit:
"Lydia, we have lost because the sand of the sea does not bear fruit;
We have lost the seeds sown on sterile soil.
What you desire, he refuses; what you wish, he does not; he claims
That what seems licit to you is illicit to him. 180
Love of his lord prevents him from attempting the love of his mistress.
Faithful love blocks faith with faith.
You dare, he fears; you hasten, but he is dilatory.
What you find right for yourself he finds wrong for him."
Pausing long to speak, grieved at being repulsed
She hesitates and, afflicted in her heart, she sighs repeatedly.
And blush and pallor come to her cheeks and infuse her countenance;
One color alters the appearance of its alternate with color.

* *Lusca:* one-eyed; *lux:* light.

Qui redit insidians rubor est accessus amoris;
190 Obiecti pallor signa pudoris habet.
Invia lascivis vibratur flamma medullis;
Ossa quatit, nervos concutit, ora premit.
Si cupit affari, cadit et sua lingua resistit,
Insidiansque demit emula verba pudor.
Nescia quid faciat, in Pirro tota vagatur;
Motibus his amens, languida fertur amans.
Egra tamen tacite subit indignatio vocis,
Et tandem questu quod fateatur habet:
"Cedamus, Lusca, dum nos urtica perurit;
200 Ecce tumet tenero lesa rubore cutis.
Cedamus, viole sordent et lilia languent;
Plus rosa vilescit que pede trita iacet.
Cedamus, nisa forsan Mopso laqueatur;
Fedari scorto non pudet, immo iuvat.
Non secus orbe novo rutilantia rura peragrans,
Qui nescit flores feda ligustra legit.
Hec est causa, patet: trepidas Deciumque vereris,
Et te, Pirre, premit non amor, immo timor."
Utque notat nomen Pirri palletque rubetque;
210 Sic quo tendit amans insidiatur Amor.
Labitur, et lapse blandus dolor impedit ora,
Et quod mente parat languida voce parit.
Passio nulla tamen potuit sopire venenum,
Vulnere quin manet quo sit amantis iter.
Ut rediit sibi mens, obliquat lumina Lusce,
Et sibi consilii perdita querit opem:
"Scire volo te, Lusca, quidem dum singula lustro,
Preter te mihi me reddere nemo potest.
Consilio solam committo me tibi soli;
220 In te stat vite spesque salusque mee.
Ergo precor subeas et adhuc cum milite fare.
Quid facit in silice stilla rotata semel?
Omen inest horis; hec est felicior illa:
Hoc illo melius tempore tempus abit.
Sit color in verbis, blando sit risus in ore,
Sic sta, sic loquere, sic tua verba loca.
Omnia promitte, promissis multa parantur:
Alludit lucris gratius omnis amor."
Digreditur Lusca: tot murmura Lidia fingit
230 Auribus, et tacitis instruit acta dolis.
Illa quidem verbis et rebus subdola, risu

The blush marks the access of love which returns to prey;
Pallor denotes the sign of struggling modesty. 190
A wanton and unquenchable flame rages in her marrow;
It attacks her bones, inflames her nerves, and overcomes her face.
If she wishes to speak, her tongue is paralyzed and refuses,
Lurking modesty cuts off the jealous words.
Not knowing what to do, she is all absorbed by Pyrrhus;
Mad with these feelings, her passion makes her faint.
But the angry indignation of speech silently rises
And she finally gives expression to her complaints:
"Very well, Lusca, since the nettle stings us; so be it.
Look how the injured skin swells with a light red. 200
Very well, the violets wilt and the lilies fade;
The rose is more despised which is trodden under foot.
Very well, he is no doubt enticed by some grasping Mopsum;
He is not ashamed to be defiled by a strumpet; rather it pleases him.
Such is the man wandering through fields gleaming with the new sun,
Who ignores the flowers and picks poor privets.
This is the cause, it is clear: you tremble and fear Decius;
Not love, Pyrrhus, but rather fear moves you."
And as she mentions the name of Pyrrhus, she pales and blushes;
Thus where the lover inclines, love lies in wait. 210
She swoons and sweet pain impedes the speech of the swooned woman,
And what she thinks in her mind she pronounces with a feeble voice.
But no passion could quell her venom,
Which rather remains in the wound by which the lover is admitted.
When she came to herself, she directed her eyes to Lusca,
And at a loss for counsel, seeks help for herself:
"Having considered at length, Lusca, I wish you to know,
That no one can restore me to myself but you.
I entrust myself alone to your sole counsel;
In you are the hope and salvation of my life. 220
Therefore, I beg you, return and speak to the knight again.
What does a drop rolling once on a stone accomplish?
Hours are propitious; one is luckier than the other.
This time will turn out better than the other time.
Let your words be vivid and let there be a pleasant smile on your face,
Stand thus, speak thus, and turn your words thus.
Promise everything, many things are procured with promises;
All love is attracted more willingly by money."
Lusca departs; Lydia whispers murmurs
To the breezes and devises deeds with secret ruses. 230
Now Lusca, crafty in word and act, with a smile,

Preveniens iuvenem, talia voce refert:
"Lidia suspirat et te suspiria produnt,
Pirre, notis, aperit lumina cecus amor;
Corporis enervat vires animumque fatigat;
Passio debilitat corpora, corda dolor.
Pallet ebur vultus, marcet decor ille genarum;
Nec flores rubet, nec rosa flore nitet.
Pirre, mihi miles non est qui magna veretur;
240 Fortior est armis quem suus aptat amor.
Pirre, potes, si vis, opibus donisque beari,
Et dare militie facta superba tue.
Hic tamen in paribus amor est, parilisque vagatur:
Pirrus ut Ypolitus, Lidia Phedra manet;
Tuque dolos animi veteres stimulosque noverce
Nosse potes, Pirre, queve cavere decet.
Non sepe Trivie virtus ulciscitur actum
Illicitum; semel est vix redivivus homo:
Femina multa potest, et scit mala multa movere:
250 Exemplo simili quod verearis habes."
Pirrus ut Ypoliti casum letumque retractat,
Multa movens imo pectore, tristis ait:
"Vel dux est deses, fateor, vel Lidia demens.
Debilitate viri femina fortis adest.
Si sedet hoc animo quod poscit Lidia, Lusca,
Dic mihi qua poterit fallere fraude virum."
"Quam miranda moves! mentem gerit illa mariti,
Quaque valet duci scit levitate ducis."
"Experiar si vera manent que, Lusca, fateris,"
260 Pirrus ait. "Si dux sit sibi nullus homo,
Augmentum poscat Pirri quod poscit amorem,
His tribus experiar." Et docet illa tria:
"Dux amat accipitrem, nec quid sibi carius illo;
Alludit celebris hac ave cura ducis.
Hanc volo quod perimat; hanc si non vindicet illa,
Ne credat leviter fallere posse virum.
Et si quinque pilos barbe de vellere vellat,
Quem trahit his precibus citius illa trahet.
Insuper excutiat quem vult de dentibus unum.
270 Si facit hec, faciet digna favore favor."
Lusca redit, properat, currit, queriturque morari;
Quod volat in votis tardat, anhela mora.
"Iamque habebit, habet mea Lidia, iamque iocatur.
Lusca labore suo iam sibi ponit onus."

Approaching the youth speaks thus:
"Lydia sighs and her sighs speak of you,
Pyrrhus, with clear signs; blind love opens her eyes;
Love weakens the strength of her body and tires her spirit;
Passion enfeebles her body and pains her heart.
The ivory of her countenance pales, the beauty of her cheeks withers;
The flower does not blush like a flower, nor the rose glow like a flower.
Pyrrhus, he who fears great enterprises is not a warrior;
He is stronger in arms whose love disposes over him. **240**
Pyrrhus, you can, if you wish, be blessed with riches and gifts
And give proud proofs of your valor.
This love has parallels and holds a similar course:
Pyrrhus is Hippolytus, Lydia is Phaedra.
You can remember the old artifices and the torments
Of the stepmother, Pyrrhus, and the things it is proper to avoid.
Infrequently does the virtue of Diana avenge illicit
Deeds. A man cannot be revived even once.
A woman is capable of much and can effect many misfortunes;
By this token you have much to fear." **250**
Pyrrhus turns over in his mind the fate and death of Hippolytus.
Considering many aspects deep in his heart, he spoke sadly:
"Either the Duke is foolish, I say, or Lydia mad.
A strong wife is joined to her husband's debility.
If Lydia has firmly in mind what she asks, Lusca,
Tell me with what trick she will be able to deceive her husband."
"What curious questions you ask! She knows the mind of her husband,
And she knows the ease with which the Duke can be led."
"I will test whether what you say, Lusca, is true,"
Pyrrhus said. "If the Duke is not the man to fend for himself, **260**
Let her demand help from Pyrrhus, since she demands love.
I will use these three tests." And he informs her of the three:
"The Duke loves a falcon, nor has he anything dearer to him than this,
And the care of a great duke is devoted to the bird.
I want her to destroy it; if she cannot kill the bird,
I doubt that she will be able to trick her husband easily.
And if she plucks five hairs from the growth of his beard,
She will attract more quickly whom she attracts with these prayers.
In addition let her pull out one tooth of her choosing.
If she does these things, her favor will be deserving of favor." **270**
Lusca returns, hastens, runs, and frets at the delay;
What, breathless, she wishes in her mind, the delay retards.
"She will have him, my Lydia has him already, the die is cast.
Lusca has now crowned her labors."

Quam procul ut vidit leto festiva labore
    Preveniens blanda voce salutat heram:
"Quando salutis opem refero tibi, Lidia, salve!
    En qua salveris digna salute salus!
Stat ratis in portu, siccatur carbasus unda!
280   Hac vice sub celis aura secunda fuit."
Militis ut mandata legens sibi rettulit, herens
    Tota sibi rapitur qua cupit illa rapi.
Mox vigor ut rediit, aperit sua lumina vultus;
    Inde sequens roseus purpurat ora nitor;
Fitque decens, ridet facies, lux ludit ocellis;
    Respondens votis, se sibi, leta, rapit:
"Quod poscit Pirrus, quod vult," ait illa, "probari,
    Sit! Licet hoc gravius quid posset esse mihi?
Accedat, properet, videat! Placet experiatur
290   Femina quod possit cum furor angit eam."
Mens ignara sue nescit presagia cladis,
    Nec videt in letis tristia posse sequi.
Dum Decius ludit, dum tractat seria letus,
    Dumque strepit variis motibus aula ducis,
Dumque sonant cithare, populus dum carminis odas,
    Dumque melos mulcent consona fila lyre,
Egreditur thalamo, sollempni veste superba,
    Lidia; qua sedit, emula captat avem:
"Hac ave peior," inquit, "cruciorque premorque
300   Nocte, die; pudor est tot mala posse pati.
Plus thalamo silva placet, plus placet herba cubili.
    Plus nemoris saltus quam mea cura duci.
Non impune feret, meriti ratione probabit
    An potior sibi sit Lidia quam sit avis."
Dixit et accipitris collum detorquet: anhelans
    Ille cadit. Pirrus obstupet, ausa notans.
Cetera turba silet; tamen hic succernitur illi;
    Alter in alterius lumine lumen agit.
Palliat illa dolum subridens, talibus usa:
310   "Dux, volo sis thalamis: ammodo linque nemus."
Hec memorans, teneris Decio subnectitur ulnis;
    More suo ludens, Lidia lambit eum.
Dum ludit lambitque virum, dum Lidia figit
    Oscula, sentitur barbara barba ducis.
Corruit in vultum, verborum conscia Lusce;
    Fit memor, et quinos succutit inde pilos.
Dux, velut excussus sompno, loca lesa pilorum

When, made gay by her happy labors, she saw her mistress
From a distance, approaching she greeted her pleasantly:
"I greet you, Lydia, as I bring a return of well-being,
And you are saluted in your well-being worthy of salvation.
The ship has reached port, the sails wet with waves are dry.
This time the breezes in the skies were favorable." 280
Restored to herself as she learns the embassy of the knight, mute,
She is utterly rapt in the way she wishes to be rapt.
Then as her vigor returned, she opened her eyes;
Immediately a rosy glow colors her face;
She is made comely, her face shines, light plays in her eyes;
She is beside herself and replies, joyful in the fulfillment of her wishes:
"What Pyrrhus demands, what he wishes," she said, "let it
Be tried! Though this be difficult, what does it matter to me?
Let him approach, let him hasten, let him see! It is well that he tests
What a woman can do when madness compels her." 290
The mind unwitting knows not the harbingers of its destruction,
Nor does it see that misfortunes can follow good fortune.
While Decius relaxes and happily discharges his business,
While the Duke's hall resounds with various activities,
While the lutes sound and the people chant songs,
While the harmonious strings of the lyre emit soothing melodies,
Proud Lydia emerges from her chamber in stately
Attire; she jealously snatches the bird where it sits:
"I am less than this bird," she said, "I suffer torment and pain
Both day and night; it is a shame to suffer so many woes. 300
He prefers the forest to my chamber and the fields to my bed.
The Duke is more concerned with glades and woods than with me.
He will not carry his falcon with impunity, he will learn by a test
Whether Lydia has more power over him than the bird."
She spoke and twisted the neck of the falcon; deprived of breath
It fell. Pyrrhus, seeing her daring, is dumbfounded.
The others are silent, but they glance at each other;
One turns his eyes to the eyes of another.
Laughing she disguises her trick, and spoke thus:
"Duke, I wish you to stay at home; henceforth abandon the forest." 310
Saying this she entwines Decius with her tender arms,
And with her accustomed game Lydia caresses him.
As she deludes and soothes her husband, as Lydia plants
Kisses, she feels the Duke's barbarous beard.
She falls on his face, mindful of the words of Lusca;
She remembers and plucks five hairs from it.
The Duke, as if shaken from slumber, touches the injured spot

Tractat et admota tractat agitque manu.
Fraudis ut astuto molimine Lidia fari
320 Incipit et solitis occupat acta dolis:
"Intempestivi fallunt tua tempora cani;
Hec tibi, dux, etas contigit ante diem;
Barba tibi iuveni fuerat que discolor ante,
His tribus ereptis, concolor ecce manet."
Dixit et emulcens animum sua brachia collo
Iactat, et illa premit que cupit ille premi.
His dux blanditiis et ficto fretus amore
Indulget factis coniugis atque silet.
Hic Pirrus risit; hic movit Lidia mentem;
330 Hic successit amor qua fuit ante timor.
Et quamvis taceat, loquitur mens intus et horret,
Respondetque malo, conqueriturque dolo.
Femina vipereis homini blandita venenis;
Est miranda suis ipsa Chimera modis:
Nunc leo, nunc serpens, nunc est capra; trux, vaga, feda:
Hoc monstro triplici fallere fraude triplex.
Artibus, ingenio, vitiis, fidens, rata, plena,
Corda trahit, mentem suscitat, ora ligat.
Mira quidem voluit lex, et natura vagatur:
340 Ecce lepus canis est et lupus ipse caper;
Musque bovem simulat et simia calva camelum;
Deridet lincis lumina talpa videns.
Aer, terra, mare mittit miranda; sed unum,
Femina, quo moveor, singula monstra movet.
Lidia, sollicitis quanquam sua guadia curis
Precipit, et differt sponte trahitque moram.
Nocte, die vigilans, magis et magis insidiatur
Qua Decii dentem demere fraude queat.
Tandem nacta locum pubem convenit herilem
350 Cui mos exstiterat pocula ferre duci:
"Vos, ait, insignes generoso germine scimus;
Sed quo nescitis degeneratis eo.
Vos reor hoc sensisse malum verumque pudorem;
Sed lateat, et vitio non strepat urna suo.
Que mihi porrigitis vos, putris anhelitus oris
Non modice fetens pocula feda facit.
Vos igitur moneo: mera cum pretenditis illi,
State retro: ciathis flectite colla procul,
Ne possit flatus Bromii turbare liquorem,
360 Et male comperto seviat ille malo."

Of the beard and rubs and rubs again with his hand.
With an astute effort at cunning Lydia began
To speak and proceeds with her usual guile: 320
"Untimely gray hairs belie your age,
This sign of age, Duke, has marked you before its time;
Now you have the beard of your youth, which was mottled before;
With these three hairs pulled out it is all of one color."
She spoke and soothing his feelings she throws her arms around
His neck, and she presses him in the way he likes to be pressed.
Trusting in these blandishments and her dissembled love
The Duke indulges the deeds of his wife and is silent.
Now Pyrrhus smiled and Lydia manipulated his heart.
Now love has followed where fear was lodged before. 330
And though she is silent, her mind is alive and bristles within
And responds with wickedness and strains with guile.
The woman caressed her husband with a viper's venom,
A chimera to be marveled at for her resources:
Now a lion, now a serpent, now a goat; fierce, crawling, and dirty;
A threefold monster, she deceives with threefold deceit.
Confident, guilty, and full of stratagems, cunning, and vices,
She governs his heart, excites his mind, and binds his attention.
A curious law and vagary of nature:
Here the hare is the hound and the wolf is the goat; 340
The mouse imitates the ox and the bald monkey the camel;
The farsighted mole laughs at the eyes of the lynx.
Air, earth, and sea produce wonders, but one thing
By which I am amazed, each woman is the cause of prodigies.
Lydia anticipates her joys, though beset by
Concern, and defers them hopefully and draws out the delay.
Vigilant night and day, she plots again and again
By what deception she can pull one of Decius's teeth.
Having finally found the opportunity, she met the youths of the house,
Whose custom it was to bear the Duke's cup at table: 350
"Distinguished youths," she said, "we know you to be of noble descent;
But to what extent you degrade it you know not.
I think you have perceived the trouble and feel genuine shame,
But let it be hidden and let the glass not sound its own shame.
The cups you hand to me, the stale breath of your mouths,
Which is utterly foul, makes distasteful.
I therefore admonish you, when you serve him with wine,
Stand back, turn your heads far from the cups
So that your breath will not disturb the Bacchic liquor,
Nor Decius be angered, ill pleased to learn of your flaw." 360

His monitis pubes in se putat esse quod audit;
Vel sit vel non sit, credulitate timet.
Discedunt, pudor ora premit, pallentque vicissim,
Vindicat umbra dolum quo trahit ipse dolus.
Alter in alterius lustrat quid sentiat ore,
Et cum nil reperit se reperire refert:
"Sta, tibi corrupto surrepunt feda palato;
Nil vitiat dentes, sed male lingua tumet."
Hic quatit illius fauces, tandemque profatur:
370 "Hic tibi dens niger est, nascitur inde malum."
Sufflat in os huius, sed nil male percipit ille,
Et tamen in partis dat sibi parte parem.
Sic erroris habet error discrimina, sicque
Incipit exemplo quisque timere suo.
Interea pubes Decio servire iubetur;
Forte Iovis aderat letior alma dies.
Fit strepitus; tectis luxu patet aula superbo;
Laudatur celebri mensa petita dape;
Ac servire mero consistit prona iuventus,
380 Quaque tenet ciathum torquet abinde caput.
Miratur quicunque videt, Deciumque tacere
Et tremit et tacite cetera turba notat.
Dux stupet his visis totiens totiensque videre;
Dissimulat visa que tamen ipse videt.
Denique (quam non vult quia que secreta latere)
Consulit uxorem visaque pandit ei.
Illa foris vultu pallorem suscitat egro,
Interius servans gaudia, tristis ait:
"Hactenus in thalamo quod novit Lidia sola,
390 Nunc agit os populi, nunc quatit aula malum.
Impedior, quid agam dubito, sileamve loquarve
Nescio." Dux inquit: "Lidia, pande mihi!"
"Pandam quo vultu, dicam qua voce pudorem
Ipsa tuum (fatear verius ipsa meum)?
Vis tamen ut pandam?" "Volo," dux ait. Illa, gementi
Incipit ore loqui, fallere nacta locum:
"Os tibi, dux, olidum fetet: sensitur et illud
Testatur pubes; pube tacente, loquor."
Miratur Decius; silet et gemit; egra vagatur
400 Vox sine voce, viam perdidit illa suam.
Sepe manu mulcet fauces, os pandit et halat;
Vix est dux de se credulus ore sibi:
"Quid mihi consilii dabit, aut quam Lidia mentem?

Instructed thus, the youths believe that they have what they are told.
Whether a thing is true or not, credulity causes fear.
They leave, and shame alternately colors and drains their faces;
The color proves the ruse in the way the ruse intends.
Each inspects the other's mouth to test what he smells,
And when he smells nothing, he says that he does:
"Stop, evil smells flow out from your rotten palate;
Your teeth are sound, but your tongue is horribly swollen."
One probes the jaws of the other and finally says:
"Here you have a black tooth, that is where the trouble begins." 370
He breathes in the face of the other, but he finds nothing wrong.
And still in distributing roles he gives himself an opposite number.
Thus error has the hazards of error, and thus
Each began to fear on his own account.
In the meantime the youths are ordered to serve Decius;
Lo, a propitious and festive Thursday was at hand.
Gaiety reigns; the hall abounds in the magnificence of the house;
The table loaded with fine dainties is praised;
And when it is time for the attentive youths to serve wine,
As they hold the cups, they turn their heads away. 380
All are amazed who look and see that Decius is silent,
And the remaining company trembles and takes silent note.
Having noticed, the Duke is astounded to see it again and again;
He pretends not to see, but sees nevertheless.
Finally, not wishing to hide the mystery from her,
He consults his wife and reveals to her what he has seen.
On the surface she dissembles pallor in her troubled face;
Repressing her joy within, she sadly spoke:
"What Lydia alone has known in her chamber until now,
Is now in the mouth of the people, now the hall echoes the fault. 390
I am speechless, I am in doubt what to do, whether to be silent or speak
I know not." The Duke said, "Lydia, speak."
"With what face should I reveal, with what voice should I myself speak
Your shame (should I not rather say my own)?
Do you insist that I speak?" "I do," said the Duke. She began
With a groan to speak, having found the means of deception:
"Oh Duke, your mouth has an evil smell; it is noticed and this
The youths prove; since the youths are silent, I will speak."
Decius is amazed; he is silent and sighs; feebly his voice wanders
Without strength, it loses its way. 400
Repeatedly he strokes his jaw, his mouth gapes, he breathes heavily;
The Duke will hardly believe it about his own mouth:
"What counsel and what solution will Lydia give me?

Ars que subveniet, que medicina mihi?"
"Si tibi dens noceat, vellatur," Lidia dixit;
"Si sit causa mali, cedet ab ore malum."
"Fortior accedat, non nostra vi cadet ille,"
Lusca refert, aderat his quia Lusca comes.
"Cuius opem petitis?" dux inquit. Lidia: "Pirri;
410 Et tibi fidus adest, et bene fortis erit."
Accitur Pirrus. Pandit que Lidia tractat
Lusca sibi, qua dux ducitur arte doli.
Succedunt thalamo quo luctans Lidia dentem
Succutit et miserum vexat agitque virum.
"Pirre, quid est? quid agis? En Lidia lassa laborat:
Subveniamus ei! Fac cito!" Lusca monet.
En, quantus dolor hunc urget, quantus labor illam!
Dux gemit et, forsan teste cruore, dolet.
Acrius insurgit multo conamine quassus;
420 Excutitur demum dens et ab ore salit.
Que rapuit rebus, sibi dat solatia verbis,
Ultra ne doleat, plus tamen ille dolet.
Pirrus abit, vix ferre valens sua gaudia risu;
Respondet votis, talia voce movens:
"Summe pater divum, qui pristina secula perdens,
Dans iterum mundum Deucalionis ope,
Omnia tu nosti forsan, sed Lidia sola
Nota tibi non est, nec sua facta patent.
Nec tantum fastu Niobe, nec carmine Circe,
430 Nec Media malis, nec levitate Lays,
Nec tantum potuit que traxit lumina ceco
A flegetonteis murmure mersa vadis."
Vix ea sic secum, thalamo cum tedia risus
Excutiens exiit Lusca levatque manus:
"De duce quid sentis?" inquit; "qua mente moveris?
Pirre, putasne? Potest Lidia, posse puta:
Dente caret Decius; quod plus est, se caret ipso;
Non es quem ludit Lidia, Lusca loquor.
Ut puto, iam veniet; an mas, an femina tu sis,
440 Pirre, probabit opus." Dixerat. Illa venit,
Tyndaridis vultum superans, formosior illa
Pro qua nox celebris est geminata Iovi.
Purpurat ora rubor velut inter lilia natus
Et gemino celi sidere visus adest.
Ludit lascivum labris libamen amoris:
Ludit et invitat gaudia a melle prope.

What art will avail and what medicine?"
"If a tooth offends you, let it be pulled," said Lydia;
"If this is the cause of the ill, let it come out of your mouth."
"Let someone stronger come; it will not yield to our strength,"
Says Lusca, for Lusca was present together with them.
"What help?" said the Duke. Lydia replied: "That of Pyrrhus;
Your faithful servant is here and will be strong enough." **410**
Pyrrhus is summoned. Lusca reveals to him what
Lydia plans, with what artifice the Duke is duped.
They enter the chamber, where Lydia struggles to pull the
Tooth and strains and torments her pitiful husband.
"Pyrrhus, what's this? What are you doing? Lydia is wearing herself out.
Let us help her! Now quickly!" Lusca urges.
As much pain as it causes him, so much labor it costs her.
The Duke groans and suffers, quite likely, from the gore in his mouth.
She attacks more vigorously and he is rocked by her efforts.
The tooth is yanked at last and pops out of the mouth. **420**
What she made off with in fact, she returns with comforting words,
Telling him to grieve no more, but he grieves nonetheless.
Pyrrhus departs, hardly containing his amusement and laughter;
He responds by swearing an oath and speaks thus:
"Great father of the gods, who destroyed the first ages
And created the world again with the aid of Deucalion,
Perhaps you know all, but Lydia alone
Is not known to you, nor are her deeds apparent to you.
Not the pride of Niobe, nor the song of Circe,
Nor the wickedness of Medea, nor the waywardness of Lais **430**
Could accomplish so much, nor Hecate who drew submerged flames
From the waves of Phlegeton with a dark murmur."
Hardly had he spoken when from the chamber bursting
With laughter Lusca emerged and threw up her hands:
"What do you think of the Duke?" she said. "How are you minded?
Are you convinced, Pyrrhus? Be assured that Lydia is capable.
Decius is without his tooth and, what is more, he is not himself.
It is not you whom Lydia mocks, I, Lusca, say so.
I think she is about to come now, and she will test, Pyrrhus,
Whether you are a man or a woman." She had spoken. Lydia came **440**
Outshining the face of Helen, more beautiful than she
For whom the illustrious night was doubled by Jove.
A blush colors her cheeks as if growing among lilies
And her eyes are like twin stars in the heavens.
On her lips plays the lascivious libation of love.
It plays and promises joys sweeter than honey.

Arte laborato crinis spatiatur in auro;
   Certat in alterius alteritate color.
Pectore compactum, gemmis rutilansque monile
450   Fulgurat et radiis alterat orbe diem.
Induitur clamidem roseam cui limbus adheret
   Aureus et gemmis insita gemma micat.
Accedit Pirrumque suis furatur ocellis,
   Et quo iam rapitur sidere rapta rapit.
Accedit, faciesque favens blanditur et orat:
   Quidquid inest facie federa velle facit.
Accedit, Pirrumque petit, pignusque salutis
   Elicit, atque manum comprimit illa manu;
Et progressa parum quo sit secretius illud,
460   Alterius thalami gaudia monstrat ei.
Posthabitis aliis, hec Pirrus: "Lidia, miror;
   Mira potes, fateor, singula mira facis.
Dum dubitant alie, tu, Lidia, nulla vereris;
   Tu, quod nulla potest, Lidia, sola potes."
"Hec sunt nulla quidem; nihil est quod, Pirre, notasti;
   Lidia que poterit, Pirre, videbis adhuc.
Nam scio posse ducem potius per inania duci,
   Ipse licet videat visa putare nihil.
Quod si me Veneris tecum deprendet in actu,
470   Non oculis credet; sic volo sicque veto."
"His tribus ergo nihil est actum, ni tribus addas
   Quartum quod superest, Lidia," Pirrus ait.
Que ratio esse queat et qua scelus arte paretur,
   Hec scribit tempus et docet illa locum.
Discedunt iterantque vices. Post basia Pirrus
   Hospitium visit, Lidia leta ducem.
Hic subitura locum; descendit questio quedam:
   Densne loco dentis crescere possit adhuc?
Lidia posse negat; sed verum Lusca fatetur
480   Dente novo vetulum sic iterasse vicem.
His ex premissis concludit Lidia: "Quanta
   Spes dabitur iuveni, si datur illa seni?"
Hac ratione suis dux dat solatia curis,
   Expectans votis tempora vana suis.
Talibus expletis mentitur Lidia morbum,
   Sponte sua morbi tedia ficta trahens.
Forte salit vena; palpat, sed phisicus heret:
   Mentitur medico sepe dolentis amor.
Morbus adest dubius et fallax passio, cum vult;

Her hair luxuriates artfully in finely wrought gold;
The color of one emulates the other.
On her breast a necklace gleaming with gems
Radiates beams and with its orb makes dark the light of day. 450
She is clothed in a rose-colored robe around which clings a border
Of gold, and one gem shines set with another.
She approaches and seizes Pyrrhus with her eyes
And seized by passion herself, she seizes the man seized by her eyes.
She approaches and her inviting face caresses and entreats;
Everything in her face makes a treaty to be wished for.
She approaches, and pleads with Pyrrhus, and asks for a pledge
Of happiness, and presses his hand with hers.
And advancing a little so that it may be more secret,
She indicates to him the joys of another chamber. 460
When all else was done, Phyrrhus said: "Lydia, I marvel;
You are capable of miracles, I say, and singular miracles.
When others hesitate, you, Lydia, fear nothing.
You, Lydia, can do alone what no one can do."
"This is nothing indeed; what you have seen, Pyrrhus, is nothing;
What Lydia can do, Pyrrhus, remains to be seen.
For I know that the Duke can be deluded more absurdly;
Though he himself sees, he will think what he sees is nothing.
If he catches me with you in the act of Venus,
He will not believe his eyes; thus I wish it and order it to be." 470
"Thus nothing is accomplished with three tests, unless you add
The fourth which remains, Lydia," said Pyrrhus.
By what means it may be and by what art the villainy done
She instructs and sets the time and assigns the place.
They take leave and renew the trials. After the kisses Pyrrhus
Returned to his house, and Lydia cheerfully to her Duke.
As she entered here, a certain question was raised:
Whether a tooth could grow again in place of the tooth?
Lydia denies it is possible, but Lusca claims it is true
That an old man had toothed anew with a new tooth. 480
From these premises Lydia concludes: "How much
Hope there is for a young man when there is hope for the old!"
By this reasoning the Duke takes comfort for his woes,
Wishfully indulging in vain hopes.
When these things had transpired, Lydia feigned illness,
Hopefully dragging out the invented discomforts of illness.
Her pulse throbs; it beats and the physician hesitates;
Love often deceives the physician of the stricken lover.
The illness is doubtful and the passion deceptive when it wishes.

490 Illa calet cum vult, friget, et egra iacet.
Sic ludens deludit Amor, sic Lidia fallit
Arte mali medicum, fraude doloque virum.
Hortus erat precinctus aquis, celeberrimus umbris
Arboreis, miti germine poma ferens.
Fons fluit in medio; ramis loca fontis opacat
Una pirus, vere gaudia veris habens.
Ut relevet febris estum vitiique calorem,
Huc tendit languens Lidia leta dolo.
Et dux et Pirrus egram comitantur euntem:
500 Dextra quod Pirro fit data leva duci.
Pone subit Lusca, tacito sibi garrula risu
Respondet, gratis fraude favente iocis.
Rictibus ora trahit Decioque ciconiat usu,
Naribus obductis cimbalat egra pedem.
Sistitur hic, faciesque loci succinnit amori!
Laudantur flores et placet unda sonans.
Visus velle notat, facies suspiria prodit.
Dux ait: "Ascende, collige, Pirre, pira."
Pirrus ad alta piri surrepit. Lusca profatur:
510 "Iam meliore piro succute, Pirre, pira."
Inque piro Pirrum succernens Lidia lustrat:
Arboris in fructu fructus amoris erat.
"Parce, precor," Pirrus clamat, "dux, parce pudorem;
Non honor est istis sollicitare locis.
Hic amor est preceps, hoc est non sana libido;
Lidia, dux, alibi posset anhela quati.
Sunt tibi, dux, thalami, sunt et loca talibus apta;
Fac, sed ne videam rusticitatis opus."
Miratur Decius, quod habent hec ludicra. Lusca
520 Subridens digitum comprimit ore suum.
"Arbor habet vitium," suspirans Lidia dixit,
"Alta quidem visum flectere sepe solent."
Dux inquit: "Descende cito, descende. Quid heres?"
"In terra poteris parcere," Pirrus ait.
Descendit Pirrus, et adhuc: "Dux, parce," precatur,
Et tanquam nolit parcere, "Parce," rogat.
Dux ait: "Experiar (totiens fantasmata fallunt!)
An moveat Pirrus ludicra sive pirus."
Scandit uterque simul at dux et Pirrus anhelans;
530 Hic repit ramis, cruribus ille subit.
Est in utroque labor, letus tamen ille laborat:
Dum quatit iste pirum, concutit ille femur.

She has fever and chills as she wishes and lies ill. 490
Thus deceptive love deceives, thus Lydia beguiles
With sham illness the doctor, her husband with cunning and fraud.
There was a garden surrounded with water, very pleasant with shady
Trees, giving root to fruit trees in its soft grass.
A spring flows in the middle; a pear tree shades the spring
With its branches, truly endowed with the joys of spring.
To relieve the heat of the fever and the burning of the illness,
Languishing Lydia, made glad by her guile, proceeds there.
The Duke and Pyrrhus accompany the invalid as she goes;
Her right hand is given to Pyrrhus, her left to the Duke. 500
Then Lusca follows, laughing silently to herself
As deception favors the pleasant game.
She grins and thumbs her nose at Decius.
With her face covered the sick woman sways on her feet.
They stop, and the appearance of the place is in tune with love.
The flowers are admirable and the sound of the stream pleasing.
Their eyes see the desire, their mouths emit sighs.
The Duke said: "Climb, Pyrrhus, and gather pears."
Pyrrhus climbs high in the tree and Lusca speaks:
"Shake pears from a better pear tree, Pyrrhus." 510
Lydia, looking up, sees Pyrrhus in the pear tree:
In the fruit of the tree was the fruit of love.
"Spare, I beg you," exclaims Pyrrhus, "oh Duke, spare decency;
It is not honorable to plough in this place.
This love is too forward, this is not rational desire;
Duke, you can thrust panting Lydia elsewhere.
You have rooms, Duke, and there are places appropriate for such things;
Please yourself, but not so that I must see this boorish display."
Decius is amazed and wonders what the spectacle is. Lusca
Bubbling with laughter holds her mouth with her hands. 520
"This tree has a defect," said Lydia sighing;
"Indeed, heights are often apt to distort vision."
The Duke said: "Descend quickly, descend. Why do you tarry?"
"On the ground, please, spare me," said Pyrrhus.
Pyrrhus climbs down, and again, "Duke, spare me," he begs,
And as if he were unwilling to spare him, "Spare me," he asks.
The Duke said: "I will test (illusions are so often false!),
Whether Pyrrhus causes the spectacle or the pear tree."
Both climb breathlessly at once, both the Duke and Pyrrhus;
The former crawls up branches, the latter up legs. 530
There is exertion in both, but the latter exertion is pleasant.
While one plies the pear tree, the other plies thighs.

Miratur Decius et vix sibi credulus heret.
    Plus stupet incertis certior illa videns.
Et notat et dubitat; tremit et gemit; insidiatur;
    Vix credens oculis desidet ipse suis.
"Aut sic est, aut fallor," ait, "aut visus inane
    Ventilat, aut vigilans sompnia visa puto.
Sic mihi, sic illi visum fuit, et mihi plus est.
540   Nescio si lusit, et, puto, ludus erat.
Tot mora dampna facit, faciet mihi iam mora dampna.
    Ut video, ludor, ludor at ipse videns."
Imputat hec ramis Decius frangitque quatitque:
    Sepe quidem Pirro sunt pira missa piro.
Labitur ergo citus et dux et Pirrus uterque
    Alterius studio fallere facta studens.
Dux ait: "Aut furor est aut hoc molimine fallor."
    Lidia: "Nec Pirrus me movet, immo pirus."
"Ut vidit, fateor, vidi, verumque putavi;
550   Sed tamen hic video certius esse nihil."
"Ut dixi tibi, dux, vitium fuit arboris; illa,
    Esse potest, alios ludificabit adhuc.
Cuius culpa manet, quia sic malus error obumbrat.
    Sit pirus excisa!" Dux iubet; icta, ruit.
Lusca tegit risum, Pirrus pira, Lidia ventrem:
    Infelix unus fit sibi fraude trium.

Decius is stunned and pauses, hardly believing his eyes.
   The more certain he is of the sight, the more he is stunned by doubt.
He sees and doubts; he trembles and groans; he peers;
   Hardly trusting his eyes he sinks in a stupor.
"Either it is so, or I err," he said, "either my eyes excite
   Fancies, or awake I think what I see is a dream.
The same thing appears to me as to him, but it means more to me.
   I do not know whether he deludes me, but it seemed delusion. **540**
Such hesitation is costly, and hesitation will cost me dear now.
   As I see, I am made sport of, and I am made sport of before my eyes."
Decius takes it out on the branches and tears and rends them;
   Again and again there fall pears from the pear tree on Pyrrhus.
Both the Duke and Pyrrhus dismount quickly,
   Each eagerly intent to trick the other.
The Duke said: "Either I'm mad or deceived by this feat."
   Lydia said: "It is not Pyrrhus but the pear tree that moves me."
"As he saw, I say, so saw I, and I thought it was true;
   But now I see more surely that it is nothing." **550**
"As I told you, Duke, it was the fault of the tree;
   Perhaps it will mislead others again.
Its guilt remains, since such an evil delusion casts its shadow,
   Let the pear tree be felled!" The Duke commands, and it falls.
Lusca hides her laughter, Pyrrhus his pears, Lydia her belly;
   One is made unhappy by the deception of three.

Adolphus' "The Blind Man and his Wife"

A small collection of fables by a certain Adolphus was found and printed by Polycarp Leyser, a professor of poetry at Helmstadt, in his *Historia Poetarum et Poematum Medii Aevi* (Halae Magdeb., 1721), pp. 2007–2036. Adolphus names himself at the end of the collection and in an acrostic at the beginning: "Adolfus me fecit." At the end he also dates his work in the year 1315. This is the extent of our information on Adolphus.

In a short preface he announces his intention of revealing the wiles of women as a warning to the reader:

> Augurio docti fraudes didici muliebres,
> De quarum fraude nemo cavere potest.

FABULA I

Caecus erat quidam, cui pulcra virago; reservans
Hanc puro pure, ne lu*d*at haec alias.
In curtis viridi resident hi cespite qu*a*dam
Luce; petit mulier robur adire pyri.
Vir favet, amplectens mox robur ubique lacertis;
Arbor adunca fuit, qua latuit juvenis.
Amplexatur eam, dans basia dulcia; terram
Incepit colere vomere cum proprio.
Audit vir strepitum, nam crebro carentia sensus
10 Unius, in reliquo, nosco, vigere solet.
"Heu miser!" clamat, "te laedit adulter ibidem;
Conqueror hoc illi, qui dedit esse mihi."
Tunc Deus omnipotens, qui condidit omnia verbo,
Qui sua membra probat vascula velut figulus,
Restituens aciem misero, tonat illico: "Fallax
Femina! Cur tanta fraude nocere cupis?
Heu mihi, quam fraude mulier mala varia sordet!
Integra jura thori non tenet illa viro.

[By learned example I have taught feminine wiles,
Whose trickery no one can elude.]

And again:

Sicut arena maris sunt sidera multa polorum:
Multa sic fraude femina prava viget.
[As numerous as the sands of the seas and the stars of the heavens
Are the deceits of a depraved woman.]

To this he curiously adds a petition to Christ to aid him in his crusade against women, and an appeal to the reader to overlook his poetic deficiencies, an indulgence of which Adolphus is sorely in need. The first fable is the pear tree story, and the others are similar. The fables were reprinted by Thomas Wright, *A Selection of Latin Stories from Manuscripts of the Thirteenth and Fourteenth Centuries* (London, 1842) and the first fable again in *Originals and Analogues* and *Sources and Analogues*. The text depends on Leyser's reading and is deficient metrically and otherwise. We have consequently taken liberties with it in a few cases (lines 2, 3, 20, 36). "Carentia" in line 9 remains a puzzle, though the sense is clear. The insertion of "ager" in line 20 leaves the verse metrically imperfect, but it is at least an improvement.

FABLE I

There was a certain blind man married to a beautiful girl, keeping
Her pure for his own pure self, lest she be fancy free.
On the green grass of their villa they sit one
Day; the wife seeks out a pear tree to climb.
Her husband gives leave, embracing the trunk round about with his arms.
The tree was forked and in the fork lurked a youth.
He embraces her, giving her sweet kisses; he began
To till the earth with his own plowshare.
The husband hears the noise; for, lacking indeed one sense,
In his remaining senses, I know, he was customarily strong. **10**
"Alas," he exclaims, "an adulterer defiles you up there;
I raise my plaints to the One who gave me being."
Then almighty God, who created all things with His word,
Who judges His creatures as the potter judges his vessels,
Returned sight to the miserable man, who at once cries out: "Deceitful
Woman! Why do you wish to afflict me with such deception?
Alas, how the evil woman is variously besmirched with deceptions!
She does not respect the laws of the marriage bed for her husband.

Alterius segetes semper putat uberiores;
20 Io confinis [ager] ubera magna tenet.
Alterius thalamo mala credit inesse sapinum,
Quamvis sit spado, nil valeatque thoro."
Percipit illa virum: vultu respondet alacri:
"Magna dedi medicis, non tibi cura fuit.
Ast, ubi lustra sua satis uda petebat Apollo,
Candida splendescens Cynthia luce mera,
Tunc sopor irrepsit mea languida corpora, quaedam
Astitit, insonuit auribus illa meis:
'Ludere cum juvene studeas in roboris alto,
30 Prisca viro dabitur lux cito, crede mihi.'
Quod feci; Dominus ideo tibi munera lucis
Contulit; idcirco munera redde mihi."
Addidit ille fidem mulieri, de prece cujus
Se sanum credit, mittit et omne nefas.
Esse solet nullum peius muliere venenum;
Excolit hanc, adamat vir, [arat] alter eam.

She always thinks that the fields of another are greener;
Lo, the neighboring field bears manifold fruits. 20
The wicked woman thinks there's a sturdy pine in the couch of another
Though he is a eunuch and is worth nothing in bed."
She hears her husband and replies with an eager expression:
"I spent much on the doctors and no cure was forthcoming.
But, when Phoebus was seeking his watery retreat
And bright Cynthia shone with pure light,
When sleep invaded my tired body, a certain woman
Appeared and her voice sounded in my ears:
'Endeavor to sport with a youth high in a tree
And your husband will quickly be given his former sight, believe me.' 30
I did so; therefore God gave you the gift of
Sight. And therefore repay me for this gift."
He put trust in the woman and at her behest
Believed himself cured and forgave all her wickedness.
No poison is ever worse than woman:
Her husband honors and loves her, but another plows her.

"A Rich Man and his Wife"

The so-called *Novellino* is the oldest collection of Italian *novelle* and seems to have been compiled around 1280. It contains a version of the pear tree story which is closer to Chaucer than to Boccaccio in that the deceived husband is blind and not simply deluded. As in the following German variant the husband's sight is restored by the Lord on Saint Peter's request. For some reason Chaucer

---

UN UOMO RICCO E LA SUA DONNA

A uno tempo era uno riccho homo, ed avea una molto bella donna per molglie; et questo homo le volea tutto il suo bene, ed erane molto geloso. Or avenne, chome piacque a Dio, che questo homo li venne uno male nelgli occhi, donde aciechò, sicchè non vedea lume. Ora avenía che questo homo no' si partía da la molglie; tuttavía la tenea sì che no' la lasciava partire da ssè, per tema ch'ella no lli facesse fallo. Ora avenne, che uno homo della contrada invaghío di questa donna, et non vedea chome le potesse favelare, però che 'l marito era tuttavía cho' lei; et questo homo moría di lei per senbianti ch'elli faciea a la donna; et la donna, vedendolo chosìe inamorato di lei, sìe ne le '(n)crebe, et disse per senbianti, "Tue vedi chome io posso, chè questi non si parte mai da me!" Sì che il buono homo non sapea che si fare nè che si dire, et parea che volese morire per senbianti; altro modo no'sapea trovare chome s'avenisse cholla donna; et la donna, vedendo i modi di questo gentile homo chome faciea, sì ne le '(n)crebe, et pensò di volere servire chostui. Ora fecie fare uno chanone di canna lungho, et puoselo a l'orecchie di questo gentile homo, et favelolli in questo modo, però che non volea che 'l marito l'odisse, et disse a questo gentile homo, "Di te m'incresce, e però oe pensato di servirti. Vattine nel giardino nostro, et sali in su 'n uno pero che v'àe molto belle pere, et aspettami là suso, ed io veròe là sùe a te." Il buono homo inchontanente n'andò nel giardino, et salíe in sul pero, ed aspettava la donna. Ora venne il tenpo che la donna era nel giardino, e volea andare a servire il buono homo, et il marito era tuttavía co' lei, et la donna disse, "E' m'è venuto volglia di quelle pere che sono in suè quello pero, che sono cosíe belle." E' marito disse, "Chiama chi ti ne cholgha." Et la donna disse, "Io me ne cholglierò pure io, ch'altri-

preferred a classical frame of reference and substituted King Pluto and Queen Proserpina for the Lord and Saint Peter (at least we take this to be Chaucer's departure). Both versions have their special ironies. In the Italian story and more particularly in the German story the Lord's wisdom and serenity administer a reproof to Saint Peter's eager and somewhat vindictive censorship. The tale thus involves a very pleasant anti-moral. On the other hand, Chaucer's use of a divine couple to supervise and debate the situation allows him to project his marriage cycle up to the level of the gods, who observe but also participate in the foibles of mankind. Both frameworks suggest the universality of the comedy and both are governed by the same tolerant good humor.

The text printed here is from Guido Biagi, ed., *Le novelle antiche dei codici panciatichiano-palatino 138 e laurenziano-gaddiano 193* (Florence, 1880), pp. 199–201.

A RICH MAN AND HIS WIFE

There was once a wealthy man and he had a very beautiful woman as his wife. And this man loved her with all his heart and was very jealous of her. Now it happened, as God ordained it, that this man contracted a malady in his eyes, from which he became blind so that he did not see the light of day. Now it came to pass that this man would not be separated from his wife; he kept her so that he did not allow her to leave him for fear that she would deceive him. Now it happened that a man in the neighborhood fell in love with this woman and did not see how he could speak to her since her husband was always with her. And this man expressed through gestures that he was dying for love of her. And the woman, seeing him so much in love with her, took pity on him and said by signs, "You see what position I am in since this man never leaves me." The good man did not know what to do or what to say and showed by his signs that he wanted to die. For he knew no way to come together with the woman. And the woman, seeing the gestures of this gentleman, took pity on him and determined to be at his disposal. Now she ordered that a long tube of reed be made and placed in the ear of this gentleman and talked to him in this way (since she did not want her husband to hear it) and said to this gentleman, "I take pity on you and have determined to be at your disposal. Go out into our garden and climb up into a pear tree, in which there are many beautiful pears, and wait for me up there and I will come up to you." The good man eagerly went out into the garden and went up into the pear tree and waited for the woman. Now the time came when the woman was in the garden and wanted to go and put herself at the man's disposal, but her husband was still with her and the woman said, "I have conceived a desire for those pears which are up in that pear tree and are so beautiful." And

menti no' mi ne gioverebe." Alotta si mosse la donna per andare in sul pero, et il marito si mosse e venne co' lei infino a piè del pero, et la donna andoe in sùe il pero; et il marito abraccia il pedale del pero, perchè non v' andasse persona dietro le'. Or avenne che la donna fue sùe pero cho' l'amico che lla aspettava, e istavano in grande solazzo, e il pero si menava tutto, sì che le pere chadevano in terra a dosso al marito. Onde disse il marito, "Che fai tue, donna, che no 'ne vieni? Tue fai cadere tante pere." Et la donna li rispuose, "Io volea delle pere d'uno ramo; non ne potea avere altrimenti." Ora volglio che sapiate che Domenedio et San Piero, vendendo questo fatto, disse San Piero a Domenedio, "No' vedi tue la beffa che quella donna fae al marito? Dè! fae che 'l marito vegha lume, sicchè elli vegha cioe che la molglie fae." Et Domenedio disse, "Io ti dicho, San Piero, che sì tosto chome elli vedrà lume, la donna averà trovata la chagione, cioè la schusa, e però volglio che vega lume, et vedrai quello ch' ella dirae." Ora vidde lume et guatò in sùe, et vidde quello che la donna faciea. Alora disse a la donna, "Che fate voi co' cotesto homo? Non è onore ned a voi ed a me, et non è lealtà di donna." Et la donna rispuose incontanente di subito, et disse, "S' io non avessi fatto chosíe con chostui, tue non n'averesti mai veduto lume." Alotta udendo il marito chosíe dire, istette contento. Et chosíe vedete chome le donne et le femine sono leali, et chome trovano tosto la schusa.

the husband said, "Call someone who will pick some for you." And the woman said, "I will pick some myself because I would not enjoy them otherwise." Then the woman went to climb the pear tree and the husband came with her to the foot of the pear tree and the woman went up into the pear tree. And the husband embraced the bottom of the pear tree so that no one would follow her up into it. Now it happened that the woman was up in the pear tree with her friend who was waiting for her, and they had great enjoyment; and the whole pear tree shook so that the pears fell down on the husband's back. For which reason the husband said, "What are you doing, woman, that you don't come down? You are making so many pears fall down." And the woman replied to him, "I wanted to get some pears from one branch and I couldn't get them any other way." Now I wish you to know that our Lord and Saint Peter having seen what had happened, Saint Peter said to our Lord, "Don't you see the trick that this woman is playing on her husband? Lord, make the husband see the light so that he can see what the woman is doing." And the Lord said, "I tell you, Saint Peter, that as soon as he sees the light the woman will have found a reason, that is an excuse, and therefore I wish him to see the light and you will see what she says." Now the husband saw the light and looked up and saw what the woman was doing. Then he said to the woman, "What are you doing with this man? It is neither honorable for you nor for me and it is not in accordance with a woman's fidelity." And the woman replied immediately and without hesitation and said, "If I had not done thus with him, you would never have seen the light." When the husband heard this, he was satisfied. And thus you see how faithful women are and how quickly they can find an excuse.

"About a Blind Man"

The following story is found in a Munich manuscript (Bayerische Staatsbibliothek, Cgm 713) from around 1460–1480 and has been assigned to the fifteenth century by the latest editor. As in the case of many such *Mären*, we have no further particulars.

The plot does not differ substantially from the *Novellino* version, but there are many differences in detail: the husband is blind from the outset; his jealousy is more extreme; the lover is less mortally impassioned; the communication with his lady is by letter and not through an ingenious hearing tube; and the pears

---

VON EINEM PLINTEN

[I]ch wil euch sagen, das ist war,
es sein mer dann zehen jar,
das ich hort sagen mer[e],
wie das einst were
ein plinter, der hett ein schöns weip;
die was im liep als sein leip.
Sie was hübsch und wol gestalt
und was darzu auch nit ser alt.
Fürwar wer sie hett gesehen,
10 der mußt mit mir die warheit jehen,
das sie was hübsch und wol gemut.
Nun forcht der selbige plint gut
also ser, das icht ein ander man
würd zu seinem weibe gan.
Er gedacht in seinem mut:
"Ich wil sie haben in guter hut,
das mir sie nimant nem,
und wil sie nemen in einem zem."
Zu nacht, als er zu pette ging,
20 ein eisen halfter er do fing
und sloß ir beide pein darein;
domit solt sie besorget sein.
Am morgen frue, do anprach der tag
(nun merket eben, was ich sag),

have become apples, which are brought along for the purpose and tossed down from a linden tree. But, most important, the intercession of the Lord and Saint Peter is greatly elaborated and expanded to occupy nearly half the tale. Saint Peter persists in his moral crusade until he is ironically slandered by the wife and chased away at knife's point by the indignant husband. He must take refuge with the Lord, who finally explains to his zealous companion the implications of the situation and declares his protection of the erring woman. The story thus deals as much with God's grace as with a woman's wiles. It has some of the warmth and charity found in the medieval miracles of the Virgin and would deserve a place of its own if the form and versification were more adroit.

The text is reprinted from Hanns Fischer, ed., *Die deutsche Märendichtung des 15. Jahrhunderts* (Munich, 1966), pp. 485–492. Fischer also prints (pp. 493–495) a low German version preserved in a Stockholm manuscript (Vu. 73) of the same period. It appears to be independent, but is fragmentary and even clumsier in form.

ABOUT A BLIND MAN

I will tell you, forsooth—
it has been more than ten years
since I heard the story told—
how there was once
a blind man, who had a beautiful wife;
she was as dear to him as his life.
She was pretty and shapely
and in addition not very old.
In truth, anyone who had seen her
would have to agree with me **10**
that she was lovely and charming.
Now this same good blind man
was very fearful that perhaps another man
would get at his wife.
He thought to himself:
"I will keep her closely guarded
so that no one will take her from me,
and will put her in fetters."
At night when he went to bed,
he took an iron halter **20**
and locked both her legs in it;
that was meant to take care of her.
Early in the morning when the sun rose
(now pay attention to what I say),

auß den panden er sie sloß.
Sein sorg die was gar groß,
und gedacht in seinem mute:
"Ach herr got, durch dein gute,
wie ich verlüre mein schönes weip,
30 das überwünt nimer mein leip."
Er sprach: "Frau, wir sullen gan.
nit lenger wil ich hie bestan
. . . .*
wan wir mugen uns began
hie nit so wol als anderswo."
Nun was ein schüler do,
der in der selben stat saß,
dem die frau von herzen holt was.
Das ward dem plinten kunt getan;
40 darumb mußt sie von dannen gan.
Der schüler ging, do er den plinten fant.
Der furt eben an seiner hant
sein minnigliches freuelein.
Nun gedacht im der schüler fein:
"Ach got, mocht ich[s] in meinem gemut
gewenden mit der frauen gut."
Er neiget sich zu ir und sprach:
"Mir ist leit fast dein ungemach."
Ein brieflein gab er ir in di hant,
50 domit tet er ir gar bekannt
seinen sin und auch seinen mut.
Das bedaucht di schönen frauen gar gut.
Do sie gelas das kleine brieflein,
sie sprach: "Ach liber meister mein,
ich sich dort einen paum stan;
wir sullen werlich darunter gan,
ob uns des obß mocht werden.
Mich gelust noch nie hie auf erden
keins dings nie also wol."
60 Er sprach: "Ich waiß nit, was ich sol
noch mit dir beginnen,
das ich es [z]war werd innen,
das es sei on alles gefere.
Mich bedunkt an deinem gepere,
du wolst an mir nit recht faren.

* The rhymes show that a line is missing from the manuscript.

he took her out of the bonds.
His worry was very great
and he thought to himself:
"Oh Lord God in Your goodness,
if I lost my beautiful wife,
I would never survive it." 30
He said: "Lady, we must go,
I wish to stay here no longer,
. . . .
for we can prosper
here less well than elsewhere."
Now there was a student at the time
who resided in the same town
and to whom the lady was devoted in her heart.
This was made known to the blind man
and therefore she was obliged to leave. 40
The student went to where he found the blind man.
He was leading by the hand
his lovely little wife.
Now the clever student thought to himself:
"Oh, Lord, if I could devise in my mind
how to make off with the good lady!"
He bowed to her and said:
"Your misfortune grieves me much."
He put a little letter in her hand,
in which he made very clear to her 50
his mind and his feelings.
This pleased the beautiful woman very much.
When she had read the little letter,
she said: "Oh, dear master mine,
I see a tree standing there;
indeed we should go under it
to see if we can get some fruit.
I never had a desire here on the earth
for anything as much as this."
He said: "I don't know 60
how I should go about
finding out from you
that there is no danger involved.
Your manner indicates to me
that you are not being honest with me.

Mag ich, ich wils bewaren.
Doch wil ich selbert dar mit dir,
ob des obs mocht werden mir,
das du so fast gelobet hast
70 und so gern darnach gast."
Sie gingen mit einander dar.
Des nam der schüler eben war,
wan er an das brieflein
hett geschriben den sin sein.
Der schüler in seiner kappen trug
schöne öpfel, der waren genug,
darmit er steigen began
auf ein linten oben hinan.
Die fraue furt den plinten dar,
80 do sie des schülers wart gewar,
das er steig auf die linten.
Sie sprach zu irem plinten:
"Nun wie sol ich es heben an,
das ich des obs müg gehan,
wan der paum ist so hoch?"
Der plint pald seinen stecken zoch
und slug aufhin an die este,
das ein apfel vil hernider veste,
den der schüler warf herab.
90 Er meinet, er slüg in mit dem stabe ab.
Die fraue den apfel balde fant,
sie gab in dem plinten in die hant.
Er sneit entzwei den apfel
und pot der frauen das ein teil.
Sie sprach: "Ich muß ir haben mee,
oder mir geschicht wirser dann wee."
Den stap er aber eins zucket,
an die est er do fluks drucket
und loset auch nach dem slag,
100 ob icht ein apfel fiel herab.
Sie sprach: "Es ist alles unmuß.
Ich gebe nicht ein haselnuß,
umb was du mir mochst abgesla[h]en,
du hettest dan ein lange gabeln.
Darumb saltu mich steigen lan
auf den paum oben hinan,
das ich fülle vol meinen sack.
Ich gewinn ir, so meinst ich mag."

If I can, I'll prevent it.
But I want to go there myself with you
to see if I can get some of the fruit
that you have praised so highly
and long for so eagerly." 70
They went there together.
The student observed this
because in the little letter
he had written his plan.
The student carried in his cloak
fine apples, of which there was a plenty,
and with which he began to climb
up onto a linden tree.
The lady led the blind man there.
When she perceived the student 80
and that he was climbing the linden tree,
she spoke to her blind husband:
"Now how should I go about
getting some fruit?
The tree is very tall."
The blind man quickly took his stick
and knocked the branches
so that an apple fell down hard,
which the student threw down.
He thought he was knocking it off with his stick. 90
The lady quickly found the apple
and handed it to the blind man.
He cut the apple in half
and gave one part to the lady.
She said: "I must have more of them,
or I will feel worse than awful."
He brandished the stick once more
and quickly knocked the branches
and listened after the blow to hear
whether perhaps an apple fell down. 100
She said: "It is all in vain.
I wouldn't give a hazelnut
for what you can knock down for me
unless you had a long hook.
Therefore you should let me climb
up into the tree
so that I can fill my sack.
I'll get as many as I can."

Er sprach: "Frau, so forcht ich mir,
110 das ein ander kum zu dir."
"Des saltu kein sorge han.
Du salt her zu dem paum gan
und mit den henden in greifen an.
So weistu, ob ein ander man
zu mir auf den paum mocht klimen.
Der solt auch wol gewinnen
lützel und wenig an der fert,
er gewünn dann doran streich hert."
Der plint gedacht: "Ja, du hast war,"
120 Und half ir auf den paumen dar.
Do sie auf den paumen kam,
do umbfing der plint den stam
und loset da vil eben.
Der schüler begund der frauen zustreben.
Mit irem schönen, stolzen leibe
wolt er nach luste kurzweil treibe.
Der plint rufen do began:
"Schüt den paumen fluks obenan,
das etswas falle herab."
130 Der schüler was ein rechter knab;
er begund sich mit der frauen rütteln
und die öpfel auß der kappen schütteln.
Er sprach, das were recht.
Unser herr und auch sein knecht
sant Peter gingen bede dafür.
Das erhoret der plint gehür.
Er sprach: "Wer get dapei?"
Wart, das er auch ein freunt sei.
Sand Peter sprach: "Herr meister, lug!
140 Sichstu nit das grosse ungefug,
wie dem plinten tut das weip?
Ich wolte gern, das sein leip
sehen solte den grossen mort."
Unser herrgot sprach: "Sie fünd wol ein antwort
danoch, ob es der man sech an."
"Herr, wie wer das aber getan?"
Sant Peter sprach: "Das höret ich gern."
Unser herr sprach: "Wiltu sein nit enpern,
so wil ich dich lassen sehen,
150 wie die fraue wirt jehen."
Den plinten er sehen ließ;

He said: "Lady, I'm afraid
that someone else will get to you." 110
"That shouldn't worry you.
You should come here to the tree
and put your arms around it
so that you will know if another man
climbs up the tree to me.
Furthermore he would get
very little from the venture,
unless it were hard blows."
The blind man thought: "Yes, you are right,"
And he helped her up the tree. 120
When she got up in the tree,
the blind man embraced the trunk
and listened very attentively.
The student began to strive for the lady.
With her proud and lovely body
he wanted to amuse himself according to his pleasure.
The blind man then began to shout:
"Shake the tree quickly up there
so that something falls down!"
The student was quite a fellow; 130
he began to shake with the lady
and shake the apples out of his cloak.
He said that was fine.
Our Lord and His servant
Saint Peter both went by.
The blind gentleman heard this;
he said: "Who is going by?"
He thought that he too was a lover.
Saint Peter said: "Lord, look!
Don't you see the great deviltry 140
the woman is practicing on the blind man?
I wish that he
could see the great crime."
Our Lord said: "She would probably find an answer
even if the man saw it."
"Lord, how could that be done?"
Saint Peter said: "I'd like to know how."
Our Lord said: "If you insist,
I'll let you see
what the woman will say." 150
He gave the blind man his sight

(der ward gar ein starker ries.)
Do er nun do über sich sach,
gern mügt ir horen, wie er sprach:
"Secht ir, frau hur, was habt ir
heut gerochen hie an mir?
Des müßt ir euer beider leben
hie umb die lieb geben."
Sand Peter sprach: "Herr meister, lug
160 und went disen ungefug,
laß desen mort nit gesche[hen]
und heiß disen plinten nit gesehen."
Die frau antworten began
auf dem paum obenan.
Sie sprach: "Lieber man mein,
diese lieb muß dir ein puß sein,
das du nimmer werdest plint.
Des half mir heut das himelisch kint
und auch darzu der schüler.
170 Der lernet mich dise mer,
das du wider hast dein augen.
Des saltu dir also taugen,
das du niderfallest auf dein knie,
und sag uns beiden gnade hie,
dem guten schüler und auch mir,
und pit got, das dein augen dir
pleiben, die du itzunt hast.
Ach du tor, wie lang du stast!"
Er vil nider auf seine knie
180 und sprach: "Frau, du lißt mich nie.
Du hast mir gutlichen getan;
des sol ich dich genißen lan
heut und zu allen stunden,
das du so eben hast funden
ein puß, das ich mein augen han.
Darumb saltu herab gan
und auch darzu der schüler;
dem sullen wir der mer
lonen hie an diser stat,
190 das er mir geholfen hat."
Die frau ging herab
und auch dazu der schön knab.
Der plint vil im zu füssen
und sprach mit worten süssen:

and a great fall was in store for him.
When now he looked up,
you may hear what he said:
"See now, Dame Whore, how you
today have taken vengeance on me!
For this you must both
give your lives for love."
Saint Peter said: "Lord, look,
and prevent this crime **160**
and keep this murder from taking place
and take this blind man's sight."
The woman began to answer
up in the tree.
She said: "My dear husband,
this love must be a cure for you
so that you will never be blind.
Today I was aided in this by Christ
and in addition by this student.
He taught me this cure **170**
so that you have your sight again.
You owe it to yourself
to fall down on your knees
and thank us both here,
the good student and also me,
and pray God that your sight
remains, that you now have.
Oh, you fool, how long you stand there!"
He fell down on his knees
and said: "Lady, you never abandoned me. **180**
You have treated me well;
I will reward you for it
today and always,
that you have found
a cure so that I have my sight.
Therefore you should come down
and the student too;
we should reward him
immediately for the fact
that he has helped me." **190**
The lady went down
and the handsome fellow too.
The blind man fell down at his feet
and said sweetly:

"Got in seinem reich
der dank euch gnedigleich.
Wir sullen in freuden leben
und sullen dem schüler geben
etswas umb sein arbeit."
200 Das was der frauen nit leit.
Zehen pfunt pfenning
die wug er also gering
und pot sie dem schüler dar.
Das nam sant Peter eben war.
Er sprach: "Herr, sol ich dem plinden sagen,
ob er das weip icht wolle slagen?"
"Ja, Peter, das sei erlaubet dir."
Zuhant ging er zu ir
und sprach: "Got grüß dich!
210 Es hat übel gemüet mich,
das du dem plinten hast getan;
das wil ich in wissen lan."
Sie sprach: "Lug, man, das ist der,
der nach mir ist geloffen her
und mir wolte gewendet han
die puß, die ich dir hab getan,
wan er sehe dich gern plint,
darumb das ich im hett zu willen gedint.
Ich sag dirs sicher, es ist war,
220 er treibs wol ein ganzes jar
mit mir an; das soltu rechen
und dein messer durch in stechen."
Der plint sein messer außzoch.
Sand Peter do fast floch
hin, do er seinen herren fant,
und klaget im die mer zuhant.
Er sprach: "Petre, du woltest anders nicht.
Vil manchem mer also geschicht,
der do saget böse mer.
230 Du warst aber also alber
und meinest nit, das dises weib
sich wol konte scheib,
das sie iren man betörte,
wie eben auch der man das hörte."
Er sprach: "Herr, und hett ich gwalt
und solt ich halt nimmer werden alt,
ich gerech mich an diser bösen haut,

"God in heaven
thank you graciously!
We shall live in joy
and give the student
something for his trouble."
The lady was not averse to this. 200
Ten pounds of money
he counted as little
and gave them to the student.
Saint Peter saw this.
He said: "Lord, shouldn't I tell the blind man
to beat the woman?"
"Yes, Peter, that is granted to you."
Immediately he went to her
and said: "God's greetings.
It has grieved me 210
what you have done to the blind man.
I am going to let him know."
She said: "Look, husband, this is the man
who ran after me here
and wanted to avert
the cure that I have performed for you
because he would like to have you blind
so that I could be at his disposal.
I tell you for a certainty, it is true.
He was at it for a whole year 220
with me; you should avenge it
and thrust your knife in him."
The blind man pulled his knife out.
Saint Peter then fled quickly
thence, to where he found his Lord,
and immediately complained of his treatment.
He said: "Peter, you insisted.
That's what happens to many people
who carry tales.
You were so foolish 230
that you didn't believe that this woman
knew enough
to fool her husband,
even though he knew all about it."
He said: "Lord, if I were able
and even if it cost my life,
I would avenge myself on this wicked witch

das sie dorft sprechen überlaut,
ich wer ir nachgestrichen.
240 Darzu so sprach sie: 'Stich in!'
Das laß ich faren, herre got,
und rich mich an ir durch dein gepot."
"Nein, Peter, ich wil dir sagen,
dem sünder sol man vil vertragen.
Weistu nicht, das ich mein leben
für den sünder hab gegeben.
Dorumb so wil ich keinen lon.
Ich wil sie in meinem schirm han.
Ee ich sie ließ in nöten,
250 ich ließ mich noch eins töten.
Wer do peichtet und bereuet
und darzu mir getrauet,
dem vergibe ich sein schuld
und laß in erwerben mein huld."
Also hot dise red ein ende.
Got sol uns sein gnade sende.

for her daring to say aloud
that I had pursued her.
In addition she said: 'Stab him!' **240**
But I'll let that go, Lord,
and avenge myself by Your command."
"No, Peter, I tell you,
one should forgive the sinner much.
Don't you know that I gave
my life for the sinner?
For this I set no price.
I want her in my protection.
Before I abandoned her to misfortune,
I would rather let myself be killed again. **250**
Whoever confesses and repents
and puts his faith in me,
I forgive him his sins
and allow him to win my grace."
Thus this story has an end.
May God be gracious to us.

Marie de France's Two Tales of "A Woman and Her Paramour"

In the epilogue to her book of fables, the authoress writes: "Marie ai num, si sui de France" ("I am called Marie, and I am from France"—that is, the Ile-de-France). This is almost all that we know for certain about Marie, the first poetess in the French language. We know that she lived and wrote in England in the last half of the twelfth century, that she was—judging from her works—a woman of good birth and education, that she wrote her *Fables* around 1170 to 1180, and that she also wrote the *Espurgatoire Saint Patriz* (*Saint Patrick's Purgatory*) and her collection of *Lais*. Her *Lais* are deservedly famous and have

---

DE MULIERE ET PROCO EIUS

D'un vilein cunte ki guaita
dedenz sun us, si espia.
Un altre hume vit sur sun lit,
od sa femme fist sun delit.
"A, las," fet il, "qu'ai jeo veü!"
Dunc l'a la femme respundu,
"Que veez vus, beals sire, amis?"
"Un altre hume; ceo m'est a vis,
sur mun lit te tint embraciee."
10 Ceo dist la femme curuciee,
"Bien sai," fet ele, "n'en dut mie,
que c'est vostre vieille folie;
tu vuels tenir mençunge a veire."
"Jel vi," fet il, "sil dei bien creire."
"Fols iés," fet ele, "se tu creiz
pur verité quan que tu veiz."
As mains le prent, od li l'en meine
a une cuve d'ewe pleine;
dedenz l'ewe le fist guarder.
20 Puis li cumence a demander
qu'il veit dedenz, e il li dit
que s'image meïsme vit.

often been translated into English; her *Fables,* often witty and delicate, deserve to be as well known. Marie tells us that her fables are translated from a version that "King Alfred" had put into English from "Greek and Latin." She probably did use an English translation of one of the medieval Latin (not Greek) versions of Aesop, and though King Alfred was not its author, she may well have thought he had written it, since Alfred's literary activities were still remembered in Marie's time and his name had become associated with didactic works of secular wisdom (such as the "Proverbs of Alfred"). Marie tells us too that she translated this work for a "Count William," but there were several Count Williams living at that time and no one knows which one she meant. Most of Marie's 102 fables are animal tales with appended "morals," but she also included tales of other sorts, such as the celebrated tale of the "Widow of Ephesus" and the two examples of the "wiles of women" included here. Our texts are taken from Karl Warnke, *Die Fabeln der Marie de France* (Halle, 1898), nos. 44–45. A more accessible recent selection of Marie's fables is that edited by A. Ewert (Oxford, 1966).

ABOUT A WOMAN AND HER PARAMOUR

I shall tell of a peasant who looked
Through his door and spied this:
He saw another man on his bed,
Doing his pleasure with his wife.
"Alas," he said, "what have I seen!"
His wife then replied to him,
"What have you seen, good sir, my love?"
"Another man, so it seemed to me,
Was on my bed and held you in his embrace."
Then said the wife, enraged, 10
"Indeed," she said, "there is no doubt at all
That this is your old foolishness;
You wish to hold a lie for the truth."
"I see," he said, "and thus I must indeed believe it."
"You are crazy," she said, "if you believe
Whatever you see is true."
She takes him by the hand and leads him with her
To a barrel filled with water;
She makes him look into the barrel.
Then she begins to ask him 20
What he sees in there, and he says to her
That he sees his own reflection.

"Pur ceo," dist ele, "n'iés tu pas
dedenz la cuve od tuz tes dras,
se tu i veiz une semblance.
Tu ne deiz pas aveir creance
en tes uiz, ki mentent sovent."
Dist li vileins, "Jeo me repent!
Chescuns deit mielz creire e saveir
ceo que sa femme dit pur veir
30 que ceo que si malvais ueil veient,
ki par veüe le foleient."

Par cest essample nus devise
que mult valt mielz sens e quointise
e plus aïde a meinte gent
que sis aveirs ne si parent.

ITERUM DE MULIERE ET PROCO EIUS

D'un vilein vueil ici cunter,
ki od sa femme vit aler
vers la forest sun dru od li.
Aprés curut; cil s'en fuï,
si s'est dedenz le bois musciez,
e il returne tuz iriez.
Sa femme laidi e blasma;
e la dame li demanda
pur quei parlot issi vers li,
10 e sis baruns li respundi
qu'il ot veü sun lecheür,
ki li fist hunte e deshonur,
aler od li vers la forest.
"Sire," fet ele, "se vus plest,
pur amur Deu, dites mei veir!
Quidastes vus hume veeir
aler od mei? Nel me celer!"
"Jel vi," fet il, "el bois entrer."
"Lasse," fet ele, "morte sui!
20 Demain murrai u uncore hui!
A m'aiuele avint altresi

"And yet," she says, "you are not
In that barrel with all your clothes on,
As it seems to you that you see there.
You should not have faith
In what you see, for appearances often lie."
Said the peasant, "I repent!
Everyone would do better to believe and to know
That what his wife says is truer
Than what is seen by his poor eyes, 30
Which so often deceive him by appearances."

By this example we learn
That intellect and trickery are worth much more
And help many people more
Than their goods or their heritage.

ANOTHER STORY OF A WOMAN AND HER PARAMOUR

I want to tell you now about a peasant
Who saw his wife going
Toward the woods with her lover.
He ran after; she was gone,
And had hidden herself in the woods,
And he went home completely enraged.
He reviled his wife and upbraided her,
And the lady asked him
Why he spoke to her in that way.
And her lord answered her, 10
That he had seen her with her lecher—
Who does shame and dishonor to her—
Going with her toward the woods.
"Sire," she said, "if you please!
For the love of God, tell me the truth!
Do you think that you saw a man
Accompanying me? Hide nothing from me!"
"I saw him," he said, "going into the woods."
"Alas!" she said, "I am dead!
I shall die tomorrow, or perhaps today! 20
It happened thus to my grandmother

e a ma mere, kar jel vi:
un poi devant lur finement,
ceo fu seü apertement,
qu'uns bachelers les cunduieit,
la u od eles rien n'aveit.
Or sai jeo bien, pres est ma fins.
Mandez, sire, tuz mes cusins,
si departiruns nostre aveir!
30 N'os el siecle plus remaneir:
od tute la meie partie
me metrai en une abeïe."
Li vileins l'ot, merci li crie.
"Lessiez ester," fet il, "amie!
Ne departez de mei einsi!
Mençunge fu quan que jeo vi."
"N'i os," fet ele, "mes ester,
kar de m'alme m'estuet penser,
ensurquetut pur la grant hunte,
40 dunt vus avez fet si grant cunte.
Tuz jurs me sereit repruvé
que malement avreie erré,
se vus ne jurez sairement,
si quel veient nostre parent,
que ne veïstes hume od mei.
Puis afiëz la vostre fei
que ja mes mot n'en sunerez
ne ja nel me repruverez."
"Voluntiers, dame," il li respunt.
50 A un mustier ensemble vunt:
la li jura ceo qu'ele quist
e plus asez qu'el ne li dist.

Pur ceo dit hum en repruvier
que femmes sevent engignier:
les veziëes nunverables
unt un art plus que li diables.

And to my mother, as I see:
A little before their deaths,
It was known to all
That a young man was seen leading them,
When no one was actually with them.
Now I know well, my end is near.
Sire, call all my kin,
For we will divide all our possessions!
I dare not remain in the world; 30
With all my share of our belongings
I shall put myself in a nunnery."
The peasant heard her, he cried for mercy.
"Let it be," he said," my dear,
Do not leave me thus!
All that I saw was a lie."
"I dare not," she said, "remain any longer,
For I must think of my soul,
Especially because of the great scandal
Of which you have made such a great story. 40
For the rest of my life it would be a reproach to me
To think that I could have behaved so wickedly,
Unless you swear on your oath,
With all our relatives watching,
That you never saw a man with me.
Then swear it by your faith
That you will never speak a word to me about it,
And will never reproach me for it."
"Willingly, lady," he answered her.
They went together to a monastery; 50
There he swore what she asked
And even more than she had told him.

Concerning this, men say as a reproach
That women know how to deceive:
Those untrustworthy schemers
Have one trick more than the devil.

"The Lady Doctor"

The tale of "The Lady Doctor" was published in *Originals and Analogues* as an analogue to "The Merchant's Tale," but it obviously has little direct rela-

---

LA SAINERESSE

D'un borgois vous acont la vie,
Qui se vanta de grant folie
Que fame n'el poroit bouler.
Sa fame en a oï parler;
Si en parla privéement,
Et en jura un serement
Qu'ele le fera mençongier,
Jà tant ne s'i saura gueter.
 I jor erent en lor meson
10 La gentil dame et le preudon;
En un banc sistrent lez à lez;
N'i furent guères demorez,
Ez-vos un pautonier à l'uis
Moult cointe et noble, et sambloit plus
Fame que home la moitié,
Vestu d'un chainsse deslié,
D'une guimple bien safrenée,
Et vint menant moult grant posnée;
Ventouses porte à ventouser,
20 Et vait le borgois saluer
En mi l'aire de sa meson.
"Diez soit o vous, sire preudon,
Et vous et vostre compaignie."
"Diex vous gart," dist cil, "bele amie;
Venez séoir lez moi icy."
"Sire," dist-il, "vostre merci,
Je ne sui mie trop lassée.
Dame, vous m'avez ci mandée
Et m'avez ci fete venir;
30 Or me dites vostre plesir."

tion to Chaucer's tale and belongs instead to the rich literature of the "wily wife." It is, however, especially interesting because of the extended *double entendre* of the sort that we encounter in the Anglo-Saxon riddles and in some of Chaucer's racier puns. It is good to be reminded of this source of humor, since the usual defense of medieval bawdry is its healthy and unashamed openness designed to evoke a guffaw rather than a snigger. As shown by "La Saineresse," our ancestors also sniggered. Our text is from Montaiglon and Raynaud, I, 289–493.

THE LADY DOCTOR

I shall tell you the life of a rich citizen
Who very foolishly boasted
That a woman could not deceive him.
  His wife heard him speaking of this
And to herself she said,
And swore an oath on it,
That she would make a liar of him
In such a way that he could not even notice it.
  One day they were in the house,
This gentle lady and the noble man; 10
They sat side by side on a bench.
They were hardly settled there
When a rogue came to the door,
Very handsome and noble, but he looked
Rather like a woman than a man in appearance.
He was dressed in a loose robe,
With a fine saffron-yellow wimple,
And he came showing great bravado.
He came carrying bleeding-cups for medicinal bleeding,
And he came in to greet this rich citizen 20
In the courtyard of his house.
"God be with you, noble sire,
With both you and your companion."
  "God save you, my dear lady," he said,
"Come sit here beside me."
  "Sire," said the other, "thank you,
But I am not at all tired.
Lady, you sent for me
And had me come here;
Now tell me your desire." 30

Cele ne fu pas esbahie:
"Vous dites voir, ma douce amie,
Montez là sus en cel solier;
Il m'estuet de vostre mestier.
Ne vous poist," dist-ele au borgois,
"Quar nous revendrons demanois;
J'ai goute ès rains moult merveillouse,
Et, por ce que sui si goutouse,
M'estuet-il fere I poi sainier."
40 Lors monte après le pautonier;
Les huis clostrent de maintenant.
Le pautonier le prent esrant;
En I lit l'avoit estendue
Tant que il l'a III fois foutue.
Quant il orent assez joué,
Foutu, besié et acolé,
Si se descendent del perrin
Contreval les degrez; en fin
Vindrent esrant en la meson.
50 Cil ne fut pas fol ni bricon,
Ainz le salua demanois:
"Sire, adieu," dist-il au borgois.
"Diez vous saut," dist-il, "bele amie;
Dame, se Diex vous benéie,
Paiez cele fame moult bien;
Ne retenez de son droit rien
De ce que vous sert en manaie."
"Sire, que vous chaut de ma paie?"
Dist la borgoise à son seignor.
60 "Je vous oi parler de folor,
Quar nous deus bien en convendra."
Cil s'en va, plus n'i demora;
La poche aus ventouses a prise.
La borgoise se r'est assise
Lez son seignor bien aboufée.
"Dame, moult estes afouée,
Et si avez trop demoré."
"Sire, merci, por amor Dé,
Jà ai-je esté trop traveillie;
70 Si ne pooie estre sainie,
Et m'a plus de c cops ferue,
Tant que je sui toute molue;
N'onques tant cop n'i sot ferir

She was not dismayed:
"You say the truth, my sweet friend;
Step upstairs to the bedroom;
I have need of your craft.
"Don't be worried," she said to the rich citizen,
"For we will return right away.
I have a most wondrous pain in my thighs
And because I am in such pain
I must be bled a bit."
Then she went up after the rogue; 40
They closed the door straightway.
The rogue immediately seized her
And stretched her on the bed
Until he had screwed her three times.
When they had thus played,
Screwed, kissed, and hugged,
Then they descend the stone steps,
Down the stairs at last,
And come into the house.
The lover was neither a simpleton nor a fool, 50
And he greeted the husband straightway.
"Sir, good day," he said to the rich citizen.
"God save you, dear lady," said the other.
"Wife, as God may bless you,
Pay this lady very well;
Hold back nothing of what she deserves
For what she freely did for you."
"Sire, don't concern yourself about my business,"
Said the lady to her husband.
"I hear you speaking foolishly, 60
For we two have already agreed on that."
She went out; she no longer delayed;
She brought a purse to the lady doctor.
Then again the wife, well out of breath,
Is seated next to her husband.
"Lady, you are all flushed,
For you stayed too long up there."
"Sire, thank you; by the love of God,
I have indeed been overworked,
Yet I could not be bled, 70
And I was given more than a hundred strokes—
So many that now I am all tender;
For no matter how many blows she could strike there,

C'onques sanc en péust issir;
Par III rebinées me prist,
Et à chascune fois m'assist
Sor mes rains deux de ses peçons,
Et me feroit uns cops si lons;
Toute me sui fet martirier,
80 Et si ne poi onques sainier.
Granz cops me feroit et sovent;
Morte fusse, mon escient,
S'un trop bon oingnement ne fust.
Qui de tel oingnement éust,
Jà ne fust mès de mal grevée.
Et, quant m'ot tant demartelée,
Si m'a après ointes mes plaies
Qui moult par erent granz et laies,
Tant que je fui toute guerie.
90 Tel oingnement ne haz-je mie,
Et il ne fet pas à haïr,
Et si ne vous en quier mentir;
L'oingnement issoit d'un tuiel,
Et si descendoit d'un forel
D'une pel moult noire et hideuse,
Mais moult par estoit savoreuse."
Dist li borgois: "Ma bèle amie,
A poi ne fustes mal baillie;
Bon oingnement avez éu."
100 Cil ne s'est pas apercéu
De la borde qu'ele conta,
Et cele nule honte n'a
De la lecherie essaucier;
Por tant le veut bien essaier;
Jà n'en fust paié à garant,
Se ne li contast maintenant.
Por ce tieng-je celui à fol
Qui jure son chief et son col
Que fame nel poroit bouler
110 Et que bien s'en sauroit garder.
Mais il n'est pas en cest païs
Cil qui tant soit de sens espris
Qui mie se péust guetier
Que fame nel puist engingnier,
Quant cele, qui ot mal ès rains,
Boula son seignor presmerains.

Not one drop of blood issued from it.
Three times in succession that one took me,
And each time placed
Upon my thighs two of her tools
And struck me with such long strokes
That I was completely martyred,
And yet I could not be bled. 80
Heavy and repeated strokes beat upon me,
And I would have died, I believe,
If it had not been for a very good ointment.
She who has any of this ointment
Is never again tormented with pain.
And when that one had hammered on me so much,
Then afterwards she anointed my wounds
(Which were very large and wide)
So well that I am completely cured.
I never dislike such an ointment, 90
And it never causes annoyance,
Providing you do not try to lie about it.
The ointment issued forth from a pipe,
And then descended into an opening
With a very black and hideous covering,
But which is very sweet indeed."
Said the rich citizen, "My sweet friend,
You were not poorly served just now;
You have had good ointment."
He did not understand 100
The trick that she had told him,
And she was not ashamed
To glorify her lechery.
Since she wanted to test him well,
She would not have been surely satisfied
If she had not told him all right away.
Therefore I consider him a fool
Who swears by his head and neck
That a woman cannot fool him
And that he knows well how to guard against it. 110
There is no one in this land
Who has acquired so much wisdom
That he can always guard himself
So that a woman cannot trick him,
Just as she, who had such pain in her thighs,
Tricked her lord at the first opportunity.

Guérin's "The Priest Who Peeked"

Guérin is known as the author of six fabliaux, including "Bérenger au long cul" (above, p. 10) and "Du Chevalier qui fist les cons parler"—the ultimate source

---

DU PRESTRE KI ABEVETE

Ichi après vous voel conter,
Se vous me volés escouter,
I flablel courtois et petit,
Si com Garis le conte et dit
D'un vilain qui ot femme prise
Sage, courtoise et bien aprise;
Biele ert et de grant parenté.
Mout le tenoit en grant certé
Li vilains et bien le servoit,
10 Et icele le prestre aimoit;
Vers lui avoit tout son cuer mis.
Li prestres ert de li souspris
Tant que I jour se pourpensa
Que à li parler en ira.
Vers le maison s'est esmeüs,
Mais ains qu'il i fust parvenus,
Fu li vilains, ce m'est avis,
Au digner o sa femme asis.
  Andoi furent tant seulement,
20 Et li prestres plus n'i atent,
Ains vint à l'uis tous abrievés,
Mais il estoit clos et fremés;
Quant il i vint, si s'aresta
Près de l'uis et si esgarda.
Par I pertruis garde et si voit
Que li vilains menguë et boit,
Et sa femme delés lui sist;
Au prestre volentiers desist
Quel vie ses maris li mainne
30 Que nul deduit de femme n'aimme.
Et, quant il ot tout esgardé,

of Diderot's *Les Bijoux indiscrets.* All of Guérin's work is notable for an almost Chaucerian skill in characterization; in "The Priest Who Peeked" the characters of the rather vicious priest and the dim-witted husband are clearly marked out in but a few deft touches. Nothing is known of Guérin's life, though it is possible that he is the "Warin" mentioned in Jean Bodel's *Congés* (see p. 88); if so, Guérin lived at the end of the twelfth and the beginning of the thirteenth centuries. Our text is from Montaiglon and Raynaud, III, 54–57.

THE PRIEST WHO PEEKED

In what follows I want to tell you,
If you will hear me out,
A courtly little fabliau,
As Guérin relates it and tells
About a peasant who had a fine wife—
Wise, courteous, and well bred;
She was beautiful and came from a good family.
He deeply loved her,
This peasant, and he served her well,
But she loved a priest; 10
To him she had given her heart completely.
The priest was so smitten by her
That one day he decided
He would go talk to her.
He proceeded to the house,
But before he arrived there,
The peasant, as I have heard,
Had sat down to dinner with his wife.
The two were all alone,
And the priest did not delay; 20
He came rapidly to the door,
But it was closed and locked.
When he came there, he stopped
By the door and looked it over.
He looked through a small opening and saw
That the peasant was eating and drinking
And that his wife was sitting next to him.
The eager priest was displeased
To see what a life was led by this husband
Who did not appreciate the pleasure of his wife. 30
And, when he had looked at everything,

Esraumment I mot a sonné:
"Que faites vous là, bone gent?"
Li vilains respondi briefment,
"Par ma foi, sire, nous mengons;
Venés ens, si vous en dourons."
"Mengiés, faites? vous i mentés,
Il m'est avis que vous foutés."
"Taisiés, sire, nous faisons voir:
40 Nous mengons, ce poés veoir."
Dist li prestres, "Je n'en dout rien,
Vous foutés, car je le voi bien,
Bien me volés ore avuler.
O moi venés cha fors ester,
Et je m'en irai là seoir;
Lors porrés bien appercevoir
Se j'ai voir dit u j'ai menti."
Li vilains tantost sus sali,
A l'uis vint, si le desfrema,
50 Et li prestres dedens entra,
Si frema l'uis à le keville;
Adont ne le prise une bille.
Jusqu'à la dame ne s'areste,
Maintenant le prent par le teste,
Si l'a desous lui enversée,
La roube li a souslevée;
Si li a fait icele cose
Que femme aimme sor toute cose.
Puis a tant feru et heurté
60 Que cele ne pot contresté
Que il fist che que il queroit.
Et li vilains abeuvuetoit
A l'huis et vit tout en apert
Le cul sa femme descouvert
Et le prestres si par desseure;
Et quist chou, "Se Dix vous sequeure,"
Fait li vilains, "est che à gas?"
Et li prestres en eslepas
Respont, "Que vous en est avis?
70 Ne veés vous? je sui assis
Pour mengier chi à ceste table."
"Par le cuer Dieu, ce samble fable,"
Dist li vilains, "ja nel creïse,
S'anchois dire nel vous oïsce,

Straightway he shouted these words:
"What are you doing there, good people?"
The peasant promptly replied,
"By my faith, sir, we are eating;
Come in and we will give you some of it."
"You're eating, you say! You are lying,
For it seems to me that you are screwing!"
"Hush, sir! We speak the truth;
We are eating, as you can see." 40
Said the priest, "I have no doubt about it;
You are screwing, for I see it clearly.
Now you are trying to trick me.
Come stand outside where I am,
And I will go sit in there,
Then you can see indeed
Whether I told the truth or lied."
The peasant quickly jumped up,
Went to the door and unlocked it,
And the priest came in; 50
He locked the door with a bolt,
And then he did not waste his time;
He did not pause until
He had grabbed the lady by the head
And pushed her down below him
And pulled up her dress.
And then he did that thing
That women love more than anything;
For he so battered and pounded
That she could not prevent 60
His doing what he wanted.
And the peasant peeked
Through the door and saw clearly
His wife's arse uncovered
And the priest on top;
And he asked, "As God may save you,"
Said the peasant, "is this a joke?"
And the priest immediately
Answered, "What do you think?
Don't you see? I have sat down 70
To eat at this table."
"By the heart of God, this is like a fabliau,"
Said the peasant; "I would certainly have believed—
If I had not heard you say otherwise—

Que vous ne foutissiés ma femme."
"Non fach, sire, taisiés; par m'ame,
Autrestel sambloit ore à moi."
Dist li vilains, "Bien vous en croi."
Ensi fu li vilains gabés
80 Et decheüs et encantés
Et par le prestre et par son sans
Qu'il n'i ot paine ne ahans,
Et, pour ce que li uis fu tuis,
Dist on encor: *Maint fol paist duis.*

Ci define li Fabliaus du Prestre.
Explicit. Amen.

That you were screwing my wife!"
"I am not, sir, hush! By my soul,
It seemed the same to me just now."
Said the peasant, "Indeed, I believe you."
Thus was the peasant tricked,
And so deceived and befuddled 80
Both by the priest and by his own weak wit
That he never felt any pain;
And because the door had a hole in it,
It is said to this day: "One hole satisfies many fools."

Here ends the fabliau of the Priest.
Explicit. Amen.

The Shipman's Tale and Its Analogues

Chaucer's story of the crafty and lecherous monk, the avaricious wife, and the compliant husband belongs to a widespread group of tales on the theme of "the lover's gift regained." J. W. Spargo, who studied this group ("Chaucer's Shipman's Tale: The Lover's Gift Regained," *FF Communications*, No. 91 [Helsinki, 1930]), found versions ranging from the ancient Orient to modern America, where the tale still circulates in oral tradition.

The basic situation is shown in its barest outlines in Bebel's *facetia*, translated below as "The Deed of a Certain Frenchman." Here we have the required cast of characters—an unscrupulous lecher, a greedy wife, and a slow-witted husband—and the basic plot, in which, as Spargo defines the theme, "a lady's favors can be won only through a gift, which the lover regains from her through a trick." Though Bebel's jest book is rather late (it appeared at the beginning of the sixteenth century), it records the story in a form probably quite close to the simple tale that had been in oral circulation for centuries.

This basic tale admits of many variations. In Bebel the crafty Frenchman is a thoroughgoing scoundrel. He initiates the action, tempts the wife with the money (which he has already borrowed from the husband), and manages to cheat everyone all around. In Boccaccio's influential version (*Decameron* 8,1), the odium is placed entirely on the woman, while the lover—the villain of Bebel's piece—becomes the hero whose trickery merits our applause for justly punishing the grasping wife. Here is a brief summary of Boccaccio's tale:

> A German soldier, Gulfardo, woos Ambruogia, the wife of a rich merchant, but she consents to lie with him only if he will pay her two hundred florins. Enraged, Gulfardo borrows the money from her husband, who is leaving town on business. He then gives Ambruogia the money in the

presence of a friend, telling her (as if to deceive his friend) that the florins are for her husband. She then goes to bed with Gulfardo. He later tells her husband that he repaid the two hundred florins to the wife; she, realizing Gulfardo has a witness to the payment, is forced to give up the money.

Sercambi's nineteenth novella printed below is obviously based on Boccaccio's tale, and in some ways Sercambi has improved it: his hero is careful to ask the merchant if he can repay the money to the wife, thus helping motivate the denouement; and Sercambi's heroine is known as a strumpet. Her demand for money is therefore less surprising than in Boccaccio, and the hero is enraged not because she asks for money but because her price is so ludicrously high.

This degeneration in the character of the lady is carried to its ultimate development in the eighteenth tale of the *Cent nouvelles nouvelles*, written around 1460, in which a gentleman, staying at an inn, agrees to pay a chambermaid for her favors, and then regains his money by simply refusing to leave her bed the next morning. She, fearful her master will discover her lucrative secret trade, is forced to return the money. A good translation of the *Cent nouvelles nouvelles* is *The Hundred Merry Tales*, R. H. Robbins, trans. (New York, 1960).

In the second traditional variation on the basic plot of "The Lover's Gift Returned," the gift is not money but an object of some value—a cloak, a piece of jewelry, a fine goose, or even, as in an eighteenth-century English version, a horse and a cart—and the gift is regained by some variation on the loan ruse; the lover pretends that the gift is a pledge left in pawn for a loan that he redeems with something belonging to the lady herself. The earliest and simplest form of the story is the brief Latin poem, "The Pepper-Mill," printed below, where the use of a pepper grinder to recover the cloak allows the poet the indecent pun that seems to be the main point of the tale.

Decameron 8,2 contains the same story and the same pun:

A priest begs the wife of a parishioner for her favors, but she will consent only for a gift of five pounds, which she needs to redeem some of her clothes that she has left in pawn. The priest has no money with him but gives her his cloak, which he promises to redeem when he fetches the money from the parsonage. They bed down in the barn and the priest goes home, where he soon repents of his bargain. He sends his servant to borrow a mortar from the lady. Then, when she is at dinner with her husband, he sends the servant to return the mortar and to explain, in the husband's presence, that the priest has left his cloak as a pledge for the return of the mortar. The husband rebukes the wife for demanding the pledge and orders her to return the cloak. She does so, and she directs the

servant to tell his master that he will never again be permitted to grind in her mortar. When the priest hears this, he laughs and sends word that he will no longer loan her his pestle.

The tale of the goldsmith's wife from Augsburg, from Frey's *Gartengesellschaft* (1556), is clearly based on Boccaccio's tale, though the pledge is a gold chain (as in Bebel's *facetia*) rather than a cloak. It is but one of a great many descendents of Boccaccio's tale, which seemed to have a special appeal, as Spargo noted, because of its indecent word-play. That clearly seems to have been the main interest of the German author, for he not only retains the pun on "mortar" but extends it with a few more of his own invention.

A third variation on the basic plot is apparent in Poggio's *facetia* of "The Peasant who Had a Goose for Sale," since here the quick-thinking peasant does not regain his gift but merely is paid for it twice—in bed by the wife and then in money by the husband. That seems to be the basic situation in the elaborately developed fabliau of "The Butcher of Abbeville," in which the cunning butcher sells the sheepskin three times over—to the maid, to the wife, and then to the priest—with the added touch that all of them have bought the priest's own sheepskin. This tale is notable too for shifting the villainous role from the seducer (as in Bebel's *facetia*) or the wife (as in almost all the other versions) to the priest/husband. His greed sets the plot in motion, and the whole elaborate tale is a fitting revenge upon the priest for his uncharitable refusal to lodge the butcher.

In the fabliau of "The Priest and the Lady" we see the basic plot of the "lover's gift regained" used as a means of extracting the lover from a difficult situation, which the witty priest then capitalizes on in an elaborate prank which, like those in the analogues to "The Merchant's Tale," involves the seduction of the wife in the husband's presence. The priest pays a fat goose for the privilege, but this has no relation to the goose in Poggio's version; it is simply the least a gentleman should do in the circumstances. It was once thought that this fabliau was a more primitive form of the story that appears in Boccaccio and Chaucer, but as Spargo argued, there is little likelihood of that, and the French tale is rather a literary adaptation of the basic tale, "worked up by a writer of no mean skill."

Probably none of the tales here discussed is the source of Chaucer's "Shipman's Tale." It was once held that "The Butcher of Abbeville" was Chaucer's source, but they are clearly quite different tales related only by their common theme. More likely is the possibility that Chaucer drew on Boccaccio, but there are difficulties with that theory too, for one cannot be positive that Chaucer knew the *Decameron*. Nor is it likely that he

knew Sercambi's *Novelliero*. Perhaps, as some believe, Chaucer drew on a now lost French fabliau; the use of French place names and of a French phrase (line 214—"Qui la?") does seem to indicate a French source. But Chaucer alone is probably responsible for the most notable characteristics of his tale, his attention to domestic comedy, such as we have noted in his other fabliaux, and his treatment of the wife's character. Almost all the tales of the "lover's gift regained" present the wife as an avaricious character who deserves the trick that is played on her. But Chaucer's tale, perhaps because he originally intended it to be told by the Wife of Bath, is told from the woman's point of view; the poor thing, we are given to understand, needs both the money and the lover, since her husband is (at least as she sees it) niggardly both in supporting his wife's extravagances and in performing his conjugal duties. Consequently, it is only just that Chaucer's heroine, unlike the wives in any of the analogues, turns her lover's trick to her own advantage; she manages to keep the money and offers to pay it back to her husband in bed. She ends with her financial and fleshly needs well provided for.

"The Pepper-Mill"

These verses appear in a collection of brief poems on popular themes preserved in an early thirteenth-century English manuscript. The poems are apparently

---

VERSUS DE MOLA PIPERIS

Militis uxorem clamidis mercede subegit
    Clericus, et piperis clam tulit inde molam;
Mane redit, referensque molam praesente marito
    Dixit, "Mantellum redde, reporto molam."
"Redde," maritus ait; respondit foemina, "reddam;
    Amplius ad nostram non molet ille molam."

elegant exercises based on vernacular tales, proverbs, and similar forms. Our text is most easily available in A.C. Lee, *The Decameron: Its Sources and Analogues* (London, 1909) and in Thomas Wright, *Essays on the Literature, Superstitions, and History of England in the Middle Ages* (London, 1846), I, 167, from which the following text is taken.

VERSES CONCERNING THE PEPPER-MILL

A clerk seduced the wife of a nobleman for the price of his cloak,
And secretly carried away her pepper-mill. [band's presence
The next day he returned, bringing back the pepper-mill, and in the hus-
He said, "Give me back my cloak; I bring back your pepper-mill."
"Give it to him," the husband said; the wife answered, "I will
Give it to him, but he will not grind again in our pepper-mill."

Eustache d'Amiens'
"The Butcher of Abbeville"

"The Butcher of Abbeville" survives in five different manuscripts, a testament to its popularity in its own time. The author is now known only from what he tells us in the epilogue to this work: his name was Eustache, and he lived in

---

DU BOUCHIER D'ABEVILE

Seignor, oiez une merveille,
C'onques n'oïstes sa pareille,
Que je vous vueil dire et conter;
Or metez cuer à l'escouter.
Parole qui n'est entendue,
Sachiez de voir, ele est perdue.
  A Abevile ot I bouchier,
Que si voisin orent mout chier;
N'estoit pas fel ne mesdisanz,
10 Mès sages, cortois et vaillanz
Et loiaus hom de son mestier,
Et s'avoit sovent grant mestier
Ses povres voisins soufraiteus;
N'estoit avers ne covoiteus.
Entor feste Toz Sains avint
Qu'à Oisemont au marchié vint
Li bouchiers bestes achater,
Mès ne fist fors voie gaster;
Trop i trova chieres les bestes,
20 Les cochons felons et rubestes,
Vilains et de mauvès afere;
Ne pot à els nul marchié fere;
Povrement sa voie emploia,
Onques denier n'i emploia;
  Après espars marchié s'en torne,
De tost aler mout bien s'atorne;
Son sorcot porte sor s'espée,

Amiens, in that area in the North of France that was so fertile a ground for the thirteenth-century fabliaux. No other works by Eustache have survived, though it seems likely that so skilled an author as this must have produced a good many works. Perhaps, like so many of his fellow writers, he produced courtly works as well as fabliaux, for he ends this tale with a mock *question d'amour* of the same sort Chaucer uses more seriously at the end of his "Franklin's Tale." Who, Eustache asks, is most worthy of the sheepskin—the priest, the servant girl, or the priest's wife? The answer, of course, is that they all get just what they deserve. Our text is from Montaiglon and Raynaud, III, 227–246. A more recent edition (based on a different manuscript) with a translation into modern French, is that of John Orr, *Le Bouchier d'Abbeville* (London and Edinburgh, 1947).

THE BUTCHER OF ABBEVILLE

Lords, listen to this marvel,
For you have never heard the like
Of what I shall tell and relate to you.
Now set your minds on listening.
A word that is not heard,
Know it well, is lost.
  At Abbeville, there was a butcher,
Much beloved by his neighbors.
He was not cruel or evil-tongued,
But wise, courteous, and of good qualities, 10
And a man loyal to his trade
Who had often been of great service
To his unfortunate poor neighbors.
He was not avaricious or covetous.
  About the time of the Feast of All Saints
It happened that this butcher went to the market
At Oisement to purchase some livestock;
But he did nothing but waste his time,
For he found the livestock too dear there,
The young pigs poor and tough, 20
Poorly-raised and in bad state.
He could not bargain for them.
He had spent his time to no purpose,
Not a penny did he spend there.
  After this thin marketing was over,
Indeed as soon as he could, he turned back.
He carried his coat over his shoulders

Quar près estoit de la vesprée.
Oiez comment il esploita:
30 Droit à Bailluel li anuita;
En mi voie de son manoir,
Quar tart estoit, si fist mout noir,
Penssa c'ui mais avant n'ira,
En la vile herbregera;
Forment doute la male gent
Que ne li toillent son argent,
Dont il avoit à grant foison.
A l'entrée d'une meson
Trueve une povre fame estant.
40 Il la salue et dist itant:
"A il en ceste vile à vendre
Riens nule où l'en peüst despendre
Le sien, por son cors aaisier,
C'onques n'amai autrui dangier?"
La bone fame li respont:
"Sire, par Dieu qui fit le mont,
Ce dist mes barons, sire Mile,
De vin n'a point en ceste vile,
Fors noz prestres sire Gautiers;
50 A II toniaus sor ses chantiers
Qui li vindrent de Nojentel;
Toz jors a il vin en tonel;
Alez à lui por ostel prendre."
"Dame, g'i vois sanz plus atendre,"
Dist li bouchiers, "et Dieus vous saut."
"A foi, sire, Dieus vous consaut!"
Atant s'en part, n'i vout plus estre;
Venuz est au manoir le prestre;
Li doiens seoit sor son sueil,
60 Qui mout fu plains de grant orgueil.
Cil le salue, et puis li dist:
"Biaus sire, que Dieus vous aït!
Herbregiez moi par charité,
Si ferez honor et bonté."
"Preudom," fet il, "Dieus vous herbert!
Quar, foi que doi à saint Herbert,
Lais hom ceenz nuit ne girra.
Bien ert qui vos herbregera
En cele vile là aval;
70 Querez tant à mont et à val

For it was almost evening.
Listen to what happened:
Right by Bailluel night fell 30
When he was still but halfway home.
Because it was late and had become very dark,
He decided he would go no further
And would lodge in the village;
He greatly feared that robbers
Would relieve him of his money,
Of which he had a good store.
At the doorway to a house
He found a poor woman standing.
He saluted her and spoke thus: 40
"Is there an inn in this town,
Or any place where a man cay pay
His money to rest his limbs?
For I never like to burden another."
The good woman answered him:
"Sir, by God who made the world,
As my lord, Sir Miles, says,
There is no wine in this village
Except at the house of Sir Walter, our priest;
He has two barrels in his cellar 50
That he brought from Nogentel.
He always has wine in barrels;
Go take your lodging from him."
"Lady, I am going there without delay,"
Says the butcher, "and God save you."
"In faith, Sir, may God guide you."
He left immediately; he had no desire to stay.
He came to the house of the priest.
The parson sat at his door;
He was filled with great pride. 60
The butcher saluted him and then he spoke:
"Good Sir, may God be with you.
Give me lodging here in charity,
For thus you will do honor and goodness."
"Bold Sir," he said, "let God grant you lodging,
For, by the faith I owe to Saint Herbert,
A layman will not spend the night here.
There will be someone who will lodge you
Down there in the village.
Seek high and low 70

Que vous puissiez ostel avoir,
Quar je vous faz bien asavoir
Ja ne girrez en cest porpris.
Autre gent i ont ostel pris,
Ne ce n'est pas coustume à prestre
Que vilains hom gise en son estre."
"Vilains! sire, qu'avez vous dit?
Tenez vous lai homme en despit?"
"Oïl," dist il, "si ai reson.
80 Alez en sus de ma meson;
Il m'est avis ce soit ramposne."
"Non est, sire, ainz seroit aumosne,
S'anuit mès me prestiez l'ostel,
Que je n'en puis trover nul tel.
Je sai mout bien le mien despendre;
Se rien nule me volez vendre,
Mout volontiers l'achaterai,
Et mout bon gré vous en saurai,
Quar je ne vous vueil rien couster."
90 "Ausi bien te vendroit hurter
Ta teste à cele dure pierre,"
Ce dist li doiens; "par saint Piere,
Ja ne girras en mon manoir."
"Deable i puissent remanoir,"
Dist li bouchiers, "fols chapelains;
Pautoniers estes et vilains."
Atant s'en part, ne volt plus dire;
Plains fu de grant couroux et d'ire.
Oiez comment il li avint:
100 Quant il fors de la vile vint
Devant une gaste meson
Dont cheü furent li chevron,
Encontre I grant tropé d'oeilles.
Por Dieu, or escoutez merveilles.
Il demanda au pastorel,
Qui mainte vache et maint torel
Avoit gardé en sa jonece:
"Paistres, que Dieus te doint leece!
Cui cist avoirs?" "Sire le prestre."
110 "De par Dieu," fet il, "puist ce estre?"
Or oiez que li bouchiers fist:
Si coiement I mouton prist
Que li paistres ne s'en perçut;

To see if you can find lodging,
For I assure you,
You will not sleep in this household.
Other people have taken lodging here,
And it is not proper for a priest
To allow a churlish person to sleep in his house."
"Churlish? Sir, what have you said?
Do you hold laymen in contempt?"
"Yes," he said, "and I am right.
Get away from my house. 80
It seems to me that this is insulting."
"Not at all, sir; rather it would be an alms-deed
To take me as a guest for this night,
For I can find nothing else.
I know well how to spend my money;
If you will offer me anything,
I will gladly pay for it,
And very good thanks I will give you for it,
For I do not want to cost you anything."
"You may as well beat your head 90
On this hard stone,"
Said the priest then. "By Saint Peter,
You will not sleep in my house!"
"Let devils stay there,"
Says the butcher, "false priest,
You are a churl and a rascal."
Straightway he left; he would say no more;
He was filled with great bitterness and anger.
Listen to what happened to him:
When he came out of the village 100
In front of an abandoned house
Whose rafters were fallen down,
He encountered a great flock of sheep.
By God, now hear a wonder!
He said to the shepherd,
Who many a cow and many a bull
Had guarded in his youth:
"Shepherd, may God give you joy;
Whose wealth is this?" "My lord the priest's."
"In the name of God," he said, "can this be?" 110
Now listen to what the butcher did.
So slyly he snatched a sheep
That the shepherd did not see a thing.

Bien l'a engingnié et deçut.
Maintenant à son col le rue;
Par mi une foraine rue
Revient à l'uis le prestre arriere,
Qui mout fu fel de grant maniere,
Si comme il dut clorre la porte,
120 Et cil, qui le mouton aporte,
Li dist: "Sire, cil Dieus vous saut,
Qui sor toz hommes puet et vaut!"
Li doiens son salu li rent;
Puis li demande isnelement:
"Dont es tu?" "D'Abevile sui;
A Oisemont au marchié fui;
N'i achetai que cest mouton,
Mès il a mout cras le crepon;
Se anuit mès me herbregiez,
130 Que bien en estes aaisiez,
Je ne sui avers ne eschars;
Anuit ert mengie la chars
De cest mouton, por qu'il vous plaise,
Quar aporté l'ai à malaise."
Li doiens pensse qu'il dit voir,
Qui mout goulouse autrui avoir;
Mieus aime I mort que IIII vis;
Dist ainsi, comme il m'est avis:
"Oïl certes, mout volentiers;
140 Se vous estiez ore vous tiers,
S'auriez vous ostel à talent;
Ainz nus hom ne me trova lent
De cortoisie et d'onor fere.
Vous me samblez mout debonere;
Dites moi comment avez non?"
"Sire, par Dieu et par son non,
J'ai non David en droit baptesme,
Quant je reçui et huile et cresme.
Traveilliez sui en ceste voie;
150 Ja Dame Dieus celui ne voie,
A foi, cui ceste beste fu;
Tans est huimès d'aler au fu."
Atant s'en vont en la meson
Où le feu estoit de seson.
Lors a sa beste mise jus,
Puis a regardé sus et jus;

He completely tricked and deceived him.
Then he threw it on his shoulders.
By another road
He returns to the door of the priest
Who was so cruel and so haughty;
Just as he was about to close the door,
He who carries the sheep 120
Says to him: "Sir, may you be saved by God
Who governs and judges all men."
The parson returns his greeting
And then quickly asks him:
"Where do you come from?" "I am from Abbeville;
I have been at the market in Oisement;
I have bought nothing except this sheep,
But it has good fat flanks.
If you will lodge me tonight,
You will be rewarded for it, 130
For I am not avaricious or miserly;
Tonight the flesh of this sheep
Will be eaten, if it pleases you,
For I have had difficulty carrying it."
The parson thought that he spoke the truth,
And he was eager to have another sheep;
He liked one dead one better than four living.
Thus he said, as I have heard:
"Yes, certainly, very willingly.
If there were three of you, 140
You would have the lodging you want.
Never has a man found me slow
In doing him courtesy and honor.
You seem to me an excellent sort;
Tell me, what is your name?"
"Sir, by God and by His name,
I am called David in true baptism,
Which I received with oil and chrism.
How I have worked on this trip!
May the Lord God not look on him, 150
In faith, whose beast this was.
It is high time it went to the fire."
They went directly into the house,
Where the fire was ready.
Then he threw down the beast,
And he looked up and down;

Une coingnie a demandée,
Et on li a tost aportée.
Sa beste tue et puis l'escorce;
160 Sor I banc en geta l'escorce,
Puis le pendi, lor ieus voiant:
"Sire, por Dieu, venez avant;
Por amor Dieu, or esgardez
Com cis moutons est amendez;
Veez comme est cras et refais,
Mès mout m'en a pesé li fais,
Que de mout loing l'ai aporté.
Or en fetes vo volonté;
Cuisiez les espaules en rost;
170 S'en fetes metre plain un pot
En essau avoec la mesnie,
Je ne di mie vilonie,
Ainz mès plus bele char ne fu,
Metez le cuire sor le fu;
Veez comme est tendre et refete:
Ainçois que la saveur soit fete
Ert ele cuite voirement."
"Biaus ostes, fetes vo talent;
Sor vous ne m'en sai entremetre."
180 "Fetes donques la table metre."
"C'est prest; n'i a fors de laver
Et des chandoiles alumer."
Seignor, ne vous mentirai mie;
Li doiens avoit une amie
Dont il si fort jalous estoit,
Toutes les nuiz qu'ostes avoit,
La fesoit en sa chambre entrer.
Mès cele nuit la fist souper
Avoec son oste liement.
190 Servi furent mout richement
De bone char et de bon vin.
De blans dras, qui erent de lin,
Fist on fere au bouchier I lit;
Mout ot leenz de son delit.
Li doiens sa meschine apele:
"Je te commant," fet il, "suer bele,
Que noz ostes soit bien et aise,
Si qu'il n'ait rien qui li desplaise."
Atant se vont couchier ensamble

He asked for a hatchet,
And it was brought to him quickly.
He killed his animal and then skinned it;
He threw the pelt on a bench, 160
Then he hung it up, as their eyes watched.
"Sir, by God, come forth;
For the love of God, now consider
How well this sheep is grown.
See how fat and fresh it is.
But he has been a heavy burden for me,
And I carried it a very long way.
Now do what you will with it;
Dress the shoulders for a roast;
Fill up the pot with it 170
As a stew for the household.
I tell you no lie,
There was never more beautiful meat.
Put it to cook on the fire;
See how tender and fine it is;
Before the sauce is ready,
It will be well cooked."
"Good guest, do as you wish;
Compared to you, I don't know how to go about this."
"Then have the table set up." 180
"It is ready, there is nothing to do but to wash
And light the candles."
Gentlemen, I will not lie to you.
The parson had a mistress
Of whom he was so very jealous
That each night he had a guest
He made her stay in her room.
But this evening he had her come dine
Joyfully with his guest.
They were richly served 190
With good meat and good wine.
With white sheets, which were linen,
The butcher's bed was prepared;
He took delight therein.
The parson calls his servant girl:
"I command you," said he, "dear girl,
To see that our guest is well at ease,
So that there is nothing to displease him."
Then they went to bed together,

200 Il et la dame, ce me samble,
Et li bouchiers remest au fu.
Ainz mès si aaisiez ne fu;
Bon ostel ot et biau samblant:
"Bele suer," fet il, "vien avant;
Trai te en ça, si parole à moi,
Et si fai ton ami de moi:
Bien i porras avoir grant preu."
"Ostes, tesiez, ne dites preu;
Ja n'apris onques tel afere."
210 "Par Dieu, or le te covient fere
Par tel couvent que je dirai."
"Dites le donc, et je l'orrai."
"Se tu veus fere mon plesir
Et tout mon bon et mon desir,
Par Dieu, que de vrai cuer apel,
De mon mouton auras la pel."
"Biaus ostes, jamès ce ne dites;
Vous n'estes mie droiz hermites,
Qui tel chose me requerez.
220 Mout estes de mal apenssez;
Dieu merci, com vous estes sos;
Vo bon feïsse, mès je n'os;
Vous le diriez demain ma dame."
"Suer, se ja Dieus ait part en m'ame,
En ma vie ne le dirai
Ne ja ne t'en encuserai."
Dont li a cele creanté
Qu'ele fera sa volenté
Toute la nuit, tant que jors fu.
230 Dont se leva et fist son fu,
Son harnois, et puis trest ses bestes.
Lors primes s'est levez li prestres;
Il et son clerc vont au moustier
Chanter et fere lor mestier,
Et la dame remest dormant.
Et ses ostes tout maintenant
Se vest et chauce sanz demeure,
Quar bien en fu et tans et eure.
En la chambre, sanz plus atendre,
240 Vint à la dame congié prendre;
La clique sache, l'uis ouvri;
Et la dame si s'esperi,

He and his lady, as I have heard, 200
And the butcher remained by the fire.
He was never so comfortable.
He had a good lodging and good treatment.
"Dear girl," he said, "come here;
Get in here and talk to me,
And if you will make me your lover,
You will have for it a good reward indeed."
"Guest, be quiet; don't speak of 'reward';
I know nothing of such business."
"By God, now you would do well to do it 210
For this promise that I will make to you."
"Say it then, and I will listen."
"If you will do my pleasure
And all my wish and desire,
By God, who judges the true heart,
You will have the pelt of my sheep."
"Good guest, say nothing more of that.
You are not well endowed with brains
To ask such a thing of me;
You are badly mistaken. 220
My God, how foolish you are!
I would do as you wish, but I don't dare;
Tomorrow you would tell my lady about it."
"My girl, as God has an interest in my soul,
Never in my life will I tell her
Nor ever accuse you of this."
She was so completely convinced
That she did his will
All the night until it was day.
Then she arose and made the fire, 230
Prepared her utensils, and tended the animals.
At prime the priest arose;
He and his clerk went to the church
To sing and perform their office,
And his lady remained sleeping.
And the guest straightway
Put on his clothes and shoes without delay,
For indeed the time was right.
To the bedroom, without waiting longer,
He came to the lady to take his leave. 240
He drew the latch, opened the door;
And the lady awoke.

Ses ieus ouvri, son oste voit
Devant s'esponde trestout droit.
Lors li demande dont il vient
Et de quel chose il li sovient:
"Dame," fet il, "graces vous rent:
Herbregié m'avez à talent
Et mout m'avez biau samblant fait."
250 Atant vers le chevès se trait;
Sa main mist sor le chaveçuel
Et tret arriere le linçuel;
Si voit la gorge blanche et bele,
Et la poitrine et la mamele:
"E! Dieus," dist il, "je voi miracles;
Sainte Marie, sainz Romacles,
Comme est li doiens bien venuz
Qui o tel dame gist toz nuz!
Que si m'aït sainz Onorez,
260 Uns rois en fust toz honorez.
Se j'avoie tant de loisir
Que g'i peüsse I poi gesir,
Refez seroie et respassez."
"Biaus ostes, ce n'est mie assez
Que vous dites; par saint Germain,
Alez en sus, ostez vo main.
Mesires aura ja chanté;
Trop se tendroit à engané
Se en sa chambre vous trovoit;
270 Jamès nul jor ne m'ameroit;
Si m'auriez mal baillie et morte."
Et cil mout bel la reconforte:
"Dame," fet il, "por Dieu merci,
Jamès ne mouverai de ci
Por nul homme vivant qui soit.
Nès se li doiens i venoit,
Por qu'il deïst une parole
Qui fust outrageuse ne fole,
Je l'ocirroie maintenant.
280 Mès or otroiez mon commant
Et fetes ce que je voudrai,
Ma piau lanue vous donrai
Et grant plenté de mon argent."
"Sire, je n'en ferai noient,
Que je vous sent si à estout

She opened her eyes, saw her guest
Right by the bed.
Then she asked him why he came there
And what it was he wanted.
"Lady," he said, "I thank you;
You have lodged me very comfortably
And you have been very kind to me."
He stepped to the head of the bed, 250
Put his hand on the bolster,
And drew back the cover.
He sees her white and lovely throat
And her bosom and breasts.
"Ah, God!" he says, "I see miracles!
Saint Mary! Saint Romacles!
What good luck it is for the parson
Who sleeps with such a lady naked!
As Saint Honorius may aid me,
A king would be well honored by this! 260
If I had enough time
To lie there but a moment
I would be healed and made new!"
"Good guest, it is not much
That you are asking! By Saint Germain,
Go away, and take your hands off me!
My lord will already have sung his Mass.
He would be terribly upset
If he found you in his bedroom.
He would never love me again. 270
You would have me ruined and destroyed."
But he very sweetly reassured her:
"Lady," he said, "by the mercy of God,
I shall never move from here
For any living man.
Even if the parson comes here,
If he should say one word
That is outrageous or foolish,
I shall kill him outright.
But now if you will do my command, 280
And do what I wish,
I will give you my sheepskin
And a great sum of money."
"Sir, I will not do that at all,
For I think that you are so indiscreet

Que demain le diriez partout."
"Dame," dist il, "ma foi tenez
Tant com je soie vis ne nez,
Ne le dirai fame ne homme,
290 Par toz les sainz qui sont à Romme."
Tant li dist et tant li promet
La dame en sa merci se met,
Et li bouchiers bien s'en refet.
Et, quant il en ot son bon fet,
D'iluec se part, n'i volt plus estre,
Ainz vint au moustier où li prestre
Ot commencié une leçon
Entre lui et I sien clerçon;
Si com il dist: *Jube, Domne,*
300 Ez le vous el moustier entré:
"Sire," fet il, "graces vous rent;
Ostel ai eü à talent,
Mout me lo de vo beau samblant,
Mès une chose vous demant
Et vous pri que vous le faciez,
Que vous ma pel achatissiez;
Si m'auriez delivré de paine;
Bien il a III livres de laine;
Mout est bone, si m'aït Dieus;
310 III sols vaut; vous l'aurez por deus,
Et mout bon gré vous en saurai."
"Biaus ostes, et je le ferai
Por l'amor de vous volentiers;
Bons compains estes et entiers;
Revenez moi veoir sovent."
Sa pel meïsme cil li vent;
Congié demande, si s'en va.
Et la dame lors se leva,
Qui mout ert jolie et mingnote;
320 Si se vest d'une verde cote
Mout bien faudée à plois rampanz.
La dame ot escorcié ses panz
A sa çainture par orgueil:
Cler et riant furent si oeil;
Bele, plaisans ert à devise,
En le caiere s'est assise.
Et la baissele, sanz atendre,
Vint à la pel; si la vout prendre,

That tomorrow you would tell it everywhere."
"Lady," he said, "take my pledge:
As ever I have face or nose,
I shall not tell it to woman or man
For all the saints in Rome." 290
He said so much and promised so much
That the lady put herself at his mercy.
And the butcher enjoyed himself well.
And when he had fulfilled his desire,
He went away; he would stay no longer;
And he came to the church where the priest
Had begun the lesson
Between him and his clerk,
And as he said: "Jube Domine,"
Behold—the butcher entered the church. 300
"Sir," he said, "God give you grace.
I have had a lodging to my taste;
I am greatly honored by your kindness,
But one thing I would ask of you—
And I pray that you will do it—
That you buy from me my sheepskin;
That would relieve me of trouble.
There are a good three pounds of wool on it;
It is a very good one, so help me God;
It is worth three pounds; you can have it for two, 310
And you will have a good bargain in it."
"Good guest, I will do it
Willingly for the love of you.
You are a good and loyal companion;
Come back and see me often."
He sold him his own pelt,
Took his leave, and went away.
And then arose the lady,
Who was very lovely and delicate.
She dresses herself in a green mantel, 320
Beautifully pressed in folded pleats.
The lady had tightly pinched her waist
With her belt, out of pride.
Clear and shining were her eyes,
Beautiful and pleasing as can be.
She is seated in her chair.
And the servant girl, without waiting,
Came to the sheepskin; she was going to take it

Quant la dame li desfendi:
330 "Di va," fet ele, "et quar me di;
Qu'as tu de cele pel à fere?"
"Dame, j'en ferai mon afere;
Je la vueil au soleil porter
Por le cuirien fere essuer."
"Non feras; lai le toute coie,
Ele pendroit trop sor la voie,
Mès fai ce que tu as à fere."
"Dame," dist el, "je n'ai que fere;
Je levai plus matin de vous,
340 A foi, maugré en aiez vous,
Vous en deüssiez bien parler."
"Trai te en sus; lai la pel ester;
Garde que plus la main n'i metes
Ne que plus ne t'en entremetes."
"En non Dieu, dame, si ferai;
Toute m'en entremeterai;
J'en ferai comme de la moie."
"Dis tu donques que ele est toie?"
"Oïl, je le di voirement."
350 "Met jus la pel, va, si te pent,
Ou tu ailles en la longaingne.
Mout me torne ore à grant engaingne
Quant tu deviens si orguilleuse;
Pute, ribaude, pooilleuse,
Va tost, si vuide ma meson."
"Dame, vous dites desreson,
Qui por le mien me ledengiez:
Se vous seur sainz juré l'aviez,
S'est ele moie." "Toutevoie
360 Vuide l'ostel, va, si te noie;
Je n'ai cure de ton service,
Que trop es pautoniere et nice:
Se mesires juré l'avoit,
Ceenz ne te garantiroit;
Si t'ai je ore cueilli en hé."
"Par mi le col ait mal dehé
Qui jamès jor vous servira.
J'atendrai tant que il vendra,
Et puis après si m'en irai;
370 De vous à lui me clamerai."

When the lady forbade her.
"Say now," she said, "tell me 330
What right you have to carry off that sheepskin."
"Lady, I am about my own business;
I want to carry it into the sun
In order to clean the hide."
"Don't do that; let it be.
It would hang too near the road.
Now get on with your own work."
"My lady, I have nothing else to do;
I got up earlier than you;
In faith, in spite of what may be wrong with you, 340
You should speak politely."
"Go away; let the hide be;
Watch that you do not set your hand on it again,
And that you meddle in this no more."
"In the name of God, lady, I will do so;
I will concern myself with it;
I will do so, since it is mine."
"You say that it is yours?"
"Yes, I tell you so truly."
"Put down that hide; go hang yourself, 350
Or go purge yourself;
It drives me to great anger
When you become so proud.
Whore, low-life, syphilitic,
Go quickly, get out of my house!"
"Lady, you speak foolishly,
And insult me about what is mine,
You may swear by the best saints,
And still it is mine." "Nevertheless,
Get out of this house, go drown yourself; 360
I have no need of your services.
You are too debauched and stupid;
If my lord himself had sworn it,
That could not keep you here,
I have taken such a hatred toward you."
"Curses be on the neck
Of whomever serves you again!
I will wait only until the priest comes home,
And then I am going away.
I will complain to him." 370

"Clameras, pute, vieus buinarde,
Pullente, ribaude, bastarde!"
"Bastarde! dame, or dites mal;
Li vostre enfant sont mout loial,
Que vous avez du prestre eüs?"
"Par la passion Dieu, met jus
La pel, ou tu le comparras."
"Mieus vous vendroit estre à Arras,
Par les sainz Dieu, voire à Coloingne."
380 Et la dame prent sa queloingne;
I cop l'en done, et ele crie:
"Par la vertu sainte Marie,
Mar m'i avez à tort batue;
La pel vous ert mout chier vendue
Ainçois que je muire de mort."
Lors pleure et fet I duel si fort.
A la noise et à la tençon
Entra li prestres en meson:
"Qu'est ce?" dist il, "Qui t'a ce fet?"
390 "Ma dame, sire, sanz mesfet."
"Sans mesfet, voir, ne fu ce mie
Qu'ele t'a fet tel vilonie."
"Par Dieu, sire, por la pel fu
Qui là pent encoste ce fu;
Biaus sire, vous me commandastes
Ersoir, quant vous couchier alastes,
Que nos ostes sire Davis
Fust aaisiez à son devis,
Et je fis vo commandement,
400 Et il me dona vraiement
La pel; sor sainz le juerrai,
Que mout bien deservie l'ai."
Li doiens ot et aperçoit,
Aus paroles qu'ele disoit,
L'avoit ses ostes culonée;
Por ce li ot sa pel donée;
S'en fu corouciez et plains d'ire,
Mès son pensser n'en osa dire.
"Dame," fet il, "se Dieus me saut,
410 Vous avez fet trop vilain saut;
Petit me prisiez et doutez,
Qui ma mesnie me batez."

"Complain? Whore! Old good-for-nothing!
Prostitute! Debauched bastard!"
"Bastard? Lady, there you are insulting!
Are your children as good,
Those you have had by the priest?"
"By the passion of God, put down
That pelt, or you will pay for it!"
"It would be better for you to be in Arras,
By the saints of God, indeed in Cologne."
Then the lady seized her distaff 380
And struck a blow, and the other cried:
"By the virtue of Saint Mary,
You are wrong to beat me!
You will buy that pelt dearly,
Though I die for it."
Then she cried and raised a great clamor.
At the noise of this quarrel
The priest came into the house:
"What is this," he said, "what is going on?"
"It is my lady, sir, for I've done nothing wrong." 390
"Nothing at all?" he said, "never before
Has she treated you so badly."
"By God, sir, it was for the pelt
That hangs there next to the fire.
Good sir, you commanded me,
Last night, when you went to bed,
That our guest, Master David,
Should be made comfortable in every way,
And I did as you commanded,
And he truly gave me 400
The sheepskin; I will swear on the saints
That I well deserved it."
The parson heard and understood
From the words that she spoke
That his guest had laid her
And for that he had given her the pelt.
He was enraged by this and filled with wrath,
But he did not dare say what he thought.
"Lady," he said, "as God saves me,
You have done a churlish trick; 410
You think too little of me and fear me too little,
You who have beaten my servants."

"Ba! qu'ele veut ma pel avoir.
Sire, se vos saviez le voir
De la honte qu'ele m'a dite,
Vous l'en renderiez la merite,
Qui voz enfanz m'a reprovez.
Mauvesement vous en provez,
Qui soufrez qu'ele me ledange
420 Et honist toute par sa jangle.
Je ne sai qu'il en avendra,
Ja ma pel ne li remaindra:
Je di qu'ele n'est mie soie."
"Qui est ce donques?" "Par foi, moie."
"Vostre, voire! par quel reson?"
"Nostre ostes jut en no meson
Sor ma coute, sor mes linceus;
Que mau gré en ait sainz Aceus
Si volez ore tout savoir."
430 "Bele dame, or me dites voir;
Par cele foi que me plevistes,
Quant vous primes ceenz venistes,
Cele pel doit ele estre vostre?"
"Oïl, par sainte patrenostre."
Et la baissele dist adonques:
"Biaus sire, ne le creez onques;
Ele me fu ainçois donée."
"Ha! pute, mal fusses tu née!
On vous dona la passion.
440 Alez tost hors de ma meson;
Que male honte vous aviegne!"
"Par le saint Signe de Compiegne,
Dame," fet il, "vous avez tort."
"Non ai, quar je la haz de mort,
Por ce qu'ele est si menterresse,
Cele ribaude larronnesse."
"Dame, que vous ai je emblé?"
"Ribaude, mon orge et mon blé,
Mes pois, mon lart, mon pain fetiz;
450 Certes, vous estes trop chetiz
Qui ceenz l'avez tant soufferte;
Sire, paiez li sa deserte;
Por Dieu, si vous en delivrez."
"Dame," fet il, "or m'entendez;

"Bah! And she wants to have my sheepskin!
Sir, if you knew the truth
About the shame that she said to me,
You would reward me for it;
She reproved me about your children.
You will suffer for it
If you allow her to insult me
And to shame all with her jangling. 420
I don't know what will happen
If my sheepskin does not remain here;
I say that it is mine alone!"
"What's this?" "In faith, mine!"
"Yours, indeed? Why is that?"
"Our guest stayed in our house,
On my mattress, on my blanket,
And St. Aceus will have the blame for it
If now you want to know all."
"Dear lady, now tell me the truth; 430
By that faith that you pledged to me
When you first came here,
Should this sheepskin be yours?"
"Yes, by the Holy Pater Noster,"
The servant girl then said:
"Good Sir, never believe it,
It was given to me first."
"Ha, whore! It was a bad day when you were born!
You were given a sore belly.
Get quickly out of my house; 440
May some shameful evil befall you!"
"By the Holy Image of Compiègne,
Lady," he said, "you are wrong."
"I am not, and I will scratch her to death,
For she is a liar,
This debauched thief!"
"Lady, what have I robbed you of?"
"Debauched creature! My barley, my wheat,
My peas, my salt pork, my bread—you took everything.
Certainly, you are too weak 450
To have put up with her for so long.
Sir, pay her what she has coming;
By God, you will be free of her!"
"Lady," he said, "now listen to me;

Par saint Denis je veuil savoir
Laquele doit la pel avoir.
Cele pel, qui la vous dona?"
"Nostre ostes, quant il s'en ala."
"Voir, por les costez saint Martin,
460 Il s'en ala dès hui matin
Ainz que fust levez li solaus.
Dieus! com vous estes desloiaus
Qui jurez si estoutement."
"Ainz prist congié mout bonement
Avant qu'il en deüst aler."
"Fu il donques à vo lever?"
"Nenil; adonc je me gisoie;
De lui garde ne me donoie;
Quant je le vi devant m'esponde . . .
470 Il estuet que je vous desponde. . . ."
"Et que dist il au congié prendre?"
"Sire, trop me volez sorprendre . . .
Il dist, 'A Jhesu vous commant.'
Adonc s'en parti à itant;
Ainz plus ne parla ne ne dist,
Ne nule rien ne me requist
Qui vous tornast à vilonie,
Mès vous i chaciez boiserie;
Onques ne fui de vous creüe,
480 Et si n'avez en moi veüe,
Grace Dieu, se mout grant bien non,
Mès vos i chaciez trahison.
Si m'avez en tel prison mise
Dont ma char est tainte et remise;
De vostre ostel ne me remue;
Mise m'avez muer en mue;
Trop ai esté en vo dangier
Por vo boivre, por vo mengier."
"Ahi!" fet il, "fole mauvaise;
490 Je t'ai norrie trop aaise;
Près va que ne te bat et tue.
Je sai de voir qu'il t'a foutue;
Di moi por quoi ne crias tu?
Il t'estuet rompre le festu;
Va, si vuide tost mon ostel,
Et je irai à mon autel;

By Saint Denis, I want to know
Who should have this sheepskin.
This sheepskin—who gave it to you?"
"Our guest, when he went away."
"Indeed! By the sides of Saint Martin,
He went away early this morning, 460
Before the sun had risen.
God, how disloyal you are
To swear so shamelessly."
"But he very sweetly took his leave
Before he had to leave."
"Was he there when you got up?"
"No, I was lying down then;
I took no notice of him
When I saw him standing by my bed . . .
I must explain. . . ." 470
"And what did he say when he took his leave?
"Sir, you are trying to trick me!
He said, 'I commend you to Jesus.'
And then he went away.
Not another word did he say,
Nor did he ask for anything
That would bring shame on you.
But you want to sniff out some folly;
You have never trusted me,
As if you have seen something wrong in me, 480
When, thank God, there is nothing wrong at all,
But you want to hunt out some treachery.
You have kept me so like a prisoner
That my flesh is grown pale and weak;
I never step outside your house;
You have shut me in a cage;
I have been too much in your power
For your drink, for your food."
"Aha!" he said, "crazy slut,
I have nourished you too well; 490
It is a near thing that I don't beat and kill you.
I can see clearly that he screwed you.
Tell me, why didn't you cry out?
You should have broken off the conversation.
Go, leave my house immediately,
And I will go to my altar;

Maintenant deseur jurerai
Jamès en ton lit ne girrai."
Par mout grant ire s'est assis,
500 Corouciez, tristes et penssis.
Quant la dame aïré le voit,
Forment li poise qu'ele avoit
Tencié ne estrivé à lui;
Mout crient que ne li face anui;
En sa chambre s'en va atant,
Et li paistres vient acourant,
Qui ses moutons avoit contez.
Ersoir l'en fu li uns emblez;
Il ne set qu'il est devenuz.
510 Grant aleüre en est venuz,
Frotant ses hines, en meson.
Li prestres ert sor sa leson
Mout corouciez et eschaufez:
"Qu'est ce? mal soies tu trovez,
Mauvès ribaus; dont reviens tu?
Qu'est ce c'on fet? Samblant fez tu,
Filz à putain, vilain rubestes;
Or deüsses garder tes bestes;
Près va ne te fier d'un baston."
520 "Sire, n'ai mie d'un mouton,
Tout le meillor de no tropé;
Je ne sai qui le m'a emblé."
"As tu donques mouton perdu?
On te deüst avoir pendu;
Mauvesement les as gardez."
"Sire," fet il, "or m'entendez:
Ersoir, quant en la vile entrai,
I estrange homme i encontrai
Que onques mès veü n'avoie
530 En champ, n'en vile, ne en voie,
Qui mout mes bestes esgarda,
Et mout m'enquist et demanda
Qui cis biaus avoirs pooit estre,
Et je li dis, 'Sire no prestre';
Cil le m'embla, ce m'est avis."
"Par les sainz Dieu, ce fu Davis,
Noz ostes, qui ceenz a jut;
Bien m'a engingnié et deçut
Qui ma mesnie m'a foutue;

I will swear that from this moment on
I will never sleep in your bed."
He sits down in great wrath,
Enraged, sad and pensive. **500**
When the lady saw him angered,
It strongly weighed on her that she had
Argued and striven against him.
She greatly feared he would harm her.
She went straightway to her bedroom,
And the shepherd came running in,
For he had just counted his sheep.
Yesterday evening one of them was stolen,
He does not know what has become of it;
With great haste he came, **510**
Rubbing his thighs, into the house.
The priest was at his reading,
Much heated with anger.
"What is this? You come at a bad time,
Damned rogue! Where do you come from,
What has happened? You are tricking me,
Whoreson, rude churl,
You had better watch your animals;
It is a near thing I don't beat you with a stick."
"Sir, I never had a better sheep **520**
In all our flock.
I don't know who stole him."
"Have you then lost a sheep?
Now you should be hanged;
You have guarded them badly."
"Sir, now listen to me;
Last night, when I came to the village,
A strange man met me there,
One whom I have never seen before,
In the fields, or in the village, or on the road. **530**
And he looked very carefully at my animals,
And he inquired closely and asked me
Whose handsome belongings these were,
And I said to him 'Our lord, the priest's.'
He stole it from me; that's what I think."
"By the saints of God, that was David,
Our guest, who stayed here last night;
He has well tricked and deceived me,
And screwed my whole household;

540 Ma pel meïsme m'a vendue;
De ma mance m'a ters mon nés;
En mal eure fuisse jou nés.
Quant je ne m'en seuch garde prendre!
On puet cascun jor mout aprendre:
De ma paste m'a fet tortel.
En connoistroies tu la pel?"
"Oïl, sire, foi que vous doi,
Bien la connoistrai, se la voi;
Je l'ai eü VII anz en garde."
550 Cil prent la pel; si la regarde;
Aus oreilles et à la teste
Connut bien la pel de sa beste:
"Harou! las," dist li pasturiaus;
"Par Dieu, sire, c'est Cornuiaus,
La beste que je plus amoie;
En mon tropé n'avoit si coie;
Foi que je doi à saint Vincent,
N'avoit si cras mouton en cent;
Mieudres de lui ne pooit estre."
560 "Venez ça, dame," dist le prestre,
"Et tu, baissele, vien avant;
Parole à moi, je te commant;
Respont à moi quant je t'apel,
Que claimes tu en ceste pel?"
"Sire, trestoute la pel cleim,"
Dist la meschine au chapelain.
"Et vous, que dites, bele dame?"
"Sire, se Dieus ait part en m'ame,
Ele doit estre par droit moie."
570 "Ele n'ert ne vostre, ne soie.
Je l'acatai de mon avoir;
Ele me doit bien remanoir.
Il m'en vint priier au moustier,
Là ù ge lisoie men sautier.
Par saint Pierre, le vrai apostre,
Ele n'iert ne soie ne vostre,
Se par jugement ne l'avés."
Seignor, vous qui les biens savez,
Huistaces d'Amiens vous demande,
580 Et prie par amors, et mande
Que vous faciez cest jugement.
Bien et à droit et leaument,

He sold me my own sheepskin! 540
'He has wiped my nose with my own sleeve';
I was born in an evil hour.
O, that I had known how to guard myself from him!
Everyday one can learn something more.
'He has made me a cake with my own dough.'
Would you recognize the skin?"
"Yes, sir, by the faith that I owe you,
I would know it well, if I saw it.
I have kept watch over it for seven years."
He took the pelt, he looked at it, 550
At the ears and at the head,
And he knew well the pelt of his animal.
"Harrow! Alas!" said the shepherd.
"By God, sir, it is Old Horny,
The animal that I love best;
There is none so docile in my flock;
By the faith that I owe to Saint Vincent
There is not so fat a sheep in a hundred;
There could not be a better one than he."
"Come here, lady," said the priest, 560
"And you, servant girl, come forward,
Speak to me, I command you—
Answer me when I ask:
What part of this sheepskin is yours?"
"Sir, I claim all the pelt,"
Said the girl to the priest.
"And you, what do you say, good lady?"
"Sir, as God has a claim on my soul,
Rightfully it should be mine."
"It will not be yours or hers. 570
I bought it with my own money;
Indeed it must remain in my keeping.
He came to ask me about it at the church,
Where I was reading my psalter.
By Saint Peter, the true apostle,
It will not be hers or yours,
Unless you have it by legal judgment."
Gentlemen, you who know well,
Eustache of Amiens asks you
And prays in the name of love and requests 580
That you render this judgment;
Indeed, both truly and loyally,

Chascuns en die son voloir
Liquels doit mieus la pel avoir,
Ou li prestres, ou la prestresse,
Ou la meschine piprenesse.

Explicit du Bouchier d'Abevile.

Let each one say his will in this matter:
Which should best have the pelt—
The priest, or Mrs. Priest,
Or the tricky servant girl?

Here ends The Butcher of Abbeville.

Sercambi's "Of Avarice and Lust"

Sercambi's book of *novelle* (see above p. 238) has intrigued students of Chaucer not so much because it contains a good analogue to "The Shipman's Tale," but because the stories are set in a frame rather reminiscent of Chaucer's Canterbury pilgrimage. During a plague in the city of Lucca a group of ladies, gentle-

---

DE AVARITIA E LUSSURIA

Carissime donne e voi omini desiderosi di udire alcuna volta l'inganni che si fanno alle donne che per denari vituperano i loro mariti e parenti, di che in nella città di Perugia, là u' stanotte siamo dimorati, fu un banchieri e mercadante nomato Pircosso, omo servente di dinari e massimamente a soldati forestieri, da'quali avea molto guadagno. Avendo il ditto Pircosso una moglie giovana di vintiquattro anni bella e balda, nomata madonna Sofia, e molte volte avendo fatto fallo al suo marito, più tosto per dinari che per amore ad altri portasse, per la qual cosa in alcuno luogo secreto fu di lei parlato. Et intra l'altre volte che di lei si dicesse si fu un giorno presso a uno carnelevale, dove era uno messer Bernardo tedesco capo di vinticinque bacinetti e soldato in Perugia. Lo qual messer Bernardo, essendo giovano, e cognoscendo madonna Sofia di Pircosso, s'innamorò di lei pensando, se costei con altri ha fatto fallo, agevolmente doverne aver diletto; et datosi a sentire e vedere in che modo potea il suo pensieri mettere in effetto, per una messetta mandò dicendo il suo volere.

La messetta, che era già stata altre volte per sì fatte cose a madonna Sofia, gli narrò la intenzione di messer Bernardo. Madonna Sofia, sentendo quello che la messetta gli avea ditto, non avendo di lei vergogna, disse, "Se messer Barnardo mi vuol dare fiorini dugento, io sono contenta et in caso sia contento vo'che gli dichi che domenica, che serà la domenica di carnelevale, dopo desinare, che 'l mio marito serà ito ad Ancona per mercanzia, vegna a me e portimi fiorini dugento et io sarò contenta che sia meco lo dì e la notte seguente et poi lo lunedì mattina si parta." La messetta, udendo quello madonna la puttana, o vuoi dire Sofia, avea ditto, si partiò et a messer Bernardo andò e tutta l'ambasciata gli disse. Messer Bernardo disse, "Troppo de'avere odorifera la sua quintana, che sare' vasto fusse

men, and prelates determine to leave the city and travel through Italy until the pestilence has subsided. The group duly elects a leader named Alvisi, who organizes the exchequer, arranges for musical and athletic entertainment during the trip, urges good manners (*onestà*) on the company, and finally appoints a member of the group as "autore et fattore di questo libro"—that is, a storyteller. The name of the appointee is revealed in an acrostic sonnet recited by Alvisi and turns out to be none other than Giovanni Sercambi, whose business it now becomes to entertain his companions with tales along the way and at their various stations. As the first sentence indicates, the following story finds the travelers at Perugia.

The text is taken from Rodolfo Renier, ed., *Novelle inedite di Giovanni Sercambi* (Turin, 1889), pp. 81–84. The text printed in *Sources and Analogues* has for some reason been bowdlerized through the exclusion of one passage.

OF AVARICE AND LUST

Dear ladies and you gentlemen wishing to hear the deceptions sometimes practiced against women who disgrace their husbands and families for money, I tell you that in the city of Perugia, where we are staying tonight, there was a banker and merchant named Pircosso, a man who lent money, principally to foreign soldiers, from whom he got great profit. The aforementioned Pircosso had a young wife of twenty-four years, beautiful and bold, named Lady Sofia, who had tricked her husband many times, rather for the money than for the love she bore others, so that she was a subject of gossip. And among many other times, she was spoken of at a carnival, at which there was a certain Bernardo, a German soldier in Perugia, captain of twenty-five men. This Bernardo was young, and having met Lady Sofia, wife of Pircosso, he fell in love with her and thought that if she had cheated with others, he should easily have his pleasure of her. And setting about discovering and determining how he could put his intention into effect, he sent word of his wishes by means of a go-between.

The go-between, who had previously been to Lady Sofia for such things, told her of Bernardo's intentions. Lady Sofia, listening to what the go-between said to her and feeling no shame, said, "If Bernardo is willing to give me two hundred florins, I will be satisfied; and in the event that he agrees, tell him to come to me on Sunday, which will be carnival Sunday, after dinner, when my husband will have gone to Ancona on business, and bring me two hundred florins; and I will be content to have him stay with me that day and the following night; and Monday morning he will depart." The go-between hearing what madam the harlot, I mean Sofia, had said, left and went to Bernardo and brought him the whole story. Bernardo said, "It would be too much for her scented charms, even if she smelled of

moscato volere tanti fiorini." E tra sè pensò un bel modo e disse alla messetta, "Va e di'a madonna Sofia che io sono contento d'arrecargli fiorini dugento et stare lo dì e la notte seco, ma perchè altri non si pensi di noi male, dille, che io merrò meco uno famiglio e senza a lui dire niente lo manderò a fare alcuna ambasciata et per questo modo persona si potrà esser accorta che io a lei sia venuto." La messetta disse, "Bene avete ordinato." E tornò alla donna e tutto le disse.

La donna contenta disse che bene avea fatto et messasi mano a borsa gli diè uno fiorino. Et a messer Bernardo mandò a dire che tutto era in punto, et che lui s'apparecchi il giorno ad andare. Messer Bernardo, avendo ordita la tela e bisognandola tessere, pensò chiedere in prestito a Pircosso, marito di madonna Sofia, fiorini dugento, et andato a lui disse, "O Pircosso, io ho alle mani una mercanzia al mio animo desiderosa, la quale m'è promessa per fiorini dugento, et senza quella al presente stare non posso a questo soldo, e però io ti prego mi debbi servire di fiorini dugento e come arò le mie prime paghe te li renderò con quello merito mi dírai." Disse Pircosso, "Volentieri," et aperta una cassa, gli prestò fiorini dugento dicendo, "A me conviene andare ad Ancona per certe mercanzie. Come arete le paghe, serbatemi li dinari." Messer Bernardo disse, "Se quello che m'è promesso inanti non facessi, volete che alla donna vostra questi fiorini renda?" Pircosso disse, "Si, presti questi dinari." E Pircosso, messosi in punto per andare ad Ancona, e' partissi di Perugia l'altro dì. Messer Bernardo sta allegro; madonna Sofia aspetta doppia piumata et per fiorini dugento, appresso la sua quintana riempiuta, sta molto contenta del partimento di Pircosso.

Venuto la domenica di carnelevale, madonna Sofia invitata dalla vicinanza alli orti [se] volea andare, ella rispondea, "Pircosso mio è ito ad Ancona e non so come si stia: io non voglio oggi uscir di casa, ma lo dì di carnelevale, se altro non sento, verrò." Le vicine acconcionsi, et se ne vanno alli orti a godere; madonna Sofia sta ad aspettare. Messer Bernardo prese uno suo stretto famiglio, avendolo di tutto il suo pensieri informato, seco lo menò in casa di madonna Sofia, e saliti in sala, dove madonna Sofia aspettava, messer Bernardo fingendosi disse, "Il vostro marito mi prestò fiorini dugento, li quali, non avendoli spesi, ve li rendo, che quando Pircosso è tornato glieli date," e misseli in sulla taula. Lo famiglio informato disse, "Messere, sapete che a casa dovete esser aspettato, et non essendovi, neuno saprà niente di voi." Or disse messer Bernardo, "Ben hai ditto, e va, e di' a chi viene che io verrò tanto che questi dinari abbia nomerati." Lo fante subito si partio. Messer Bernardo disse come avvenne fatto che il fante si

oriental spices, to ask for so many florins for them!" And thinking up a good trick, he said to the go-between, "Go and say to Lady Sofia that I will be happy to give her two hundred florins and to remain the day and the night with her; but so that others will not think ill of us, tell her that I will bring a servant with me, and without telling him anything, I will send him on some errand; and in this way, no one will be aware that I have come to her." The go-between said, "You have made a good decision." And she returned to the lady and told her everything.

The lady was pleased and said that she had done well and, putting her hand into her purse, gave her a florin. And she sent her to Bernardo to say that everything was arranged and that he should on that day prepare to go to her. Bernardo, having arranged the plot and busy weaving it, determined to borrow from Pircosso, the husband of Lady Sofia, two hundred florins. And going to him he said, "Oh Pircosso, I have in hand a transaction which to my mind is very desirable and which is promised to me for two hundred florins; and without it I cannot now remain in this service. And for this reason I ask you to oblige me with two hundred florins. And when I have my first pay, I will return them to you with whatever interest you say." Pircosso said, "Gladly." And opening a chest, he lent him two hundred florins, saying, "I must go to Ancona on business. When you have your pay, keep the money for me." Bernardo said, "If what has been promised me should not be fulfilled, do you wish me to return these florins to your wife?" Pircosso said, "Yes, return this money." And Pircosso got ready to go to Ancona and left Perugia the next day. Bernardo is delighted. After having perfumed herself, Lady Sofia waits all decked out in her finery for the two hundred florins, very pleased by the departure of Pircosso.

When the Sunday of the carnival was at hand, Lady Sofia, invited by the neighbors to go to the gardens, replied, "My Pircosso has gone to Ancona and I don't know how he will manage; I don't want to go out of the house today, but on the day of the carnival, if I don't hear anything new, I will come." The neighbors, having attired themselves, go out to the gardens to enjoy themselves. Lady Sofia stays behind to wait. Bernardo, having taken a close servant of his and having informed him of the whole plan, took him along to the house of Lady Sofia and, going up to the room where Lady Sofia was waiting, Bernardo said by way of pretense, "Your husband lent me two hundred florins, which I have not used, and therefore I am returning them to you so that when Pircosso returns, you will give them to him." And he put them on the table. The servant, who had been instructed, said, "Sir, you know that you are expected at home, and not finding you, no one will know what has become of you." Now Bernardo said, "You do well to remind me of this; go and tell anyone who comes that I will come as soon as I have counted this money." The

ricordoe di quello avea a fare. Madonna Sofia disse per arte ogni cosa avere fatto. "Prima il mio marito esser fuori, apresso voi addutti li fiorini dugento, et in contrada non esser persona che veduto v'abbia, e però noi possiamo stare in buono agio oggi e stanotte." Messer Bernardo dice, "Voi dite il vero," e nomerati li dinari, messer Bernardo prese madonna Sofia et basciandola disse che le piacesse contentarlo di quello che più volte ha disiato. Madonna Sofia, apparecchiata la sua quintana a rimover li colpi della punta della lancia di messer Bernardo, montato a cavallo colla lancia ritta percosse in quintana et fu di tutta la quintana vincitore et quante volte prima che sera fusse la punta della sua lancia in nella quintana di Sofia misse e quella dentro tenendovi tanto che da sè stessa la lancia n'usciva. E come il dì venuto vincitore della giostra, così la notte più di sei colpi colla sua lancia in nella quintana percosse. La mattina, coronato di vittoria, si partio.

E madonna Sofia, allegra che la sua quintana avea portato l'onore sopra tutte le quintane di Perugia et rallegrandosi de'fiorini auti e molte volte innomeratoli, et passato alquanti giorni della quaresima, Pircosso tornò d'Ancona. Messer Bernardo, ciò sentendo, subito prese il suo secreto famiglio et a casa di Pircosso se n'andò et fatto richiedere Pircosso. [Quando] sente che messer Bernardo lo richiede, disse che venisse su. Messer Bernardo, che avea al suo [famiglio] fatto comprare alquante anguille grosse et alcuna tinca del lago di Perugia, è montato in sala; subito a Pircosso disse, presente madonna Sofia, "Voi sapete che mi prestaste fiorini dugento quando vi partiste per alcuno mio bisogno e io quelli non potendo spender li addussi a madonna Sofia vostra donna, come mi diceste, presente questo mio famiglio, e perchè a me fu sommo servizio, posto che io quelli non spendesse, vo' che voi con madonna abbiate queste anguille e questa tinca et che le ricordate per mio amore, non per rispetto del servizio, ma per domestichezza." Pircosso, che ode che alla moglie ha renduto li fiorini dugento, non avendogli nulla ditto, le disse, "O tu non me n'hai ditto nulla?" Lo famiglio astuto disse a Pircosso, "In mia presenzia messer Bernardo glieli diè." La donna subito comprese la malizia di messer Bernardo e disse, "Io pensavo dirtelo a più agio, ma poi che messer Bernardo dice che a me li rendeo egli dice vero. Ben credea che fusseno stati d'altra mercanzia che di prestito, et arei voluto che alla ragione della mercanzia tu li avessi messi." Pircosso disse, "Io glieli prestai il giorno che di qui mi partii." Messer Bernardo, "Voi dite vero et per certo il servizio fu a me grande e però sempre mi vi tengo obbligato." La donna come baldanzosa disse, "Oimè non vi tenete obbligato, già sapete che io sono una volta moglie di Pircosso et così dovete esser obbligato a me come a lui." Messer Bernardo, che di lei avea avuto quello volea, cognoscendola

servant went away immediately. Bernardo explained how it came about that the servant remembered what he had to do. Lady Sofia said that everything had been worked out artfully: "First, my husband is away from home; the florins have been brought, and there is no one in the neighborhood who has seen us. And therefore we can be at our ease today and tonight." Bernardo said, "You are right." And having counted the money, Bernardo took Lady Sofia and kissing her said that she should be so good as to satisfy him in the way he had mentioned several times. Lady Sofia having prepared her charms to receive the blows of the point of Sir Bernardo's lance, he mounted and, with his lance erect, drove into her and was victor over all her charms, and as many times, both early and late, as the point of his lance was placed in the charms of Sofia, she grasped it so eagerly that it hardly left her. And when the day came, he emerged as victor in the joust and had thus struck more than six blows with his lance. In the morning, crowned with victory, he departed.

And Lady Sofia, delighted that her charms had taken precedence over all the charms of Perugia and pleased with so many florins, counted them many times; and after several days of Lent, Pircosso returned from Ancona. Bernardo, hearing this, immediately took his intimate servant and went out to Pircosso's house and asked for Pircosso. When he heard that Bernardo was asking for him, he had him come up. Bernardo, who had made his servant buy several large eels and a tench from the lake of Perugia and having gone upstairs to the parlor, quickly said to Pircosso, in the presence of Lady Sofia, "You know that you lent me two hundred florins when you departed, for a certain transaction of mine, and I, not being able to spend them, brought them to Lady Sofia, your wife, as you told me, in the presence of this servant of mine; and since this was a great service to me, although I did not spend them, I want you and Lady Sofia to accept these eels and this tench and enjoy them for my sake, not because of the service but for our friendship." Pircosso, who heard that the two hundred florins had been returned to his wife and knowing that she had said nothing to him, said to her, "You have told me nothing of this." The clever servant said to Pircosso, "Bernardo gave them to her in my presence." The lady immediately understood Bernardo's fraud and said, "I intended to tell you at a more convenient moment, but what Bernardo is saying is the truth. I thought indeed that they were from another transaction rather than from a loan and I would have wished that you had invested them in your business." Pircosso said, "I lent them to him the day I left here." Bernardo: "You are right and indeed you did me a great service and therefore I will always be obliged to you." The lady, who was nothing daunted, said, "Dear me, don't be obligated thus; you know that I am Pircosso's wife and therefore you should be obliged to me as well as to him." Bernardo, who had had what he wanted from her and knowing her to be

cattiva, disse, "Madonna, in nelle nostre contrade li mariti portano le brache et a loro si de' rendere reverenzia, et io vo' osservare la legge del mio paese, però che a Pircosso de' denari prestati gli sono sempre obbligato et non a voi." Pircosso, che ode sì bel parlare, dice alla donna, "Messer Bernardo ha ditto quello che si conviene," et preso l'anguille colla tinca, messer Bernardo si partio e Pircosso colla moglie rimane. Madonna Sofia, vedendosi così beffata, pensò di non cadere in tal fallo mai con persona che per quel modo si abbia quello che dato gli avesse. E così osservò poi.

worthless, said, "Lady, in our regions the husbands wear the trousers and reverence is owed to them, and I wish to observe the law of my country; and therefore I will always be obliged to Pircosso and not to you for the borrowed money." Pircosso, hearing such fine words, said to the lady, "Bernardo has spoken as is fitting." And the eels and the tench having been taken, Bernardo departed and Pircosso remained with his wife. Lady Sofia, seeing herself thus duped, resolved never to fall into such a trap again with a person who got back what he had given her in this way; and this she kept thereafter.

Two Facetiae

A *facetia* is a brief, preferably well-turned, joke or anecdote. Though the joke is itself presumably immemorial, the *facetia* as a literary form is the creation of Giovanni Francesco Bracciolini, called Poggio (1380–1459). Poggio was a Florentine of great literary accomplishments who served as secretary at the Papal Court in Rome. He was one of the most active humanists and the author of a large number of historical, moral, rhetorical, and polemical works. In addition he was a keen manuscript hunter and was responsible for turning up works of

---

POGGIO: DE RUSTICO QUI ANSEREM VENALEM DEFEREBAT

Rusticum adolescentem, qui Florentiae anserem deferebat venalem, conspicata mulier, quae sibi faceta videbatur, ridendi hominis gratia rogavit, quanti anserem faceret. At ille, "Quod facillime," inquit, "persolvas." "Quid est?" inquit mulier. "Unico," ait ille, "coitu." "Jocaris," respondit mulier, "sed domum ingredere, et de pretio conveniemus."

Ingressus domum, cum perstaret in sententia, mulier pretio annuit. Verum cum superiores partes egisset, petito ansere, rusticus se negat daturum; non enim se mulierem subagitasse, sed se ab ea compressum dixit. Igitur, reintegrata pugna, munere sessoris fungitur adolescens. Iterum ex conventu mulier cum anserem postulasset, renuit adolescens, pari ratione se cum illa esse asserens; non enim se pretium accepisse, sed repulisse injuriam illatam; nam se prius a muliere subactum.

Cum longior progrederetur contentio, superveniens vir sciscitatur, quaenam haec sit controversia. "Cupiebam," inquit uxor, "tibi coenam opiparem parare, nisi hic maledictus impediret; convenerat enim mecum in viginti solidis; nunc, postquam introiit domum, mutata est sententia, duos amplius requirit."

"Eia," inquit vir, "tam parva res impedit coenam nostram! Accipe," inquit, "quodlibet." Ita rusticus pretium abstulit et concubitum uxoris.

such classical authors as Quintilian, Lucretius, Statius, Ammianus Marcellinus, Cicero, and Plautus. But his fame among nonhumanists rests on his *Liber facetiarum* (1438–1452), a collection of topical, historical, satirical, bawdy, and often funny anecdotes.

Poggio's *facetiae* were a great literary success and were soon imitated abroad. Our second example of the genre comes from the most prominent German imitator, Heinrich Bebel (1472–1518), whose *Libri facetiarum* appeared from 1508 to 1512. The text of Poggio's *facetia* is from *The Facetiae or Jocose Tales of Poggio* (Paris, 1879), pp. 111–113, and the text of Bebel's *facetia* is from *Facetiarum Henrici Bebelii poetae a D. Maximiliano laureati libri tres a mendis repurgati et in lucem rursus redditi* (Tübingen, 1542), p. 80. Poggio's collection has recently become available in paperback: Bernhardt J. Hurwood, trans., *The Facetiae of Giovanni Francesco Poggio Bracciolini* (New York: Award Books; London: Tandem Books, 1968).

POGGIO: THE PEASANT WHO HAD A GOOSE FOR SALE

A young peasant, who was carrying a goose to Florence to sell, was spied by a lady, who fancied herself witty and, who, for a joke, asked him how much he wanted for the goose. "What you can very easily pay," he said. "What is that?" asked the woman. "One screw," he said. "You are joking," she replied, "but let's go into the house and we will agree on a price."

When they went into the house, he persisted in his intention, and the lady agreed to the price. But, since she had been on top, when she claimed the goose, the peasant refused to give it up; he said it was not he who had pushed her down but she who had lain upon him. Therefore, the struggle was renewed, and the youth performed like a prize rider. According to the agreement, the woman again asked for the goose, but the young man again refused, asserting that now they were even, for he had not received the agreed price but had only avenged the insult the woman had done him when she first got on top of him.

The argument had continued for a long time when the husband came home and asked what the argument was about. "I was eager," said the wife, "to get you a good meal, if it had not been for this cursed wretch; he agreed with me on twenty pence, but when he came into the house, he changed his mind, and he insists on two more."

"Gracious!" said the husband, "should so small an amount delay our dinner? Here," he said, "take what you want." Thus the peasant carried off both the cash and the favors of the wife.

BEBEL: FACTUM CUIUSDAM FRANCIGENAE

Quidam Francigena (ut est genus hominum fallax et versutum) in civitate Ticino a quodam cive centum aureos mutuo accepit, oppignorando ei aureum torquem: atque illius uxorem accedens, dixit: "Hos accipe centum, atque unam noctem voluntati meae obsequaris." Mulier praedae dulcedine capta (sum sit nummus optimum expugnandae pudicitiae instrumentum), consensit. Francus postridie expleta libidine virum accessit, suum torquem exegit, quoniam aureos omnes uxori illius reddiderit. Quae conventa non potuit negare, frustraque Franco fuit obsequiosa.

BEBEL: THE DEED OF A CERTAIN FRENCHMAN

A certain Frenchman, since the French are a deceitful and crafty race, received a hundred gold pieces from a certain citizen of the city of Pavia by giving him a golden chain as a pledge. And approaching this man's wife, he said: "Accept these hundred gold pieces and consent to do my will for one night." The woman, succumbing to the temptation of the prize, since money is the best instrument for overcoming virtue, consented. The Frenchman, having satisfied his lust, went to her husband the next day and demanded his chain inasmuch as he had returned all the gold to his wife. She could not deny the claim and was thus obliged to comply with the Frenchman's request despite herself.

Jacob Frey's "A Goldsmith's Wife in Augsburg"

The sixteenth-century German collections of *Schwänke* have been mentioned already (p. 65), and there is not much to be added about Frey and his *Gartengesellschaft.* Archival researches have revealed only that he was born in

---

VON EINER GOLDTSCHMIDIN ZU AUGSBURG UND EINEM JUNGEN EDELMAN, WIE SIE IM EIN GULDIN KETTIN AB ERBULET UND WIDER GAB

Uff dem reichsstag zu Augspurg was ein edelman, der des keisers hoff nach zohe, in einer schönen, grossen herberg, der het 4 oder 5 pferd. Wann er wolt spatzieren reiten, so sass er im hoff uff und rannt für die thür, warff das ross ein mal oder etliche herumb. Es was ein hüpscher, geradner edelman und het ein schöne guldine ketten am halss. Nun was neben der herberg ein goldschmid, ein reicher burger, der het ein schönes weib; und wann der edelman also für das hauss rant, macht gute bössle, so lag des goldtschmids fraw am fenster, sagt, "Ich wolt, das ich mit dem edelmann solt ein par leinlachen zerreissen." Das hört der edelman, der sprach, "Da wolt ich mein guldin ketten umb geben." Das vermarckt die fraw.

Als nun über drey oder vier tag ir man nit daheimen was, liess sie den edelman beschicken, sagt, "Junckherr, sind ir noch der wort, die ir das ander mal geredt haben, eingedenck?" "Ja, fraw," sagt der edelman. Damit furt sie ihn an ein besonder gemach, zohe sich auss bitz auff das hembd, sprach, "Junckherr, ir wisst wol, warumb es zu thun ist." Der edelman sprach, "Ja, es ist umb die ketten zu thun," zohe sie von dem hals, gab sie der frawen. Sie beschloss die ketten behend in einen trog uff ire kleider. Wolan, die zwey tantzten die nacht den Dannheuser.

Morgends frü der edelman ward ausgelassen, was traurig umb sein ketten. Sein knecht sahe, das der junckherr traurig was, sprach, "Juncker, was ligt euch an?" Der edelman sagt, "Mein anligen kan ich niemands klagen." Der knecht sprach, "Ey junckherr, es ist allwegen gewesen, wann einer bekümmert ist, das er solchs seinen guten freunden klaget unnd offenbaret. Nun binn ich ewer diener, ich will mein haut dran strecken,

Strassburg sometime before 1520. He was a notary in the Alsatian town of Maursmünster and died in 1562. Five other works bearing his name are extant, an allegorical dialogue, two plays with Biblical themes (Abraham and Lazarus), a *Fastnachtspiel*, and a collection of brief lives in the manner of Plutarch. About Frey himself we know nothing except what a contemporary noted next to his name in an administrative document after his death: "God bless him, he was a boon companion!"

The text printed here is no. 76 in the collection and is taken from *Jakob Freys Gartengesellschaft*, ed. Johannes Bolte (Tübingen, 1896), pp. 90–92. It contains a somewhat less elaborate example of the *double entendre* developed at length in "The Lady Doctor."

ABOUT A GOLDSMITH'S WIFE IN AUGSBURG AND A YOUNG NOBLEMAN, HOW SHE GAINED A GOLDEN CHAIN FROM HIM FOR LOVE AND GAVE IT BACK

At the Reichstag in Augsburg there was a nobleman in the following of the Emperor's court, who lived in a fine big inn and had four or five horses. When he wanted to go riding, he mounted in the court and trotted out the gate and threw the horse's head about a few times. He was a handsome, stately nobleman and had a beautiful gold chain around his neck. Now next to the inn there was a goldsmith, a rich burgher, who had a beautiful wife. And when the nobleman cantered by the house this way and made a couple of neat turns, the goldsmith's wife was at the window and said, "I'd like to tear a few bedsheets with that nobleman." The nobleman heard this and said, "I'd give my gold chain for that." The woman took note of this.

Now, when three or four days later her husband was not at home, she had the nobleman sent for and said, "Sir, do you still remember the words that you spoke before?" "Yes, lady," said the nobleman. With that she led him to a separate chamber, undressed to her shift, and said, "Sir, you know what it is a question of." The nobleman said, "Yes, it is a question of the chain," took it from his neck, and gave it to the woman. She quickly locked the chain in a chest on top of her clothes. Well, the two of them danced to Tannhäuser's tune that night.

The next morning the nobleman was let out and was grieved by the loss of his chain. His servant saw that the nobleman was grieved and said, "Sir, what is troubling you?" The nobleman said, "I cannot complain of this affair to anyone." The servant said, "Oh sir, it has always been that when someone is grieved, he tells it and complains to his good friends. Now, I am your servant and I will put my life at stake to help you." The

es muss euch geholffen werden." Der junckherr erzalt dem knecht, wie es im mit der goldtschmidin und der guldin ketten gangen seye. Der knecht sagt, "Dem ist wol zu thun. Die fraw hat uns zum nechsten ein mürselstein geluhen, da ein gaul kranck war, ettwas darinn zu stossen; den will ich ihr wider bringen. Land mich machen, ewer ketten soll euch wider werden."

Am andern tag zu dem imbis, als der goldtschmid und sein fraw zu tisch sassend, klopffet der knecht an der thür, ward eingelassen, stund für den tisch und sagt, "Herr, da schickt euch mein junckherr den mürselstein, danckt euch sehr und begert die guldin ketten, die er ewer frawen darfür zu pfand hat gelassen." Der goldtschmid war zornig über die fraw, sagt, warumb sie imb ein so klein ding also ein kostlich pfand nem. Die fraw sprach, "Herr, ich hab kein ketten empfangen." Sagt der herr, "Nu hörst du wol, was der knecht sagt." Die fraw leucknet wie ein mörder, aber der knecht sprach, "Zu wortzeichen legt sie die ketten in ein trog unden am beth auff die kleider." Der herr ward zornig, nam die schlüssel, schloss den trog uff, fand die ketten und gab sie dem knecht; der nam sie, gienge sein strass.

Die fraw gienge dem knecht nach unnd sprach, "Sag deinem junckherrn, er müss mir zum nechsten nimer meh in meinem mürselstein stossen. Ich will im auch kein häffely mehr leihen, das er darin kochen solle, und solt er hungers sterben. Wie ers gewölt unnd im gefallen hatt, habe ich ihm geschirr geluhen; das hat er mir gelöchert und zerstossen. Nun muss ich die stuck mir selbs behalten." Der knecht gab dem junckherrn die ketten; der reit hinweg mitt freuden, unnd warend das par leinlachen auch zerrissen.

nobleman told the servant what had happened with the goldsmith's wife and the chain. The servant said, "There is a solution. The woman recently loaned us a mortar, when a horse was sick, to crush something in; I will return it to her. Leave it up to me; you'll get your chain back again."

The next day at mealtime, when the goldsmith and his wife were sitting at table, the servant knocked at the door, was admitted, stood before the table, and said, "Sir, my master sends you your mortar, thanks you very much and requests the golden chain that he left with your wife as a pledge." The goldsmith was angry at the woman and asked why she had taken such a valuable pledge for so small a thing. The woman said, "Sir, I have received no chain." The master said, "Now you hear perfectly well what the servant says." The woman denied it for all she was worth, but the servant said, "As a proof of my words, she put the chain in a chest at the foot of the bed on top of her clothes." The master became angry, took the key, opened the chest, found the chain, and gave it to the servant. He took it and went on his way.

The woman followed the servant and said, "Tell your master he may never again pound in my mortar. Nor will I lend any pot to cook in, even if he dies of hunger. Just as he desired and as it pleased him, I lent him dishes, and he has poked them full of holes. Now I have to keep the pieces myself." The servant gave his master the chain; he rode away joyfully, and the bedsheets were ripped too.

"The Priest and the Lady"

This anonymous thirteenth-century fabliau is preserved in but one manuscript, but it must have been fairly popular, for prose adaptations of it appear in a

---

DU PRESTRE ET DE LA DAME

Icil, qui les mençonges trueve,
A fait ceste trestote nueve,
Quar il avint, à un mardi,
Que uns Prestres, devers Lardi,
S'aloit à Estanpes deduire;
Mais ses deduiz li dut bien nuire
Ainsi com vos m'orroiz ja dire.
Mais conter vos vueil tot à tire
Comment une cointe borgoise,
10 Qui estoit mignote et cortoise,
Li ot mandé, n'est mie guile,
Que ses sires à une vile
Devoit cel jor au marchié estre:
Bien li ot tot conté son estre.
Que vos iroie plus contant?
Li Prestres si esploita tant,
Et tant de la Dame s'aprime
Qu'il fu à l'ostel devant prime,
Où fu receü sanz dangier.
20 La baiesse atorne à mengier
Char cuite en pot, pastez au poivre,
Et bon vin cler et sain à boivre,
Et li bains estoit ja chauffez,
Quant uns deables, uns mauffez,
Le seignor la Dame amena,
Quant au marchié ot esté ja.
Le cheval qui soef le porte,
Il s'en vint droit devant la porte;
Si la trouva molt bien fermée,
30 Que la barre ert tote coulée.
Quand il parla, si dit, "Ovrez
Errant et point n'i demorez;
Por qoi m'avez la porte close?"

number of Renaissance French collections, such as the *Nouveaux contes à rire.* One explanatory remark is necessary on the setting of the tale: the husband enters on horseback and sees his wife in the bathtub, because the house, like most prosperous dwellings of the period, opens onto a walled courtyard, and the bath is set up in the courtyard rather than in the house itself. Our text is from Montaiglon and Raynaud, II, 235–241.

THE PRIEST AND THE LADY

He who composed this fiction
Has made it altogether new.
It happened on a Thursday
That a priest, near Lardi,
Went off to Etampes to amuse herself;
But his amusement came close to harming him,
As you will now hear me tell.
But I want to tell you first of all
How a merchant's lovely wife,
Who was attractive and courteous, 10
Sent word to this priest—it is no lie—
That her husband one day
Had to be out of town on business;
Indeed, she told him her whole situation.
What more should I tell you?
The priest rushed so fast
And came so quickly to the lady
That he was at the house before prime,
Where he was received without any coyness.
The maidservant started to get dinner— 20
Meat cooked in a stew, pies with pepper,
And good clear wine, healthy to drink.
And the bath water was already heated
When a devil, a misbegotten spirit,
Brought the husband home to the wife,
Since he had already finished his business.
The horse that gently carried him
Brought him right to the gate,
Which he found closed fast,
For the bar was locked tight. 30
Then he spoke and said, "Open
Quickly and don't delay in there!
Why have you shut the gate on me?"

Et la borgoise molt en poise,
Qui li covient la porte ovrir;
Mais cele fist avant covrir
Les pastez soz une touaille,
Et puis après se retravaille
De repondre le chanteor,
40 Qui de soi avoit grant paor.
Au Provoire loe et conseille
Qu'il entrast en une corbeille,
Qui ert mise dedenz la porte.
Et cil, qui ne se desconforte,
Cel conseil ne refusa mie,
Ainz i entra, sanz nule aïe,
Que geter se velt de la frape;
Mais il laissa aval sa chape.
Plus ne repostent ne ne firent,
50 Tot maintenant la porte ovrirent
Au borgois qui tendoit la muse.
Cil entra enz et partot muse,
Tant qu'il a la cuve veüe
Où la Dame estoit tote nue;
Ainz nul barat n'i estendi.
Tantost du cheval descendi,
Si l'a fait molt tost establer:
Et cil, qui n'a soing de fabler,
Qui repoz ert en la corbeille,
60 Icil ne dort ne ne someille,
Mais si fort de paor trestranble,
Que la corbeille et lui ensanble
Encontre terre aval chaïrent;
Cil de l'ostel pas ne le virent.
Quant il vit qu'il estoit cheüz
Et qu'il n'estoit mie veüz,
Si s'en vient enmi la meson;
Hardiement dist sa raison,
Ne parla pas comme noienz,
70 "Diex," fait li Prestres, "soit ceanz;
Ge vos raport vostre corbeille."
Au borgois molt a grant merveille
Quant il vit ainsi le Provoire,
Et la Dame li fait acroire
Que ele le li avoit prestée.
Bien est la dame asseürée,

And the wife was greatly upset,
For she had to open the gate;
But first she had the pies
Covered with a towel,
And then she worked fiercely
To hide the priest,
Who was very afraid for himself. 40
She advised and urged the parson
To get into a wicker basket
That was set behind the gate,
And he, who was in despair,
Did not refuse this advice,
But got in there, without any help,
For he wanted to get out of this mess;
But he left his cape behind.
They hid nothing more nor did anything else,
But straightway opened the door 50
For the merchant, who was wasting his time.
He came in and looked about
Until he saw the bathtub,
Where the lady was, stark naked;
But he saw no harm in that.
Then he got down from his horse,
And had it quickly taken to the stable.
And he who had no desire to tell tales—
He who was resting in the basket
Where he could neither snooze nor sleep— 60
He trembled so violently from fear
That he and the basket together
Tumbled onto the ground.
Those in the house did not see him.
When he realized that he had fallen
And had not been seen,
He went straight into the house.
Boldly he spoke out these words,
And he did not sound as though he were desperate;
Said the priest, "God be in this house! 70
I have brought you back your basket."
The merchant was greatly surprised
When he saw the parson like this,
And the lady made him believe
That she had loaned it to him;
She was as self-assured as you please.

"Certes que ge en ai bon gaige."
"Dame, vos feïstes outraige,"
Fait li borgois, "quant en preïstes
80 Son gaige, ne ne retenistes."
Or est li Prestres fors de foire,
"Dame," fait il, "ma chape noire,
Se vos plaist, quar me faites rendre,
Ge n'ai mestier de plus atendre,
Et ma toaille et mes pastez."
"Sire Prestres, trop vos hastez,
Mais mengiez avuec mon seignor;
Si li faites itant d'ennor."
Et li Prestres dit, "Je l'otroie,"
90 Qui du remanoir ot grant joie:
Il est remés sanz grant dangier.
Lors vont laver et puis mengier.
La table sist sor deus coussins;
Desor la table ot deus broissins
Où il avoit cierges d'argent;
Molt estoient bel et gent.
Lors despiecent pastez et froissent;
La Dame et li Prestres s'engoissent
De verser vin à grant foison:
100 Tant qu'au seignor de la maison
Ont tant doné de vin à boivre
Et mengier des pastez au poivre
Que il fu maintenant toz yvres.
Si ot vaillant plus de mil livres
En son chatel que au matin.
Lors commence à paller latin
Et postroillaz et alemant,
Et puis tyois et puis flemmanc,
Et se ventoit de sa largesce,
110 Et d'une trop fiere proesce
Que il soloit faire en s'anfance;
Li vins l'avoit fet roi de France.
  Lors dist li Prestres, ce me sanble,
Que trois genz leveroit ensanble;
Mais li borgois li contredist,
Et dit, "Merveilles avez dit;
Ice ne porroit pas voir estre;
Merveille avez dit, sire Prestre."
Fait li Prestres, "Et g'i metroie."

"Certainly, I have had a good pledge for it."
  "Lady, you do wrong,"
Said the merchant, "when for this you ask
His pledge, as if you would not get it back." 80
Now the priest is bold in turn,
"Lady," he said, "my black cape,
If you please, since you made me give it;
I have no need to wait any longer,
And give me back my towel and my pies."
  "Sir Priest, you are too hasty;
You should have dinner with my husband,
If you would do him so great an honor."
  And the priest said, "I grant it,"
And he was very glad at the outcome: 90
He stayed without much resistance.
Next they went to wash themselves and then to eat.
The table rested on two cushions;
Upon the table were two candlestick holders
Where there were two silver candlesticks;
Everything was noble and elegant.
  Then they cut up pies and handed them around;
The lady and the priest busied themselves
In pouring out wine in great abundance;
To the lord of the house 100
They gave so much wine to drink
And so many pies with pepper to eat
That quickly he was dead drunk.
He was worth a thousand pounds
More than he was in the morning.
Then he began to speak Latin
And gibberish and German
And then Dutch and Flemish,
And he boasted of his generosity,
And of the terrible deeds of prowess 110
That he used to do in his younger days;
The wine had made him the King of France.
  Then the priest said, as I have heard,
That he could pick up three people at once.
But the merchant denied this
And said, "You speak fantasies.
Indeed, it could not be done here;
You speak fantasies, Sir Priest."
  Said the priest, "I will bet on it."

120 "Et qui metroiz?" fait il. "Une oie,"
Fait li Prestres, "se vos volez."
"Ce est gas, quant ainsinc pallez,"
Fait li borgois, qui le devée.
La parole au Provoire agrée
Et molt li plaist et atalente.
Lors vient au borgois; si l'adente
Tot estendu encontre terre,
Et puis va la baiasse querre;
S'il l'a mise sor son seignor;
130 A la Dame fist tant d'onor
Que sor lui lieve la chemise;
Après si l'a enverse mise;
Entre les cuisses si li entre;
Par le pertuis li entre el ventre;
Là a mis son fuiron privé:
Molt seroit malvais au civé
Li connins que li fuirons chace.
Molt est fox qui tel connin trace;
Mielz li venroit trover deus lievres,
140 Quar cil connins est si enrievres
Qu'il ne puet faire bele chiere
S'il n'a fuiron en sa tesniere.
De ci au borjois vos rameine,
De lui relever molt se paine,
Que, quant li Prestres boute et saiche,
Li borgois dit qu'il les esquasche
Et que desor lui a deus rosches,
Et li Prestres sone deus cloches,
Qui avoit faite sa besoigne.
150 Au borgois a dit sanz aloigne,
"Levez sus, que ge ne porroie
Ces trois lever por riens que j'oie:
Por quant s'en ai tel paine eüe
Que tote la coille m'en sue
Et de l'angoisse et de l'efforz."
Dist la Dame, "N'estes si forz
Que ausi forz ou plus ne soit;
Or paiez l'oie, quar c'est droit."
"Dame," fait il, "par bone estraine,
160 Soffrez vos jusqu'à diemaine,
Vos l'aurez grasse par ma foi."
Dit le borgois, "Et ge l'otroi,

"And what will you bet?" he said. 120
"A goose," said the priest, "if you are willing."
"That is foolish, when you talk like that,"
Said the merchant, who accepted the challenge.
This speech was agreeable to the parson,
And it greatly pleased and satisfied him.
Then he went to the merchant, and he arranged him
All stretched out on the floor;
And then he went to get the maidservant,
And he placed her upon her lord;
To the lady he did such honor 130
That he lifted her dress
After he had stretched her out
And he entered between her thighs.
Through the little opening he entered the belly;
There he put his own special ferret;
It would be straight to the stew-pot
For the poor little hare that this ferret chased.
It is very tricky to chase such a hare;
It would be easier to catch two rabbits,
For this hare is so clever 140
That it could put on a good front
If it had a ferret in its nest.
From this I return to the merchant,
Who was very eager to get up,
Since, when the priest pushed and pulled,
The merchant said that he was squashing them
And that there were two stones upon him,
And that the priest was tolling two bells
When he did his business.
At last he said to the merchant, 150
"Get up, for I could not
Lift these three for anything that I could try,
And I have worked so hard at it
My balls are all sweaty
From the labor and the effort."
Said the lady, "You are not so strong
For one who should be as strong or stronger.
Now hand over the goose, for that was agreed."
"Lady," he said, "by a happy chance,
If you will wait until tomorrow, 160
You will have a fat one, by my faith."
Said the merchant, "And I agree,

Si l'achaterez au marchié:
Bien ai eü le col charchié.
Alez à Dieu beneïçon!"
Atant s'en vait en sa maison,
Que saigement a esploitié;
C'est de tel vente tel marchié.
Par cest flabel poez savoir
170 Molt sont femes de grant savoir:
Tex i a et de grant voisdie;
Molt set feme de renardie,
Quant en tel maniere servi
Son bon seignor par son ami.

Explicit du Prestre et de la Dame

If you will buy it at the market;
I have carried a heavy burden.
Go with God's blessing."
  Straightway he went to his house,
He who had succeeded so cleverly;
It is a matter of buying and selling.
  From this fabliau you can learn
That many women are very clever; **170**
There are women like this of great trickery.
A woman knows much of foxiness
When she has served in this way
Her good husband by means of her lover.

Here ends The Priest and the Lady.

Some Analogues of Chaucer's Other Tales

In this final section we have included two analogues of "The Summoner's Tale," one analogue of "The Manciple's Tale," one analogue of "The Friar's Tale," and "Dame Sirith."

The central episode in Chaucer's "Summoner's Tale," the "satiric legacy," is based on a theme that has long been popular in folk and literary traditions. F. J. Child, in *English and Scottish Popular Ballads,* I, 143–144, lists many examples from English and European balladry; students of English literature will recall such literary examples as Donne's "The Will" or the final lines of Jonathan Swift's "Verses on the Death of Dr. Swift." Likewise, the theme of deception in relation to an inheritance is at least as ancient as the biblical theme of Jacob and Esau. But such deceptions as Esau practices are devised by the would-be heirs rather than the dying maker of the will, and in popular ballads or literary treatments such as Swift's, the satiric legacies exist apart from what might be called the "great expectations" theme, which is the main source of comedy in "The Summoner's Tale."

The story on which the "legacy" in "The Summoner's Tale" is based was probably current in popular tradition. There was a story that Jean de Meun, the author of the second part of the *Roman de la rose,* left a heavy chest to the Jacobin friars in Paris on condition that they bury him in their church and not open the coffer until after his burial. The friars, thinking Jean had repented for the many insulting things he had written about them (even in his *Testament*), rushed to open the coffer as soon as Jean's burial service was finished. When they opened it, they found it was filled with lead. They were so angry they wanted to dig poor Jean up and throw him out of the church, and they were prevented from doing so only by the intervention of Parliament. At least that is the story (for a full account see Méon, *Le Roman de la rose,* I, 57 ff.); we can trace it back no farther than

the sixteenth-century writer Bouchet, who claims as his authority an "old chronicle of Aquitaine." But that such a story was current in the Middle Ages is shown by its appearance in the book of *Til Eulenspiegel.* Til, we are told, bequeathed the contents of a heavy chest to be divided among his friends, the town council of Mölln, and the priest. But when the eager heirs opened the chest, they found it contained only heavy stones.

Aside from these anecdotes, the only extended analogue known to scholars has been "The Tale of the Priest's Bladder," by Jacques de Baisieux, which we have printed below. Scholars such as Skeat once thought that Chaucer knew this French fabliau and used it as his source. But there are few exact resemblances, and as W. M. Hart wrote (*Sources and Analogues,* p. 276), "the very excellences of *Le Dis de la vescie à prestre* might well lead one to think that Chaucer had never seen it; had he encountered the character of the priest, had his attention been called to the possibilities for irony in speech and situation, he would surely have developed them in 'The Summoner's Tale.' " "The Tale of the Priest's Bladder" is therefore best read simply as an example of how another very talented fourteenth-century poet used the same themes as Chaucer employed in his "Summoner's Tale."

However, what these common themes were and how they were transmitted remains a mystery, for no one has ever made a thorough study of the backgrounds of this tale. The situation seems an inevitable one, and it seems likely there were a great many versions of the tale, but the only popular analogues to "The Summoner's Tale" of which we know are those cited by Heinrich von Wlislocki (in *Zeitschrift für vergleichende Literaturgeschichte und Renaissance-Literatur,* Neue Folge, II, 194–199) from Hungarian tradition, and these Hungarian stories are based on Chaucer's tale, unexpected examples of his far-ranging influence rather than testimony to the tradition on which he drew. Therefore, students of Chaucer will be especially interested in the tale from *Til Eulenspiegel,* printed below, which is obviously based on the sort of story that underlies both "The Summoner's Tale" and "The Tale of the Priest's Bladder." *Til Eulenspiegel* has been generally overlooked by students of Chaucer, probably because of its late date (the first edition is dated at the end of the fifteenth century, though the stories it contains are probably older), but it contains three analogues to Chaucer's *Canterbury Tales.* In the earliest editions there is the story of Til's adventure as a false pardoner, which parallels the account that Chaucer's Pardoner gives of himself, even to the trick of warning his audience that adulterous women may not make offerings to his relic (thereby guaranteeing that no woman will fail to make an offering). This is, however, a widespread theme. Equally widespread is the story that Chaucer uses as his "Friar's Tale," which appears

in the 1532 German edition of *Til Eulenspiegel*. Usually it is a farmer or a lawyer that is carried off by the devil, but in *Til Eulenspiegel*, as in Chaucer, it is a summoner (see J. M. Lappenberg, *Dr. Thomas Murners Til Eulenspiegel*, Leipzig, 1854, pp. 142–143). However, the third analogue to Chaucer, "How Howleglas Deceived His Ghostly Father," which we print below, is not so widespread a tale, and is known only from Chaucer, from Jacques de Baisieux's poem, and from *Til Eulenspiegel*.

It seems likely that Til's adventure is based on some fabliau of the same sort that Chaucer knew, and it is significant that Jacques claims that his French work is a translation from a Flemish fabliau. However, only a full study would reveal the nature of the relation among the three tales, and we print *Til Eulenspiegel* only as an example of how this tale could be handled by another writer, who by combining it with a second theme managed to give the "great expectations" tale an additional and even more disgusting outcome.

As an analogue to "The Friar's Tale," we include the story by Caesarius of Heisterbach about "An Administrator Who Was Carried Off Alive by the Devil When He Was on His Way to Collect His Fees." There is no exact analogue to Chaucer's tale, although, as we point out in the introduction to Caesarius' tale, a mistake in translation by previous scholars has obscured the relation between Chaucer's tale and Caesarius' *exemplum*. The editors of *Originals and Analogues* printed two Latin tales (both based on Caesarius' *exemplum*); these are translated by R. D. French in *A Chaucer Handbook* (New York, 1927), pp. 285–286. Both tales were reprinted in *Sources and Analogues* along with another derivative of Caesarius' tale, a story about a farmer and the devil, first printed by Archer Taylor in "The Devil and the Advocate," *PMLA*, XXXVI (1921), 35–59. Taylor adduces a variety of German vernacular and modern folk versions of the story. Since Caesarius' exemplum is the source of all the medieval versions and of most of the modern ones, we have printed his version.

The fourth tale in this section is an analogue to "The Manciple's Tale." The story that the Manciple tells is often classified with Chaucer's fabliaux, but it has relatively little in common with the other works we have considered, and its principal source is not medieval story but classical legend: Ovid's *Metamorphoses* (II, 531–562), as reinterpreted in medieval adaptations such as the early fourteenth-century *Ovide moralisé* and Guillaume de Machaut's *Le Livre du voir dit*. However, Chaucer's version also owes something to the tale of the talking bird in the popular *Seven Sages of Rome*, which stems ultimately from Oriental sources and which clearly belongs in the category with which this volume is concerned. Chaucer may have known that tale in the Middle English translation, since the English *Seven Sages* was very popular in the fourteenth century. How-

ever, we have chosen to print the earliest French prose version, which was the source for the Middle English version and which, unlike the English *Seven Sages,* is now unobtainable in all but the largest libraries, for it was unknown to the compilers of *Originals and Analogues,* who printed a late French verse version, and consequently has not been reprinted since the early nineteenth century.

Finally, we have printed the thirteenth-century English fabliau "Dame Sirith," not as an analogue to Chaucer's works but as an illustration of what another English writer, a talented one at that, could do in this genre before it had been touched by the master hand of Geoffrey Chaucer. "Dame Sirith" is a skillful work, and as the reader will see, it holds its own in this distinguished company.

Jacques de Baisieux's "Tale of the Priest's Bladder"

Jacques de Baisieux probably lived in the first quarter of the fourteenth century and was a native of the small Belgian town of Baisieux near Mons. He wrote a number of courtly and allegorical poems as well as "The Tale of the Priest's

---

LI DIS DE LE VESCIE A PRESTRE

En lieu de fable vos dirai
Un voir, ensi k'oï dire ai,
D'un prestre ki astoit manans
Deleis Anwiers; li remanans
Estoit mut biaus de son avoir,
Car plains estoit de grant savoir.
Si n'avoit pas tot despendut,
A amasser avoit tendut,
S'estoit riches hons et moblés;
10 Buez et vaches, brebis et bleiz
Avoit tant c'on n'en savoit conte,
Mais li Mors, qui roi, duc ne conte
N'espargne, l'ot par son message
Somont al naturel passage:
Eutropikes ert devenus;
De nul home n'estoit tenus
Ki li promesist longe vie.
Li prestes, qui out grant envie
De bien morir et justement,
20 Manda tost et isnelement
Son doiien et toz ses amis,
Son avoir entre lor main mis
Por donner et por departir
Cant ilh verront que departir
De son cors estovera l'ame:
Jouuel, cossin, pot ne escame,
Cuete, tuelle, neiz une nape,

Bladder" and "The Three Knights and the Chemise" ("Des Trois Chevaliers et del chainse" in Montaiglon and Raynaud, III, 123–136). This latter tale, which was translated into English verse by G.L. Way in the eighteenth century, is more like a Breton lay than a fabliau, for it is, as Gaston Paris wrote, "filled with the spirit of the poems of the Round Table," and it ends like Chaucer's "Franklin's Tale" with the author turning to the audience to ask which was the most worthy, the knight or his lady. In short, Jaques was a skilled poet, capable of writing well in a variety of modes, and it is curious that he has received so little attention from critics and literary historians. His "Tale of the Priest's Bladder" is one of the best of the fabliaux. Our text is from Montaiglon and Raynaud, III, 106–117.

THE TALE OF THE PRIEST'S BLADDER

Instead of a fabliau, I shall tell you
A true story, as I have heard tell,
Of a priest who dwelt
Near Antwerp. What he had acquired
In the way of possessions was very great,
For he was filled with good sense.
He had not spent everything;
He had taken care to save,
And thus he was a rich and prosperous man.
Of beef cattle, and cows, and grain 10
He had so much that one could not count them.
    But Death, who spares neither
Duke nor count, had summoned him with his messenger
To the inevitable departure.
He became dropsical;
By no one was it believed
That he had promise of a long life.
This priest, who had a deep desire
To die well and justly,
Sent right away 20
For his dean and all his friends,
And put his possessions into their hands
To give out and divide up
When they should see that his soul
Was striving to leave his body.
Not jewels, cushions, pots, nor benches,
Mattresses, linens, not even a tablecloth,

Brebis, moutons, buef, ne sa chape
Ne li remaint que tot ne donne,
30 Et nome chascune persone
A qui ilh vuet c'on doinst ses chozes.
Descovertes, et non pas clozes,
Lettres saeler et escrire
En fist, que ne le vos puis dire;
Plus briément, quant que il avoit
Ilh dona tot quant qu'il savoit,
Con chil qui n'avoit esperance
D'avoir de son mal aligance,
Car sa maladie ert amere.
40 Atant se sont d'Anwier dui Frere
De Saint Jake issu por prechier,
Qui mut se vuelent estachier
Cant aucun desviiet ravoient.
Cele part tot droit en lor voie
Si sont chés le prestre venus.
I estre quidarent retenus
Al mangier, à joie et à feste
. . . . *
Si c'autrefois esté i furent
50 Mais ne mengierent ne ne burent,
Car malade ont trové le prestre.
Non porquant li ont de son estre
Demandé et de son afaire.
Ses mains manient, son viaire,
Ses piés, ses jambes regarderent
Et tot son cors mut bien tansterent;
Si lor sembla bien par droiture
C'awoir ne poist de son mal cure
Ke ne l'en coviengne morir:
60 Trop lonc tans l'a laisié norrir,
Si n'est pas legiers à curer.
"Mais des or nos covient curer,"
Dist l'uns à l'autre, "c'est passé
Ke de l'avoir k'a amassé
Doinst à nostre maison xx livres
A lé, por refaire nos livres;
Se nos le poons ensi faire,
A no Prius devera plaire
Et si en seront liet no Frere."

* The rhyme indicates a line has been lost.

Sheep, mutton, beef, not even his cape—
Nothing remained to him that he did not give away.
And he named each person 30
To whom he wished his things to be given.
He had public, not private,
Letters written and notarized
On this—more I can't tell you.
In short, whatever he had
He gave away as best he knew how.
Since he had no hope
Of any relief from his illness,
For his disease was severe.
At this time two Jacobin friars 40
Had set out from Antwerp to preach;
They greatly desired to profit themselves
By putting back on the right path any who strayed.
They came directly forth on their way
Until they arrived at the priest's house.
They expected to be invited in there
For eating, for pleasure, and for a feast,
. . . .
For they had been there before.
But they will neither eat nor drink, 50
For they have found the priest ill.
Nevertheless, they ask him
About his state and about his condition;
They feel his hands, his face,
His feet, and they look at his legs
And carefully examine his whole body.
Thus it was clear to them indeed
That he could not be cured of his malady,
And that surely he must die of it;
It had been allowed to develop for such a long time 60
That it is not easy to cure.
"Although we should care for him,"
Said the one to the other, "it is too late for that.
Yet, from the possessions he has amassed
He should leave our house twenty pounds
As a bequest for repairing our books;
If we could manage that
It would be pleasing to our prior
And our brothers would rejoice."

70 "Vos dites voir, par Dieu no pere,
Frere Louuiz; or i para
Liqueis miez à lui parlera
Et mostrera nostre besongne."
Al prestre, ki out grant esoingne
De maladie, ont dit sans faille,
"Sire, chis maus mut vos travaille,
Vos nos sambleis mut agreveis,
De vostre ame penser deveis;
Doneis por Dieu de vostre avoir."
80 Dist li prestes, "Ne puis savoir
K'aie caché sortout ne cote
Neis les linchuès à coi me frote,
Ke tout n'aie por Dieu doné."
"Comment aveis vos ordené,"
Dient li Frere, "vo besongne?
Li Escriture nos temongne
C'on doit garder à cui on done,
S'emploiiet est à la persone
A cui on vuet aumone faire."
90 Li prestes respont, sans contraire,
"J'ai à mes povres parentiaus
Doné brebis, vaces et viaus,
Et à povres de cele vilhe
Ai doné ausi, par saint Gilhe,
De bleis qui vaut plus de x livres:
Por ce ke je soie delivres
De ce ke j'ai vers iaus mespris,
Car entor iaus mon vivre ai pris:
Si ai doné as orfenines,
100 A orfenins et à beguines
Et à gens de povre puissance,
Et si ai laisiet, por pitance,
c souz as Freres des Cordeles."
"Ces amuenes si sont mut beles;
Et as Freres de no maison,
Aveis vos fait nule raison?"
Ce dient li doi Frere al prestre.
"Naie, voir." "Ce comment peut estre?
En maison a tant de preudomes,
110 Et à vos prochain voisien somes,
Et si vivons mut sobrement,
Vos ne moreis pas justement

"You speak the truth, by God our Father, 70
Friar Louis. Now I shall prepare
My best snares, and I shall speak to him
And reveal our need to him."
To the priest, who was in grave danger
From his illness, they said straightway,
"Sir, your illness afflicts you severely,
And you seem to us gravely ill.
You must think of your soul;
Give something from your possessions for God."
Said the priest, "I cannot think 80
That I have held back anything—not a coat
Nor even the sheets against which I rub myself.
I have given all for God."
"But," say the friars, "how have you
Ordered your business?
The Scriptures warn us
That one must be careful to whom one makes gifts
And be sure that they are given to the person
To whom one wishes to give alms."
The priest answered agreeably, 90
"To my poor relations I have given
Sheep, and cows, and calves,
And to the poor of this town
I have also given, by Saint Giles,
Some grain that is worth more than ten pounds,
So that I might be delivered
From any wrongs that I have done them,
Since I have made my living among them;
And I have given to orphan girls
And to orphaned lads and to nuns 100
And to people with small means,
And I have also left, for their daily bread,
One hundred sous to the Franciscan friars."
"These alms are very fine,
But have you had no thought
For the friars of our house?"
This the two friars said to the priest.
"No indeed." "How could this be?
In our house there are so many good men,
And we are such close neighbors to you 110
And we live so soberly
That you will not die justly

Se del vostre ne nos laiiés."
Li prestes trestous esmaiiés
Respont, "Par les oelz de ma teste,
A doner n'ai ne bleif ne beste,
Or ne argent, hanap ne cope."
Chascuns des Freres li rencope
Et li mostre par exemplaire
120 K'ilh puet un de ses dons retraire
Et rapeler por iaus doner,
"Nos nos vorimes mut pener
Ke vostre ame fust adrechie,
Car chaiens a esté drechie
Soventes fois bien nostre escuele,
Et li amuene si est biele
Ki est à nostre maison mise.
Nos ne vestons nule chemise
Et si vivomes en pitance.
130 Ce sache Dieus, por la valhance
De vostre argent nel disons mie."
Li prestes l'ot, si s'en gramie
Et pense qu'il s'en vengera,
S'ilh puet, et k'ilh les trufera,
Mar le vont or si près tenant.
As Freres respont maintenant,
"Appenseis sui, doner vos voelh
I jouuel ke mut amer suel
Et aime encore. Par saint Piere,
140 Je n'ai chose gaires plus chiere;
Milh mars d'argent n'en prenderoie,
Et, se je bien haitiés estoie,
Je n'en voroie mie avoir
II^{c} marchies d'autre avoir;
Diez vos a chaiiens asseneis.
Vostre Prieus me ramineis;
Si vos en ferai conissanche
Ains que de vie aie faillance."
Li Frere, sans duel et sans ire,
150 Ont respondut, "Dieus le vos mire!
Cant voleis vos que revenons,
Et nostre Prieuz ramenrons?"
"Demain, je sui ou Dieu plaisir,
Vo promesse deveis saisir
Ains que je trop agreveis soie."

If you do not leave us something of yours."
  The priest, completely astonished,
Answered, "By the eyes of my head,
I have nothing to give, neither grain nor beast,
Gold nor silver, cup nor bowl."
  Each of the friars reproaches him
And shows him by examples
That he could retract one of his gifts **120**
And call it back to give to them,
"We have been willing to take great pains
That your soul should be set right,
For in this place has been set forth—
Many times and well—our teaching;
And the alms are especially good
Which are given to our house.
We do not wear fine shirts,
And we live on poor food.
God knows, as to the value **130**
Of your money, we say nothing."
  The priest hears this and is enraged by it,
And he thinks that he will be avenged for it
If he can, and that he will trick them;
They are going to suffer for pressing him so closely.
Then he answers the friars,
"I have decided that I should give you
A jewel that I have always loved very much
And love still. By Saint Peter,
I have nothing nearly so valuable. **140**
I would not take a thousand marks of silver for it,
And, if I were in good health,
I would not let another have it
For two hundred marks.
God directed you here;
Bring your prior to me,
And I shall tell you about it
Before my life fails me."
  The friars, without sadness or wrath,
Answer, "God bless you for this! **150**
When do you want us to return
And bring our prior?"
  "Tomorrow, if it pleases God I am here,
You shall take your bequest,
Although I shall be greatly troubled."

Atant ont acueilli lor voie
Li Frere; à Anwier sont venu,
Si ont lor chapitre tenu.
Chascuns s'aventure raconte,
160 Mais chil n'ont cure de lonc conte,
Ains ont dit haut en audience,
"Faites venir bone pitance.
II^{c} livres gaangniet avons
A I prestre ke nos savons
Malade chi à une vilhe."
Frere Nichole et Frere Gilhe,
Frere Guilhiame et Frere Ansiaus
Vinrent oïr ces nos nouviauz,
Ki mut forment lor abelissent.
170 De ces grans poisons mander fisent,
Viez vin, novel, flons et pasteis.
Chil grans mangier fu mut hasteis;
Chascuns de lui bien aisier pense;
Ne burent pas vin de despense,
De boire et de mangier bien s'aisent,
Por le prestre le hanap baisent
Ki le jouuel lor ot promis.
Cant en lor testes orent mis
De ce bon vin, grant feste fisent;
180 Lor cloches sovent en bondissent
Ansi con ilh auuist cors saint;
N'i a voisin qui ne se saint,
Et se merveillent qui la voient,
Qui miez miés as preschors s'avoient
Por la grant merveilhe esgarder.
Nus d'iauz ne se savoit garder
De mener vie deshoneste,
Car chascuns a serré la teste
De bon vin et de lor pitance.
190 A lor diverse contenance
Et al maintieng et à lor estre
Semblerent bien hors de sens estre.
Chascuns ki les voit s'en merveilhe,
Et Frere Louuis s'aparailhe
De demander con faitement
Il poroient plus sagement
Al prestre querre lor promesse.
"Demain, auchois c'on chante messe,

Straightway the friars were
On their way; to Antwerp they came
And called together their chapter.
Each told what befell,
But they had no concern for making a long tale, **160**
But shouted out in the assembly,
"Bring forth a good feast!
We have gained two hundred pounds
From a priest whom we know,
Ill in a small village."
Friar Nicholas and Friar Giles,
Friar William and Friar Ansel,
Came to hear this news,
Which very greatly pleased them.
They ordered huge fishes, **170**
Old wine and new, custards and pastries.
This great feast was quickly brought forth;
Each thinks himself well at ease;
They do not drink cheap wine;
With drinking and eating they are well entertained,
And they kiss their cups for the priest
Who promised them the jewel.
When they had poured in their heads
This good wine, they made a great festival:
They rang their bells resoundingly **180**
As if for the relics of a saint.
There was not a neighbor who did not bless himself
And wonder whom the feast honored.
They came racing to the preachers
To see the great marvel.
None of the friars could keep
From acting in a disorderly way,
For each of them had befuddled his head
With good wine and with their food.
By their bizarre looks **190**
And their postures and their manners
They seemed indeed to be out of their minds;
All who saw it wondered at it.
Then Friar Louis draws himself up
To ask exactly how
They could best
Obtain their bequest from the priest.
"Tomorrow, before Mass is sung,

Se fera bon metre à la voie,"
200 Dist chascuns, "se Jhesus m'avoie,
Anchois ke li Mors le sorprengne,
Si comment ke la choze prengne,
De no don aions conissance;
Nos i arons mainte pitance:
Si s'en doit on mut bien pener.
Frere Louuis, lesqueis miner
I voreis vos? Or le nos dites."
"Frere Guilhiames, li ermites,
En venrạ et Frere Nichole,
210 Bien saront dire la parole,
Et si venra Frere Robiers;
Çaiens n'a si sage Convers,
Si portera no breviaire;
De no Prieus n'avons ke faire."
Ensi ont le plait otriiet.
L'endemain se sont avoiiet
Tot droit vers la maison le prestre,
Ja n'i cuidierent à tans estre;
Mais, ains ke li jors fu passeis,
220 Amassent ilh mieus estre asseis
A Anwiers dedens lor maison.
Atant ont le prestre à raison
Mis, et de Deu l'ont salué;
Puis demandent s'il a mué
Son mal en nul aligement.
Li prestes mut trés sagement
Lor dit, "Bien soiiés vos venu,
Je n'ai mie desconneü
Le don ke promis vos avoie,
230 Encore en sui je bien en voie;
Faites les eschevins venir
Et le maieur, si k'awenir
Ne vos puist nule grevance;
Devant iaus la reconissance
Mut volentiers vos en ferai
Et la choze vos nomerai,
Et vos dirai u ele ert prise."
Entrues que li prestes devise,
Freres Robers a tant pené
240 K'ilh a le maieur aminé
Et toz les eschevins ensemble.

It will be well to be on our way."
Each says, "As Jesus may save me, 200
Before Death seizes him,
We must have knowledge of our gift,
Of how one gets the thing.
We will have a great alms-gift there,
But one must take great trouble for it.
Friar Louis, whom do you want
To take with you? Tell us now!"
"Friar William, the hermit,
Will go there, and Friar Nicholas,
For they know how to speak well, 210
And also Friar Robert will come,
For there is no wiser convert here,
And he will carry our breviary.
We need not bother with our prior."
Thus the business is settled.
The next day they were on their way
Straight to the priest's house.
They did not worry about being early,
But, before the day had ended,
They wished they had stayed 220
In their house at Antwerp.
Straightway they greeted
The priest and saluted him in God's name;
Then they asked if he felt any change,
Any easing of his illness.
The priest very politely
Said, "You are indeed welcome;
I have not forgotten
The gift that I promised you,
For indeed I am still so inclined; 230
Have the town councillors come
And the mayor, so that in the future
There will be no trouble for you.
In their presence I shall gladly
Do this for you,
And I shall name this thing to you
And I shall tell you where it is."
While the priest was yet speaking,
Friar Robert so busied himself
That he brought the mayor 240
And all the councillors as well.

Li IIII Frere, ce me samble,
Les ont hautement benvigniés.
Li prestes ki fu ensigniés,
Si a parlé premierement
Et lor a dit si faitement,
"Sangnor, vos estes mi ami,
Por Dieu, or entendeis à mi;
Frere Louuis, Frere Symons
250 Vinrent ier chi faire sermons,
K'ilh me cuidoient en santé,
Mais Dieus par sa grasce a planté
En moi maladie si grieve
C'aparant est ke mais n'en lieve.
Il me virent et esgarderent,
Et après si me demanderent
Se j'avoie pensé de m'ame,
Et je lor dis, par Nostre Dame,
Ke j'avoie trestot donet.
260 Ilh demanderent s'ordiné
A lor maison riens née avoie,
Et je dis non; se Dieus m'avoie,
Il ne m'en estoit sovenu,
Or estoient trop tart venu;
Je n'avoie mais que doner.
'Non,' dissent ilh, 'trop malmener
Vos voi, mavaisement moreis
S'en cestui propoz demoreis,
Se vos ne nos doneis del vostre.'
270 Et je, par sainte patenostre,
Ne vuelh pas morir malement.
Si ai pensé si longement
K'apenseis me sui d'une coze
Ke j'ai en mon porpris encloze,
Ke j'aime mut et tieng mut chiere,
Mais je lor doin en tel maniere
K'ilh ne l'aront tant con vivrai,
Car onkes ne le delivrai
En autrui garde k'en la moie.
280 Sachiés ke durement l'amoie
Et amerai tote ma vie:
Sans convoitise et sans envie
Lor done chi en vo presence,
Et ke nus n'i amene tenche."

The four friars, as I have heard,
Nobly greeted them.
The priest, who was very clever,
Then straightway spoke out
And said to them exactly thus,
"My lords, you are my friends;
By God, now listen to me:
Friar Louis and Friar Simon
Came to me yesterday to give a sermon 250
That they might bring me back to health,
But God in His providence had planted
In me a disease so severe
That it is clear I will never recover from it.
They came and looked at me,
And then they asked me
If I had thought of my soul
And I said to them, by our Lady,
That I had given away everything.
They asked if I had provided 260
Any gift for their house,
And I said no; as God may save me,
I had not thought of it,
And now they had come too late.
I had nothing more to give.
'No?' they said, 'You are going
Too far astray; you will die in a state of sin
If you persist in this intent
And do not give us something of your goods.'
And I, by the holy Our Father, 270
Did not wish to die in a state of sin.
I therefore considered this for so long
That I thought of a thing
That I have locked in my possession
That I greatly love and hold very dear,
But I grant it to them in such a manner
That they will not have it as long as I live,
For I have never given it
Into anyone's keeping save my own.
Know you that I deeply love it 280
And will love it all my life;
Without covetousness or envy
I give it to them in your presence,
And let no one raise any dispute about it."

Dient al prestre li IIII Frere,
"Dites quel choze c'est, biaz pere."
"Volentiers voir, c'est me vesie.
Se la voiiés bien netoiie,
Mieus ke de corduan varra
290 Et plus longement vos dura:
Se poreis ens metre vo poivre."
"Nos aveis vos ci por dechoivre
Mandeis, foz prestes entesteis?
Avoir nos cuidiés ahonteis,
Mais n'en aveis, par saint Obert,
Bien nos teneis or por bobert."
"Mais vos, por beste me teneis,
Cant les dons que je ai doneis
Me voleis faire recolhir.
300 Bien me faites le sanc bolir
Ki voleis ke je le rapiele;
Bien vos dis ke pot ne paele
Ne riens née à doner n'avoie;
Or me voleis metre en tel voie
K'en vos soit mieus l'amouene asise
K'en lieu u je l'euuise mise,
Por ce ke de tos melhor estes."
Li Jacobin baisent les testes,
Si se sunt retorné arriere
310 Vers lor maison à triste chiere,
Et tot chil ki là demorerent
De ris en aise se pamerent
Por la trufe de la vesie,
Ke li prestes ot tant prisie
As Jacobins, ki bien en burent
Et mangierent et en rechurent
De vin et de poissons pitance.
Jakes de Baisiu, sans dotance,
L'a de Tieus en Romanc rimée
Por la trufe qu'il a amée.

The four friars say to the priest,
"Good father, tell us what this thing is!"
"Indeed, I will; it is my bladder.
If you see that it is well cleaned,
It will be better than leather
And last you much longer. 290
You can put your pepper in it."
"Have you brought us here
To fool us, false stubborn priest?
You intended to shame us,
But you will never profit from this, by St. Obert,
Though you now consider us fools."
"But you considered me a beast
When you wanted me to take back
The gifts that I had given.
Indeed, you made my blood boil 300
When you wanted me to recall them.
Indeed, I told you that I had
Neither pot nor pail nor anything to give;
But you wanted to convince me
That the alms would be better bestowed on you
Than in any place I would have given them,
Because you are the best of all."
The Jacobins hang their heads,
And then turned themselves back
Toward their house with sorry faces; 310
And all those who lived around there
Nearly fainted from laughing
At the trick of the bladder
Which the priest had so praised
To the Jacobins, who drank on it,
And feasted, and received for it
Rations of wine and fish.
Jacques de Baisieux, in truth,
Translated this from Flemish into French
Because he so enjoyed the trick.

"How Howleglas Deceived His Ghostly Father"

The most famous of all literary clowns, Til Eulenspiegel, lived in the early fourteenth century and, according to a tradition at least as old as the middle of the fifteenth century, he died in 1350 in his native town of Mölln, near Lübeck in Germany. However, all we know of his celebrated life are the fictional stories preserved in the *Adventures of Til Eulenspiegel,* which was apparently first written down in Low German (the dialect of the area in which Mölln lies) in 1483, though the stories it contains may be much older. The Low German version of 1483 has not survived and is known only through the many translations

---

HOW HOWLEGLAS DECEIVED HIS GHOSTLY FATHER

And as Howleglas was thus sick, and then they brought to him a priest, and when the priest was come here he thought in his mind, "This hath been a great deceiver of the people and beguiler, wherewith he hath got much money."

And then came the priest unto him and said, "Howleglas, remember yourself, for you have done many sins, and now you must remember that you have a soul to keep and how you have gotten much money by deceit and falsehood, and now bestow that money to the worship of God and poor priests as I am. And that I counsel you for to do, and I shall order it well and remember you hereafter and do many Masses for you."

Then said Howleglas, "Good father, if it pleases you to come at noon again, then shall I make ready some money for you."

Then was the priest glad and then departed. Then took Howleglas an earthen pot and filled it half full with turds and he strewed thereon a little money, so that the dirt was covered.

And when it was noon, the priest came, and he said to Howleglas, "Friend, shall I have that that you promised me?"

And Howleglas said, "Yes." Then he set the pot before him and said, "Take now yourself, but be not too hasty nor put your hand too deep."

Then said the priest, "I shall do as you bid me."

And Howleglas did open the pot and he bade the priest to grip softly, for it was almost full. Then was the priest hasty and put his hand into the pot, and he gripped a great handful. And when he felt it soft, he pulled out his hand, and it was all tobeshitten. Then the priest said, "Ye may well be

that appeared at the beginning of the sixteenth century. Among the earliest was the English version, *Tyl Howleglas,* printed about 1519 by Jean van Doesborough in Antwerp, where many early English books were printed. This English version was evidently based directly on the Low German original and thus preserves the book in more authentic form than the slightly earlier High German version of 1515 (see F.W.D. Brie, *Eulenspiegel in England* [*Palaestra,* XXVII], Berlin, 1903). The few fragments of this earliest English version that now survive show that the next editions, by William Copland (*A Merrye Jest of a Man That Was Called Howleglas,* 1528 and 1530), are simply reprintings of the Antwerp version. We have therefore printed the relevant chapter from Copland's edition, as transcribed by Frederic Ouvry, *Howleglas* (London, 1867), with corrections from a microfilm of the damaged British Museum version. We have modernized some spellings, supplied punctuation and paragraphing, and made some silent corrections.

---

called a deceiver and beguiler that have deceived his ghostly father, and when ye be at the point of death!"

Then said Howleglas to the priest, "Good sir, did I not show unto you before that you should not grip too deep? And if that ye were covetous, it was not my fault."

Then said the priest, "Ye pass in ungraciousness all other that ever I saw. In faith, it was great pity that thou scaped from hanging when thou shouldest have been hanged at Lübeck." And then the priest departed from thence.

Then Howleglas called the priest again, and he said to him, "Master Parson, come again and take your money with you!"

But he went his way and made as he heard it not.

Caesarius of Heisterbach's Tale "Of An Administrator Who Was Carried Off Alive by the Devil When He Was on His Way to Collect His Fees"

Caesarius of Heisterbach was born around 1180 in the vicinity of Cologne, where he received his education. The abbot of the monastery of Heisterbach, so the story goes, convinced Caesarius to become a monk by telling him a pious tale—an *exemplum* such as the tale printed below. Caesarius entered the Cistercian monastery at Heisterbach and remained there the rest of his life, teaching the novices and composing some 36 books of sermons, saints' lives, histories, and works of devotion and instruction, until he died in 1240. His most popular work, the *Dialogus miraculorum,* was a widely read collection of *exempla,* and a great storehouse of popular lore. It has been translated into English as *The Dialogue on Miracles* by H. von E. Scott and C. C. Swinton Bland, with an introduction by G. G. Coulton (London, 1921). The *Libri VIII miraculorum,* from which this selection is taken, survives only in fragmentary form (only three of the eight books are known to exist), but the number of Renaissance adaptations shows its popularity and it still has its admirers: in the 1920's the celebrated German writer Hermann Hesse translated many of the tales in the *Libri VIII miraculorum* into modern German.

As explained below in the introduction to "The Merchant and His Magpie," the *exemplum* was a very popular genre in medieval times, especially in the

---

DE ADVOCATO, QUEM DIABOLUS VIVUM RAPUIT, DUM IRET FACERE EXACTIONEM

Retulit mihi quidam abbas ordinis Cisterciensis ante annos paucos in diocesi Bremensi militem quendam fuisse diversarum villarum advocatum. Hic erat homo sine ulla misericordia neque timens deum neque diabolum; avarus enim erat supra modum, frequentes et graves in sibi subiectos faciens exactiones.

Die quadam cum propter exactionem faciendam ad villam quandam properaret, diabolus in specie hominis se illi in itinere sociavit. Quem cum

thirteenth and fourteenth centuries, when collections of *exempla* such as those by Caesarius were written and widely disseminated for the use of preachers. Chaucer evidently appreciated this genre—his "Nun's Priest's Tale" and "Pardoner's Tale" are *exempla*—and, if he indeed based his "Friar's Tale" on Caesarius' work, he may well have heard it used as an *exemplum* to illustrate the point of a sermon.

The relation of "The Friar's Tale" to this *exemplum* has been obscured by the fact that Chaucerian scholars have almost always translated *advocatus* as "lawyer," and it has therefore seemed significant that Chaucer's protagonist is an ecclesiastical official rather than a man of law. However, *advocatus,* as used in this tale, means not "lawyer" but an ecclesiastical official, a layman (usually noble) who acted as the judicial administrator of church estates. His task was to defend the interests of the estate, often by the sword rather than in a court of law. He had the power to visit the tenants of the estate three times a year, and he could collect a fee for doing so; on his visits, he could exact fines for any offenses, and he was allowed to keep one-third of the fine. (For details see Du Cange, *Glossarium mediae et infimae latinitatis* and F. Lucii Ferraris, *Bibliotheca canonica iuridica moralis theologica,* both s.v. *advocati ecclesiarum.*) In short, the *advocatus* combined the duties of a seneschal of a feudal estate, and some of those of a summoner, who could mulct the people for their crimes (in one later version of Caesarius' tale, he is called *senescallus et placitator*—seneschal and collector of fines for ecclesiastical offenses). The office seems to have been more common on the Continent than in England, and Chaucer's change of the protagonist from *advocatus* to summoner seems to have been a change simply to the closest fourteenth-century English equivalent of this official. We have been tempted to translate *advocatus* by "summoner," but have settled for "administrator," since the duties of an *advocatus* were those of a judicial administrator, and administrators have always been in bad odor.

Our text is from *Die Fragmente der Libri VIII Miraculorum des Caesarius von Heisterbach,* ed. Aloys Meister, *Römische Quartalschrift für christliche Alterthumskunde und für Kirchengeschichte,* Supplement, XIII (1901), 90–91.

OF AN ADMINISTRATOR WHO WAS CARRIED OFF ALIVE BY THE DEVIL WHEN HE WAS ON HIS WAY TO COLLECT HIS FEES

A certain abbot of the Cistercian order in the diocese of Bremen told me a few years ago about a certain gentleman who was the Administrator of an abbey and had charge of a number of small towns. He was a man without any pity, and he feared neither God nor the devil; he was avaricious beyond measure, and he collected frequent and heavy fees from those who were subject to him.

One day he was going to a certain town to collect his fees and, as he was going along, he met the devil in the guise of a man. When—as much from

ille tam ex horrore quam ex mutua collocutione diabolum esse intellexisset, ire cum illo vehementer timuit, nullo tamen modo neque orando neque se signando ab eo separari potuit, quia damnatus et ei traditus a summo iudice fuit peccatis suis exigentibus.

Cumque simul pergerent, occurrit eis homo quidam pauper porcum in laqueo ducens. Cum idem animal huc illucque se diverteret, clamavit homo ille iratus: Diabolus te habeat.

Quo verbo audito advocatus sperans tali occasione liberari ab illo ait illi: Audi amice, porcus tibi datus est; vade, et tolle illum.

Respondit diabolus: Nequaquam mihi ex intimo corde donavit, et ideo eum tollere non possum.

Deinde transeuntes per aliquam villam, cum infans fleret, mater in foribus domus stans turbida atque irata voce dicebat: Diabolus te habeat. Quid me fletibus tuis inquietas?

Tunc miles iterum sperans a suo socio liberari ait: Ecce hic lucratus es animam! tolle infantem hunc, quia tuus est. Ecce, mater eius tradidit eum tibi.

Cui diabolus respondit ut prius. Non enim donavit illum mihi ex corde, sed talis est consuetudo hominibus loqui, cum irascuntur.

Incipientes autem appropinquare loco, ad quem proparabant, homines villae advocatum a longe videntes et causam adventus non ignorantes simul una voce clamabant: Diabolus te habeat! diabolo bene venias.

Quo audito diabolus caput movens et cachinnans ait militi: Ecce! isti dederunt te mihi ex intimo corde et idcirco meus es. Et rapuit eum diabolus in ipsa hora; sed quid de eo gestum sit, vel quo eum direxerit, usque in hodiernum diem ignoratur. Verba mutuae confabulationis militis cum diabolo per famulum eiusdem militis dicta et manifestata sunt.

Audiant hoc exemplum pauperum exactores, quorum hodie infinitus est numerus. Quid horribilius, quam hominem impoenitentem rapere vivum et in ipso actu scelerum deducere ad infernum aeternis poenis sine fine cruciandis.

the stranger's horrible appearance as from the conversation—he understood that this was the devil, he greatly feared to go along with him; yet by no means, neither by prayers nor by crossing himself, could he get away from him, because he was damned and delivered to the devil by the Highest Judge because of his sinful demands.

And so as they went along together, a man approached them, leading a pig by a rope. When this animal tried to wander off here and there, the man was enraged and shouted, "May the devil have you!"

When the Administrator heard these words, hoping by this chance to be free from the devil, he said to him, "Listen, friend; that pig was given to you; go and take it."

The devil answered, "He did not give it to me from the bottom of his heart, and therefore I can't take it."

Next, as they were passing through a small town, a baby was crying; its mother, standing in the door of the house, was upset, and in an angry voice she said, "May the devil take you! Why do you bother me with your crying?"

Thereupon the gentleman, again hoping to free himself from his comrade, said, "Look, you've gained a soul! Take that baby, for it is yours. Look, the mother has given it to you!"

The devil answered him as before, "But she did not give it to me from her heart; this is just the way people talk when they are angry."

When they were finally approaching the place to which they were travelling, the men of the town saw the Administrator from afar and, knowing why he was coming, they cried with one voice, "May the devil have you, and he is welcome to you!"

When he heard this, the devil, nodding his head and snickering, said to the gentleman, "Aha! They gave you to me with all their heart, and so you are mine!" And at that very moment the devil grabbed him, but what he did with him or where he took him is not known to this very day. The words of the conversation between the gentleman and the devil were revealed and told by the servant of this gentleman.

May those who rob the poor listen to this *exemplum,* for their number is infinite in these days! What is more terrible than an unrepentant man whom the devil carries off alive, taking him away in the very act of crime to the eternal punishment and endless tortures of hell!

"The Merchant and His Magpie"

Chaucer evidently knew this story of the tell-tale bird, for he seems to refer to it in "The Wife of Bath's Prologue" (D,232), and there are some details (such as the cage in which the bird is kept) in Chaucer's "Manciple's Tale" that seem to have been drawn from the story in *The Seven Sages of Rome.* Like *The Canterbury Tales,* the *Seven Sages* is a collection of stories told by various tellers within a narrative framework. Here the tellers are Roman sages, such as the Cato who tells this story, and the narrative framework is supplied by the postponed execution of the emperor's son. The emperor, Diocletian, entrusts his son to seven philosophers, who are to instruct the boy in the seven liberal arts for seven years. While the son is away, the emperor (a widower) marries a vicious woman. When the son returns she attempts to seduce him, and when she fails she accuses him of rape. Each day for a week, the son is led out to execution, but one of the philosophers steps forward to tell a story that dissuades the emperor from carrying out the sentence. Each night the empress tells him a story that persuades him to get on with the execution the next day. Finally the sages win, and the evil empress is burned.

Each of the tales that the philosophers tell is an *exemplum,* a brief story told

---

LI BOURJOUS QUI AVOIT UNE PIE

Sire, fait-il, il ot en ceste vile, I bourjous qui avoit I pie qui disoit ce que l'en li demandeit que il avoit véu, qu'ele parloit moult bien la langue romainne. Et la fame au bourjois n'esteit mie sages, qu'ele amoit en la vile. Et quant li preudons venoit dehors, la pie li disoit ce que ele avoit véu, et sovent avenoit que la pie li disoit voir au predome, que li amis sa fame i avoist esté. Et il l'en créoit moult bien, qu'ele ne savoit mentir, ains disoit à son seingneur toz jorz ce qu'ele véoit.

Tant que li sires fu hors en sa marchandise; il ne revint pas cele nuit; la dame manda son ami. La pie estoit en une cage en haut attachiée, en une perche, en mi le porche de la meson. Et cil vint très qu'à l'uis, et n'osa entrer anz, pour la pie. Si manda la dame, ele vint à lui. "Dame," dist-il, "ge n'ose antrer anz, por la pie, qu'ele le diroit à vostre seingnor."

"Venez avant," fet-elle, "g'en panseré bien."

to illustrate a moral point, as in the following tale, which proves the danger of listening to evil advice. The *exemplum* was a very popular genre of the medieval tale, and collections of *exempla* such as the *Gesta Romanorum* and the *Disciplina Clericalis* (see "Dame Sirith," p. 372) were very popular. *Exempla* were frequently used in sermons, and many of the late collections were made for the use of preachers. They were also popular in secular literature, however, as shown by the fables of Marie de France (see p. 256), which are cast in the form of *exempla,* as well as by many of the other tales in this book which end, as the *exemplum* conventionally does, with a statement of the moral point of the tale.

The *Seven Sages* is based on an Oriental work, known as *The Book of Sindibad,* which may have been composed as early as the fifth century B.C., and which was transmitted into Western literature in the twelfth century, when the earliest European version of the *Seven Sages* was composed. There are versions of that book in almost every language of Europe, and it remained a favorite long after the Middle Ages. A popular edition, for example, was printed in Boston in 1794. Chaucer may have known the *Seven Sages* either in the Middle English verse version or the French prose version from which the English work was translated. Since the Middle English version is easily available in Brunner's edition (Early English Text Society, 191) and in *Sources and Analogues,* we have chosen to print the twelfth-century French version on which the Middle English tale is based. It has not been reprinted since 1838, and our text is from that edition: Auguste Louis Armand Loiseleur Deslongchamps, *Essai sur les fables indiennes et sur leur introduction en Europe suivi du roman des sept sages de Rome en prose . . . ,* ed. Le Roux de Lincy (Paris, 1838), pp. 55–58.

THE MERCHANT AND HIS MAGPIE

In this town there was once a merchant who owned a magpie that would tell whatever one asked her about what she had seen, for she spoke the French language very well. The wife of this merchant was not very well-behaved, for she had a lover in the town. And when the good man went out, the magpie would tell him what she had seen, and it often happened that the magpie told the good man truly that his wife's lover had been there. And he believed her completely, for she did not know how to lie and always told her lord what she had seen.

Once this husband was away on business; he did not return that night; the lady sent for her lover. The magpie was in a cage hung up high on a perch in the middle of the entrance hall of the house. And the lover came right to the door, but he did not dare enter, because of the magpie. He sent for the lady; she came to him. "Lady," he said, "I do not dare come in because of the magpie, for she will tell everything to your husband."

"Come on," she said. "I will think of something to do."

"Dame," dist-il, "volantiers." Il s'en passe outre et vient en la chambre.

La pie le regarde, si le conut bien, car froiterie li avoit fait aucune foiz, si s'escria, "Ha! sire, qui en la chambre estes repos, por coi n'i venez vos tant comme mes sires i est?"

A tant se tut; et la dame s'apansa de male guille. Quant il fu annuitié, ele prant sa chamberière, si li baille I grant plomme plein d'eve et I cierge tout ardant, et I maillet de fust. Quant vint vers la mienuit, ele la fet monter sur la meson, ileuc endroit où la pie estoit; si commance à férir du maillet sur les essanles; et quant ele avoit assez féru, si reprenoit le cierge, le boutoit par entre essanles, que la clarté en venoit à la pie, enmi les eulz. Après si prenoit le plomme et versoit l'eve sus la pie. Et tele vie mena de si au jor; et quant il fu ajornez, si descent, le maillet en sa main, et le cierge en l'autre. Li amis à la dame s'en ala.

Ne demora guères que li sires vint. Il vint tout droit à sa pie. "Amie," dist-il, "conment vous est? menjastes vous hui?"

"Sire, li amis ma dame a été céenz, en nuit, toute nuit, et geu o lui; n'a guères qu'il s'en parti. Je l'en vi ore droit aler par ci."

Li sires regarda la dame de felons eulz. Lors retorna vers la pie, et li dist, "Certes, belle douce amie, ge vos en croi moult bien."

"Sire, jà a il à nuit, fet si male nuit, et pléu toute nuit; et a tonné, et esparti, et fait de moult grant escrois; et li esparz me venoit en mi les eulz. Pou s'en fault que ge n'ai esté morte."

Li sires regarda la dame, et la dame lui. "Par la foi que je doi Dieu, dame," dist li sires, "il a fet moult belle nuit, annuit, et mout clere."

"Certes, sire, ça mon fet," ce dist la dame, "une des plus belles et des plus clères de l'an."

Li sires demanda à ses voisins et il distrent autresint qu'il avoit fet moult belle nuit. Li sires fu irés; la dame le vit en ire, et vit bien son point qu'ele pot parler, si dist, "Seingnor, or poez vooir de coi mi sires m'a toz jorz blasmée et férue et chaciée, qu'il créoit sa pie de quan qu'ele disoit. Or androit, li dist-ele que mes amis a an nui jéu avec moi; certes ele ment ausint bien comme ele avoit fet du tens." Li sire fu irez de ce que la pie li avoit menti de la nuit; si cuide que ausint li mantit-ele de sa fame. Il vient à sa pie. "Par mon chief!" fait-il, "vos ne me mentiroiz jamès." Si la prant, si li ront le col.

"Lady," he said, "willingly." He walked in beside her and went into the bedroom.

The magpie looked at him and recognized him, for he had done an evil deed there once before, and she cried out, "Aha, sir! You who are at ease in that bedroom, why don't you come here like that when my lord is here?"

Then she was quiet; and the lady thought of a dirty trick. When it was night she called to her chambermaid and gave her a great basin filled with water, a brightly burning candle, and a wooden mallet. When it was about midnight she had the maid climb up on top of the house, near to the place where the magpie was. Then she began to beat on the shingles with the mallet and when she had beaten them enough, she picked up the candle and thrust it between the shingles so that its light hit the magpie right in the eyes. Then she took the basin and emptied the water on the magpie. She carried on in that manner until it was day, and when it was daylight, she came down, the mallet in one hand, the candle in the other. The lady's lover went away.

It was not long before the husband returned. He came straight to his magpie. "Friend," he said, "how are you? Have you eaten today?"

"Sir, my lady's lover has been here, last night—all night—and he slept with her; he went away just now. I just now saw him go straight through here."

The husband looked at his wife with angry eyes. Then he turned back toward the magpie and said to her, "Of course, my pretty sweet friend, I believe you completely in this."

"Sire, what a night it was, such a foul night, and it rained all night, and it thundered, and crackled with lightning, and made great noises; and the lightening struck me right in the eyes. I was very nearly killed."

The husband looked at the wife, and the wife at him. "By the faith that I owe to God, lady," says the husband, "it was a very good night last night, and very clear."

"Certainly, sir, by my faith," replies the lady, "one of the most lovely and most clear of the year."

The husband asked his neighbors and they all agreed that it had been a very lovely night. The lord was enraged; the lady saw him angered and saw well her chance to speak, and she said, "Lord, now you can see why my husband has always blamed and beaten and chastised me, because he believes his magpie whatever she may say. Now see, she told him that my lover slept with me last night; indeed, she is lying now just as she has so many other times."

The husband was enraged because his magpie had lied to him about the night; he believed that she had also lied to him about his wife. He went to his magpie. "By my head," he says, "you will never lie to me again!" Then he grabbed her and wrung her neck.

Quant il ot ce fait, il fu si esbahiz que nus plus. Il regarda la cage où la pie estoit; et regarde contremont les essanlles, si les vit desaouées. Il prant une eschiele, si monte sus la meson, si vit le plomme que la chamberière i ot porté et vit la cire dégoutée desus les essanlles, et regarde que la couverture fu toute desavoiée, et vit le grant pertuis par où elle botoit le cierge tout ardant; si s'apensa de la traïson que sa fame li avoit fete; si commença à fere son duel. "Hilas!" fait-il, "pour coi l'ai-ge tuée? Por coi crui-ge ma fame?" Il s'en devalle jus, si chace sa fame hors de sa meson; si se commence à demanter et à destordre ses poinz ensemble.

When he had done this, he was more abashed than ever before. He looked at the cage where the magpie was; he looked up at the shingles and saw them pushed aside, he took a ladder, climbed up on top of the house; and he saw the basin that the chambermaid had carried there, and he saw the wax that had dripped on the shingles, and he saw that the roof was all disarranged, and he saw the large hole through which the chambermaid had thrust the brightly burning candle; and he realized the treachery that his wife had done. Then he began to make his lament. "Alas," he said, "why did I kill her? Why did I believe my wife?" He then immediately came down and chased his wife out of the house. Then he began to lament and to wring his hands.

"Dame Sirith"

Chaucer probably never read "Dame Sirith," though he almost certainly knew the story on which it was based. Its use of magic as a means of seduction may recall scenes in "The Miller's Tale" or "The Franklin's Tale," and the theme of the wife outwitted has a faint relation to "The Shipman's Tale," but we have included it in our collection not so much because of these themes but because it is the earliest fabliau in English and the only surviving example of the genre before Chaucer. "Dame Sirith," which was probably written in the thirteenth

---

DAME SIRITH

As I com by an waye,
Of on Ich herde saye,
  Ful mody man and proud;
Wis he was of lore,
An goodlich under gore,
  And clothed in fair shroud.

To lovien he bigon
And wedded wimmon;
  Therof he hevede wrong!
10 His herte hire was al on,
That reste nevede he non—
  The love was so strong.

Wel yerne he him bithoute
How he hire gete moute,
  In any cunnes wise.
That befel on a day
The loverd wend away

3. **mody man** spirited man 4. **lore** learning 5. **goodlich under gore** goodly (handsome) in dress 6. **shroud** clothing 8. **An wedded wimmon** a wedded woman 9. **hevede** had 10. **His herte hire was al on** His heart was entirely set on her 11. **That reste nevede he non** So that he had no rest 13–14. **Wel . . . moute** He earnestly considered how he could get her 15. **In any cunnes wise** In any sort of way 17. **Loverd** Lord (husband)

century, is preserved in only one manuscript, but there is another version of the same story, a fragment of a secular play, the "Interludium de Clerico et Puella," which may be based on another version of "Dame Sirith" or may simply be based on the same source (the tale of "Dame Sirith" is taken from the popular *Disciplina Clericalis* by the twelfth-century writer, Petrus Alphonsus). The form of "Dame Sirith" is essentially dramatic, and in the manuscript marginal notations assign the speeches to the three characters, as if the tale were meant for dramatic presentation. "Dame Sirith" was first printed by E. Mätzner, *Altenglische Sprachproben,* I, i (Berlin, 1867) 103–113, on whose edition we have based our text. The best and most recent edition is J.A.W. Bennett and G.V. Smithers, *Early Middle English Verse and Prose* (Oxford, 1966), pp. 77–95. We have liberally regularized the spelling in the text and substituted Chaucerian forms for many of the earlier and dialectical forms that make the poem difficult, and we have adapted two readings from Bennett and Smithers.

On his merchandise.

He wente him to then inne
Ther hoe wonede inne— 20
That was riche won!—
And come into then halle,
Ther hoe was shrud with palle
And thus he bigon:

"God almightten be herinne!"
"Welcome, so Ich ever bide wynne!"
Quod this wif.
"Is it thy wille, come and site,
And what is thy wille let me wite,
My leve lif. 30

"By oure Loverd, hevene-king,
If I may don anything
That thee is lef,
Thou might finden me ful fre;
Fol blethely will I don for thee
Withouten gref."

19. **then inne** the house 20. **hoe** she **wonede** dwelled 21. **won** dwelling 23. **Ther hoe was shrud with palle** Where she was dressed in rich material 25. **God . . . herinne** God almighty be herein 26. **So . . . wynne** As I ever hope for bliss 28. **Is it thy wille** if it is your wish 29. **wite** know 30. **My leve lif** my dear 33. **thee is lef** is pleasing to you 34. **fre** generous 35. **Fol blethely** full gladly

"Dame, God thee foryelde!
Bote on that thou me nought bimelde
  Ne make thee wroth,
40 Min ernde will I to thee bede.
But wrathen thee for my dede
  Were me loth."

"Nay, iwis, Wilekin!
For nothing that ever is min,
  Thau thou it yerne,
Uncurteys ne will I be.
Ne con I nought on vilté,
  Ne nought I nille lerne.

"Thou mayst sayen al thine wille,
50 And I shal herknen and sitten stille
  That thou have told.
And if that thou me tellest skil,
I shal don after thy wil,
  That thou be bold.

"And thau thou saye me any shame,
Ne shal I thee nowight blame
  For thy sawe."
"Nou Ich have wonne leve,
Yif that I me shulde greve
60   It were unlawe.

"Certes, dame, thou seyst as hende,
And I shal setten spel on ende
  And tellen thee al:
What Ich wolde and why Ich come.
Ne con Ich sayen non falsdom,
  Ne non I ne shal.

37. **foryelde** reward 38. **Bote on** providing **me nought bimelde** not complain of me 39. **Ne make thee wroth** nor become angry 40. **Min . . . bede** I will tell my errand to you 41. **But wrathen thee** but to anger you 42. **loth** unpleasant 45. **Thau thou it yerne** though you desire it 47. **Ne . . . vilte** I know nothing about filthy conduct 48. **Ne . . . lerne** nor do I want to learn anything 52. **skil** something reasonable 53. **after** according to 54. **That thou be bold** be sure of that 55. **thau** though 56. **nowight** in any way 57. **sawe** speech 58. **leve** leave, permission 59. **Yif . . . greve** if I should come to grief 60. **It were unlawe** it would be wrong 61. **thou seyst as hende** you speak graciously 62. **shal setten spel on ende** shall speak my piece right out 64. **What . . . come** what I want and why I came

"Ich habbe iloved thee many yer,
Thau Ich nabbe noght ben her,
My love to showe.
While thy loverd is in towne, 70
Ne may no man with thee holden roune,
With no thewe.

"Yurstenday Ich herde saye,
As Ich wende by the waye,
Of oure sire;
Me tolde me that he was gon
To the faire of Botolfston
In Lincolnshire.

"And for Ich wiste that he was oute,
Tharfore Ich am igon aboute 80
To speken with thee.
Him burth to liken wel his lif
That mighte welde such a wif
In privité.

"Dame, if it is thy wille,
Both dernelike and stille
Ich wille thee love."
"That wold I don for non thing,
By oure Loverd, hevene-king,
That us is bove! 90

"Ich have my loverd that is my spouse,
That maiden broughte me to house
Mid menske inou.
He loveth me and Ich him wel;
Oure love is also trewe as stel,
Withouten wou.

"Thau he be from hom on his ernde,
Ich were unsely if Ich lernede

68. **Thau . . . her** though I have not been here 71. **roune** conversation 72. **With no thewe** in any way 73. **Yurstanday** yesterday 76. **Me** men 77. **Botolfston** Boston 79. **for Ich wiste** because I knew 82. **Him burth** he ought 83. **mighte welde** can possess 86. **dernelike** secretly 90. **That us is bove** Who is above us 93. **Mid menske inou** with much honor 95. **also** as 96. **wou** woe 97. **ernde** errand 98. **unsely** evil

To be an hore.
100 That ne shal nevere be
That I shal don silk falseté
On bedde ne on flore.

"Nevermore his life while
Thau he were on hondred mile
Biyonde Rome,
For nothing ne shold I take
Man on erthe to ben my make
Ar his hom-come."

"Dame, dame, torn thy mod!
110 Thy curteysy was ever god,
And yet shal be;
For the Loverd that us haveth wrought
Amend thy mod, and torn thy thought,
And rew on me!"

"We, we! holdest thou me a fol?
So Ich ever mote biden Yol,
Thou art unwis!
My thought ne shalt thou never wende.
My loverd is curteys man and hende,
120 And man of pris,

"And Ich am wife bothe god and trewe.
Trewer woman ne may no man knowe
Than Ich am.
Thilke time ne shal never bitide
That man for wowing ne thoru pride
Schal do me sham."

"Swete levemon, mercy!
Shame ne vilany
Ne bede I thee non;
130 Bote derne love I thee bede,

99. **hore** whore 101. **silk** such 106. **nothing . . . take** I would be no means take to me 107. **make** mate 108. **Ar** ere 109. **torn thy mod** change your mind 114. **rew** have pity
115. **We, we** alas, alas 116. **So . . . Yol** as I ever expect Christmas 117. **unwis** unwise, foolish 119. **hende** gracious 124. **bitide** happen 127. **lemmon** sweetheart 129. **bede** asked 130. **Bote derne** only secret

As man that wolde of love spede
  And finde won."

"So bide Ich evere mete other drink,
Her thou losest al thy swinke.
Thou mayst gon home, leve brother,
For nille Ich the love ne non other
Bote my wedde housebonde;
To tellen it thee ne wille Ich wonde."

"Certes, dame, that me forthinketh.
On wo is the man that muchel swinketh **140**
And at the last loseth his sped.
To maken monis is him ned.
By me I saye, ful iwis,
That love the love that I shal mis.
And dame, have now godneday!
And thilke Loverd that al welde may
Leve that thy thought so tourne
That Ich for thee no leng ne mourne."

Drerymod he wente away,
And thoughte bothe night and day **150**
  Hir al forto wende.
A frend him radde forto fare
(And leven al his muchele care)
  To Dame Sirith the hende.

Thider he wente him anon
So swithe so he mighte gon;
  No man he ne imette.
Ful he was of tene and treye.
With wordes milde and eke sleye
  Faire he hire grette: **160**

131. **As . . . spede** as one who wanted to succeed in love 132. **And finde won** and to find joy 133. **So . . . drink** as I ever hope for food or drink 134. **swinke** labor 135. **leve** dear 136. **nille . . . other** I will not love you or any other 137. **Bote** except for 138. **wonde** change 139. **me forthinketh** disappoints me 140. **wo . . . swinketh** woe is the man who works hard 141. **sped** profit 142. **To . . . ned** he must make moans (complain) 144. **shal mis** must miss 145. **godneday** good-day 146. **that al welde may** who can control everything 147. **Leve** grant 148. **leng** longer 149. **Drerymod** sad-hearted 151. **Hir . . . wende** to change her completely 152. **radde** advised 153. **muchele** great 154. **hende** clever 156. **so swithe so** as quickly as 157. **No . . . imette** he met no one 158. **tene and treye** grief and pain 159. **sleye** clever 160. **grette** greeted

"God thee iblessi, dame Sirith!
Ich am icom to speken thee with,
For ful muchele nede.
And Ich may have help of thee,
Thou shalt have—that thou shalt see—
Ful riche mede."

"Welcomen art thou, leve sone!
And if Ich may other cone
In any wise for thee do,
170 I shal strengthen me therto.
Forthy, leve sone, tel thou me,
What thou woldest I dide for thee?"

"Bote, leve nelde! Ful evele I fare,
I lede my lif with tene and care.

"With muchel unsele Ich lede my lif,
And that is for an swete wif
That heighte Margery.
Ich have iloved hire many day
And of hire love hoe says me nay;
180 Hider Ich com forthy.

"Bote if hoe wende hire mod,
For sorewe mon I waxe wod
Other myselve quelle.
Ich havede ithought myself to slo;
Forth then radde a frend me go
To thee my sorewe telle.

"He saide, withouten faille,
That thou me couthest help and vaile,
And bringen me of wo,
190 Thoru thine craftes and thine dedes.
And Ich wile give thee riche mede,
With that it be so."

161. **iblessi** bless 164. **And** if 166. **mede** reward 167. **leve** dear 168. **other** or **cone** can 171. **Forthy** therefore 173. **Bote** help **leve nelde** dear old lady 174 **tene** grief 175. **unsele** unhappiness 177. **That heighte** was named 179. **hoe** she 181. **if . . . mod** unless she change her mind 182. **mon I waxe wod** must I go mad 183 **Other myselve quelle** or kill myself 184. **slo** slay 185. **radde** advised 188. **couthest** could **vaile** avail 189. **of wo** out of woe 191. **mede** reward 192. **With that** providing that

"Benedicite be herinne!
Her havest thou, sone, muchel sinne.
Loverd, for His swete name,
Lete thee thefore haven no shame!
Thou servest after Godes grame
When thou sayst on me silk blame.
For ich am old, and sick, and lame;
Siknesse haveth maked me ful tame. 200
Bless thee, bless thee, leve knave,
Leste thou mesaventer have
For this lesing that is founden
Oppon me, that am harde ibonden.
Ich am an holy womon;
On witchecraft nought I ne con,
Bote with goode men almesdede
Ilke day my lif I fede,
And bidde my Paternoster and my Crede
That God hem help at here nede 210
That helpen me my lif to lede,
And leve that hem mote wel spede
(His lif and his soule worthe ishend
That thee to me this ernde haveth send!)
And leve me to ben iwreken
On him this shame me haveth speken."

"Leve nelde, bilef al this!
Me thinketh that thou art onwis.
The man that me to the taute,
He wiste that thou us couthest saute. 220
Help, Dame Sirith, if thou maut,
To make me with the sweeting saut,
And Ich will geve thee gift ful stark—
Many a pound and many a mark,

193. **Benedicite be herinne** bessings be herein 196. **Lete . . . sham** grant that you not have shame because of this 197. **servest after** deserve **grame** anger 198. **silk** such 201. **leve knave** dear boy 202. **mesaventer** misfortune 203. **lesing** lying 204. **harde ibonden** hard pressed, in difficult circumstances 206. **On . . . con** I know nothing of witchcraft 207. **gode men almesdede** the alms of good men 208. **Ilke** each 209. **bidde** pray **Paternoster** Lord's Prayer 210. **God . . . nede** God help them in their need 212. **And . . . spede** an grant that they well prosper 213. **Worthe ishend** be damned 214. **That . . . send** who sent you to me on this errand 215. **leve . . . iwreken** grant that I be avenged 216. **On . . . speken** on him who spoke this shame about me 217. **Leve . . . this** dear old lady, leave all this 219. **taute** directed 220. **wiste** thought **us couthest saute** could reconcile us (the clerk and the lady) 221. **maut** can 222. **To . . . saut** to reconcile me with the dear girl 223. **stark** great

Warme pilche and warme shon,
With that min ernde be wel don.
Of muchel godlec might thou yelpe
If it be so that thou me help."

"Liy me nought, Wilekin, by thy leuté;
230 Is it thin ernest thou tellest me?"

"Ye, nelde, witerly,
Ich hire love! It mot me spille,
Bote Ich gete hire to my wille."

"Wat God, Wilekin, me reweth thy scathe;
Oure Loverd sende thee help rathe!
Wiste Ich hit mighte ben forholen,
Me wolde thinke wel folen
Thy wille forto fullen.
240 Make me siker with word on honde
That thou wolt helen, and I wile fonde
If Ich may hire tellen.

"For al the world ne wold I nought
That Ich were to chapitre ibrought,
For non silke werkes.
My jugement were son igiven
To ben with shame somer-driven
With the prestes and with clarkes."

"Iwis, nelde, ne wold I
That thou havedest vilany
250 Ne shame for my god.
Her I thee my trouthe plight:
Ich shal helen by my mighte,
By the holy Rod!"

"Welcome, Wilekin, hiderward!

225. **pilche** fur coat **shon** shoes 226. **With that** providing that 227. **godlec** goodness **yelpe** boast 229. **Liy** lie **leuté** oath 231. **Ye, nelde, witerly** yes, old lady, certainly 232. **It mot me spille** it must kill me 233. **Bote** unless 234. **Wat . . . scathe** God knows, Wilekin, I pity your distress 235. **rathe** quickly 236. **Wiste . . . forholen** if I were sure it could be hidden 237. **Me . . . folen** it would seem to me well done 238. **fullen** fulfill 239. **siker** sure 240. **wolt helen** will keep it quiet **fonde** try 243. **chapitre** ecclesiastical court 244. **silke** such 246. **somer-driven** driven on a packhorse (as a punishment) 251. **my trouthe plight** pledge my word 252. **helen** keep it quiet 253. **holy Rod** cross

Her havest imaked a foreward
   That thee may ful wel like.
Thou might blesse thilke sith
For thou might make thee ful blith;
   Thar thou namore sike.

To goder-hele ever come thou hider, 260
For sone wil I gange thider
   And maken her understande.
I shal kenne hire silke a lore
That hoe shal lovien thee muchele more
   Than any man in lande."

"Also hav I Godes grith,
Wel havest thou said, Dame Sirith,
   And goder-hele shal ben thine!
Have her twenty shiling:
This Ich give thee to meding, 270
   To buyen thee sheep and swine."

"So Ich evere brouke hous other flet,
Neren never penes beter biset
   Than thes shulen ben!
For I shal don a juperti
And a ferly maistri
   That thou shalt ful wel sen."

[*To her dog Dame Sirith says:*]
"Pepir nou shalt thou eten;
This mustard shal ben thy mete, 280
   And gar thin eyen to rene;
I shal make a lesing
Of thin eye renning,
   Ich wot wel wher and whenne."

   "What! Now const thou no good!

255. **foreward** agreement 257. **thilke sith** such a time 259. **Thar** need **sike** sigh 260. **goder-hele** good fortune 261. **gange** go 263. **I . . . lore** I shall teach her such a doctrine 264. **hoe** she 266. **Al . . . grith** as I may have God's protection 268. **goder-hele** good fortune 270. **to meding** as payment 272. **So . . . flet** as I ever enjoy house or floor 273. **Neren . . . biset** Pennies were never better employed 275. **juperti** deed 276. **ferly maistri** wondrous feat 279. **Pepir** pepper 281. **gar** cause **rene** run 282. **lesing** lie 284. **wot** know

Me thinketh that thou art wod.
Givest thou the whelpe mustard?"

"Be stille, boynard!
I shal with this ilke gin
290 Gar hire love to ben al thine.
Ne shal Ich never have reste ne ro
Til Ich have told how thou shalt do;
Abid me her til min hom-come."

"Yis, by the somer blome!
Hethen nill I ben benomen
Til thou be agein comen."

Dame Sirith bigon to go
As a wretche that is wo,
That hoe com hire to then inne
300 Ther this gode wif was inne.
Tho hoe to the dore com,
Swithe rewliche hoe begon:
"Loverd," hoe sayth, "Wo is olde wives
That in poverté ledeth ay lives!
Not no man so muchel of pine
As poure wif that falleth in nausine.
That may ilke man by me wite,
For may I nouther gange ne site;
Ded wold I ben ful fain!
310 Hunger and thirst me haveth ney slain;
Ich ne may mine limes onwold
For muchel hunger and thirst and cold.
Wharto liveth silke a wretche?
Why nil God my soule fetche?"

"Sely wif, God thee unbinde!
Today wille I thee mete finde
For love of God.
Ich have rewthe of thy wo,

286. **wod** crazy 288. **boynard** fool 289. **ilke gin** same trick 290. **Gar** cause 291. **ro** peace 294. **by the somer blome** by the bloom of summer 295. **Hethen . . . benomen** I will not be dragged away from here 299. **That . . . inne** so that she came to the house 301. **Tho hoe** when she 302. **Swithe . . . begon** very sadly she began 303. **hoe** she 305. **Not no man** no man knows 306. **nausine** distress 307. **wite** know 308. **For . . . site** for I can neither walk nor sit 311. **Ich . . . onwold** I cannot control my limbs 314. **Why nil** will not 315. **Sely wif** good woman

For evele iclothed I se thee go
  And evele ishod. 320
Com herin—Ich wile thee fede."

"God almighten do thee mede
And the Loverd that was on rode idon,
And faste fourty dayes to non
And hevene and erthe haveth to welde."

"As thilke Loverd thee foryelde,
Have her flesh and eke bred,
And make thee glad—it is my red—
And have her the coppe with the drinke—
God do thee mede for thy swinke!" 330

Thanne spak that olde wif
(Crist awarie hire lif!):
"Alas, alas, that ever I live!
Al the sinne Ich wolde forgive
The man that smite of min heved;
Ich wolde my lif me were bireved."

"Sely wif, what ailleth thee?"
"Bote ethe may I sory be!
Ich havede a doughter fair and fre—
Fairer ne mighte no man se. 340
Hoe havede a curteys housebonde,
Freer man might no man fonde.
My doughter lovede him al to wel;
Forthy mak I sory del.
Oppon a day he was out wend,
And tharthoru was my doughter shend.
He hade an ernde out of toune,
And com a mody clerc with croune,
To my doughter his love bed,
And hoe nolde nought folewe his red. 350

322. **do thee mede** reward you 323. **on rode idon** placed on the cross 324. **And . . . non** and fasted forty days until the ninth hour (3 P.M.) 325. **welde** rule 326. **foryelde** reward 327. **flesh** meat 328. **red** advice 332. **awarie** curse 335. **The . . . heved** to the man that would smite off my head 336. **Ich . . . bireved** I wish my life were taken from me 338. **ethe** easily 341. **Hoe** she 342. **fonde** find 344. **del** lament 346. **shend** ruined 348. **mody** high-spirited **croune** tonsure 349. **bed** offered 350. **And . . . red** and she would not follow his advice

He ne mighte his wille have,
For nothing he mighte crave.
Thenne bigon the clerc to witch
And shop my daughter til a bitch.
This is my doughter that Ich of speke!
For del of hire min herte breketh.
Loke how hire eyen greten;
On hire cheken the teres meten.
Forthy, dame, were it no wonder
360 Thau min herte burste asunder.
A, whoso ever is yong housewif,
Hoe loveth ful litel hire lif,
And any clerc of love hire bede,
Bote hoe grant and lete him spede!"

"A! Loverd Crist, what may I thenne do?
This enderday com a clerc me to
And bede me love on his manere
And Ich him nolde nought ihere.
Ich trowe he wolle me foreshape.
370 How trowstu, nelde, Ich mowe ascape?"

"God almighten be thin help,
That thou ne be nouther bitch ne whelp
Leve dame, if any clerc
Bedeth thee that love-werc,
Ich rede that thou grante his bone
And bicom his lefmon sone.
And if that thou so ne dost,
A worse red thou underfost."

"Loverd Crist, that me is wo,
380 That the clerc me hade fro
Ar he me havede biwonne!
Me were levere than any fe

354. **shop . . . bitch** changed my daughter into a bitch 356. **del** sorrow 357. **greten** weep 358. **cheken** cheeks 363. **And** if **bede** prays 364. **Bote** unless **spede** succeed 366. **enderday** other day 367. **bede** pray 368. **And . . . ihere** and I would not listen to him 369. **Ich . . . forshape** I am sure he will transform me 370. **How . . . ascape** how do you think, old lady, I can escape 372. **nouther** neither 374. **Bedeth . . . love-werc** asks you for that love-work 375. **rede** advise **bone** plea 376. **lefmon** sweetheart 377. **And . . . dost** and if you do not do thus 378. **A . . . underfost** you take a worse course of action 380. **me hade fro** had gone away from me 381. **Ar . . . biwonne** before he won me 382. **Me . . . fe** I would rather than any amount of wealth

That he havede ones layen by me
  And efftsones bigunne.

"Evermore, nelde, Ich will be thine,
With that thou fetch me Wilekin,
  The clerc of whom I telle.
Giftes will I give thee
That thou might ever the bettere be,
  By Godes owne belle!" 390

"Sothliche, my swete dame,
And if I may withoute blame
  Fain Ich wille fonde,
And if Ich may with him mete
By any way other by strete
  Nought ne will I wonde.

"Have god-day, dame, forth will I go."
"Allegate looke that thou do so
  As Ich thee bad.
Bote that thou me Wilekin bringe, 400
Ne may I never lawe ne singe
  Ne be glad."

"Iwis, dame, if I may,
Ich wille bringen him yet today,
  By mine mighte."
Hoe wente hire to hire inne:
Ther hoe founde Wilekinne,
  Bi oure Drighte.

"Swete Wilekin, be thou nought dred,
For of thin ernde Ich have wel sped. 410
Swithe come forth thider with me,
For hoe haveth send after thee.
Iwis, now mayst thou ben above,
For thou havest grantise of hire love!"

384. **efftsones** immediately 386. **With that** providing that 391. **Sothliche** truly 393. **Fain . . . fonde** I will gladly try 395. **other by strete** or by street 396. **Nought . . . wonde** I will not delay 398. **Allegate** by all means 400. **Bote that** unless 401. **lawe** laugh 406. **Hoe . . . inne** she went to her house 408. **Dirghte** Lord 409. **dred** afraid 411. **Swithe** quickly 414. **grantise** the grant

"God thee foryelde, leve nelde,
That hevene and erthe haveth to welde."

This mody man bigon to gon
With Sirith to his levemon
In thilke stounde.
Dame Sirith bigon to telle
And swor by Godes Owne belle,
Hoe havede him founde.

"Dame, so have ich Wilekin sought,
For now have Ich him ibrought."

"Welcome, Wilekin, swete thing,
Thou art welcomere than the king.

"Wilekin the swete,
My love I thee bihete,
To don al thine wille!
Turnd Ich have my thought,
For I ne wolde nought
That thou thee shuldest spille."

"Dame, so Ich evere bide non,
And Ich am redy and ibon,
To don al that thou saye.
Nelde, *par ma fai!*
Thou most gange away
While Ich and hoe shulen playe."

"Goddot, so I wille;
And loke that thou hire tille
And strek out hire thes;
God give thee muchel care
Yif that thou hire spare
The while thou with hire bes.

And whoso is onwis

415. **foryelde** reward 418. **levemon** sweetheart 419. **In thilke stounde** that very moment 432. **spille** kill 433. **so . . . non** as I ever hope for dinner 434. **ibon** prepared 436. **par ma fai** by my faith 439. **Goddot** God knows 440. **And . . . tille** and see that you plow her 441. **And . . . thes** And stretch out her thighs 444. **The . . . bes** For the time you are with her

And for non pris
    Ne con geten his lefmon,
I shal, for my mede,
Garen him go spede,
    For ful wel I con." 50

Explicit.

448. **mede** reward, pay 449. **Garen . . . spede** cause him to understand

Index of Authors, Works, and Genres